Comparative Ethics Series /
Collection d'Éthique Comparée :

Comparative Ethics Series /
Collection d'Éthique Comparée

As Religious Studies in its various branches has spread out in recent years, it has met with a newly emergent discipline: Comparative Ethics as the study of moralities as cultural systems, rather than as the philosophical investigation of particular moral issues. To study a morality as a dynamic whole in its social nature and functioning requires a context in which other instances of a comparable kind are considered. Moral action-guides and religious action-guides have historically been brought together in mixed, moral-religious or religious-moral systems. The different paths followed by moralities as cultural systems in the varying contexts demand comparative study.

The series embraces three kinds of studies: (1) methodological studies, which will endeavour to elaborate and discuss principles, concepts and models for the new discipline; (2) studies which aim at deepening our knowledge of the nature and functioning, the scope and content of particular moral systems, such as the Islamic, the Hindu, the Christian and so on; (3) studies of a directly comparative kind, which bring differing moral systems or elements of systems into relationship.

GENERAL EDITOR: *Paul Bowlby* Saint Mary's University (Halifax)

ADVISORY BOARD: *Charles Adams* McGill University (Montreal)
Ernest Best University of Toronto
Antonio R. Gualtieri Carleton University (Ottawa)
Roger Hutchinson University of Toronto
Patrick Kerans Dalhousie University (Halifax)
Jack Lightstone Concordia University (Montreal)
David Little University of Virginia (Charlottesville)
Thierry Maertens Université Laval (Québec)
Ronald W. Neufeldt University of Calgary
David Roy Bioethical Institute (Montreal)
Max T. Stackhouse Andover Newton Theological
School (Newton Centre, MA)

Contents

COMPARATIVE ETHICS

Volume 4

In Good Faith

Canadian Churches
Against Apartheid

Renate Pratt

Published for the Canadian Corporation for Studies in
Religion / Corporation Canadienne des Sciences Religieuses
by Wilfrid Laurier University Press

1997

Wilfrid Laurier University Press acknowledges the support of the Canada Council for the Arts for our publishing program. We acknowledge the financial support of the Government of Canada through the Canada Book Fund for our publishing activities.

Library and Archives Canada Cataloguing in Publication

Pratt, Renate
    In good faith : Canadian churches against apartheid

(Comparative ethics series ; v. 4)

Includes bibliographical references and index.

ISBN 978-0-88920-280-1 (paper)
ISBN 978-0-88920-645-8 (PDF)

1. Apartheid – Religious aspects – Christianity. 2. Apartheid – Moral and ethical aspects. 3. Social responsibility of business – Canada. 4. Social responsibility of business – South Africa. 5. Taskforce on the Churches and Corporate Responsibility. 6. Church and industry – Canada. 7. Church and industry – South Africa. 8. Christianity and politics – Canada. I. Canadian Corporation for Studies in Religion. II. Title. III. Series.

HF5388.P72 1997   261.8′5   C96-931980-0

Cover design by Leslie Macredie using a photograph by Paul Weinberg entitled *Soweto Unrest*, 1985

Preface

We have experienced nothing short of a miracle in South Africa as we have seen apartheid disappear from the scene; as we have watched incredulous, the long lines of South Africans taking part in their first democratic elections; the inauguration of Nelson Mandela as the first-ever democratically chosen president of this new South Africa and the installation of a government of national unity.

We have scored a spectacular victory over one of the most vicious systems the world has known, as vicious as Nazism ever was. Its perpetrators had sought to control every aspect of the lives of the victims of this totally evil system and the perpetrators were not averse to using the most violent and repressive measures to enforce their hegemony—there were bannings that condemned people to a twilight existence as prisoners at their own expense, when a gathering meant one other person and they were not permitted to attend a gathering!—there were detentions without trial for lengthy periods and people often died mysteriously in those detentions, as in the notorious brutal murder of Steve Biko. People were incarcerated for having had the audacity to imagine that they too were human beings with inalienable rights—such as the Mandelas, the Sisulus and others. Many others went into exile, and there was the constant harassment, the public vilification of those who opposed apartheid. This was a powerful system supported by many Western governments because the perpetrators were White and the victims were largely Black and because this South African government was smart enough to exploit the often strange obsession with Communism by its declaration that it was the last bastion of Western civilisation against soviet communist expansionism.

The struggle against this powerful regime was rough, but we have notched up our spectacular victory over the injustice and oppression of apartheid. But our victory would have been totally impossible without the remarkable and courageous support and commitment of many in the international community. We could not have made it without the imposition of sanctions against the apartheid monster. It is a great privilege to be able to say thank you very much to you all who supported us. Our victory is your victory.

Renate Pratt's book is a ringing account of how one group in Canada struggled to galvanise Canadian public opinion to pressure business and government to take a moral stand against apartheid. It was never easy to do this. We can read what it cost the anti-apartheid stalwarts whose names must be written in letters of gold in any authentic history of the struggle for justice, peace, democracy and reconciliation in South Africa. I am honoured to have been asked to write this short preface and to urge many to read this fascinating account.

Goodness, justice, love, peace—these ultimately prevail against their awful counterparts because this is a moral universe and God is in charge.

The Most Reverend Desmond M. Tutu

Foreword

When the Centre for the Study of Religion in Canada received a grant from the Lilly Endowment, Inc. to study the social justice activities of the United Church of Canada and its ecumenical partners, a topic with obvious relevance for our project was the Canadian churches' role in the struggle against apartheid in South Africa. Our initial hope was that Renate Pratt would write a background paper and give the keynote address at a consultation on this topic. It soon became evident that our modest request had lured her into a major project. The book she ended up writing provides a detailed reconstruction of the faithful witness of the Canadian churches and the Taskforce on the Churches and Corporate Responsibility against Canadian support for the unjust and racist apartheid policies of the South African government.

The way the story is told reflects the perseverance and scrupulous attention to detail that characterized the approach taken by the Taskforce in the campaign against apartheid. The Centre for the Study of Religion in Canada is grateful to Renate for this labour of love, and to the Lilly Endowment for its contribution to publication costs. We share Renate's gratitude to Sandra Woolfrey and Wilfrid Laurier University Press for making publication both possible and a pleasant experience.

This rich account of the Canadian churches' role in the struggle against apartheid will appeal to readers with a general interest in the South African policies of Canadian governments and corporations and in the public role of the Canadian churches. It will also interest different types of specialists. It speaks directly and concretely to issues such as the effectiveness of economic sanctions, the ability of non-governmental organizations to influence public policies and the continuing relevance of religion in a so-called secular age. (For an interesting illustration of the rediscovery of the role of religion by international relations scholars, see the 1994 publication of the Washington Center for Strategic and International Studies, *Religion, The Missing Dimension in Statecraft*, edited by Douglas Johnston and Cynthia Sampson and published by Oxford University Press.)

Until the middle of the twentieth century it would have been common to interpret this type of church-sponsored social justice activity as part of a program to Christianize the social order. Christians are now more conscious of living in a religiously diverse society. Our neighbours are Buddhists, Hindus, Jews, Muslims, members of other traditions and persons with no explicit religious affiliation. In the public space within which Canada's role in the world is debated, the churches translate the concerns grounded in the faith of their members into the shared language of fairness, justice, peace, human rights, environmental protection and so forth. This does not mean, however, that religious beliefs and values and church-sponsored activities are no longer relevant factors in the conduct of nations and in campaigns for justice and human rights.

Apartheid policies in South Africa provide a particularly striking illustration of the continuing role of religion in the conduct of nations. The Dutch Reformed Church of South Africa used Christian beliefs and biblical stories to justify the separate development of black and white races and the suppression of the rights and freedoms of the black majority.

The Canadian churches challenged Canadian governments and corporations to justify their support for the unjust policies of the South African government without presuming that Canada is or ought to be a Christian society. Nor did they exaggerate their power or authority to influence government or corporate policies. As the title of this study points out, they acted in good faith in response to the unjustifiable assault on the dignity and rights of the South African black majority because it was the right thing to do.

While the churches' primary motive was to be faithful, they were also effective. Their persistent challenges and calls for accountability might not have made corporations and governments more moral. However, as this study demonstrates, these social justice activities helped to alter the climate within which businesses and governments decided whether or not it made economic and political sense to continue to support the unjust and racist policies of the South African government.

Roger Hutchinson
Centre for the Study of Religion in Canada
Emmanuel College, Toronto

Acknowledgments

When Mandela walked out of prison in 1990, many activists, myself included, said that they had not believed that this would happen in their lifetime. I decided to write this book with a sense of gratitude that I was allowed to witness the ending of apartheid rule and with a sense of obligation that the story of the Taskforce be told. *In Good Faith* is, I hope, a testament to the high level of shared commitment and to the close and collegial relationship between the representatives of the member churches and religious orders and the staff of the Taskforce.

The book spans nearly two decades of anti-apartheid work of this community of purpose. The years 1975–85 provide a rich record of Canadian politics and corporate investments preceding the final stages of the liberation struggle. Mulroney's initiatives in 1985 then heralded a period of Canadian leadership in the Commonwealth and introduced economic sanctions as policy alternatives, which saw the members of the Taskforce briefly at the centre of this change before they resumed their role as authoritative critics when the government abandoned its commitments all too early.

In Good Faith, however, begins with *Investment in Oppression* (1973), published by the YWCA of Canada. It was the first publication that examined Canadian economic links with South Africa. As a member of the board and chair of the Study and Action Committee that produced the study, I gratefully remember the support I received from the board and in particular from Agnes Roy, Jean Campbell and Mabel Aplin, then senior staff members of the YWCA of Canada.

I express my sincere thanks to Roger Hutchinson, principal of Emmanuel College, University of Toronto, and director of the Centre for the Study of Religion in Canada for welcoming and encouraging the writing of this book. I am deeply grateful to the Centre for its generous grant toward the cost of the preparation and publication of this volume.

I am indebted to my friend and colleague Moira Hutchinson, who succeeded me as coordinator of the Taskforce in May 1986. The years 1981–86, during which we were both on the staff, were marked by close consultations and fruitful exchanges that helped shape the work of the Taskforce, including its anti-apartheid activities. I owe much to her wisdom and advice. I thank Moira for her encouragement, her reading of the manuscript at various stages, her sound counsel and practical assistance. She sifted through the Taskforce's files and organized the delivery to my home of boxes from the archives, making it easy for me to retrieve relevant files.

These archives provide a lively record of the years traversed. They show how significant were the relationships with the churches and other organizations in South Africa and Namibia. The wealth of press clippings bears witness to the quality reporting of Canadian and international journalists. I gratefully acknowledge their contribution to the work of the Taskforce and to this volume, be it through reporting on Canadian government or corporate positions or through accounts of events in South Africa often produced in defiance of emergency rule and censorship. A debt is owed as well to the South African "alternative press" such as *Southscan*, whose clandestine reports were, at times, the only credible source of South African news. As praiseworthy were the international clipping services on Southern Africa, such as *Facts & Reports* in the Netherlands, or the ANC *Sechaba*, news clippings that reproduced a wealth of detailed, worldwide information for the international anti-apartheid network.

I thank Jeralyn Towne for her diligent and helpful research into sources of information that had stayed in my mind only as vague memories; Jeralyn was able to trace and provide missing names, dates and other details. I am indebted to my friend and one-time colleague Allen Cook, for his willingness to discuss details of South African events and to come up with relevant newspaper articles. I thank my family on both sides of the Atlantic for sustaining over the years their interest in and patience with my preoccupation.

My special thanks go to Carroll Klein of Wilfrid Laurier University Press for her patient and sensitive editing and for her encouragement and reassurances throughout the process of production.

Finally I thank Cran Pratt, my husband and best friend, for his tireless support, interest and enthusiasm for the book. He served many times as my sounding board for ideas, assumptions and theories. His readiness to discuss problems has often restored the self-confidence of this flagging writer. His enduring patience in reading and rereading the manuscript and in proposing changes have helped tighten the prose and have contributed to greater clarity.

I count myself fortunate to have been given the opportunity to pull together the record of the Taskforce's contribution to the struggle against apartheid. Any errors or omissions are mine alone.

Introduction

Large corporations are powerful members of Canadian society. Their policies and practices affect the well-being of millions of people in Canada and around the world. Many Canadian Christians see, as part of their concern to promote social justice, an obligation to challenge corporate activities that contribute to social injustice, to violations of human rights, to increased militarism or to ecological abuse. Reflecting this concern, the Canadian churches created the Taskforce on the Churches and Corporate Responsibility in January 1975 in order to respond more effectively and in a coordinated manner to the requirements of this mandate.

A two-year planning process had preceded the formal establishment of the Taskforce. In December 1972 the Joint Working Group of the Canadian Catholic Conference and the Canadian Council of Churches adopted a resolution asking that ecumenical church staff and laity explore the impact of corporate activity in developing countries and the possibility of dialogue with corporate management about the moral dimensions of doing business. In response an ad hoc task force was formed, chaired by Reverend Tom Anthony, director, National and World Program of the Anglican Church of Canada. It met regularly and continued to report to the Joint Working Group. Two years later, it was decided to establish the Taskforce. The author was hired in December 1974 as its first coordinator; the first chair was Tom Anthony. Almost all of the representatives of the churches and religious orders who had served on the ad hoc task force and had shaped the design and the objectives of the Taskforce then joined the new ecumenical coalition as members. The churches and religious orders

---

Notes for the Introduction are found on p. 4.

1

that they represented committed themselves jointly to fund the organization and to appoint representatives to its board and committees.

The founding churches and organizations comprised the Anglican Church of Canada, the Baptist Federation of Canada, the Canadian Conference of Catholic Bishops, the Canadian Council of Churches (in a non-funding observer capacity), the Lutheran Church in America, Canada Section,[1] the Presbyterian Church in Canada and the United Church of Canada. The founding religious orders were the Canadian Religious Conference of Ontario, the Jesuit Fathers of Upper Canada, the Redemptorist Fathers, the Scarborough Foreign Mission Society, the Sisters of Charity of Mount St. Vincent, Halifax, and the Sisterhood of St. John the Divine. By 1994, twenty years later, the original church membership remained the same but for the withdrawal of the Baptist Federation of Canada. The number of individual religious orders with membership in the Taskforce had increased to eighteen; in addition, three associations or conferences of religious orders, each of whom appointed representatives, were involved. CUSO and the National Board of the YWCA enjoyed consultative membership.[2]

Originally the founders of the Taskforce had been influenced by the example of their American sister churches who, as shareholders, had earlier begun to protest American corporate involvement in the Vietnam War and in the apartheid system in South Africa. Since the late 1960s, Canadian churches had been asked as shareholders to respond to proxy solicitations from their American colleagues on issues of corporate social responsibility. Although some Canadian churches had traditionally refrained from investing in alcohol and tobacco companies, the active involvement of church shareholders in corporate decision making presented the founding members of the Taskforce with altogether new and complex challenges which the Taskforce set out to meet.

Official representatives of the member churches and religious orders who make up the Taskforce board and its executive determine the activities in which they wish to participate, and Taskforce briefs, letters and policy statements reflect their considered views and policy positions. The Taskforce itself is not an investor; it owns no shares. Thus shareholder interventions and other corporate initiatives can occur only when the shareholding denominations or religious orders decide to undertake such actions.

Church activity related to South Africa's system of apartheid consistently shared a crowded Taskforce agenda with other pressing issues. In the early years these involved investment in and loans to human rights violator regimes in Latin America and East Asia. In time the Taskforce also became concerned about Canadian military exports, international loans and debt, ecological abuses and questions about corporate governance. Nevertheless, apartheid remained a major preoccupation of the churches and religious orders. Indeed, church positions opposing the apartheid system in Southern Africa had been a strong early element in ecumenical collaboration, even before the formal establishment of the Taskforce. This is partly to be explained by the sheer tenacity of the apartheid system, aided by the irresolute responses to it by Western powers and investors. As well, the commitment of the member churches to work for fundamental changes was constantly fortified by their close ties with colleagues in Southern Africa. They shared with each other a firm and absolute rejection of the thesis that the white minority regime's creation of the apartheid state was based on Christian principles and could be justified and defended on those grounds. The struggle for the birthright of black South Africans thus involved for the South African churches, and by extension for the Canadian churches, a reaffirmation of their Christian faith and its social justice implications.

The close formal and informal relations between the members of the Taskforce and their Southern African partners have inspired and shaped much of the work of the Taskforce. As we shall see, reciprocal visits of church people and exchanges of views with delegations from South African community organizations, trade unions and liberation movements have made it possible for the Taskforce to be confident that its actions were grounded in solidarity with these South African and Namibian partners. Member churches agreed with their Southern African partners that apartheid represented a state system of constitutionally entrenched racism and repression of its black majority citizens and of all serious opponents of the regime.

In their early discussions about possible Canadian actions, members of the Taskforce resolved primarily to address the systemic manifestations of apartheid. The churches were persuaded that they must in particular seek to stem the inflow of foreign capital and must expose, and seek to prevent, the provision of foreign technology and military equipment for South Africa's security apparatus. These were initially the principle objectives of the churches when they addressed the government as well as the corporations and banks in which they were investors.

The churches' endeavour to bring into harmony their social teachings with their responsibility as investors had sharpened their awareness of the social impact of corporate activity and of their own shared responsibility as co-owners of these enterprises. In other words, the churches were becoming proactive shareholders. They sought through negotiations with senior management to present their views and policy positions and to persuade management to change its policy or practice. These meetings would be followed by direct shareholder action if such "quiet diplomacy" proved ineffective.

The Taskforce also sought to clarify the position of the Canadian government, in part because corporations and banks frequently invoked government legislation or the lack of it in defence of their own policy positions.

As well, the frequent convergence of corporate and government positions on South Africa's apartheid system explains the churches' close scrutiny of government policy. The Taskforce addressed in particular those aspects of Canadian corporate and government policies that the churches could reasonably expect to change once the inherent contradictions in these policies had been exposed. They took at face value corporate and government assurances that they, too, abhorred apartheid and that they, too, agreed that apartheid should be ended, if at all possible, by peaceful means. The churches urged that as proponents of this view, corporations and government had an obligation to use all peaceful means available to bring about fundamental change. How the corporations and government reacted to the churches' positions during the long years of detailed probings through shareholder actions, management meetings, briefs and public and private discussions, is the story of these pages.

The volume is organized into four parts, covering the periods of events from 1975 to 1980; 1980 to 1984; 1985 to 1987; and from 1987 to 1990. Canadian corporate and government policy towards Namibia until its independence in 1990 is woven into the main body of the narrative.

Notes

1 Renamed Evangelical Lutheran Church in Canada in 1986.
2 At no time have the activities of the Taskforce been funded by government or business. The Taskforce publishes an *Annual Report* with a list of its members and an audited statement of its accounts.

Part One   1975–80

1   Prelude to Action

The Taskforce "opened its office for business" on 2 January 1975 with a sense of urgency to respond to a long agenda that had been accumulating during the preceding two years of planning. The participating churches and religious orders each brought to the new coalition a priority list of proposals, and every list contained a request to develop a program for action regarding South Africa's system of apartheid.[1] The churches considered only briefly whether they should defer action under the new mandate to allow time for developing a common approach. It was quickly agreed however, that as there already existed a significant consensus among the churches on this issue, it was more important to begin discussions with Canadian corporations. On the basis of these first experiences, the Taskforce could then reflect on subsequent steps and on the lessons learned for additional church initiatives.

Investment in Oppression

There was more to the church consensus on South Africa than merely a shared sense of urgency. *Investment in Oppression*, the first Canadian study about the impact of Canadian and other foreign investment on the system of apartheid in South Africa and Namibia, had been published by the YWCA of Canada in May 1973.[2] At that time a number of the founding churches of the Taskforce had helped to fund the publication.[3] It provided the Taskforce with a systematic review of the incremental imposition of oppressive laws that had been imposed in South Africa and Namibia since 1948. These laws and their effect on the South African population are briefly sketched below to remind us of the conditions that had compelled the churches to act.

Notes for chapter 1 are found on pp. 20–21.

White Supremacy Legislation

The key apartheid laws included the Native Trust and Land Act, limiting black land rights to 13 percent of South Africa's territory; the Population Registration Act and the Group Areas Act, providing for enforced geographical separation of the races; a host of laws that restricted black union activity and determined black wage levels; the Suppression of Communism Act, which provided a legal basis for very extensive political repression;[4] the hated "Pass Laws" that obliged all blacks to be able to produce at all times a bulky identity book or face fines and/or imprisonment; and the Terrorism Act of 1967, known for its retroactive application to Namibia and for its clause permitting indefinite detention without trial. Taken together, the laws constituted the basic components of the doctrine of white supremacy:

- exclusive white control of the national political institutions;

- denial of all civil and political liberties to Africans;

- the confinement of the majority African population to land rights in only 13.6 percent of the land area;

- stringent restrictions upon African rights to live, to work and to travel within their country;

- an educational system for Africans which equipped them only for the subordinate role whites had intended for them; and

- a pervasive state security system in the service of racism.

The "Homelands"

The "homelands" policy of the South African government, from its beginning, has been the cause of unending suffering for millions of black South Africans. It has also featured prominently in the arsenal of South Africa's international propaganda. Understanding this issue was important, for there were Canadian corporations with investment in the "homelands."

When *Investment in Oppression* was published, there were ten designated tribal "homelands" in the 13 percent of the land set aside for permanent black residency. Most were fragmented pieces of land separated by "white" settlements. They were vast rural slums—overpopulated and impoverished—where around twenty million, that is some 80 percent of black South Africans, were required to live except for those periods when they were employed in the white economy. During these periods they became foreigners in "white" South Africa, without their families, and tolerated only as long as their labour was needed. Apart from those employed by the administration of the "homelands," almost all their permanent populations consisted of the old, the very young, the sick, the maimed and the unemployed.

These rural slums provided the rationale for the withdrawal of citizenship and the denial of political and civil rights to blacks anywhere else in South Africa. Under the grand apartheid design of the early sixties all blacks—but for a few exempted by complicated rules—were recognized as citizens only of one or the other of these artificially created "homelands." Pretoria's propaganda had the "homelands" developing into independent "nations," which would be granted "independence" by the white government. Blacks therefore needed to be conceded no political rights in the "white" areas nor in the national South African institutions.

This rationale also provided the pretext for massive population removals of black communities in order to "clear" areas for "white" occupancy. Between the mid-1960s and mid-1980s, 3.5 million black South Africans were driven from their homes and off their land. Police bulldozers destroyed their homes; the people and what possessions they could salvage were loaded on police trucks for a journey of often hundreds of kilometres away. They were then literally dumped into the arid areas of one or another of the "homelands," which most of them had never seen before. Some were moved again and again when their designation was arbitrarily changed or the assigned "homeland" refused them. Many perished. Whoever visited "The Discarded People" described so movingly by Cosmas Desmond in his book of that title,[5] will be haunted forever by the sight of despair and broken lives.[6]

The South African churches recognized at once the calamitous consequences for black South Africans of both the Group Areas' Act and the establishment of the black "homelands." They and their partners abroad, including the Canadian churches, continued to call urgent attention to the dehumanization and wholesale destruction of African families by the forced removals and the "homelands" policies.

In 1973 no "homeland" had yet been declared "independent." In 1979 the Taskforce updated and republished *Investment in Oppression*. By this time the Transkei, in 1976, and Bophutatswana, in 1977, had "gained independence." Since then the Ciskei and Venda similarly accepted nominal independence from Pretoria, while Gazankulu, Lebowa, KaNgwane, KwaNdebele, KwaZulu and Qwaqwa were designated "self-governing states." Usually acceptance of "independence" was induced by the South African government through promises of economic benefits and financial pledges attractive to the "homeland" leaders.

From the start, the "homelands" displayed despotic leadership and high levels of oppression and corruption. They were subject to a number of attempted, as well as some successful military coups, always accompanied by behind-the-scenes involvement from Pretoria in a role that either favoured or prevented a change in leadership. The South African government used the "homeland" leaders for its own purpose, creating black collaborators whose very survival depended on the continuation of the system of apartheid that kept them in power and paid their bills. Even the otherwise cooperative Western states could not bring themselves to concede diplomatic recognition to these fictional states; and only South Africa opened its "foreign missions" in each of them.

Black Working Conditions

The original study of *Investment in Oppression* carefully reviewed wage levels and working conditions in major South African industries.[7] All South African surveys showed consistent and strict racial segregation in every aspect of the working environment with the poorest facilities accorded to blacks who also had inferior, if any, health services, accident compensation or pension coverage. Comparisons between wages by categories of work and race demonstrated the wide gap existing between the top categories held by white workers, and the lowest occupied invariably by black workers. Black or mixed-race trade unions were outlawed. Specific categories of work were reserved for whites only.

Contract Labour

Blacks seeking work had to apply at labour bureaus in the "homelands," which would assign them to a one-year contract—renewable—to wherever black labour was needed. These black workers, called "sojourners" in "white South Africa," had to leave their families behind and were housed in "single" men's hostels.[8] For each contract renewal they had to return to their "homeland," which could be hundreds of kilometres away from their place of work. South Africa's most lucrative resource industries, the gold, diamond, platinum, copper, coal and uranium mines, were kept going, year in and year out, by this infamous contract labour system.

The South African churches and their allied organizations, together with their international partners, protested this inhuman and family-destroying system. They found it deeply offensive that the white minority regime, capable of such brutal racism, continued to find sympathy and support in the capitals and boardrooms—and, it must be said, in many a cathedral of the Western world—as a Christian bulwark against Communism.

Corporate and Government Attitudes

Since 1948 there had also been sustained economic growth and rising prosperity for white South Africans, thanks to a rapid inflow of foreign capital and technology and a great increase in foreign investment and international trade. Given this combination of economic growth in the white community, and racial subjugation and poverty for South Africa's black citizens, *Investment in Oppression* asked:

Can it be argued that Western economic involvement in South Africa has in fact constituted a liberalizing influence? Although the substantial increase of Western economic interests in South Africa over the last two decades has coincided with a major augmentation of repressive measures, can it still be hoped that its presence is now going to expose the contradictions of apartheid? Is there any evidence that Canadian business, or foreign investment in general, has challenged the South African government at all to move in a more liberal direction? (p. 4)

Investment in Oppression had tried to answer these questions and to evaluate the attitudes, policies and employment practices of Canadian investors. It had sent out a detailed questionnaire to thirteen Canadian corporations which, at the time, held a controlling interest in companies operating in South Africa or Namibia. Not all replied and those that did were not as forthcoming as had been hoped. Members of the Taskforce were to become familiar with these corporations, in particular with Alcan, Ford and Massey-Ferguson (later renamed Varity), three important corporate investors that had been on the original YWCA list of companies.

The vice-president of Falconbridge Nickel Mines replied in full to the YWCA questionnaire, but asked that his responses be kept confidential. Three executives took the view that the questions posed were not legitimate subjects for public concern, or at least not for the YWCA. The president of the Manufacturers Life-Insurance Company for example, wrote: "I have always wondered why the YWCA has concentrated its attention on South Africa ... there are many other areas in greater need of your attention." The Sun Life Insurance Company of Canada wrote that it failed to understand that there were any special concerns relating to investments in South Africa. The president of Consolidated Bathurst Ltd. upbraided the committee about "a certain smugness in one imperfect society judging another by its own standards" and advised that "if the main objective of the exercise is to see the Republic of South Africa evolve into a more racially equitable society then I would argue that any program designed to put pressure on the government of the day simply hastens their resolve [*sic*]." The company, not having provided a single response to the questionnaire, suspected the committee's motives: "I must question the propriety of using the YWCA for such a vehicle in respect to South Africa."[9]

A final and by now classic quote belongs to R. John Scott, American managing director of Ford South Africa, in 1970. When asked whether he had any acquaintances in the African, Asian or Coloured communities in South Africa, he replied, "I don't mix with them here and if I move back to America I wouldn't mix with them there either."[10]

Investment in Oppression had reviewed as well the policy position of the Canadian government. The 1970 government white paper *Foreign Policy for Canadians* declared "South Africa is possessed by the cancer of Apartheid." It identified two conflicting Canadian reactions to the apartheid system: "One is a broad revulsion against the racial discrimination practised in southern Africa and a general agreement that self-determination of Africans is a principle that cannot be denied." This reaction was attributed mainly to "the Canadian churches, other organizations and concerned individuals." The white paper ascribed the second reaction to "businessmen [*sic*] who see better-than-normal opportunities for trade and investment in the growing economy of the Republic of South Africa" and to Canadians who doubted that outside influences could effectively press the pace of "developments in South Africa."[11]

Cancer or not, the Trudeau government decided to leave its policy unchanged. Canadian public funds continued to maintain five commercial officers in South Africa to promote trade between Canadian and South African enterprises.[12]

In contrast, *Investment in Oppression* concluded: "Foreign investment has been an extremely important contributing factor to the sustained economic growth enjoyed by the South African economy since 1948. This expansion has coincided with an equally sustained and massive effort to entrench white supremacy and racial separation in the political and social institutions of South Africa" (p. 38). There had been no evidence that foreign investors objected to South Africa's increasingly harsh measures. On the contrary, the study found that the apartheid system and foreign investors served each other's interests. Investors contributed to the growth of the white economy while repression, to the degree that it was successful, provided the "stability" that attracted foreign investors. *Investment in Oppression* also warned that foreign investors served South Africa in yet another way: they strengthened the pro-South African lobby abroad, inviting tolerance for South Africa's apartheid system.

These 1973 conclusions place *Investment in Oppression*, the YWCA which undertook the study and the churches and non-governmental organizations who sponsored it, ahead of all other Canadian inquiries into the role of foreign investment in South Africa. They were the first in Canada to argue that there should be no further investment in Southern Africa. "We urge Canadian companies to cease all further investments in South Africa ... and to withdraw their investment from Namibia."[13]

The authors concluded that for all who favoured pressure by peaceful means, such a policy would be the most effective in forcing the regime into fundamental social and political changes. For the member churches of the new Taskforce, *Investment in Oppression* became a valuable resource as they began policy discussions with Canadian corporate managers engaged in business with South Africa.

Early Critics of the Taskforce

The new determination of the churches to exercise their shareholder rights in annual general meetings and to call attention to corporate decisions affecting social justice and human rights had raised eyebrows in the board rooms and angered prominent shareholders and a number of senior clergy. The novelty of the approach was all the more irritating as church question-ers obeyed the rules and were without exception polite and deferential. Corporate management lays great stress on ensuring that shareholder meetings are totally predictable. Even the briefest and most routine share-holder motions and seconding statements required in the by-laws are pre-arranged and read out by designated shareholders to eliminate the slightest glitch in the proceedings. The Taskforce did its best to accommodate these corporate wishes by regularly giving notice of the churches' intention to speak and by indicating the general nature of their concerns, but it was not prepared to withdraw from the scene.

Church shareholders knew that the issues they were raising were current and important. To make any impact, they needed to be discussed in the presence of the directors and fellow shareholders during the one annual occasion permitting public discussion. Participation in shareholder meet-ings has always been just a brief annual event in a continuum of Taskforce activity, but particularly in the early years, its controversial aspects attracted more attention, including media attention, than other ongoing pursuits.

In 1977 the very existence of the Taskforce gave rise to corporate anger and volatile charges when a sustained effort to neutralize the activities of the Taskforce began. Senior members of the business community estab-lished the Confederation of Church and Business People (CCBP) and could boast to have among its members prominent church leaders. The CCBP championed corporate decisions that were being challenged by the churches. By doing so, inevitably, they became apologists for regimes such as apartheid in South Africa and Pinochet's rule in Chile. Through its inter-nal network, a regular newsletter and organized meetings, members of the CCBP charged that the Taskforce was distributing biased information and alleged that it was manipulating official church policy in favour of an anti-business ideology.

This powerful attempt to silence the Taskforce was met by the individual member churches of the Taskforce. Since the CCBP included business peo-ple who were members of their congregations, church representatives on the Taskforce board were anxious to deal with their critics themselves. They sought to disabuse CCBP members of their frequently voiced but erroneous conviction that actions taken ecumenically within the Taskforce did not represent decisions of the appropriate structures of their own denominations. By meeting this open hostility of business members and of colleagues within their own congregations, church representatives were protecting the staff and the ongoing programs of the Taskforce from time-consuming and energy-draining involvement in this controversy.

In 1979 the Taskforce published a revised edition of *Investment in Oppression*.[14] While this revision was in progress, the member churches decided to review and update their denominational policy positions on South Africa. The Taskforce was asked to prepare a working draft as a contribution to the formal discussions that took place within each denomination. These policy statements, reflecting in their style and emphases the different traditions of the denominations, provided the Taskforce with solid endorsement and a common basis for its ongoing work. The revised positions of 1978 were included in the 1979 edition of *Investment in Oppression*.[15]

By the mid-1980s much of the early criticism of the Taskforce had dissipated. Thanks to the resolute commitment of the member churches, the right of all shareholders to challenge corporate policy was now more widely accepted if not always welcomed.

New Oppression and Fresh Resistance

Events in South Africa quickly established the need for accelerated international initiatives in support of anti-apartheid movements in South Africa and Namibia. On 16 June 1976 Soweto's school children began a protest that changed fundamentally the direction of South Africa's history. Towards the end of 1975 the government had imposed Afrikaans as the medium of instruction in African secondary schools. For senior black students studying for their final exams and already victimized by the inferior "Bantu" education, this abrupt switch from English or Zulu to Afrikaans was the last straw. Few African teachers could speak the language and even fewer students could understand it. Anxious teachers, parents and students had in vain pleaded against this edict that would further block black advancement.[16]

Soweto high-school students, supported by the Black Parents' Association, called a rally for 16 June. The police confronted the peaceful march of about 20,000 students and used tear gas to disperse them. When the students retaliated with stones, the police lost their nerve and fired live ammunition at the children. When the shooting stopped, seventy-eight students lay dead. The picture shown around the world of a young boy carrying a dead child, Hector Pieterson, became the international symbol for Soweto Day.

What was to have been a students' rally developed into an outraged uprising, still led by the schoolchildren, first against the Bantu education system and soon against everything apartheid stood for. The revolt spread rapidly throughout the country and touched most black and many other student bodies. Police terror was unleashed with enormous force, resulting in more than 700 deaths by 1977. Thousands were arrested and many were detained without charge or trial. The outrage mobilized black community and civic organizations who joined the unending and—of course—illegal demonstrations. Workers staged sympathy strikes protesting police killings of the demonstrators and in turn joined those already detained. Black youths in their thousands fled the country to join Umkhonto we Sizwe, the armed wing of the African National Congress (ANC).

Several members of the South African Council of Churches (SACC), and in particular the Christian Institute (CI), urged their Christian colleagues to take their place alongside those struggling against apartheid. By the end of 1976 the CI promised support for all peaceful efforts to bring change to South Africa and specifically to support workers' stayaways and economic sanctions and to discourage white immigration.[17] Such statements promptly provoked hostility from the South African business community and their international associates. For the member churches and religious orders of the Taskforce however, this engagement of prominent South African church leaders was an important signal that they were in step with their South African partners.

Annex: Policy Positions on Apartheid of the Canadian Churches and Religious Orders by 1978[18]

Anglican Church of Canada

At its meeting on 8–11 November 1977 the Executive Council of the Anglican Church of Canada ratified the following resolution adopted a few days earlier by the House of Bishops:

> The House of Bishops is appalled at the increase of rule by decree, and at the further denial of human rights for the great majority of people in South Africa by a government which has made a total travesty of its claim to be ruling in the name of Christian civilization. In our view, opposition can only be effective by the isolation of that government at all levels. The House of Bishops calls on the Canadian Government, which with other western nations continues to sustain the apartheid system through extensive economic, diplomatic (and in some cases military) links, to sever all connection with the South African Government until apartheid is eradicated.

Canadian Conference of Catholic Bishops

The position of the Conference was expressed in a public letter of 11 May 1978 from Archbishop Gilles Ouellet, then president of the Canadian

Conference of Catholic Bishops, to Fred McNeil, at the time chair of the Bank of Montreal. The bank was one of the largest Canadian lenders to South Africa. We reproduce here excerpts from this letter:

> [T]he Catholic Church throughout the world has condemned apartheid in South Africa as a cruel offense against humanity. In solidarity with the Churches in South Africa ... the major Christian churches in Canada [are] urging Canadian institutions ... to use their economic and moral influence to dismantle the apartheid system. These Church interventions have focused on Canada's trade relations with South Africa, the operations of several Canadian-based corporations in that country as well as bank loans to the Government of South Africa and its agencies.
>
> [W]e have been concerned primarily about the impact of foreign investment on apartheid itself. For us the record clearly shows that foreign investment has not (as some western business leaders initially predicted) had a liberalizing impact on the apartheid regime. ... [W]e believe that a significant number of Canadian bank loans ... serve to strengthen the structures of apartheid and prolong the day when justice will be realized for the black majority. ... [C]an doubt any longer be cast on the evidence indicating that western bank loans contribute to the military and defense purposes of the South African government?

The Lutheran Church in America, Canada Section (LCA-CS)

Between June 1974 and 1978 various decision-making structures of the Lutheran Church in America adopted positions on South Africa and Namibia that strengthened the mandate of the Canada Section to act on corporate and government involvement in Southern Africa.

In June 1974 the Eastern Canada Synod resolved "That the Eastern Canada Synod approach the Canadian Government ... to explore the possibility of ceasing Canadian commerce with South Africa as long as effective Apartheid remains a policy of South Africa" and that the Synod "urge the people of Canada to take a careful look at their investments and purchases of products from companies operating in South Africa which take unfair advantage of black and coloured African labour." (The Synod purchased a number of shares in Falconbridge Nickel Mines to be able to raise its concerns at annual meetings of the company.)

In August 1975 the Executive Committee of the Canada Section instructed the executive secretary to promote understanding of the role played by Falconbridge in Namibia and to review the position of the Canadian government in the United Nations on Namibian resource depletion with the aim of urging the government and the company to better protect the interests of the Namibian people.

At its 1977 biennial convention the LCA-CS officially endorsed as its own position the statement made by the Anglican, Roman Catholic and United Churches to Alcan Aluminium Ltd., and to the Canadian banks.

On a visit to North America in 1978 Bishop Joseph Kibira, president of the Lutheran World Federation, called on all churches to encourage governments to withdraw financial investments that supported South Africa's apartheid system.

Presbyterian Church in Canada

In 1977 the 103rd General Assembly of the Presbyterian Church in Canada reaffirmed an earlier statement that "all forms of racism and apartheid are contrary to the mind and will of Christ." The Assembly then asked the Administrative Council to instruct the Trustee Board, as responsible shareholders "to recommend actions towards just employment practices by such companies as have direct activity and/or influence in countries which have declared, or apparent discriminatory policies, particularly in South Africa;" and to request that the federal government "reconsider the extent of its program of trade promotion in South Africa in relation to the need of other African states for trade facilities."

The United Church of Canada

Based on a report offered by the Church's own "South African Task Force," the Executive of General Council of the United Church of Canada in April 1979 passed two sets of detailed resolutions. One dealt with the Church's position on government policies and the second with its position on private sector involvement in South Africa in April 1979.

Affirming its Gospel understanding that apartheid "is a sin and blasphemy against God ... which must be resisted with every morally acceptable, political economic and social means at our disposal," the Executive of General Council recognized that "a high level of economic alignment between the Canadian and white South African interests serves to strengthen the economic and military power of the South African government and tends to inhibit the adoption of forthright policy positions on the part of the Canadian government and the Canadian private sector and to neutralize opposition to the apartheid system." The United Church body also noted the importance for its decisions of the positions adopted by the South African Council of Churches which, in July 1978, stated "that foreign investment and loans have largely been used to support the prevailing patterns of power" and urgently requested "that foreign countries and organizations for the sake of justice revise radically their investment policies in regard to South Africa."

The United Church Position on the Government of Canada

The Executive of General Council resolved that the Canadian government should be asked to:

- publicly discourage new and expanding investments;
- instruct the Export Development Corporation to withhold its corporate account facility to all commercial transactions with South Africa;
- abrogate the bilateral British Preferential Tariff agreement;
- close the program for export market development to trade missions to South Africa; and
- revise the Canadian Code of Conduct for companies operating in South Africa to provide that such companies
  (a) insist on the right of workers to have their families near the place of work;
  (b) recognize and bargain with black trade unions;
  (c) press for and financially support efforts in South Africa to bring about equal education programs over and above the company's in-service training; and
  (d) disclose annually to a monitoring committee their sales to the South African government of equipment and products intended for or easily adapted for military or police use.

The Executive of General Council asked that compliance with the Canadian Code be mandatory and enforced by legislation; that companies issue annually detailed progress reports to a monitoring and enforcement committee (to be established) which should make such company reports available to the public.

The United Church body further resolved that the Canadian government be urged to support initiatives in the United Nations in favour of economic or other sanctions—partial or complete—in areas such as communications, air, trade or oil.

Regarding Canadian economic activity in Namibia, the United Church body advised the government to "[remove] all tax concessions from companies operating in Namibia until a representative government recognized by the United Nations has been established there."

United Church Position on Private Sector Activities

The Executive of General Council resolved to convince the private sector

- that all Canadian participation in direct or indirect financial investment of any form to the Government of South Africa or its agencies be suspended until apartheid has been abandoned; and
- that Canadian companies operating in South Africa commit themselves to management policies which are actively non-supportive of apartheid policies.

Such policies should include giving legal assistance to employees detained without charge and company implementation of points a) to d) listed above under Canadian Code of Conduct for Companies Operating in South Africa.

The United Church of Canada should request of the private sector that

- there be no expansion of existing business and no further investment in South Africa by companies incorporated in Canada or their subsidiaries until there is clear evidence that apartheid is terminated; and

- companies making sales to the South African government of equipment or products intended for, or easily adapted for military or police use, commit themselves to terminate such sales, and, in cases where this is not a possible option, that companies be asked to initiate a phased termination of this aspect of their operations.

The Executive of General Council resolved that the United Church

- continue to use its leverage as shareholder to urge corporations to adopt positions as set out in the foregoing sections;

- request its Investment Committee to assess effectiveness of actions, noting that the option of disinvestment when the corporate response is largely negative has always been a part of investment strategy. (Particular attention was drawn to Falconbridge Nickel Mines and the Bank of Montreal.)

- recognize that there is no escape from responsibility and that on moral issues Christians cannot be neutral, that the Church courts, Church affiliate institutions, local congregations and individual members be encouraged to evaluate their own relationship through their bank accounts, their political activity, their use of share ownership and other assets to this particular question and take appropriate actions.

Finally, the Division of World Outreach and the Division of Finance were encouraged to expand their efforts to train black South Africans to prepare them for a future South Africa of "their own shaping" and "to explore ways in which the church and corporations can expand their efforts in this directions."

Young Women's Christian Association of Canada (YWCA)

The National Convention of the YWCA meeting in Vancouver 29 May to 3 June 1977 recommended that the national board direct its attention to the implementation of World YWCA resolutions on racism and human rights, which were passed in Australia in 1967, in Ghana in 1971 and in Vancouver in 1975. The last resolutions had urged National Associations to concentrate their efforts in the next four-year period on:

- the identification and elimination of all legalized forms of discrimination based on colour, race, religion, language and sex; and
- the implementation of anti-discrimination laws that have been passed but are not yet effective.

Regarding racism, the 1975 World YWCA Vancouver meeting had also called on National Associations "to affect foreign policies and trade policies" to bring about change recognizing that such measures can be effective only if nations cooperate in applying them. It therefore called upon its National Associations to urge their governments to apply the strongest economic measures against nations which, as a matter of national policy, flagrantly violate, on the basis of race, the economic, political and social rights of a large segment of their population.[19]

In implementation of the earlier resolutions, the YWCA of Canada published *Investment in Oppression* in 1973, and requested a public commitment by Canadian banks to make no further loans to the South African government until apartheid was ended.

Notes

1 Other agenda items included corporate investment plans in and loans to Chile after the 1973 coup d'état; conditions in Canadian operations in Brazil, then under a military junta, and a presentation and appearance before "The Commission on Corporate Concentration in Canada" meeting during the year.

2 *Investment in Oppression*, Report of the Study and Action Committee of the World Relationships Committee of the YWCA of Canada on Canadian Economic Links with South Africa (Toronto: Young Women's Christian Association of Canada, 1973).

3 The Anglican and United Churches of Canada; the Presbyterian Church in Canada; the Canadian Council of Churches; the Co-Directors, the Canadian Catholic Conference, Social Action Office; the Canadian Catholic Organization for Development and Peace. Other organizations that helped fund the publication were the Canadian Council for International Co-operation and the United Nations Association of Canada. I had chaired the committee of the YWCA of Canada that had researched and written this Report. Thus the churches and religious orders whose representatives made up the first board of the Taskforce, with me as coordinator, were already familiar with the arguments of the study and were in broad agreement with its recommendations.

4 This act, amended several times over the years, created thousands upon thousands of political prisoners simply because of the wide definition of "Communists." The state "deemed" persons to be Communists if their aim had been "the bringing about of any political, industrial, social or economic change within the Union [of South Africa] by unlawful acts or omissions or by the threat of such acts or omissions or by means which include the promotion of disturbance or disorder," which the state judged to be in the service of Communism and to be causing hostility between the races of South Africa (Muriel Horrell, *Action, Reaction and Counteraction* [Johannesburg: The South African Institute of Race Relations, 1971], p. 22, quoted in *Investment in Oppression*, p. 13.

5 Cosmas Desmond, *The Discarded People* (Harmondsworth: Penguin Books, 1971).

6 Despite the government's assurance that forced removals had been halted in 1985, they were still going on in January 1986, when the Canadian Catholic Mission met with people in a vast and treeless field in the "homeland" of KwaNdebele. They had just been dumped here. We saw their numbed despair and disbelief as they stared at the barrenness around them and saw absolutely nothing but row upon symmetric row of galvanized latrines reflecting back the glaring sun.

7 We relied almost exclusively on information from South African sources. I take this occasion to honour the late Muriel Horrell, author of most of the publications in the sixties and early seventies of the South African Institute of Race Relations, which helped us so immeasurably to get a rounded picture at this distance of events in South Africa. The Institute published annually *A Survey of South African Race Relations* and specialized studies such as *South Africa's Workers* (1969), and *Action, Reaction and Counteraction and Legislation* and *Race Relations* (1971).

8 There were also "single" women's hostels, but the overwhelming number of hostel dwellers were men.

9 Appendix II, "Questionnaire of the Study and Action Committee to Canadian Companies and Replies Thereto," in *Investment in Oppression*, pp. 40–45.

10 Timothy Smith, "Chrysler, Ford, and General Motors in South Africa," *Newsletter, Council on Economic Priorities*, 1, no. 5 (October-November 1970), 20–23, quoted in *Investment in Oppression*, p. 45.

11 *Foreign Policy for Canadians: United Nations*, published by authority of the Hon. Mitchell Sharp, secretary of state for External Affairs (Ottawa: Queen's Printer for Canada, 1970), pp. 18–19.

12 To put this in perspective, at the time Canada had nine commercial representatives in the rest of Africa's forty-one states.

13 *Investment in Oppression*, p. 41.

14 The Taskforce engaged Hilary Pearson to do the detailed research that this revision required.

15 Substantial excerpts from these policy statements are reproduced at the end of chapter 1.

16 See Fatima Meer, *Higher than Hope: The Authorized Biography of Nelson Mandela* (London: Penguin Books, 1990), pp. 303–4.

17 Resolution adopted by the Annual General Meeting of the Christian Institute of Southern Africa, Edendale, Natal, 18 September 1976 (Colleen Ryan, *Beyers Naudé: Pilgrimage of Faith* [Claremont, SA: David Philip Publishers, 1990], p. 181).

18 Extracts from "Appendix E, Policy Positions of Canadian Churches and Related Organizations," in *Investment in Oppression*, pp. i–iv.

19 The language of the resolutions on racism were kept deliberately general to avoid jeopardizing the work of the YWCA of South Africa (mixed race). After 1976 Joyce Soroke, its dynamic executive director, and other staff were detained on several occasions for their courageous stand against the apartheid regime.

2   Canadian Business Ties

Historic partnerships between a number of Canadian denominations and religious orders and their South African sister churches had of course preceded the establishment of the Taskforce. The new coalition simply facilitated cooperation among the Canadian churches and religious orders and between them and the South African Council of Churches (SACC), the Southern African Catholic Conference of Bishops (SACCB) and related anti-apartheid organizations. As public concern grew, the shared analysis of *Investment in Oppression* provided an immediate focus on Canadian investment in South Africa. The Taskforce was thus able to give expression to a general impatience with the corporate sector for profiting from the system of apartheid and with the Canadian government for the timidity of its policy toward it.

The Bank Campaign

The first interaction between members of the Taskforce and the business community involved Canada's major banks. In 1974 a printout had been sent anonymously from the Frankfurt office of the European American Banking Corporation to the Interfaith Center on Corporate Responsibility (ICCR) in New York. It revealed multi-million dollar syndicated loans to the South African government and its state agencies between 1970–73. These, and subsequent loans, had been advanced by European and North American, including Canadian, banks. The ICCR in turn published "The Frankfurt Documents," which catalogued by borrower, lender, type of loan and maturity date, the involvement of Canadian and other banks in these large long-term loans to South African state agencies.[1] We also learned that, undaunted by the intensified repression that followed the Soweto school-

---

Notes for chapter 2 are found on pp. 57–61.

children's revolt, international banks had extended additional long-term loans to the apartheid state. Of the five major loans in 1976, only one, a $200-million loan for the Electricity Supply Commission, had been concluded in March, before "Soweto." All others coincided with the terror that reigned throughout the year. In July 1976 the state-controlled South African Broadcasting Corporation and South African Airways received $20 million and $99 million respectively. In October the state-owned South African Development Corporation received a $25 million loan, and in November a loan of $110 million went directly into the South African treasury for balance of payment support.[2]

Disclosure of the dimensions and frequency of these commercial loans involving as they did a very large number of international lenders, left no doubt about the significant role played by private bankers in underpinning the system of apartheid, a role that is generally concealed by client/banker confidentiality. As shareholders and clients of Canadian banks, member churches and religious orders sought confirmation from each bank of the accuracy of the loan disclosures and asked for a commitment from senior management to cease lending to South African state agencies until apartheid was abandoned.

There were some initial difficulties in gaining access to senior bank executives—rather than their public relations officers—and a first round of meetings with the "big five" were conducted in an atmosphere which varied between tense hostility and condescending bonhomie. At one point one bank chairman conceded that meeting with church shareholders had been a real challenge to him as there was nothing in a bankers' experience or training that had prepared him for meeting organizations such as the Taskforce. The same could be said for the majority of church representatives on the board of the Taskforce, few of whom were versed in international lending. In this instance though, church representatives had the advantage that they—rather than the bankers—knew the details of South Africa's apartheid system. We explained to the banks that loans to the South African government constituted support for the system of apartheid and a vote of confidence in racism. Although the bankers agreed that apartheid was abhorrent and that change would have to take place, they believed that withholding loans would not have the desired effect and might even hurt those we wanted to help.

This argument was to become the nearly automatic response offered to church criticisms of Canadian investments in South Africa. In responding to the banks, the churches explained that there was an important difference between bank loans to the South African government and its agencies and the operations of foreign companies in South Africa. The latter could, if they wished, lessen some of the burden of apartheid for their black employees. They could, for example, raise wages and improve working conditions;

they could initiate meaningful training and educational programs; offer housing loans and conclude private wage agreements with black unions although these were not yet allowed to be officially registered. Activities such as these could conceivably be cited as a liberalizing influence on apartheid. In the case of international bank loans however, the recipient was the very regime that had imposed the racist laws, enforced them relentlessly and could be counted upon uncompromisingly to defend them.

Some bank executives made a distinction between one South African government department and another. For example, one bank chairman felt that the South African Post—recipient of one of his bank's loans—was more benign than South Africa's Ministry of Justice.[3] During this particular discussion, we tried to discover whether the bank had overall lending criteria that would preclude, as a matter of principle, specific loan applicants. This led to a very curious conversation, which concluded with church representatives suggesting that if the bank would not lend to "houses of ill repute," neither should it lend to South Africa, for South Africa itself was a "house of ill repute." We had scored a few debating points and had learned more about the psychology of bankers, but we had not made any discernible impact.

Taskforce members began to participate in annual meetings of shareholders in the winter of 1975–76, seeking to inform their fellow shareholders of their concern. They explained their position as best they could within the few minutes allowed them during question period.

Question period in a shareholder meeting comes at the end of a lengthy meeting filled with speeches and routine procedures. By the time questions may be asked, many shareholders want to leave. They have little patience for prolonging a meeting on issues extraneous to their interests. Dissident shareholders are thus always at the mercy of the chair, who sets the tone by either expressing his own impatience, thereby encouraging shareholders to be discourteous, or by inviting respect for the right of the questioner. Over the years church shareholders experienced many styles of handling their concerns, none quite as hostile as during their first appearance at the annual general meeting of the Bank of Montreal in December 1975. Fellow shareholders and the chair got so enraged at the churches' request to halt loans to the South African government that, amidst calls of "go back to Moscow" from the shareholders, the chair had the microphone switched off during a question by W. R. Davis, then assistant treasurer of the United Church of Canada. This incident earned the Taskforce its first prominent press report. *The Montreal Gazette*, described the churches' action rather patronizingly as "Lilliputian Darts"—forgetting perhaps the ultimate mastery of the Lilliputians over Gulliver. More important, the *Gazette* gave publicity to the Bank of Montreal's South African loans and the churches' opposition to them.

Where shareholder discussion was permitted, bank chairmen by and large expressed abhorrence of apartheid, but were unyielding on the question of halting loans to the apartheid regime. To avoid any further discussions, some retreated into the near "sacrosanct" client/banker confidentiality.[4] The churches countered that while this might legitimately rule out disclosure of the details of individual loans, it could not apply to the banks' overall policy of lending to the South African government. Some bankers rejected discussion of South African loans on the grounds that this was a political issue and therefore foreign to the banks' business; yet others held that the loans to South Africa were made from international funds and should therefore not really concern Canadians. There were also those who thought that the loans would still somehow benefit black South Africans.

As shareholders left these meetings, some of us would make for the exits and stand beside bank employees who were distributing bank literature. There, we pressed our statements about the banks' complicity in apartheid into the outstretched hands of departing shareholders. There is no telling how many were read once our fact sheets were found, tucked away along with the chair's speech.

Public Education

After the first round of management and shareholder meetings, during which not a single banker had been won over, the Taskforce decided to garner support for its actions from their constituencies and the general public. Member churches and religious orders reasoned that a large segment of their constituencies were likely to be clients of banks, and that widespread mobilization could render the banks sufficiently vulnerable to make it worth their while to halt the loans. There were, after all, many smaller banks and credit unions that provided alternative banking services. One bank or another, we hoped, might thereby be induced to become itself such an alternative institution. The Taskforce board therefore approved "Banking on Apartheid," an eight-sided pamphlet describing conditions for black citizens under apartheid; giving information about known participation by Canadian banks in international loans to South Africa; setting out the rationale and policy position of the churches and the responses received from each bank. The churches appealed to their members and to the general public to protest the banks' involvement in apartheid. We took care in this campaign not to blame branch managers for policy decisions taken at head office. We suggested that they be asked to make inquiries about their bank's South African lending policy and to forward to head office requests from local customers that South African loans be halted. By this process we hoped to sensitize these individuals to the issue while causing a minimum of antagonism. The pamphlet was an instant success;

50,000 copies were distributed upon request in 1976; responding to popular demand, the Taskforce updated and reprinted the pamphlet in 1977.

By the spring of 1976 the members of the Taskforce were beginning to
appreciate the dimensions of the task they had set for themselves. We also
began to feel part of an international movement to end loans to South
Africa. The World Council of Churches (WCC) had established The Programme to Combat Racism (PCR) under Baldwin Sjollema, its first ener-
getic Dutch director. Thanks to his encouragement, organizations such as
ours were strengthened in Britain, Belgium, France, Germany, Holland
and Sweden. In Europe, under pressure from church and organizational
clients, two of the largest Dutch banks, the Algemene Bank Nederland and
the Amsterdam-Rotterdam Bank, were the first to announce that they
would no longer lend to South Africa. In North America, the ICCR in New
York gave leadership to the South African bank campaign and played a liai-
son role with specialized units of the United Nations concerned with apartheid. Over the years the Taskforce gave evidence on Canadian corporate
and bank involvement in South Africa and Namibia during hearings organized by the United Nations Centre against Apartheid.

In March 1977 the Taskforce mounted a highly successful Public Forum
on Bank Loans to South Africa. We were able to arrange for visits to Canada by Baldwin Sjollema, director of PCR, and Tim Smith, director of ICCR
to address the Forum.[5] Canadian bank representatives had been invited to
present their views, but had declined. We left a symbolic empty chair on
the platform. Yet the Forum did not at all lack voices from within the Canadian churches' vocal opposition to the Taskforce. Their challenge greatly
contributed to the educational value the Forum was meant to have.

In October 1977 renewed waves of oppression swept over South Africa,
culminating in another turning point. Eighteen of the remaining anti-
apartheid organizations still at liberty, among them the Christian Institute,
were declared unlawful and their staff banned. Mass arrests of several hundred people took place throughout the country. Those protesting police
actions, many of them church people, were silenced by the same means.
News of continued arrests arrived throughout that autumn.

Increasingly, the connections between Canadian banks and South
Africa's repression found public currency. Telex communication between
the Canadian churches and their South African partners had helped us to
keep track of events there. On 12 October we learned of the murder in
police custody of Steve Biko, leader of the Black Consciousness Movement,
followed by further repression a few days later. We organized a "service of
witness" at the intersection of King and Bay streets in downtown Toronto,
in front of Canada's major banks just opposite the South African trade mission. On only one day's notice more than 200 people joined us on the wide
sidewalks skirting the towering skyscrapers where many pedestrians

stopped to "learn" the reason for a Christian service in Toronto's financial district and many joined us. Nothing could have symbolized quite as sharply the approach to justice taken by our member churches and religious orders. I shall always remember the poignant moment when Sister Beryl Stein of the Sisters of St. John the Divine stood on a box and, holding a bullhorn, recited the Magnificat.

In the United States as well, Soweto and its aftermath had prompted more intensive mobilization against South African loans by dissident shareholders and customers. The Chase Manhattan was the first North American bank to respond to this pressure. In the same year it adopted a code of ethics that excluded loans that "tend to support the apartheid policies of the South African government or reinforce discriminatory business practices."[6]

The Chase, its timing and its circumspect code, were likely the role model for the Royal Bank, Canada's largest bank. On 31 March 1978 it became the first Canadian bank to issue a statement on South African loans. It declared that it had not made loans to the South African government or its state agencies for almost two years and that "under current circumstances it will not make general purpose loans or balance of payment loans and that it will not make loans if these are judged to support apartheid or South Africa's pass-law system."

Members of the Taskforce were pleased that the logjam of tight-lipped responses had been loosened. Yet we recognized that the actual phrasing of the statement did not mean very much—under the prevailing chaos in South Africa, few banks would be tempted to make "general purpose loans." As well, we disagreed that there could be loans to the South African government that would not benefit apartheid. International research had confirmed that the bank had not, indeed, extended South African loans for quite some time. What really mattered was the recognition that enough public pressure had led the Royal Bank to make this public statement. Also, a useful precedent had been created by the Royal's judgement that to disclose *no* new loans evidently did not breach client/banker confidentiality.

In November 1978 Corporate Data Exchange, Inc., an independent research institute in New York, provided the Taskforce with new figures of known Canadian loans to the South African government and its state agencies. The data, covering the period 1972–76, showed a total of US$636.3 million, most of which was due for repayment in the early 1980s. The Canadian Imperial Bank of Commerce, the Toronto Dominion Bank and the Bank of Montreal had participated in these loans and had acted as lead managers of some of the loan consortia. Most prominent among South African borrowers were three state-owned corporations: the Iron and Steel Corporation (ISCOR), an important component of South Africa's military-industrial complex; the Electricity Supply Commission (ESCOM), responsible inter alia for South Africa's nuclear development program; and the

South African Railway and Harbour Commission (SARH)—renamed the South African Transport Services, SATS—responsible not only for South Africa's transportation infrastructure but also for the levelling of black dwellings and forced removals by the police.

The Royal Bank was not itself listed, but the Orion Bank in London, England, in which the Royal held a 20 percent interest, was named by Corporate Data Exchange as a substantial lender during the period reviewed. This did not conflict with the wording of Royal's statement, but it did raise the question of whether associated and controlled subsidiaries were respecting the bank's new policy. We discussed this matter with senior officials of the Royal Bank. They gave us assurances that the Orion's position on loans to South Africa was not "inconsistent" with their own, and that the Royal Bank of Canada would not knowingly make or participate indirectly in loans that it would not make directly.

No arguments in private meetings with bank executives nor questions at shareholder meetings had at all moved the other four major banks. Indeed, the Bank of Montreal showed itself to be a spirited defender of its loans to South Africa. During the December 1977 annual general meeting, the chairman, Mr. Fred McNeil, who had recently visited South Africa, said that the loans of the Bank to South Africa were "insignificant in amount and effect on profitability" but that conceding to the churches' request to halt these loans "would not be morally defensible nor morally consistent."

So pleased was Mr. McNeil with his address on the topic that he had it duplicated and sent to every shareholder. In addition, copies were sent to Roman Catholic bishops and to the Confederation of Church and Business People. Archbishop Gilles Ouellet, then President of the Canadian Conference of Catholic Bishops, wrote a detailed response, which served as a thoughtful policy statement of the Canadian Conference of Catholic Bishops regarding corporate social responsibility on bank loans and related questions.[7]

The late Senator Eugene Forsey, a shareholder of both the Royal Bank and the Bank of Montreal, had previously sent his proxies to the Taskforce for our use. In 1978 he decided to accompany us in person to the annual meeting of the Bank of Montreal. We were proud to have the support of this remarkable Canadian. Speaking in English and in French to his overwhelmingly English audience (except for the ushers), he proposed a complete loan embargo against South Africa to be relaxed only in exceptional cases. This policy, he suggested, should gradually be adopted for all repressive regimes. The Senator's words were received in frigid silence.

A few months later, in May 1978, Dawson College of Montreal removed its account from the Bank of Montreal in protest of the bank's refusal to halt South African loans. Dawson thus became one of the first of a substantial number of universities and colleges who were to take similar decisions over the next few years.

Public Pressure

By 1979 Canadian banks were under increasing public pressure. Alterca-
tions on racial and social justice issues between the chair of a major bank
and dissident church shareholders were a completely new phenomenon in
Canada. They attracted growing—in time even sympathetic—media attention. Each piece of publicity added to the number of unsolicited shareholder proxies sent to the Taskforce from across Canada for use by its
members. International research on additional South African loans, undertaken by such organizations as the New York Corporate Data Exchange,
Inc., the World Council of Churches' "Programme to Combat Racism" or
the British-based "End Loans to South Africa," proliferated and created its
own publicity.

To help people understand the importance of bank support for the
apartheid system, the Taskforce published and periodically updated "A
Few Words from the Canadian Banks." This new brochure simply detailed
the amounts, recipients and due dates of Canadian loans to the South African government and its agencies and added statements made by the banks
regarding these loans and their positions on future lending. There was
great demand for such straightforward factual information. It was used for
years by many different Canadian organizations—church and secular—as
a basis for their own statements and actions. We also produced an even sim-
pler but equally popular device. We printed gummed sheets of "NO LOANS
TO SOUTH AFRICA" stickers, the size of "air mail" labels, which could be
affixed to cheques.[8] They were widely used and left a paper trail from local
merchants and restaurants to bank employees. The United Church of Canada used them on their pay cheques. In addition, we circulated petitions
inviting shareholders and depositors to support the churches' position and
gathered thousands of signatures. We also solicited "role model" Canadians to support our efforts. We collected a list of wonderful signatories,
among them Chester Ronning, Margaret Laurence, Emmett Hall, Rose-
mary Brown, George Erasmus, June Callwood, William Hutt, Christina
McCall and Eugene Forsey.

Canadian bank loans to South Africa were provoking public protest from
many organizations. An audacious action by the Toronto Committee for
the Liberation of Southern Africa's Colonies mixed faked cheques among
the banks' stacks of deposit and withdrawal slips which read "pay to the
order of John Balthasar Vorster, prime minister of South Africa, the sum of
$50 million." Each commemorative day—such as 21 March (Sharpeville
Day), 16 June (Soweto Day) or 18 July (Mandela's birthday)—were occasions for demonstrations or pickets in front of bank buildings. Soon important organizations and individuals publicized the transfer of their accounts
from banks still unprepared to announce a no-loans policy to alternative
lending institutions. CUSO, then Canada's largest non-governmental inter-

national development agency, led the way in 1977 when it withdrew all its short-term investments from the Royal Bank and placed its $11-million annual budget in an alternative financial institution. CUSO was looking for an institution with a "no loans to South Africa" policy.

Not all the initiatives on South African loans were taken by anti-apartheid activists. After some years during which no new Canadian loans had appeared in international research documents, the Toronto Dominion Bank announced during its 1979 shareholder meeting that the previous August it had participated in a loan to the Electricity Supply Commission of South Africa (ESCOM). The Bank argued that this loan would be used for the electrification of black communities. The churches protested that ESCOM's program to develop South Africa's nuclear industry was the more likely beneficiary of this international loan than the black townships.

When the churches met with officials of the Toronto Dominion bank in January 1980, both parties agreed to postpone the publication of the updated brochure on Canadian bank loans while the bank reviewed its South African loans policy. In March 1980 the chair of the Toronto Dominion announced that "this loan [to ESCOM] will not be renewed, nor will the Bank make new loans to the Government of South Africa or its agencies under present conditions."

By 1980 even the Bank of Montreal, now with William Mulholland as chair, moved away from its previous vigorous defence of South African loans. However, the new chair did not advance matters when he declared categorically that issues relating to client business would not be a matter for public—meaning shareholder—discussion.

Krugerrand Sales

The churches had initially believed that of the Canadian banks, the Bank of Nova Scotia was the least involved with South Africa. This turned out to have been an error. In 1978 Canadian bank sales of Krugerrand, South Africa's gold coin, became a public concern. With this, the Bank of Nova Scotia moved to centre stage. Cedric Ritchie, head of the Bank of Nova Scotia, informed the Taskforce in 1979: "The Bank of Nova Scotia is the largest and in fact virtually the only significant Canadian intermediary in the gold markets of the world ... we deal in over fifty different items of gold coins and bullion to fill the orders of our customers."[9] "The Krugerrand was designed for international marketing by the South African Chamber of Mines. To name the coin after Paulus Kruger, a legendary nineteenth-century Afrikaner leader with biblical beliefs rooted in the Old Testament, gives history a paradoxical twist. Kruger distrusted all non-Afrikaners and opposed the (mainly English) industrialists and mine owners whom he thought to be in league with the devil. He prophesied: "Every ounce of gold taken from the bowels of our soil, will yet have to be weighed against rivers of tears."[10]

His prophesy came true, but not in the way he had foreseen. In 1979 the average monthly earnings for black miners, who made up 90 percent of the workforce in South Africa's gold mines, were $142; those of whites were $1,163. Only white miners were unionized; the vast majority of black miners were contract workers who lived as "single" men in company compounds.

While most of the refined gold was sold in the form of bullion on international markets by the government itself, Krugerrands were sold to international customers by the Chamber of Mines. The coins were sold either as collector items or were crafted into pieces of jewellery. Advertisements for the coin emphasized the "stability" and "security" value of gold as investment and its glamour and elegance when combined with jewellery. Given the conditions under which Krugerrands were produced, there was hardly a more direct investment in oppression than in the purchase of the gold coin.

Members of the Taskforce joined the international campaigns already under way in the United States, Britain and continental Europe. They took the matter of Krugerrand sales to the Canadian chartered banks, requesting that they not sell the Krugerrand, but instead vigorously promote Canada's Maple Leaf coin as an alternative for gold-buying customers. It seemed to us a straightforward proposal, making sense to most Canadians. Yet the banks made it sound like an impossible proposition. The Scotiabank said that it was selling the Krugerrand for the South African Chamber of Mines only with great reluctance:

> In 1969, Scotiabank was chosen as the official distributor in Canada of Krugerrands. There were then eighteen Krugerrand distributors worldwide; there still are only eighteen and we know we are in last position as regards volume of transactions.
>
> We did not seek the Krugerrand appointment; we were chosen because we were then the only dealer in gold in Canada. Moreover, we have reason to believe the Canadian Mint pressured for an appointment of a distributor in Canada.[11]

Scotiabank did not think it was its place to propose a ban on the distribution of the coin to the government. Other Canadian banks wishing to purchase Krugerrands for their customers obtained these from the Bank of Nova Scotia. In all other respects they echoed the Bank of Nova Scotia, pleading that failing a government ban, they were obliged to respond to customers' requests for the South African coins.

The appointment in early 1980 of Cedric Ritchie, chair of the Bank of Nova Scotia, to the board of directors of the Mineral and Resources Corporation (Minorco), a company controlled by Anglo American Corporation of South Africa, went some way to explain the logic behind the Scotiabank's role in the Krugerrand marketing. In the seventies Minorco was incorporated in Bermuda. By camouflaging its South African origin, Minorco was able to aid Anglo's penetration of the international market. On Minorco's board Ritchie was joining Walter Wriston, chair of Citycorp., a major lender to South Africa. Thus Ritchie came to work closely with South Africa's largest corporation, whose chairman, Harry Oppenheimer—succeeded by Gavin Relly—was a natural and powerful opponent to any restrictions on loans to South Africa. The Canadian churches strongly protested Ritchie's acceptance of the directorship at a time of heightened oppression in South Africa and unsuccessfully urged him to step down from this position.

Bid to Influence the Lawmakers

When the Bank Act was revised between 1978 and 1980, the Taskforce presented a brief to the House of Commons Standing Committee on Finance, Trade and Economic Affairs, calling for greater transparency of international lending by Canadian commercial banks. Under the watchful eye of a delegate from the Canadian Bankers Association, the Taskforce argued that in the interest of public and shareholder accountability, a revised Bank Act should require uniform and equitable disclosure of Canadian bank loans over $1 million to foreign governments or their agencies. In the late spring of 1980 church delegates met with members of Parliament from all political parties, government officials and members of the Standing Committee to solicit their support. The churches made the point that international loans were a growing and significant part of Canadian bank operations. As such, they had foreign policy implications and were of interest to shareholders and the government and indeed to parliamentarians and the public. Such information was necessary in order to assess both the risks being incurred and the corporate citizenship being practised.

The churches also noted that "[T]here is the principle of stewardship which compels shareholders and depositors to know how the bank uses money, and the principle of accountability which makes it impossible to treat loans to foreign governments as merely loans to a client."[12]

The recommendations and arguments of the Taskforce fell on deaf ears. The report of the Standing Committee on Finance, Trade and Economic Affairs was unmoved by them.

Positions of Canadian Banks by 1980

There was by 1980 a distinct diversity in the positions taken by the Canadian banks regarding their lending to the apartheid regime. These positions can be summarized as follows:

- The Royal Bank reserved the right to consider all loan requests; it had not renewed or made new loans since 1976; under current circumstances, no general purpose or balance of payment loans would be made; and it would not knowingly make or participate in loans indirectly which it would not make directly;

- The Canadian Imperial Bank of Commerce held that Canadian loans to South Africa benefited black South Africans and that revealing such loans would violate client/banker confidentiality;

- The Bank of Nova Scotia felt obliged to protect client/banker confidentiality and did not reply to questions about South African loans; it noted that it complied with Canadian law, which permitted these loans;

- The Bank of Montreal turned back all inquiries, declaring that matters related to client business would not be discussed in public;

- Since 1979 the policy of the Toronto Dominion Bank stated that it would not renew or make new loans to the South African government or its agencies under present conditions.[13]

When the churches began their joint activities on Canadian investments in South Africa and Namibia, they had not been aware of the dimensions presented by Canadian bank loans to the apartheid government and its agencies. Once known, they became a challenge that was difficult to research and hard to broach with the banks. However, the issue itself was uncomplicated and the relationship between bank and customer lent immediacy to public education and mobilization for action. The Taskforce had made real progress but there was a long way to go yet.

Corporate Investment in South Africa and Namibia

A preliminary list of Canadian manufacturing and mining companies operating in South Africa and Namibia had been presented to the churches in *Investment in Oppression*. These operations were as important to the South African regime as were the bank loans, but the complexities of their corporate entanglements hid them from public awareness and made mobilization against their specific activities more difficult. This section reviews the activities of these companies and the early responses of the Taskforce to them.

Alcan Aluminium Ltd.

The churches had begun conversations with Alcan even before the formal establishment of the Taskforce. They were anxious to discuss the company's responses to the YWCA questionnaire of 1973 and were disturbed by Alcan's expansion of its South African investment. The company had just joined African Oxygen and Foote Minerals to establish the Silicon Smelters in the border area of the Lebowa "homeland." At this time the South African government was offering incentives for "industrial decentralization" that would make maximum use of cheap black labour without an influx of blacks into "white" areas. Such border industries were ideally suited for this purpose; Africans continued to live in the "homelands" away from "white" residential areas, yet worked for "white" industries. Employers were exempted from minimum wage requirements; working conditions were "out of sight" and worse than elsewhere. Given the poverty of the "home-lands," workers who protested were easily replaced.

In their early discussions with Alcan management and in their questions during Alcan's 1975 shareholder meeting, church representatives addressed these features of the company's South African expansion. By its investment in the Silicon Smelters, they argued, Alcan affirmed its toler-ance for the racist regime. More than that, by locating the smelter in a border area, the company was accommodating apartheid's decentraliza-tion policy and was taking unfair advantage of the huge pool of unem-ployed labour.

Over the next few years the churches requested, and Alcan secured for them from its South African managers, information about wages and employment conditions at the Smelters. The Smelters' grim record turned out to be appalling enough to embarrass Alcan's senior management in Montreal. They could hardly be defended as an illustration of the liberal-izing influence that foreign investment was thought to be bringing to South Africa. Nathanael Davis, chair of Alcan, told the 1977 annual meet-ing that the Silicon Smelters "is encountering difficulties at the moment ... I do not think that this is a reason not to pay proper wages but their preoccupations have been in other directions."[14]

By April 1979 Alcan had sold its interest in the Silicon Smelters. Bob Rosane, Alcan's incoming area general manager for Africa, had clearly not been happy with this particular association and described Alcan's 1973 decision to invest in the Smelters as "a piece of euphoric nonsense."

Alcan's relationship with the giant South African Tongaat Hulett Group of companies was an altogether different matter. In the mid-seventies Alcan had sold down its South African investment and opted for a 24 percent minority partnership in Hulett Aluminium Ltd., an aluminum fabricator and one of Tongaat Hulett's many companies. Initially the Taskforce had set out to test the thesis that foreign companies in South Africa represented a liberalizing influence and had therefore inquired about black wages and working conditions in South African companies with Canadian investment. The partnership between Hulett Aluminium and Alcan tilted enquiries into a new direction as members of the Taskforce began to recognize the strategic importance of the alliance of these two powerful corporations. The leadership of Tongaat Hulett was deeply immersed in white South African politics and steeped in the written and unwritten rules of apartheid society. Alcan brought to the partnership not only capital and technology but also its extensive international experience in markets for aluminum products and a successful record of military contracts.

In July 1975 the Taskforce sent to Alcan the churches' position on apartheid and their perception of Alcan's role as a foreign investor in South Africa. They asked Alcan to respond and to correct the churches' impressions where these were wrong. In their statement, the churches were critical of Alcan's acquiescence in the apartheid system. They felt that Alcan, by becoming a minority partner in Hulett Aluminium, had removed itself from the responsibility of initiating liberalizing measures.[15] These impressions had been deepened, the Taskforce wrote, by Alcan's acceptance of Hulett's judgement of South African organizations that would most likely achieve desired changes. Alcan and Hulett shared a negative assessment of the Christian Institute of South Africa, an interdenominational organization under the dynamic leadership of Reverend Beyers Naudé which sought to dismantle apartheid by non-violent means.[16] Instead, Alcan and Hulett backed the South African Foundation, claiming it as a vehicle for liberal change.[17]

A brief detour is in order to place the South African Foundation in its historical context. It had been created after the March 1960 Sharpeville shootings, where sixty-nine unarmed civilians were killed while staging a peaceful demonstration against the pass laws. International investors panicked, and for a brief period South Africa experienced a net outflow of private capital and faced a severe financial crisis. In a swift move, powerful South African and international business interests established the South African Foundation to stem the financial drain and to counter the beginnings of unfavourable global reaction to apartheid. The Foundation's role was to undertake "the promotion of international understanding of the South African way of life, achievements, and aspirations ... and positive campaigns which shall present to the world at large the true picture of South Africa."[18]

Increasingly the Taskforce also questioned Alcan about the production in South Africa of specialized aluminum products for military purposes. It disagreed with the company that the 1963 UN voluntary arms embargo against South Africa did not apply to its operation there. The Resolution had called for an end to investment in, or technical assistance to, South African manufacturing industries of military equipment.[19] The voluntary nature of the arms embargo meant, of course, that it was observed only by those already predisposed not to arm the apartheid state.

The fact was that Pretoria had taken seriously the warning signals implicit in the voluntary embargo. In anticipation of an eventual mandatory arms ban, the regime sought to lessen its dependence on foreign sources. It had begun not only to assemble military equipment in South Africa under licensing agreements with international suppliers of parts and technology, but had also, by the end of the 1960s, established ARMSCOR, its state-owned armament corporation. ARMSCOR coordinated research and production among a myriad of public and private companies to achieve self-sufficiency in South Africa's military preparedness.[20] The Taskforce began to be troubled about Alcan's role in this network.

The first public discussion of Alcan's South African involvement took place during the 1975 shareholder meeting. To our surprise several shareholders approached us immediately after the meeting to express their support for our involvement. The following year unsolicited proxies began to arrive at the Taskforce office; their owners asked church delegates to represent their shares on this issue.

At the 1976 annual meeting, church representatives pressed Alcan to produce information on wages and working conditions in Hulett's operations and to answer the churches' concerns about Alcan's possible involvement in military production. Alcan dispatched a senior officer to South Africa to seek responses to these questions and, on his return, made available the details of employment practices of its majority partner in South Africa.

On 16 June 1976 members of the Taskforce were in Montreal for a meeting with Alcan's senior executives to discuss these details. Unknown to us, this was also the first, calamitous day of protest by black schoolchildren in Soweto, marking the start of sustained black defiance and state repression. Yet here we were going through the grotesque exercise of reviewing categories of jobs by race and wage levels to determine whether some minuscule progress in black working conditions was evidence of Alcan's liberalizing influence in South Africa.

On several occasions the churches had, without success, asked Alcan to make a donation to the South African Council of Churches (SACC) as acknowledgement of the devastating effect apartheid had on people's lives and to assist financially SACC's relief programs. Members of the Taskforce were surprised and pleased, therefore, that Alcan's Bob Rosane chose October 1977, a period of heightened repression, for a visit to the South African Council of Churches. This impeccable corporate manager must have cut a singular figure amidst the frightened and bewildered people and the overworked and harassed staff of the SACC, which had escaped recent government bannings. Rosane made a small but important financial contribution on behalf of Alcan to help people who had just been orphaned by a ban on eighteen organizations that had previously assisted them. Although much more pressure would be needed before Alcan turned its back on apartheid, the churches appreciated this gesture—unique among the companies with whom they were dealing.

Toward the end of 1977 international anger over South Africa's conduct had reached a new level. Unprovoked, South Africa's army had invaded Angola; the Soweto uprisings had been brutally dealt with; Black Consciousness leader Steve Biko had been murdered by the police; and nearly twenty anti-apartheid organizations had been outlawed, their staff imprisoned or banned. On 4 November 1977 the UN Security Council adopted Resolution 418, declaring that "the acquisition by South Africa of arms and related matériel constitutes a threat to the maintenance of international peace and security." The Security Council instructed all states "to cease forthwith any provision to South Africa of arms and related matériel, to review licences granted for the manufacture and maintenance of arms and to refrain from any co-operation . . . in the manufacture and development of nuclear weapons." However, UNSCR 418 made no mention of direct and indirect supplies to ARMSCOR of military technology and components by foreign investors *in* South Africa. Nor did it call for an end to licensing agreements, but only for their "review." The Taskforce was to become acutely aware of these inadequacies when they remonstrated with Alcan, other Canadian investors and the Canadian government about the applicability of UNSCR 418 to Canadian involvement in South Africa.

The mandatory arms embargo replaced the 1963 voluntary measure. In addition to the establishment of South Africa's own arms industry, South Africa had enacted several pieces of legislation designed to lessen the impact of the mandatory embargo. The National Supplies Procurement Act of 1970 gave the minister of defence the power "when necessary for the security of South Africa" to order any individual or industry to "manufacture, produce, process or treat and to supply or deliver or to sell" any goods or services to the South African Defence Forces.[21] The Internal Security Act and the Publications Act greatly increased the secrecy required of corporations engaged in these activities; in addition the Atomic Energy Act and the Petroleum Products Act constrained industries in these sectors to supply the armed forces and the police.[22]

One latecomer in this series of South Africa's protective legislation was the 1980 National Key Points Act, which became an added factor in Alcan's South African investment. Under this law South Africa's minister of defence could designate any place or area a "Key Point." Industries located in these areas were then required to implement, at their own expense, security arrangements detailed by the minister of defence. These usually included the training of white workers as militia reserve units and the storage on the premises of arms and ammunition for the defence of the plant in cases of serious unrest. Key Point industries were obliged to be open for inspection by the minister of defence or his agents at all times. Information about Key Point security measures were secret. Owners who failed to comply with the Act faced prison sentences of up to three years and fines of up to (approx.) $20,000.[23]

Some of the Taskforce's discoveries were made in rather round-about ways. In August 1980, during an international seminar, we learned that the

London-based Orion Bank—in which the Royal Bank of Canada held a 20 percent share—had recently participated in a major Eurobond purchase for the Standard Bank of South Africa. At issue here was not the Royal Bank but rather the beneficiary—the Standard Bank of South Africa—with its connections to the South African military establishment. In June 1980 Ian MacKenzie, chair of the Standard Bank, had joined Prime Minister Botha's Defense Advisory Board.

And there were other implications. The June 1980 issue of *Paratus*, the journal of South Africa's armed forces, reported that there were three other directors of the Standard Bank of South Africa on Botha's Defence Advisory Board. These were Gavin A. Relly of Anglo American, A. Michael Rosholt of Barlow Rand and Christopher J. Saunders, chair of Hulett Corporation—Alcan's South African partner.[24]

During a tense exchange we pressed Alcan about Saunders' membership on the Defence Advisory Board and suggested that it was likely that Hulett Aluminium was sufficiently defence-related to be designated a "Key Point" industry. A half nod from Bob Rosane confirmed this. We began to feel very uncomfortable. Here we had been accepting, in good faith, Alcan's claim that its South African investment was a "liberalizing influence" when it had in fact opted some time previous to locate itself within Prime Minister Botha's inner circle.

Before we return in a later section to the churches' continuing actions concerning Alcan's South African investments, we turn to other early encounters with potential and actual corporate investors in South Africa.

Seagram's plans for KwaZulu

In late 1975 an American consulting firm[25] invited the Taskforce to react to a proposal for a $10 million whisky distillery in KwaZulu as a joint venture between the Canadian Seagram Company and Stellenbosch Wine Trust of South Africa Breweries. Mindful that this was a Canadian company, we wrote to Charles Bronfman in Montreal to tell him of our existence and interest in the matter. He replied to assure us that in the final decision our comments would definitely be taken into account.[26] The Taskforce had, in fact, major reservations related to the nature of the investment, its product and its ultimate destination, none of which contributed to black development. The investment would be capital intensive with a low yield of employment opportunities; it would be located in a "homeland," thus helping to legitimize this aspect of apartheid doctrine; it would not meet the people's basic needs and its ultimate destination was the export market, benefiting the foreign exchange position of the apartheid regime.

The Taskforce was not won over by the consultants' assurance that the investment would forge links between black South African and black American business people. Such links, the churches said, would be no substitute for the lack of fundamental civil and political freedoms and would serve to create a new black elite that South African strategists of white supremacy saw as a potential ally against popularly based resistance movements.[27] Finally, the churches said, they feared that the more Canadian economic interests were tied to the status quo in South Africa, the less prepared they would be to support any social and political changes. The Taskforce forwarded these comments in a further letter to Charles Bronfman.

In early May 1976, Reverend Thomas Anthony, chair of the Taskforce, myself and members of the American Committee on Africa, met in New York with Seagram's consultants in the unexplained presence of an official of the US State Department. We reviewed the arguments already offered by the Canadian churches and assured Seagram's consultants that we would give maximum publicity should Seagram invest in KwaZulu. Unconvinced, the consultants recommended that Seagram go ahead with its investment plans.

On 27 May Bronfman phoned the Taskforce to say that for business reasons Seagram was not proceeding with the South African investment. At the time Bronfman was on the board of directors of the Bank of Montreal and would have been acquainted with the publicity caused by the Bank's loans to South Africa. We liked to think that the $10 million of controversial investment in a South African "homeland" was not worth the public squabble and possible boycott of Seagram's products which, although never directly threatened, could reasonably have been anticipated had the investment taken place.[28]

Titanium Mining at Richards Bay

Early in 1976 the Quebec Iron and Titanium Corporation/QIT-Fer et Titane announced its intention to participate in a $300 million development of the iron- and titanium-bearing beaches in Richards Bay, Natal. At the time the corporation was two-thirds owned by Kennecott and one-third by Gulf and Western. Nevertheless it was legally a Canadian company with a postal address in Sorel, Quebec. QIT-Fer et Titane announced that it would enter into partnership with the South African government's Industrial Development Corporation (IDC) and several private South African enterprises. The initial investment would give QIT-Fer et Titane, with a nearly 40 percent interest, control of the smelting operations, and IDC and its South African affiliates control of mining in a new company called Richards Bay Heavy Minerals. Richards Bay and its surrounding land and beaches had belonged to the "homeland" of KwaZulu until it had been summarily excised in 1974 and declared "white" after the discovery of the mineral resource in the sands.

The Taskforce wrote to QIT-Fer et Titane that it was opposed to its investment plans, and church representatives went to New York in February 1976 to join their American colleagues in discussions with the company. Together they advanced some of the same arguments given to Seagram, but with less success. QIT-Fer et Titane's stake in its South African investment plans were much higher and the company's vulnerability to product boycott was almost nil. Titanium is used in the paint and pigment industries and the ostensible plan was to develop for South Africa a viable export market for the European textile, paint and paper industries. The churches opposed the venture in the first instance because they were opposed to any new foreign investment in apartheid South Africa. There was, however, a further dimension to their opposition. Depending on the conversion process, Titanium could serve as a strategic metal. Because of its versatile combination of lightness, strength and heat resistant properties, the metal is ideally suited for aircraft components, energy systems and nuclear installations, as well as for modern weapons systems. The management of QIT-Fer et Titane granted that this conversion process was possible, but asserted that its costs would be prohibitive.

The US churches had presented a formal shareholder proposal to the 1976 annual meeting in New York, asking the directors of QIT-Fer et Titane to oppose the South African investment. Member churches of the Taskforce, none of whom held shares in the company, were at the meeting and had issued a statement in support of this motion to both Kennecott Corporation and QIT-Fer et Titane.

When the proposal was discussed, Frank Milliken, chair of the company, made public a letter from M. Gatsha Buthelezi, written in his capacity as chief executive councillor of KwaZulu. Buthelezi confirmed that the Kwa-Zulu "homeland" favoured Kennecott's investment. His comments give a rare insight into the subservient role played by even the most powerful and prominent of South Africa's "homeland" leaders. Although he had just been swindled out of a valuable piece of industrial real estate for blatant racist reasons, Buthelezi echoed the view of the apartheid government who paid his salary: "This we have asked for not just on any terms as we have always emphasized with every new investment. We need job opportunities for our people particularly in this area where they will be able to live with their families and work where the ravages of migratory labour will be avoided."[29] The shareholder proposal of the American churches was defeated. Still, it received support from 3.65 percent of Kennecott voting shares. Given the tendency of institutional and individual shareholders to support management, this early vote on a South African issue ranked fairly high and, under US law, could be resubmitted the following year.

Further research was to reinforce the churches scepticism about the non-strategic nature of the titanium produced at the Richard's Bay smelter. In 1985 the story of QIT-Fer et Titane and its South African investment resurfaced for the Taskforce and is discussed below.

Ford South Africa

Ford Canada had been one of the companies on the original list of *Investment in Oppression*. At the time it was 88.4 percent owned by the US-based Ford Motor Company, which held its South African investments through the Canadian subsidiary.[30] The Taskforce initiated contact with Ford Canada in 1979. It became immediately obvious that all Ford South Africa policy decisions were made in the office of the vice-president for Mid-East and Africa of the Ford Motor Company, USA. Ford Canada's role was limited to the inclusion in its annual report of Ford South Africa's annual financial statement. Everyone from the management of the Ford Motor Company to its shareholders, including our American partner churches, ignored the Canadian dimension.

In response to our first letter in June 1979, Ford Canada put up a brave front. We had expressed support for a carefully conceived US shareholder proposal from the American churches requesting Ford South Africa to terminate its contracts with the South African police and military. Ford Canada replied that Ford South Africa had been a leader in fostering progressive change in South Africa. It had improved labour/management relations, adhered to the Canadian Code of Conduct (see below) and made generous contributions towards black housing. Ford Canada also warned that implementation of the US church shareholder proposal could damage their operations in South Africa. Ford Canada did not address the matter of Ford South Africa's sales to the military and police.[31]

This changed in July when, at the request of the Ford Motor Company, members of the Taskforce met with a public relations officer from Ford Canada and the vice-president for International and Governmental Affairs of Ford's head office. Ford officers repeated the claim that their company was now a leader among progressive South African employers, contributing to gradual liberal changes. Regarding government contracts however, Ford management held that a loss of police and military contracts could result in layoffs of their Ford workers and could evoke retaliatory measures from the South African government involving possibly the loss of all other government contracts. These, Ford estimated, were about 5 to 8 percent of its South African market. Indeed, Ford officials feared that termination of the contracts might lead to a South African consumer boycott of Ford vehicles altogether. They invited members of the Taskforce to recognize that these risks would more than offset the perceived advantage of not selling to the police or military.[32]

The Taskforce was astonished that the company would so misjudge the misgivings of the churches about Ford's collaboration with the South African military and police. Church representatives had not expected Ford to argue that being a model employer—if in fact it was—would morally compensate for its collaboration with the enforcement agencies of the apartheid state. When church representatives suggested that Ford's sales to the South African military and police amounted to circumvention of the mandatory arms embargo against South Africa, Bill Broderick of the Ford Motor Company was able to recite from memory the relevant sections of UNSCR 418. It said that governments should "cease forthwith any provision of . . . military vehicles and equipment, paramilitary police equipment and spare parts . . . ." Broderick argued quite correctly, that no government had interpreted this resolution to include non-military vehicles or equipment purchased for use by the police or the military.

We agreed that this was evidently the interpretation favoured by governments. The churches sought to convince Ford that the very sale of Ford's "non-military" vehicles to the police and military, converted them into "military and police equipment." Taskforce members however, did not so much quarrel with the legality of the contracts; rather they wished them terminated because of de facto support they gave to the apartheid regime. We put to Ford's executives that their corporation, whose South African operations at the time represented less than 1 percent of its world-wide business, could well afford to distance itself from apartheid and that it should retire from the scene.[33]

On 4 September 1979 the leaders of five Canadian churches issued an "Open Letter to Ford" in response to Ford's refusal to move on the issue. They argued that "Ford's decision to keep its military and police contracts will serve to assist the South African Government in its imposition of apartheid." The church leaders expressed the fear that Ford had become hostage to apartheid, rather than the liberalizing force it had claimed to be."[34]

A month later even Ford South Africa's image as a model employer was severely tarnished. Workers in its Port Elizabeth plant near Cape Town went on strike in support of Thozamile Botha, a foreman who had been fired for his activities—not as a Ford employee but as chair of the Port Elizabeth Black Civic Organization. Increased tensions had been caused by forced removals of approximately ten thousand black people after their residential area was declared "white" under South Africa's Group Areas Act. Ford's black workers, whose families and friends were being "endorsed out," joined the community protests to stop the removals. Not surprisingly, the "Group Areas" ruling also affected the workplace, and hostilities erupted between black and white workers at the Ford plant.

Fired by Ford, Thozamile Botha and his supporters were detained without charge by the police. All through November industrial action continued, leading to Ford's summary dismissal and replacements of 15,000 black workers in Port Elizabeth and in two neighbouring plants which had also been affected. At this point American diplomats visited Ford's management in Port Elizabeth and appear to have urged the company to contain the situation. In December 1979 negotiations opened with Thozamile Botha and other representatives of the dismissed workers. In January 1980, four days after an agreement for reinstatement was reached, security police raided black townships and detained three black civic leaders, Botha among them. They were released in February and immediately banned. Thozamile Botha eventually escaped and was able to tell this story to the international community, among others, at a meeting called by the Taskforce on the Churches and Corporate Responsibility.[35] Reverend Tom Anthony, the director of the National and World Program of the Anglican Church of Canada, visited Ford South Africa in June 1980. Despite specific and repeated requests, he was not allowed to meet with the workers in the plant.

To give publicity to Ford South Africa's activities, the Taskforce combined in a flyer a news item on Ford South Africa, which had been published in *Catholic New Times*, with a photograph showing a black student being arrested before a waiting Ford police van and the record of the chronology of events during the Port Elizabeth industrial dispute.[36] These Taskforce actions were supplementary to the main pressure on the Ford Motor Company, which continued to be exerted in the USA by members of the ICCR. Their shareholder actions and company negotiations about Ford South Africa's operations received proxy support from the United Church of Canada, a Ford shareholder, while the Taskforce gave publicity to these actions.

"Black on Black"

Massey-Ferguson had also been identified by *Investment in Oppression* as a company with South African investment. In 1973 Massey-Ferguson (South Africa) manufactured farm, industrial and construction machinery; Perkins Engines (Pty) Ltd., Massey-Ferguson's British subsidiary, produced diesel engines.

The story began in 1977 with a visit to the Taskforce office of a young woman from Crossroads in Capetown. She described to us how the Department of Railways and Harbours (SARH) "cleared" African squatter camps that had been erected by family members from the "homelands." These families had come to Crossroads to be with their breadwinners—mostly their husbands and fathers—in defiance of South African law. Our visitor told us that the bulldozers used by SAHR to level the camps had Massey-Ferguson markings. This was important information. A number of international bank loans had been extended to the SARH and the case against such loans was strengthened by this news. Further, it suggested that Massey-Ferguson (South Africa), like Ford South Africa, provided agencies of the South African government with equipment used to enforce the apartheid system.

Additional information about Massey-Ferguson's activities in South Africa reached us through more conventional sources. In May 1979 *Business Week* carried an article that explained that as a direct result of the integration of political, military and economic planning in implementation of Botha's total strategy, diesel engines were going to be manufactured in South Africa, rather than imported. *Business Week* reported that Massey-Ferguson's UK subsidiary, Perkins Engines, was tipped to supply technology to the new South African government-owned company, Atlantis Diesel Engines:

> Part of the economic underpinning for Pretoria's new "fortress Southern Africa" policy will be a sustained drive for self-sufficiency in essential heavy industries, especially those that serve South Africa's military. Even before the government of Prime Minister P.W. Botha launched its latest effort to reduce Pretoria's strategic dependence on the West, plans were announced for the construction of a diesel engine plant to produce heavy truck engines for, among other customers, the South African Defence Force.[37]

The Taskforce wrote to Massey-Ferguson and expressed its concern that the company appeared to be assisting the South African government to maintain and defend its oppressive rule. After an exchange of letters with senior management, Conrad Black, then chair of Massey-Ferguson, wrote to the Taskforce on 12 July 1979. We were anxious to reproduce his letter in our *Annual Report*, but also mindful that our 1979 budget was just short of $45,000: a good reason to seek advice on the rules of libel. Through the mediation of a friend, a libel lawyer agreed to see Reverend Jim Webb, S.J. and me to give us twenty minutes of free advice. He explained the possible grounds for libel and then marked the exact portion of the letter that we could reproduce without fear of consequences. He warned us sternly to refrain from any comment. Here is that portion of the letter:

> The policy that your organization is promoting, which apparently strenuously opposes "any arrangements which would strengthen South Africa's military preparedness," is not one with which we agree. The forebears of the majority of the white population of South Africa settled in the Cape colony in that country more than three hundred and fifty years ago, when there were no blacks in that area. Even if we had the means to reduce the ability of the South African whites to become more economically and technologically self-sufficient, which we do not, we would certainly not be inclined to do so. Like all other peoples, they have a perfect right to self-preservation, and like all other respectable nationalities, they should be commended for having the collective pride and motivation to defend themselves. I have not the slightest doubt that, were your recommendations to be followed by the international community and the white population of South Africa left without any modern means of self-defence, they, who almost alone have populated and developed that remarkable country, would be eliminated as an ethnic entity by the gruesome

combination of subjection, massacre and expulsion. Discouraging people from a sense of self-reliance is no answer to the evils of the world.

Though I am sure I find racial policy in South Africa quite as distasteful as you do, it would not be a collective improvement, even if any activity of ours were of the slightest influence, to replace the oppressions of the current regime with the barbarism that would eagerly replace them. In any case, nothing that we are doing could be fairly described as likely to "strengthen South Africa's military preparedness."

In 1982 the Taskforce resumed action regarding the sale of bulldozers to the South African government and technology transfers for diesel engines by Massey Ferguson's subsidiary.

Falconbridge in Namibia

Falconbridge Nickel Mines, we noted, was one of the Canadian companies that had replied fully to the YWCA questionnaire, though requesting confidentiality. Falconbridge owned 25 percent of Western Platinum Mines, located in South Africa. It also held a majority 75 percent interest in the Oamites (copper) Mine in Namibia. The Taskforce decided to focus on the company's Namibian investment.

In 1966 the United Nations had voted that South Africa's rule in Namibia was illegal. The Taskforce therefore took the view that mining concessions granted by this illegal regime were null and void, and that companies that continued to operate there were doing so in defiance of international law. In this the Taskforce felt supported by a decision of the United Nations Council for Namibia. On 27 September 1974, under Sean McBride, the first and very remarkable commissioner for Namibia, the Council had adopted *Decree No. 1 for the Protection of Natural Resources of Namibia.* In essence the Decree called on companies not to deplete Namibia's natural resources prior to an international settlement unless they successfully negotiated their licences with the UN Council for Namibia.

In 1975 the churches thus began their long relationship with successive senior executives of Falconbridge. The very first issue, however, concerned the company's continued operations in Rhodesia (now Zimbabwe), then under United Nations mandatory economic sanctions and involved in a war of liberation for a black majority government. During the 1975 annual meeting of shareholders, church representatives questioned the chair about the omission in the company's annual report for 1974 of a financial statement for its wholly owned Blanket Mine in Rhodesia. To the amusement of most shareholders, the chair replied that the majority of the mines' employees had gone to war and there had been no time to issue reports. Intrigued by this flippant reply, members of the Taskforce requested an investigation by the Department of Industry, Trade and Commerce to establish whether repatriated earnings from the Blanket Mine and taxes paid by it to the embargoed government were violating Canadian United Nations Rhodesia Regulations (PC 1968—2339). A fairly extensive investigation was undertaken by the department involving company documents and the United Nations' Rhodesia Sanctions Committee. Fourteen months later, the Taskforce was informed that it did not appear at this time that an offence had been committed by Falconbridge.[38]

A more lasting disagreement with Falconbridge arose from its decision to establish the Oamites Mines in Namibia in partnership with the South African Industrial Development Corporation (IDC). The decision was made in 1971, five years after the UN vote that terminated South Africa's rule in Namibia, and at the very time as the International Court of Justice (ICJ) confirmed the legality of the UN decision under international law. The ICJ also enjoined member states to refrain from any act that would imply recognition of the illegal regime. Falconbridge had great difficulty in accepting the position of the churches that extracting non-renewable resources in Namibia while its people were held in bondage under an illegal occupation, amounted to theft. Indeed, Falconbridge insisted that it was merely obeying the laws of the land; it never questioned South Africa's right to issue laws for Namibia.

Moreover, Falconbridge sought to convince us of South Africa's sensible rule in Namibia and in doing so used the regime's terminology and ideology. Its executives warned against an Ovambo-SWAPO hegemony, in which a large tribe occupying a small area would dominate the many smaller tribes scattered throughout the rest of the country. Falconbridge explained that SWAPO would not take into account, as South Africa did, the many differences among the "nations" for which a federal constitution would be best suited. This defence of apartheid, as transplanted into Namibia, confirmed our concern that corporations investing in the apartheid system become its foremost international apologists.

We attempted to obtain information on wages and working conditions at the Oamites Mines. The company insisted that it did not pay by race but by job classification and that, therefore, its employment practices were "non-racial." This argument was used frequently by South African employers. It was a transparent subterfuge, for all the lower job categories were filled by blacks and all the highest by whites.

A generous information service in the secretariat of the UN Council for Namibia, run by Betsy Landis, a competent and committed lawyer, kept us regularly updated with news from Namibian press clippings and answered our more urgent questions promptly and patiently by telephone. We thus learned that Falconbridge—like other resource-extracting companies—was anxious to deplete the Oamites mine in record time before "uncertainties" in the disputed territory overtook them. In this, Falconbridge appears to have been successful. The Oamites Mines, practically exhausted, was sold in 1983 to a South African owner and collapsed the following year. Falconbridge disclosed that between 1972–82 it had paid $5,319,614 in taxes to the illegal regime and between 1969–82 had netted $4,368,214 in profits.[39]

Rio Algom

Another Canadian company had been active in Namibia since 1971. Rio Algom, a subsidiary of Rio Tinto Zinc, had joined its British parent, the South African Development Corporation, Total of France, South Africa's General Mining and Finance Corporation and a number of smaller companies to develop Rossing Uranium, the largest open-cast uranium mine in the world. One of Rossing's directors was George Albino, chair of Rio Algom. Rossing's development had been facilitated by major long-term uranium contracts with Britain, France, West Germany, Japan and others. In time these contracts were also to benefit Canada's Crown corporation Eldorado Nuclear (later CAMECO), for it became the major processor of substantial quantities of uranium, imported from Namibia. Rossing's tax payments were deferred for seven years. As they began to fall due, Rio Algom and other companies who paid taxes to the illegal regime in Namibia were allowed to deduct these from their Canadian taxes. Thus for years Canadian taxpayers underwrote the pillage of Namibian resources.

Our efforts to meet with Rio Algom about its involvement in Namibia were not successful until March 1984. We knew, though, that the company had not forgotten us—every year its library ordered two copies of our *Annual Report*.

At the end of 1980 the Taskforce took stock of the situation. The Canadian government clearly tolerated corporate activity in Namibia despite its support for the 1966 United Nations vote that terminated South Africa's rule over Namibia and in defiance of the ICJ ruling that UN member states should refrain from any acts implying recognition of the illegal administration. Foreign, including Canadian companies, continued to profit from the depletion of Namibia's non-renewable resources and the Canadian government played midwife to the theft by allowing tax deductions for companies that paid taxes to the illegal regime.

As we had done in the case of Canadian bank loans to South Africa, we sought to mobilize public opinion on the issue of Canadian investment in Namibia. In 1982 we issued 18,000 copies of "Canada, Namibia and You," a pamphlet in English and French that set out the history of oppression in Namibia and the pertinent facts on Canadian corporate activity not readily available elsewhere in Canada. It included names and addresses of corporate executives, and departments of government and their ministers. The pamphlet was updated regularly and widely used as the Canadian anti-apartheid movement gathered momentum.

The members of the Taskforce had scored very few successes in their efforts to cut Canadian corporate involvement in South Africa and Namibia. The self-interest of corporations, their resentment toward church pressures and their uncritical recapitulation of even the most transparently ideological rationalizations of the apartheid regime, clearly contradicted corporate assertions that they should be looked upon as the champions of progressive change.

The Taskforce and Government Policy

Development of a Position

The common denominator in the endeavours of the Taskforce has been to seek improvement in social justice and human rights in areas where corporate policy can make a difference. If approaches to corporations through discussions and proactive shareholdership promised fruitful negotiations, this route was preferred. It would simultaneously assist in the alleviation of specific social injuries while also setting precedents for the particular corporations. It was hoped that such precedents would also create a climate more generally conducive to corporate social responsibility. We have seen a glimmer of this possibility during the bank campaign, first with the Royal's and even more so with the Toronto Dominion Bank's statements on lending to the South African government.

These, however, were the exceptions. Most companies and banks rejected any suggestion that social harm was perpetuated or created by their operations. Even where the evidence seemed incontrovertible—that doing business with such governments as South Africa's strengthened the staying power of the regime and prolonged repression—the corporations almost always felt that their position was unassailable. They protested that they acted as good corporate citizens and were not violating any law in Canada or elsewhere. In this they were no doubt right. They also rejected the notion that companies should distance themselves from regimes such as apartheid in South Africa, even in the absence of a Canadian government policy or a specific request to them. The impact of the churches on corporate policies concerning their Southern African investments was thus weakened by the near total silence of the Canadian government on the specific issues of bank lending to and corporate activity in South Africa and Namibia.

It became important therefore that the members of the Taskforce determined for themselves what exactly were the relevant Canadian laws, regulations, policies and guidelines that applied to Canadian investment in Southern Africa. In addition, the churches were led by their basic commitments to examine the whole range of Canadian policies towards South Africa and Namibia, whether articulated in Ottawa, the United Nations, the Commonwealth, international financial institutions or other multilateral organizations.

The churches wanted to know to what extent Canadian diplomatic positions in such forums were in turn reflected in specific policies at home. For example, did Canada's 1966 vote in the United Nations to terminate South African rule in Namibia have consequences for Canadian companies operating there under licence from South Africa? Or again, did the 1977 Security Council Resolution 418, declaring a mandatory arms embargo against South Africa, cause the Canadian government to restrict sales to the military and police of specialized material from Canadian subsidiaries in South Africa? As the earlier discussions illustrated, these questions were not academic, but had very practical applications. The Taskforce began to press for changes in both legislation and public policies where it found government rhetoric and action to be in disharmony. The frequency of Taskforce briefs to successive governments and the large volume of correspondence that the Taskforce initiated testify to the importance of this dimension of the work of the Taskforce.

The first brief was submitted in November 1975 to Allan MacEachen, secretary of state for External Affairs, and Don Jamieson, minister of Industry, Trade and Commerce.[40] The brief, *Canadian Policy on Southern Africa: An Ecumenical Consensus Paper,* was the first successful effort by the member churches of the Taskforce jointly to formulate policy proposals. The use of the term "consensus," reflected the "opting-in" philosophy underlying much of the work of the Taskforce. This did not mean that each member church or order was committed to each recommendation, but that all important points put forward by one or another of our members had been sufficiently accommodated that each was comfortable to support the "Consensus Paper."

The greater difficulty in the "Consensus Paper" had been to formulate an opening statement of the Christian rationale for the churches' involvement in social justice questions in general and in regard to South Africa's apartheid system in particular. The problem was, of course, not a lack of exegeses of Christian principles for the type of social action undertaken by the Taskforce. Each denomination was very clear on these for itself but they differed one from the other. The difficulty in developing a common Christian rationale accounts also for the rather sketchy appearance of such texts in later Taskforce briefs and other public documents. Time and again it proved easier to reach agreement on specific inter-church social action initiatives than it was to find a common formulation of the faith foundation for such initiatives.

The 1975 Consensus Paper already noted that the long partnership between the member churches of the Taskforce and "their sister churches in South Africa and other church-related agencies" assured that the Taskforce had "a realistic picture of the racial tensions involved . . . and reflect the thinking and positions of a wide spectrum of white and black liberal opinion in Southern Africa."[41]

At this point, church representatives wrote, they were not at all convinced that the Canadian government took seriously its own opposition to the system of apartheid nor its own confirmation of support for fundamental change in South Africa and Namibia.

The 1975 Consensus Paper developed a series of detailed policy recommendations which the Taskforce argued were both morally compelling and politically feasible. It called for a halt to formal and informal links between South Africa and NATO; for the withdrawal of Canadian commercial officers from South Africa; and for a strong code of practices that Canadian companies operating in South Africa would need to respect. It asked that Canadian diplomats be present at political trials in South Africa and that they protest the continuing detentions without trial. The churches asked for official Canadian recognition of the authority of the UN Council for Namibia and enforcement by the Canadian government of UN Decree No. 1 of 1974; it called for an end to the practice of allowing Canadian corporations in Namibia to deduct from their Canadian tax obligations, the taxes paid to the South African regime which occupied Namibia illegally.[42]

Allan MacEachen received us on 12 November 1975 with bemused indifference, but had his officials prepare a detailed written response for him. The government firmly rejected all proposals related to corporate activity, whether in South Africa or Namibia. A particularly lengthy argument accompanied the minister's response on Namibia. An entry in our first *Annual Report* notes that "it took the Minister three single-typed pages to explain Canada's policy and to explain why it cannot support 'unrealistic measures' such as the 1974 UN Decree on the Protection of Natural Resources of Namibia since Canada 'considers its implications very far-reaching'."[43] We wondered at the time whether this edginess about policy proposals on Namibia was at all related to the government's emphatic rejection in Canada of demands made by its aboriginal peoples—which paralleled the Decree—that industrial development be deferred until land claims were settled unless they were themselves involved in the negotiations with the developer.

1977 Policy Changes

In November 1977 Taskforce members were back in Ottawa with another brief under the title "Canadian Policy towards Southern Africa," a title that was retained for all subsequent briefs. Waves of new repression in South Africa had followed the Soweto students' uprisings in June 1976. Steven Biko's murder in police custody and mass arrests in October 1977 gave new urgency to many of the recommendations that had been made in the 1975 brief. As before, the draft of the new brief was circulated among the member churches and religious orders for their comments and for confirmation of their support for the policy positions being advocated.[44] Such care makes good sense at all times. However, prevailing circumstances in 1977 made it even more important. The Taskforce was only two years old, yet it was already subjected to strident criticism from senior members of the business community and of clergy close to them, who accused the members of the Taskforce of distorting both church policies and factual data. The Taskforce brief was circulated to all members of parliament and distributed to the press. In the light of the government policy changes that soon followed, the churches' presentation received considerable media attention.

After the non-committal reception by MacEachen in 1975, we were hardly prepared for the extraordinarily accommodating encounter two years later with Don Jamieson, the secretary of state in External Affairs.[45] Jamieson told us that he was about to announce major policy changes which he felt would go a long way to satisfy the members of the Taskforce. He appeared to be pleased to test the reaction of government critics to the changes he had in mind. The timing of our brief and the meeting with the minister had created the impression that the churches' prompting had convinced the government to reshape its policies in very short order. But this was not the case. Although the government policy changes resembled in their general outline the recommendations of the Taskforce, they differed in many important details. We examine these below.

On 19 December 1977 Donald Jamieson announced in the House of Commons that Canada was to phase out "all its Government-sponsored, commercial-support activities in South Africa." The detailed policy announcements included the following:

- Commercial counsellors would be withdrawn from Johannesburg and Cape Town and the Consulate General would be closed;
- The government account of the Export Development Corporation (EDC) would no longer be available for any transaction relating to South Africa;
- Visas would be required for South Africans travelling to Canada;
- The Department of Finance and others would review the implications of tax concessions that companies obtain for their operations in Namibia under "what is essentially an illegal regime";
- An examination of the impact and capacity to renounce the British Preferential Tariff with South Africa (a remnant of South Africa's Commonwealth membership); and
- A code of conduct for Canadian companies operating in South Africa would be developed.[46]

The Taskforce was slowly learning to "deconstruct" such fine-sounding policy statements. It took a critical look at Canada's new Southern African policy, which had won international and domestic acclaim quite disproportionate to its importance. The two changes that appeared to be the most significant were the closing of the EDC government account to South African transactions and the withdrawal of commercial counsellors. Yet the closing of the EDC government account—that portion of EDC activity at the discretion of cabinet—was a symbolic gesture at best. The government account had in fact not been used for South African business in ten years. The EDC's corporate account, on the other hand, continued to be open to concessional financing and insurance for trade with South Africa, though the minister had made no reference to this.

A Taskforce internal memo on the new measures concluded bluntly: "For reasons of political expediency (possibly Canada's participation in the Namibia negotiations) the cabinet has decided that Jamieson should take a public stand on South Africa without effectively jeopardizing the interest of those with a stake in the *status quo*."[47] A 1982 study by Professor T. A. Keenleyside on the impact of the 1977 policy changes has since confirmed this judgement. About the consequences of the new government policy for EDC South African trade credits, he wrote that "... rather than abating, the role of the EDC in facilitating trade with South Africa has actually expanded ... Canada's exports continued to increase [after 1977] and at a rate not only higher than its exports worldwide but also higher than the rate of increase in exports to South Africa of other OECD countries collectively."[48] In August 1981, the government quietly extended to the EDC's corporate account its ban on concessional lending for South African transactions. An External Affairs official told the Taskforce of this "administrative determination" and suggested that this was a major concession to pressure. In fact, like the government account, the corporate account had hardly been used for South African trade financing and the last significant credits from it had been extended in 1976, interestingly enough, for Canadian exports to the Hulett Aluminium Company and to ISCOR, South Africa's state-owned steel company.[49] The 1977 announcement on the EDC as well as the subsequent additional restriction on EDC lending, each obscured the fact that the EDC facility most valuable to Canada-South Africa trade, namely the coverage of export insurance, remained open for a steady stream of Canadian exports to South Africa right up to Canada's first sanctions in July 1985.

The impact of the withdrawal of Canadian commercial counsellors from South Africa was also minimized. By 1979 the three Canadian trade commissioners had indeed been withdrawn, but a commercial officer had been engaged locally and was working out of Canada's embassy in Pretoria. Don Jamieson justified the appointment in response to a Taskforce enquiry:

our Embassy would have to have some means of dealing with these [commercial matters] particularly if confronted by a visiting Canadian businessman [*sic*] expecting co-operation from his Government's representative on the spot . . . . Our existing Embassy staff is quite small and would not normally be expected to cope with complex commercial questions ... [the Commercial Officer] would not engage in trade promotion.[50]

Further, one could have expected that "phasing out of all government sponsored commercial support activities in South Africa" would have included as well the termination of any activities in South Africa under the Program for Export Market Development (PEMD). This was not the case; the government in fact continued to support Canadian business in the exploration of South African markets through PEMD funding.[51]

Canada's Code of Business Practices

South Africa's bloody response to the 1976–77 black uprisings had created an international scandal and had caused deep embarrassment among South Africa's friends abroad. A formula had to be found that would permit rhetorical condemnation of the system of apartheid but would avoid, at the same time, condemning foreign companies for their continued involvement in this system. Thus, for the first time in the history of South Africa, foreign investors began to be portrayed, by themselves and by their governments, as agents for change in South Africa. To create this new corporate image, governments established codes of conduct for foreign companies operating in South Africa; these codes began appearing in North America, Britain and Europe during 1977 and 1978. In the United States the Reverend Leon Sullivan, the first black director of General Motors, established the "Sullivan Principles," a private rather than a government project. All codes were voluntary and enjoined foreign corporations in South Africa to report annually on their efforts to improve the wages, benefits and working conditions of their black employees; desegregate facilities; pay equal wages for equal work; accept black union activities and free collective bargaining; assist with housing, education and training and generally contribute toward a higher living standard for their black workers.

Canada followed in April 1978 with its own code. After consultations with the appropriate Canadian companies and other interested commercial organizations, External Affairs developed the "Code of Conduct Concerning the Employment Practices of Canadian Companies Operating in South Africa." Although the members of the Taskforce did not believe that such a code could contribute to the dismantling of apartheid, they nevertheless felt that if sufficiently strong, a code might make a real difference to black workers employed by Canadian companies. During a lengthy telephone conference with External Affairs officials, we made an unsuccessful attempt to strengthen External's draft.[52]

When we saw the final text, we issued a press release expressing disappointment that the code was voluntary and lacked any enforcement and monitoring mechanism. Moreover, neither the Canadian nor any other codes addressed the unavoidable integration of foreign companies into the structures of the apartheid system and its military and police apparatus. The Canadian government nevertheless cheerfully believed that "by promoting the achievement of the [code's] objectives, Canadian companies will be able to make an important contribution towards improving the working conditions generally of Black and other non-white workers in South Africa."[53] The guidelines for company reports on their implementation of the Canadian code were so vague that by 1981 only one out of the original twenty-eight companies identified by the government was submitting reports. The one company was Alcan, which submitted reports prepared by Hulett Aluminium. In response to a parliamentary question on 14 October 1981, Mark MacGuigan, then secretary of state for External Affairs tried to place responsibility for monitoring the code's implementation on interested Canadians: "[T]he annual public reports which the government believes should be made by companies on their implementation of the code of conduct are intended to provide pertinent information to interested Canadians. The extent of progress in realizing the objectives of the code is a matter for their judgement."[54] External Affairs, having launched the code with much fanfare, neither ensured that companies submitted code implementation reports nor reviewed those that had been presented. Indeed, when the Taskforce enquired, no one was sure what had happened to them.

This analysis of the 1977 government announcement and its ultimate vacuity still leaves us searching for the rationale of the exercise: why bother to go through all the hoops of announcing change if everything remained the same? The answer is that everything did not remain the same. In 1977 there were potent reasons why it was in the interest of the Canadian government to enhance its international profile on apartheid. In January 1977 Canada, together with the Federal Republic of Germany, took its seat for two years on the United Nations Security Council. The Council's permanent Western members, the USA, Britain and France, were united in their opposition to economic sanctions against South Africa. They were now joined by two non-permanent members who shared their commercial and geo-political interests in Southern Africa and an adamant opposition to economic sanctions.

At the same time international patience with South Africa was running out, and Third World and some Western middle powers were pressing for censure. South Africa's callous repression in 1976 and 1977 had provoked international outrage, as had its defiance of all attempts to dislodge it from Namibia. South Africa's unprovoked 1975 military invasion deep into newly independent Angola had prompted the unanimous adoption by the United Nations Security Council of Resolution 385 on 30 January 1976. It provided for a process of transition to Namibian independence through free and fair elections under the supervision and control of the United Nations. This too had been brusquely rejected by South Africa. As a result, mobilization within the United Nations for mandatory economic sanctions against the apartheid state was gathering momentum. In early 1977 there were already four draft sanctions resolutions before the Security Council, which the United States and its allies were bound to veto.[55] They were therefore anxious to find a way to preclude new sanction proposals and the inevitable, recurrent and politically awkward vetoes.

The announcement in December 1977 of lame but high-profile policy changes towards Southern Africa were key to facilitating Canada's initiative in the Security Council to promote an alternative strategy to sanctions. Canada therefore needed to embark on a crash program of policy changes to demonstrate that it was a credible critic of South Africa's apartheid system. That done, Canada could argue that its opposition to mandatory economic sanctions was not because it supported the status quo but because it believed that direct negotiations would be more effective. In April 1978 Don Jamieson spoke to the United Nations General Assembly Special Session on Namibia on behalf of the governments of France, Germany, Britain, the United States and Canada. He told the General Assembly that "our five countries decided to make a concerted effort to investigate whether by means of the existing relations between themselves and South Africa, it might not be possible to find a practical way of implementing Security Council resolution 385."[56] By September 1978 the "Contact Group of States," with Canada, France, Germany, the United Kingdom, and the USA as members had been formally established and Security Council Resolution 435 adopted, giving the Contact Group the authority to negotiate South Africa's early withdrawal from Namibia and to satisfy the provisions of UNSCR 385. Although the five Western states succeeded in gaining the good will and support of the Front Line States and SWAPO, they failed totally to implement UNSCR 385 of 1976 and UNSCR 435 of 1978. They failed to negotiate an early transfer of power to the people of Namibia whose struggle for independence went on for another twelve years; long after the Contact Group had ceased to function. But the Contact Group had indeed succeeded in holding off demands for new mandatory economic sanctions.

Seen in this light and particularly with the aid of hindsight, the ineffectiveness of the 1977 changes in Canadian policy toward South Africa take on a deeply disturbing complexion. Yet it is difficult to interpret these events in any other way.

Notes

1 The Royal Bank of Canada, The Canadian Imperial Bank of Commerce, The Toronto Dominion Bank, The Bank of Nova Scotia and the Bank of Montreal. There were also minor loan involvements of smaller banks, and correspondence was conducted with them as well.

2 "Banking on Apartheid," pamphlet published by the Taskforce on the Churches and Corporate Responsibility, June 1977.

3 When it was pointed out that mail in South Africa was routinely opened by security officers working in the postal services, he was sure that this would only happen in the case of enemies to the government!

4 This is not an exaggerated description. One bank chair actually responded to questions about South African loans, that client/banker confidentiality did not permit him to respond. It was, he said, "the banks' equivalent to the confessional."

5 The World Council of Churches had produced a booklet in 1977, *The W.C.C. and Bank Loans to South Africa*, which had further confirmed for the Taskforce the importance and international nature of the bank loans campaign. In addition, an education action kit, *Canadian Banks & South African Apartheid: A Strategy for Christian Action*, had been developed by the Hamilton Conference of the United Church of Canada of which several hundred copies were purchased and distributed by members of the Taskforce. This was important as well, reassuring us that there was also local and regional support for the action.

6 Anthony Sampson, *Black and Gold: Tycoons, Revolutionaries and Apartheid* (Sevenoaks: Hodder and Stoughton, 1987), p. 171.

7 See Appendix to Part I, chapter 1, for the letter to Fred McNeil of the Bank of Montreal from Archbishop Ouelette, 11 May 1978. The letter also covered the objections to loans by the Bank to Chile under Pinochet, a parallel action with Canadian banks, also coordinated by the Taskforce.

8 The Taskforce, similarly engaged in opposing continued bank loans to Chile under the Pinochet dictatorship, had also printed NO LOANS TO CHILE stickers.

9 Letter from C.E. Ritchie, Chairman of the Board, President and Chief Executive Officer of the Bank of Nova Scotia, to Jim Webb, S.J., Chair of the Taskforce on the Churches and Corporate Responsibility, 16 November 1979.

10 Paul Emden, *Randlords* (Hodder and Stoughton, 1935), p. 142, quoted in Sampson, *Black and Gold*, p. 66.

11 Letter from C.E. Ritchie to J. Webb, S.J., 16 November 1979.

12 Canada, House of Commons, Standing Committee on Finance, Trade and Economic Affairs, *Minutes of Proceedings and Evidence*, 23 January 1979, and Taskforce on the Churches and Corporate Responsibility, *Annual Report, 1978–1979* and *1979–1980*, pp. 24 and 23–24 respectively.

13 Of the smaller banks surveyed, the following information was obtained: The Bank of British Columbia—the Bank's lending policy is confidential; Canadian Commercial and Industrial Bank—no public or private loans outstanding, no formal policy; Continental Bank—not involved in international lending; Mercantile Bank—never extended any credit to any entity in South Africa, no policy; Northland Bank—no loans to date ("We question the usefulness of an economic boycott. . . . [W]e do not evaluate the legitimacy of governments in whose jurisdiction the borrower resides"); La Banque Canadienne Nationale—has had outstanding loans since 1973, 1974 and 1975. It will no longer lend directly or through bank-loan syndications to private- or state-owned corporations in South Africa. It has no formal policy; and La Banque Provinciale du Canada—no outstanding loans, no loans made for five years ("country limit" for South Africa was nil).

After the November 1979 merger of the last two banks into The National Bank of Canada, the South African loan policy remained unchanged.

14 See Transcript of Proceedings of portions involving discussions with members of the Taskforce at Alcan's 17 March 1977 annual shareholder meeting; typescript, 11 pages (Taskforce Archives), pp. 6–7.

15 This position was confirmed in October 1977 when, in reference to the large number of arrests and the murder of Steve Biko, Alcan's chair wrote: "[T]he events of recent weeks will not deter us from continuing our encouragement of the liberalizing policies which the companies in which we have an interest are following. . . . Our long established policy as an investor and a multinational has been to avoid interference in the political affairs of host countries."

Letter from Nathanael V. Davis, chair, Alcan Aluminum Ltd., to Dr. John Zimmerman, chair, Taskforce on the Churches and Corporate Responsibility, 16 December 1977 (Taskforce Archives), p. 19.

16 The Christian Institute was a trusted partner organization of the Taskforce and was financially supported by several of its member churches. The C.I.'s leadership and its activities were frequent targets of police harassment and censorship.

17 Taskforce on the Churches and Corporate Responsibility, *Annual Report, 1975–1976* (mimeograph), 29 pages (Taskforce Archives), p. 12. After the 1976 annual meeting, Nathanael V. Davis, chair of Alcan, told church representatives that he disagreed with them; that the Foundation was a liberal association working for change rather than an "image-maker" for the South African government (Taskforce on the Churches and Corporate Responsibility, Report on the Annual Shareholder Meeting of Alcan Aluminum Ltd., 11 March 1976).

18 Brian Bunting, *The Rise of the South African Reich*, rev. ed. (Harmondsworth: Penguin Books, 1969), pp. 335–36; p. 336 gives a *Rand Daily Mail* (21 June 1967) quotation attributed to Dr. H.J. van Eck, Deputy President of the Foundation. At a Foundation banquet van Eck spoke of the "personal contact at the top" which had won for South Africa "good friends and reliable supporters in key positions in the power structures of the world. When one looks at the many vicious attacks that have been launched on South Africa in the past seven years, it must be obvious that without behind the scenes intervention on our behalf at crucial stages of these several campaigns, we could never have won through to the position of international respect and domestic peace and prosperity which we enjoy today."

19 United Nations Security Council Resolution 181, 7 August 1963.

20 See also Gavin Cawthra, *Brutal Force: The Apartheid War Machine* (London: International Defence and Aid Fund for Southern Africa, 1986), p. 16.

21 As quoted in ibid., p. 89.

22 See ibid., pp. 87–89.

23 Republic of South Africa, "National Key Points Act," *Government Gazette*, 181, no. 7134, 25 July 1980.

24 Botha's Defence Advisory Board had been established in 1977 to assist in the implementation of his announced "total strategy" for the preservation of apartheid. Thirteen top South African business leaders had joined military and police chiefs to come to an agreement and to advise Botha on how best to integrate South Africa's security planning and its economic objectives. Ian MacKenzie's appointment had provoked widespread protests in Britain, and during its May 1981 annual meeting the British parent bank announced the resignation of MacKenzie from Botha's Defence Advisory Board.

25 Clark, Phipps, Clark & Harris, Inc. of New York.

26 Letter from the Rev. Thomas M. Anthony, chair of the Taskforce on the Churches and Corporate Responsibility, to Charles Bronfman, president, The Seagram Company Ltd.,

17 December 1975; reply from Bronfman to the Rev. John M. Zimmerman, vice-chair of the Taskforce, 12 April 1976.

27 That this was in fact P.W. Botha's idea as early as 1975 when, as defence minister, he formulated the "total strategy" concept, is discussed in Robert M. Price, *The Apartheid State in Crisis: Political Transformation in South Africa 1975–1990* (New York and Oxford: Oxford University Press, 1991), p. 85.

28 A further conversation between Bronfman and Anthony revealed that information and analyses provided by the Taskforce had indeed contributed to Seagram's decision to forego investment in South Africa and that South African and other sources had offered misleading and unhelpful information (letter from the Rev. Thomas M. Anthony to Charles R. Bronfman confirming the content of their 15 September 1976 telephone conversation, 5 October 1976).

29 Letter to Frank Milliken, chairman of the Board, Kennecott Copper, from M. Gatsha Buthelezi, chief executive councillor of KwaZulu, written on "KwaZulu Government Service" stationery, 20 January 1976.

30 In 1924, when Ford South Africa was established, the Ford Motor Company made this investment through Ford Canada to profit from special Commonwealth tariffs due to South Africa's and Canada's membership in the Commonwealth.

31 Letter from R.F. Bennett, president and chief executive Officer of Ford Motor Company of Canada Ltd., to Jim Webb, S.J., chair, Taskforce on the Churches and Corporate Responsibility, 11 May 1979.

32 "Position Paper in Response to the Taskforce on the Churches and Corporate Responsibility's Letter of June 1, 1979" (mimeograph), 10 July 1979, 4 pages. The Paper was prepared by the Ford Motor Company and circulated at the 11 July meeting with the Taskforce (Taskforce Archives).

33 Taskforce on the Churches and Corporate Responsibility, "Meeting with Representatives of the Ford Motor Company Held on 11 July 1979" (mimeograph), 4 pages (Taskforce Archives).

34 The letter to Ford by Taskforce participants was signed by the Rev. Clarke Raymond, Executive Director of Program, the Anglican Church of Canada, the Rev. G.W. Leutkhehoelter, President of the Lutheran Church of America (Canada Section), Dr. Donald Ray, Secretary of the General Council of the United Church of Canada, Sister Angelina Shannon, IBVM, Mother General of the Sisters of Loretto and President of the Canadian Religious Conference of Ontario, and the Rev. Dennis Murphy, General Secretary of the Canadian Conference of Catholic Bishops ("Open Letter to Ford," 4 September 1979 [Taskforce Archives]).

35 An unmarked copy of *The Port Elizabeth Strike and Beyond*, outlining these events, arrived at the Taskforce on 17 March 1980. Thozamile Botha spoke to a meeting called by the Taskforce in September 1980 (Taskforce Archives). Thozamile Botha moved to Britain where he attained a PhD at Essex University. He chaired the ANC in the UK and returned to South Africa in 1990 where he was elected to the ANC national executive specializing in regional and local government and housing (Anton Harber and Barbara Ludman, eds., *A-Z of South African Politics, Weekly Mail & Guardian* [Harmondsworth: Penguin Books, 1994], pp. 10–11).

36 "Canada's Church Leaders Question Ford's South African Connections," Catholic New Times, 16 September 1979; RNS Photograph (June 23, 1977), "Police hold student during demonstration while their Ford truck is parked nearby"; chronology of events: "News Update on Ford South Africa." Thozamile Botha spoke to a meeting of the Taskforce in September 1980.

37 "South Africa, A Drive for Strength to Offset Sanctions," *Business Week*, 21 May 1979.

38 "[I]t does not appear at this time that an offence has been committed by Falconbridge Nickel Mines Ltd. . . . [W]e have no proof that such a transfer of funds has occurred or that other prohibited activities have taken place" (letter from Denis Evans, chief, Export and Imports Division, Department of Industry Trade and Commerce, to the Rev. Thomas Anthony, chair, Taskforce on the Churches and Corporate Responsibility, 1 June 1976).

39 Taskforce on the Churches and Corporate Responsibility, *Annual Report, 1983–1984* (Toronto), p. 46.

40 "Canadian Policy towards Southern Africa: An Ecumenical Consensus Paper." A meeting took place on 12 November 1975 between MacEachen and representatives from the Anglican Church of Canada, the Canadian Council of Churches, the Canadian Catholic Conference of Bishops, the Lutheran Church in America (Canada Section) and the United Church of Canada. See "Report on the Meeting with the Secretary of State for External Affairs," 12 November 1975 (mimeograph), 8 pages (Taskforce Archives).

41 Ibid., p. 1.

42 Ibid., pp. 3–6.

43 Taskforce, *Annual Report, 1975–1976,* p. 20.

44 There was some careful phrasing that made clear the distinction between "representing" and "reflecting." The annual report notes: "The brief reflected (emphasis added) the official policy positions of several member churches of the Taskforce and [the brief] was adopted (emphasis added) by the Anglican Church of Canada, the Canadian Religious Conference of Ontario, the Lutheran Church in America, Canada Section, the Social Action Department of the Canadian Conference of Catholic Bishops and the United Church of Canada."

45 Archbishop E.W. Scott informed Jamieson that the House of Bishops of the Anglican Church in Canada had formulated a strong resolution, later adopted by the National Executive Council, which called for a severance of all links with South Africa, including economic, social, cultural and diplomatic relations. Taskforce on the Churches and Corporate Responsibility, Report on the Views of the Secretary of State for External Affairs, the Hon. Don Jamieson, at a meeting with representatives of the Taskforce, 15 November 1977 (mimeograph), 6 pages (Taskforce Archives).

46 Statement by the Secretary of State for External Affairs, the Hon. Donald C. Jamieson (Canada, House of Commons, *Debates,* 19 December 1977, pp. 1999–2001).

47 Taskforce on the Churches and Corporate Responsibility, "Assessment of the Effectiveness of Government Announced Measures Regarding South Africa," 27 January 1978 (mimeograph), 6 pages (Taskforce Archives).

48 T.A. Keenleyside, "Canada-South Africa Commercial Relations: 1977–1982: Business as Usual?" *Canadian Journal of African Studies,* 17, no. 3 (1983), 450, 464.

49 See Export Development Corporation, *Annual Report, 1976* (Ottawa, 1977).

50 Letter from the Hon. Don Jamieson, secretary of state for External Affairs, to the Rev. Dr. John Zimmerman, chair, Taskforce on the Churches and Corporate Responsibility, 9 June 1978. Six years later, members of the Taskforce met with Marc Breault, then Director General, Africa Bureau of External Affairs. He confirmed that Bruce Fraser, the locally employed commercial officer, was an ex-Rhodesian public servant. To a Taskforce query about the man's sanctions-breaking activities during mandatory sanctions against Rhodesia, Breault observed that most Rhodesian public servants had done this. Fraser, Breault said, promoted trade with independent African states, not with South Africa. Should Canadians want help with South African trade, Fraser would hand them a street map and a telephone directory, that was all! (Taskforce on the Churches and Corporate Responsibility, "Notes on the Meeting with Marc Breault", Toronto, 2 November 1984, 9:45–10:30 a.m. [mimeograph, Taskforce Archives]).

51 Keenleyside, "Canada-South Africa Commercial Relations," p. 453.
52 Taskforce on the Churches and Corporate Responsibility, record of 14 March 1978 telephone conference with officials of the Department of External Affairs (Taskforce Archives).
53 "Code of Conduct Concerning the Employment Practices of Canadian Companies Operating in South Africa," External Affairs Memorandum, undated [April 1978], p. 1.
54 Canada, House of Commons, *Debates*, 14 October 1981, p. 11764.
55 Patrick Laurence, "Shuttle Diplomacy for Namibia," *The Nation*, 25 February 1978.
56 Canada Communiqué, "Notes for a Speech by the Secretary of States for External Affairs of Canada, the Hon. Don Jamieson, to the Ninth Special Session of the United Nations General Assembly on behalf of the Governments of France, the Federal Republic of Germany, the United Kingdom, the United States and Canada," Canadian Delegation to the United Nations, Press Release no. 5, Tuesday, 25 April 1978.

Part Two   1981–84

3 Apartheid and the Canadian Government

Prologue

This volume does not purport to portray the developments in South Africa with anything like the authority to which it aspires in its presentation and analysis of the work of the Taskforce, the policies and practices of the Canadian banks and corporations involved in South Africa and the policies of the Canadian government. Nevertheless, the growth of a determined internal resistance to the increasing repression in South Africa was an important factor that shaped and galvanized Taskforce activities. It was therefore decided to include in Parts Two and Three a review of pertinent South African developments. The principal sources for these narratives have been documentation collected at the time by the Taskforce. These included foremost the authoritative monthly reports and annual reviews of South African and Namibian developments published by the International Defence and Aid Fund for Southern Africa of London (UK); reports of the *Ecumenical News* services; clipping services of *Facts & Reports* from the Netherlands; *Sechaba*, a clipping service of the ANC, and information conveyed to the member churches from their South African partner churches. It is hoped that these chapters will provide not only a useful overview of South African events in the periods covered, but also a good indication of how those events were seen and understood by the Taskforce at the time.

The Emergence of Apartheid's "Total Strategy"

The years following the Soweto uprisings were marked by jails that were overcrowded with political prisoners, by detentions without trial, by ban-

---

Notes for chapter 3 are found on pp. 93–96.

nings in the hundreds and by a new phenomenon, the growing numbers of unsolved murders of opponents to the regime. Potential new investors hesitated at the same time as young professional whites began to look for opportunities abroad. Then came South Africa's information scandal, which was revealed in September 1978. It rocked the government of John Vorster and eventually forced his resignation.

In order to better control the domestic news media, to improve international opinion of apartheid and to discredit its opponents, the Department of Information had been spending millions of dollars on more than 130 secret projects. It had bought the South African newspaper *The Citizen* in order to have an English language newspaper favourable to its views; had launched its own news magazine, *To the Point*, bought the Sacramento, California *Union* newspaper and a 50 percent share in the United Press International television news agency and had attempted but failed to acquire the Washington *Star*. Of particular interest to the churches were South Africa's attempts to undermine the credibility of the World Council of Churches, a long-time critic of apartheid, particularly through its Program to Combat Racism. The Department of Information had made an annual grant of $400,000 to the Christian League of Southern Africa, a pro-government organization, which was used to step up its travel and guest program to bring supporters to South Africa and to expand *Encounter*, the League's magazine, to better "expose" the WCC's "marxist" ties.[1] The Taskforce was alerted by these revelations and took note of the political and financial powers behind the pro-South African propagandists and their determination to discredit and destroy its critics.

There was in fact little international repercussion to the scandal. Rather, the very replacement of Vorster by P.W. Botha, who had been minister of defence, was welcomed as a positive sign. Indeed, Canadian corporate and bank executives noted that Botha had permitted black trade union activity and was reviewing influx control regulations for urban blacks. They suggested that it was time to ease the pressure on the regime to give it a chance to prove itself. Given these sentiments, the Taskforce looked more carefully into these recent South African initiatives.

The Wiehan and Riekert Commissions

Two South African commissions that had been appointed in 1977 submitted their reports in 1978 and rekindled hopes, particularly among the dispirited South African business community, that their confidence in the apartheid government was after all well placed. The Wiehan Commission had examined and now recommended changes to industrial relations and trade unions rights. Although black union activity was outlawed, black unions had established themselves. They had given leadership to demands for better wages and working conditions and had led illegal strikes in key economic sectors such as transportation, engineering, chemical and automobile industries. Faced with these determined extra-legal workers' organizations, many employers had little choice but to negotiate with them. Because grievances of black workers were inseparable from the oppression they experienced in their homes and communities, leaders of these unregistered union also became politically active. As we saw in the example of the strike at Ford South Africa, (see p. 43) they organized against the ever-present threat of population removals and police harassment and demanded better housing, education and health services. Black unions supported organized resistance to apartheid with work stoppages, stay-aways and other solidarity actions.

Wiehan correctly assessed that the vigorous black unions now posed a considerable threat to the apartheid system. He warned that they were becoming "vehicles for change" in matters far beyond the strict confines of labour rights. Despite bannings, imprisonment, harassment and self-exile, de facto black unions had slipped away from government control. Wiehan was not anxious to recommend a total ban on black trade union activity. This would have prompted strong reaction in South Africa, would have invited international condemnation and caused extreme embarrassment to foreign companies. Wiehan recommended instead, and the government accepted, that black trade unions be brought under government control by legalizing them. Henceforth black unions could register and enjoy all union rights, including the right to strike. Dues were collected and their accounts audited. Unregistered unions were outlawed.

Thus the black unions owed their new legal status to the militancy and determination of their members while the regime in turn reasserted its control by conceding union rights. The sting was in the conditions under which union registration could take place. Unions had to be apolitical and free from foreign interference, including foreign funding. As well, union activity was constrained to the promotion of peace and harmony, clearly to the exclusion of political organizing against population removals and other political demands. The black unions welcomed their legal recognition, confidently predicting that in time they would shake off the government's constraints.

The Riekert commission had been charged to examine and to recommend changes to influx control, the state system that regulated the movement of African workers from the "homelands" to industries in "white" cities. "Grand apartheid" the total separation of the races, was in fact breaking down. Extreme poverty in the "homelands" was forcing millions of black workers to seek work in "white" industries. White employers became angry when police arrested their employees for working illegally.

White workers were angry because the situation no longer protected them from cheap black competition, and black workers became increasingly resentful that they could not live with their families near their workplace.

Riekert did not seek to dismantle influx control; rather he streamlined and, by detailing specific elements of control, he strengthened it. He argued that it was essential for the preservation of social security measures that the rate of urbanization be controlled. Riekert's solution, a careful adaptation of the ideas of the late Hendrik Verwoerd, called for rational planning in the supply and demand of black labour; for black manpower training of the right number and quality of workers "in accordance with expected demand conditions."[2] He proposed, and Botha accepted, that the myriad of previous criteria for legal black residency be replaced by only two qualifying conditions: the availability of housing and suitable employment. In reality these twin conditions served to restore absolute state control and put Africans in a very precarious position.

Black housing, exclusively controlled by state authorities, was notoriously inadequate. Housing inspectors, by mercilessly enforcing overcrowding rules, could and did remove in their thousands, destitutes who had been taken in by friends and relatives to escape the absolute poverty of the "homelands." Housing inspectors also tracked down political opponents of the regime, using infractions of the housing rules as grounds to send them back to their "homelands."[3]

A close dovetailing of the recommendations of the two commissions produced a further important control mechanism. Wiehan had said that workers who engaged in political activity or who were accused of violating the terms of union activity could be summarily dismissed. Riekert recommended that unemployed blacks be returned to the "homelands." Taken together, these two sets of recommendations meant that a threat of dismissal would become a threat of deportation. Finally, Riekert's proposals made the employer of illegal black workers liable for a (approx.) $700 fine for each offence.

In 1984 a new law, the Aliens and Immigration Laws Amendment Act, further limited the movement of South Africans from the "homelands" to the Republic. It required a bank deposit from any "alien" before a temporary entry permit into South Africa was issued. The onus on enforcement of the new law was placed on the employer not to hire "aliens" without an entry permit on pain of a fine or two years in jail. Conforming with the general thrust of these policies to minimize the presence of blacks in areas other than the "homelands," forced population removals were stepped up to clear "black spots" from designated "white areas."[4]

The widespread notion in the international business community that the new measures were "liberalizing the apartheid system" reflected the erroneous belief that any adjustments to the system must benefit black South

Africans. This error was matched only by the convictions of members within the South African National Party. Although the white-only elections of April 1981 still gave Botha and the National party a comfortable majority, there were serious defections of Afrikaner votes to the new conservative parties. They feared that Botha was selling out the *volk*.

Botha's "Total Strategy"

The two measures just discussed were part of a larger strategy to ensure the consolidation and survival of white supremacy. P.W. Botha first conceived the concept of "total strategy" in 1977 when he was minister of defence. He was driven by the spectre of an African continent that was rapidly being decolonialized and feared in particular the radicalization of South Africa's black struggle, which had escalated considerably following the collapse of the Portuguese colonial power in Mozambique and Angola.

He devised a multipronged national plan to create a viable black middle class that was dependent on the perpetuation of the white power structure. Such a black middle class, he calculated, would feel threatened by a radical transformation of South Africa's power relationships and would act as a buffer against it. Botha began by gathering into a powerful State Security Council (SSC) the chiefs of staff of the intelligence and security services and the minister of defence as well as non-military politicians from the departments of justice and foreign affairs. The SSC identified eleven areas of national activity to be included in the total strategy planning process. Each of these areas in turn required subcommittees and advisory boards. We have already seen that prominent members of South Africa's business community had joined Botha's Defence Advisory Board (see chap. 2, p. 39). Other talents were recruited from among the supportive socio-political academic community and from among South Africa's propagandists.[5] Robert Price describes how these military and police officers, government officials, academics and businessmen worked together through three specialist committees: "one to deal with security matters; another to handle political, economic and social problems, and the third to manage communications and propaganda. . . . These functional divisions reflect the essence of the 'total strategy' . . . combining socio-economic policy and ideological or psychological warfare with more conventional police activities."[6] P.W. Botha's total strategy also demanded resolute repression of those who resisted his so-called reforms in order, on the one hand, to show the white electorate that the regime was determined to be tough with "radical revolutionaries," and on the other, to daunt these "radicals" with their own hopeless powerlessness.

The regime's attempt to destroy black resistance was aimed as well at the newly independent black states on its borders. The SSC, under a policy of "proactive defence," authorized overt military and economic destabilization campaigns designed to terrorize South Africa's neighbours and to consolidate its military hold on Namibia. The raids were exploited for their propaganda value, seeking to demonstrate the inability of the new states to govern effectively.

Encouraged by the West's extraordinary indulgence toward South Africa during this period, Botha's terror campaigns grew bolder with every raid. In a not-so-veiled reference to South Africa's recruitment and training of mercenaries for destabilization activities, General Malan, who served as both defence minister and chief of South Africa's defence forces, declared that South Africa would defend itself "even if it means we will have to support anti-communist movements . . . and allow them to act from our territory."[7]

The South African military made deep and lasting incursions into Angola, causing enormous loss in human life and destroying with ruthless abandon much of Angola's vital infrastructure. South Africa also admitted to several air attacks on Mozambique and a devastating commando raid on Maseru, Lesotho. All this it justified as strikes against military bases of the African National Congress (ANC). Yet journalists visiting the sites shortly after these gruesome raids reported routinely that the evidence suggested that innocent civilians were the main if not the only victims.[8] The continuing military attacks, particularly against Angola, a country not at war with South Africa, were tolerated by Western governments without the slightest diplomatic reprimand.[9] The legacy of the desolation and grief caused by South Africa's genocidal acts is still visited on the impoverished peoples of this erstwhile prosperous and functioning state, leaving behind a generation maimed by exploded land mines.

Destruction in Mozambique was intended not only to destabilize this fragile country, but was as well pointedly aimed at landlocked Zimbabwe—despite the fact that its government had declared its country out of bounds for ANC bases. In December 1982 commandos destroyed an oil depot in Beira that contained supplies for Zimbabwe which were to be conveyed there by a previously sabotaged and recently repaired pipeline. This forced a reluctant and angry Zimbabwe to request urgently needed oil supplies from South Africa. Before that, in July 1982, South African equipment had been used by Zimbabwe-based saboteurs to destroy two-thirds of Zimbabwe's air force. One month later three dead South African soldiers were left behind at Sengwe after another attempted commando raid. South Africa had also been at the centre of the much-publicized botched coup in the Seychelles in 1981, demonstrating to the world South Africa's easy and almost casual willingness to overthrow any independent African government not to its liking.[10]

The most revealing element of the "total strategy" was the new constitution. It was approved in 1983 in a referendum in which only whites could vote. It took effect in September 1984 and was inaugurated in 1985. The new constitution provided for three separate parliamentary chambers, one for each of the participating population groups—whites, Asians and "coloureds" in apartheid's terminology. These three racially exclusive chambers met together only on ceremonial occasions. Each chamber legislated on matters of "communal interest," while legislation of interest to all three chambers had to be adopted by each chamber separately. In case of conflicting decisions resulting from the tri-cameral procedure, the state president (replacing the prime minister) and his council made the final decision.

The president's council comprised twenty members elected by the white chamber; ten elected by the "coloured" chamber and five elected by the Indian chamber. The president nominated twenty-five additional members, thus ensuring that the centrally important president's council had a white majority. The president himself was elected by an electoral college of fifty white, twenty-five coloured and thirteen Indian members in turn elected by each chamber.

The new constitution was obvious and unsubtle in its message for black South Africans. Except for carefully crafted and limited exemptions, their future was confined to the "homelands" whose populations had doubled over the last twenty years. By 1983 there were eleven million who were eking out a living in these rural slums.[11] All black South Africans, both those confined to the "homelands" and those permitted to live in the white areas, were to be excluded from participating in the national democratic institutions of South Africa.

We saw that only those black South Africans who were in legal employment and lived in approved housing qualified for residence in the urban areas. Implicit in the new constitution that had adapted and reshaped white supremacy to suit a new South African reality was Botha's expectation that the relative prosperity these urban blacks would enjoy in contrast to those in the "homelands" would induce them to support the constitution even though it denied them any representation in the new parliamentary chambers. Grotesquely, Botha saw himself as a reformer. In 1982 when he gave a major speech explaining the new constitutional changes, he announced that "I have come to the realization and conviction that the struggle in South Africa is not between Whites and Blacks and Browns, but between Christian civilized standards and the powers of chaos."[12]

The words "reform" and "power sharing" reverberated in the South African and international corridors of power where the new constitution won wide acceptance and support. Apologists for the white minority regime saw it as a "good start" and "the beginning of the end of apartheid."

Black South Africans, in contrast, were profoundly hostile and alienated. Archbishop Tutu reflected the depth of their bitterness when, in 1986, he told the Ontario legislature that South Africa's 1984 constitution "mentions 73 percent of the population of South Africa in one sentence. We are mentioned in one sentence of a constitution which some said was a step in the right direction: 'All matters relating to blacks will be dealt with by the state president by decree.' "[13] The strong popular reaction against the new constitution throughout South Africa focused on the irrevocable exclusion of black political participation. Our South African partners, already deeply troubled by the increasing scope and devastating impact of population removals, had just completed a major study that pleaded with the international Christian community to heed their appeal.

> The removal and relocation of people in South Africa is a process so destructive of people and communities that it challenges us to action. Removals continue to take place on an immense scale, while the manner in which particular removals are carried out usually causes great suffering. This tragic process affects the lives of each one of us in some way.
>
> For this reason we, the leaders of Christian churches in South Africa, address this report in the first instance to everyone who lives in our country. If we remained silent we would betray our responsibility to God and His people. Secondly, we address Christians outside South Africa. We want the whole human family to know how division and suffering are inflicted upon the people of our land. For whatever injures one sector of humanity injures humankind as a whole.[14]

Two months before the white-only referendum on the constitution, both the South African Council of Churches and the Southern African Conference of Catholic Bishops issued strong statements rejecting the new constitution. The reforms, the churches said, failed in justice, truth, love and freedom: "Africans will still have no representation in the central government, which will continue to make laws affecting them. This is a serious moral failure. It is an affront to the people concerned and assures that racial discrimination will continue."[15] A pastoral letter from the Roman Catholic bishops making these points was read out in every Catholic Church in South Africa on 25 September 1983. The South African Council of Churches reaffirmed its call for the maintenance of a unitary state and rejected any participation in political arrangements that provided for separate black states. The SACC saw this as a design to legitimate the exclusion of the majority black population from genuine participation in South Africa's national political institutions.

On 20 August 1983 an event of major political importance took place. One thousand five hundred delegates representing 400 organizations gathered in Cape Town. They were united in their opposition to the new constitution and resolved to campaign against the Asian and "Coloured" elections scheduled for the following year. They formed a single national organization, the multiracial United Democratic Front (UDF), which advocated a non-racial unitary and democratic South Africa. Within a year the

UDF grew to include 590 organizational affiliates of labour unions, community, professional and students' organizations and a variety of church-related bodies, and became the vehicle for coordinated expression of popular resistance to the "new dispensation."

Although the UDF and its activities were not proscribed, and despite the organization's strict commitment to non-violence, it became at once the target of police harassment. Numbers of senior leaders were detained without charge or trial, some soon to be released, others to be detained for weeks and months. During the campaigns leading up to the Indian and "coloured" elections, speakers were arrested, permits for protest demonstrations were withdrawn at the last moment and public meetings were arbitrarily banned. The night before the "coloured" election, twenty UDF leaders were arrested in pre-dawn raids and a further 150 were arrested during the day.

The "coloured" elections took place on 22 August 1984. The government announced that there had been a low—30 percent—turn out. In effect, since only 60 percent of "coloured" voters had registered, the actual participation rate was no more than 18 percent. The white government attributed the low turn-out to UDF intimidation. The more likely explanation was that those who voted had done so for fear of reprisals from the government or their employers. A week later the Indian population similarly rejected the new constitution when less than 15 percent of eligible Indian voters cast their ballots. In January 1985 the inaugural ceremony was held for P.W. Botha's investiture as state president. To his credit, Canada's ambassador to South Africa did not attend it. Although several other diplomats stayed away, the Canadian and Swedish envoys were alone in voicing their disapproval of the new constitution publicly.

In discussion with members of the Taskforce, senior business executives expressed support for the new South African constitution. They believed that the changes it had brought were important first steps. They did criticize the ongoing "homelands" policy, but failed to see that it was integral to the new structures they applauded. In truth the 1984 constitution offered "coloureds" and Asians very little political influence, certainly less than had been exercised by the "Cape Coloureds" until 1956. (That year they had lost their vote by being taken off the common voters roll.) Twenty-eight years later Asian and "coloureds" were limited to electing members for separate chambers with limited powers. Their votes could not affect the chances of election of supportive and more powerful white candidates. The separate chamber system deliberately excluded any interracial collaboration among progressive parliamentarians—each remained a powerless minority. Those who had argued for changing the system from within found themselves outmanoeuvred by the very system they had joined for this purpose.

For the Botha regime the new constitution had unforeseen consequences. Having designed a parliament which subdivided South Africa's
minorities into white, Indian and "coloured" structures and separated
these from the majority black population, which in turn was subdivided
into separate "homelands," the Botha government had unintentionally
created a powerful and tenacious multi-racial opposition. Symbolizing the
widespread outrage over the exclusion of blacks from the constitutional
changes, dissident Asian and "coloured" South Africans began to ignore
official racial categories, calling themselves "blacks." They were joined by
white support organizations in local, regional and national structures
within the rapidly growing UDF.

There were civil protests and black unrest in the townships throughout
South Africa as soon as the terms of the new constitution had sunk in.
These were met by brutal police and army responses in cycles of increasing
repression and violence reminiscent of the Sharpeville massacre twenty-
four years earlier and the Soweto uprisings of 1976. The rise in black anger,
the organized and determined protests of the UDF and the state's reaction
to them extracted increasing costs in human lives and injuries. Hundreds
were killed, thousands—including growing numbers of children—were
detained and many organizations working for peaceful change were outlawed. Charges of treason were still the favourite response to black
demands for democratic rights. Although the UDF held to its non-violent
policy and was not banned, twenty-two of its leaders and prominent members were charged with treason and faced a possible death penalty. South
Africa was heading towards disintegration and social chaos, sparked not
least by Botha's most ill-conceived constitution.

Canadian Policy Responses

By 1981 the parameters for the future work of the Taskforce had been
mapped out. Member churches had opened a large arena for corporate and
bank actions and had begun seriously to monitor the Southern African policies of the Canadian government. The churches had reviewed and revised
their own policy positions on apartheid and found in the Taskforce an ecumenical unit through which they could act together in pursuit of their
objectives.

In 1980 South Africa and its illegal administration in Namibia were the
remaining bastions of white supremacy in Africa. They faced not only a
hostile African continent but, in addition, a growing body of determined
opponents in the international community. Anti-apartheid inter-govern-
mental initiatives were led by Third World and Scandinavian governments
and were matched by a growing activism within international non-governmental organizations and the churches.

The United Nations, through its specialized committees and agencies such as the UN Centre against Apartheid, the Fourth Committee, the UN Trust Fund for Southern Africa and at times the UN Centre on Transnational Corporations, played a major support role. The UN Centre against Apartheid in particular frequently provided opportunities for the liberation movements, international NGOs and representatives of sympathetic governments to meet and exchange views and experiences; to discuss courses of action and to agree on solidarity statements.[16] The Taskforce participated in many of these events and through them found new friends, new networks, new sources of information and importantly, fresh affirmation that the Canadian churches were part of an international community that mattered in the struggle against apartheid.

The churches had meanwhile come to recognize just how collegial was the acceptance of white South Africa, its apartheid system notwithstanding, in the economic and political power structures of Canadian and other industrialized societies. Western tolerance for black repression in South Africa was strongly reinforced by the prevailing political tendency to exonerate almost any state for its human rights infractions as long as it was fiercely anti-communist. The flip side of this attitude was the notion that those who criticized Western tolerance of the apartheid system—or other repressions in non-communist states—were "soft" on Communism, and their criticism could be dismissed on those grounds alone.

The churches' campaign to reduce Canadian complicity in apartheid presented specific difficulties for the Canadian government. As substantial social institutions, the churches could not be peremptorily dismissed. Moreover, the Canadian government presented itself internationally as a firm critic of apartheid so that it had to handle rather carefully the arguments of the churches that its opposition had but little bite. As a result government leaders and senior External Affairs officials tended to assume a tone of patronizing reproof, suggesting that the churches understood neither the unacceptable implications of their policy demands nor the wisdom of existing government policies. It took the Taskforce some time before it could draw from the government a detailed response to its critical analysis of Canadian policies. An exchange of views finally took place in the first half of the 1980s and provides an excellent and comprehensive summary of both the position of the government and the criticisms and recommendations of the churches as these were defined at the time.

The 1981–83 Exchange between the Government and the Taskforce.

In analyzing the 1977 government measures that had promised much but had done little, members of the Taskforce sought to discern certain patterns in the positions taken by different government departments. By 1981 it seemed clear to them that those measures announced in 1977 by the secretary of state for External Affairs, whose implementation required the cooperation of the departments of Finance and Industry, Trade and Commerce—a review of tax allowances for companies operating in Namibia, or a halt to the PEMD for business in South Africa—had largely been ignored. Members of the Taskforce therefore prepared a major brief which they addressed to both the secretary of state for External Affairs and the minister of Industry, Trade and Commerce. The brief was submitted in early May 1981 and a meeting with Mark MacGuigan, the secretary of state for External Affairs and Ed Lumley, the minister for Industry, Trade and Commerce took place in Ottawa on 15 July 1981.

At the meeting in the splendid new External Affairs building, the two ministers sat a little cramped side by side at the narrow end of a large oblong table, presumably to symbolize their close and equal relationship concerning the issue. As MacEachen had done in 1975, MacGuigan and Lumley, six years later, allocated too little time for an adequate discussion of the churches' agenda. The ministers agreed to formulate their responses in a written reply to the Taskforce.

This detailed rejoinder was nearly a year in preparation and was dated 15 June 1982. At the time it constituted the fullest statement of the government's policy towards Southern Africa.[17] In March 1983 the churches responded in turn with a critique of that policy.

In their opening paragraphs the ministers suggested that the Taskforce and the government held the same aspirations for social justice in Southern Africa and that the government's position left South Africa in no doubt about its opposition to apartheid. However, the ministers added,

> it would be self-defeating to ignore that South Africa is a technically advanced, resource-rich state well able to sustain itself. These considerations have shaped our policy, not—as you suggest—inter-departmental conflict and differing priorities. . . . We remain convinced that societies which are isolated and deprived of external contact find it most difficult to change and to adopt new conceptions and new approaches. Here, we have deliberately sought to maintain a balanced approach which leaves no doubt, through our statements and actions, of our opposition to and abhorrence of apartheid, but which also leaves the way open for contacts (including trade and investment) and dialogue which, in themselves, strengthen Canada's capacity to encourage the process of change in South Africa.

The ministers stressed that they preferred peaceful change to "sudden conflict and destructive violence."

The churches replied that sharing the same objective—an end to the system of apartheid—was important. However "[i]t is in the means selected that the reality and seriousness of the commitment to the common objective is tested." The churches noted that the ministers had rejected every one of their nine recommendations. They were also discouraged that the ministers' response had not taken into account events that had occurred since their meeting in 1981. In the intervening year "sudden violence and destructive conflict," which the ministers deplored, had been unleashed by the white minority government against those seeking an end to apartheid.

The Taskforce referred to tough new security laws that placed increased restrictions on anti-apartheid organizations and to evidence of the continued interrogation by torture of political prisoners that caused rising numbers of deaths in police custody. The Taskforce warned that the proposed South African constitutional changes would concentrate even more powers in the hands of the apartheid regime. Meanwhile South Africa had also carried out several military raids into neighbouring states and had continued its war in Namibia, carrying it deep into Angola where it now occupied large tracts of territory. South Africa was bringing death and destruction to Mozambique through training and logistical support for the insurgents there. In December 1982 South African commando raids were also launched against Lesotho. "All these acts" the Taskforce contended, "must now be considered when we talk about 'peaceful change' in this part of Africa."[18]

In preparing the initial brief in 1981 the Taskforce had sought to articulate a set of policy proposals for the Canadian government which could not easily be dismissed as extravagant or far in advance of what would be acceptable to the Canadian public. The government in turn responded to the proposals rather more fully and carefully than has sometimes been the case. For this reason, the following close analysis of the recommendations presented by the Taskforce in 1981, the ministers' 1982 responses and the final comments from the Taskforce in 1983 review both the position being taken by the government and that advocated by the churches. It illustrates the Taskforce's determined effort to be fully in command of the detailed complexities of the issues it chose to raise.

Recommendation One: Export Development Corporation

We ask that the Export Development Corporation (edc) be instructed to withdraw its corporate account support from any transaction relating to South Africa.

The ministers replied that they were always looking for constructive ways to express their opposition to South Africa and had asked the EDC to suspend its lending facilities for South African buyers of Canadian goods. On the other hand the EDC would continue to extend EDC credit insurance and guarantees to Canadian suppliers for their exports to South Africa. The ministers declared that such insurance policies were issued for global coverage of total export sales and specific exports could therefore not be excluded. In addition they wrote that "it is not deemed feasible nor desirable to alter the provision of the export credits insurance or guarantees to Canadian exporters at this time."

While total EDC loans for South African buyers between 1961 and 1976 had amounted to only $3.8 million and none had been made since 1976, EDC export credit insurance and guarantees were highly valued as a safeguard against non-payment and political risk. In 1981 alone, EDC insurance and guarantees for goods destined for South Africa amounted to just over $45 million.[19] The churches concluded, therefore, that the Canadian government had suspended the facility that had fallen into disuse, but retained its most important support activity for Canadian commerce with South Africa.

The members of the Taskforce were sceptical about the government's claim that it would not be "feasible" to suspend the EDC export insurance coverage for South Africa. They noted that other states were able to do this with apparent ease. For example, in 1978 the United States, Denmark, Norway and Holland, and in 1979 Sweden as well, had excluded South Africa from their global coverage of export credit insurance and guaranties.[20] Members of the Taskforce in 1983 reiterated their original recommendation, that the only defensible policy position regarding the EDC was to withdraw its corporate account support from *any* transaction related to South Africa.

Recommendation Three:[21] *Ford South Africa*

> We ask the Canadian government publicly to inform the Ford Motor Company of Canada and all other Canadian companies operating in South Africa:
>
> (a) that it considers contracts with the South African police and military a contravention of the mandatory arms embargo;
>
> (b) that it will disallow as normal operating expenses for purposes of Canadian tax deductions taxes paid to the South African government on military and police contracts and costs incurred through the organization of white militia units and the storage of weapons.
>
> We further ask that the Canadian government request Ford Canada that it instruct its South African subsidiary to cancel all existing police and military contracts and not to enter into new contracts; and that the Canadian displeasure about the military and police contracts be communicated to the Ford Motor Company in the United States and to the South African government.

In response to point a) the ministers made full use of the fact that the wording of UNSCR 418, the 1977 mandatory arms embargo against South Africa, did not cover military and police equipment that was produced by foreign subsidiaries *in* South Africa.[22] The ministers wrote: "It is very doubtful that the Ford Motor Company of Canada Ltd. ... can be judged to be in violation of the UN embargo ... [P]roducts manufactured in South

Africa by Ford South Africa fall outside the scope of Resolution 418." The churches noted that this decision of the Canadian government was contrary to the obvious intent of UNSCR 418, namely to deprive the South African military and police of international supplies. Canada had supported this resolution under Article 7 of the United Nations Charter, which designated the embargoed state as a serious threat to international peace.[23] Yet External Affairs chose the narrowest possible interpretation of the mandatory embargo.

The ministers also rejected Recommendation Three (b) on similarly narrow grounds. They said that tax deductions allowed to Canadian companies for taxes paid by their subsidiaries to foreign governments were applied universally. No special provisions existed for South Africa. Moreover, even if they did, External Affairs foresaw problems for Key Point industries: "[T]he impossibility of identifying operating expenses incurred in fulfilling the requirements of the National Key Points Committee would make such a policy unenforceable.... A South African subsidiary which did report the costs involved ... might well be deemed to be in breach of [South Africa's] defence regulations." The ministers thus conceded that Canadian investment, particularly when involved in strategic production— far from encouraging the process of change—was part of South Africa's "total strategy" in defence of the system of apartheid. The ministers rejected out of hand the final part of the recommendation regarding Ford South Africa. They wrote that these recommendations were contrary to the government's policy not to exercise (or seek to exercise) extra-territorial jurisdiction. "We believe," the ministers said, "that there are better and more effective ways of promoting fundamental change in South Africa," but nowhere in their lengthy response did they indicate what these might be. The Taskforce expressed its dismay at the ease with which the Canadian government had slipped away from its putative dedication to promote change in South Africa. When faced with a concrete policy issue, the Canadian government would rather discover reasons for inaction.

Recommendation Four: Massey-Ferguson

> We ask the Canadian Government to inform Massey-Ferguson that it considers the company's sale of technology to the South African military as a breach of the mandatory arms embargo, and to insist that it cancel its contract with Atlantis Diesel Engine Company of South Africa (ADE).

The ministers' response referred again to their policy in regard to extra-territorial jurisdiction. The ministers pointed out that Perkins Ltd. was a British subsidiary of Massey-Ferguson. They then explained that

> [I]t is Canadian policy, in compliance with the U.N. arms embargo, not to allow the sale of goods which are on the Export Control List to military and

para-military organizations in South Africa. It is, however, an open question whether the Perkins diesel engine, given its relatively small size, would fall within the ambit of the Export and Imports Permits Act. It must be noted, in any event, that Perkins is a foreign subsidiary of a Canadian company and that Canada has strongly objected to attempts by other countries to impose their laws on Canadian subsidiaries through the parent companies of these firms. Any attempt by the Canadian government to make use of its recent financial agreements with Massey-Ferguson to require a company that is incorporated and doing business in the United Kingdom to follow Canadian government trade policies would, in our view, be regarded by the U.K. as an infringement of its jurisdiction.

After *Business Week* had given publicity to Perkins' technology sale in 1979, members of the Taskforce had raised this issue with the company itself. The answer that they had received from its CEO had been unsettling (see pp. 45–46 above). At about that time Massey-Ferguson was experiencing major financial difficulties, and the Canadian government—among others—had stepped in to keep Massey-Ferguson financially afloat. In 1981 the Taskforce therefore asked the Canadian government to use the leverage of its assistance to bring Massey-Ferguson's activities into line with the clear intent of the arms embargo.

We were puzzled by the response. The Taskforce had not suggested that Perkins engines were actually shipped from Canada to ADE in South Africa, nor had we asked that the government stop any such shipments from Britain. We had asked that the government convince Massey-Ferguson to rescind Perkins' technology licensee agreement with ADE on the grounds that ADE was a South African government enterprise using the technology inter alia for military purposes. The ministers' reply did not at all address this issue.

And what did the ministers mean when they declared that it was an open question whether "the Perkins' diesel engine, given its relatively small size, would fall within the ambit of the Export and Import Permits Act"? It was more than an "open" question, it was a new question that only the government could answer since the guidelines for the exports of strategic equipment were classified.[24] Did Perkins sell not only diesel engine technology but also actual diesel engines, and were these shipped from Canada to ADE in South Africa? The Taskforce only knew that at the end of 1981 Massey-Ferguson had shipped "machinery and parts" worth nearly $3 million to South Africa and neither Massey-Ferguson nor the government gave further details.[25]

The Perkins story nevertheless circulated for quite some time. In November 1982 *The Ottawa Citizen* quoted J. Battersby, an executive of ADE and former general manager of Perkins South Africa (before it moved to Britain), that Perkins had been well aware of the military aspects of the project. *The Ottawa Citizen* also revealed the total indifference of senior government officials to the military implications of the South African trans-action. Ray Billard, director general of the machinery branch of the Department of Industry, Trade and Commerce was quoted to say that the government was not interested in "what this particular subsidiary was cooking up with somebody . . . Perkins is a British company. If it does not bother the British government, why should it bother Canada?[26]

Recommendation Five: Krugerrand Sales

> We ask the Canadian Government to institute measures to prevent the Krugerrand from being sold in Canada.

The ministers replied that a proposal from the International Gold Corporation[27] to establish itself in Canada had been turned down by the Foreign Investment Review Agency because it lacked significant benefit to Canada. The sale of Krugerrand in general, however, was considered as trade in peaceful goods with South Africa and the government would not stand in the way of "the legitimate overseas activities of Canadian compa-nies and individuals . . . [unless they] contravened sanctions imposed by the United Nations Security Council."

The ministers had ignored altogether our inquiry as to which depart-ment of government was authorizing the sale of Krugerrand in Canada. Inquiries had been made first to the Bank of Nova Scotia, the distributing agent for the South African Chamber of Mines, and then to the master of the Royal Mint. He had directed us to the Department of External Affairs and to the Ministry of Industry, Trade and Commerce. The latter then advised us to write to the minister of Supply and Services who in turn closed the circle by directing us back to the master of the Royal Mint. None could or would tell us who authorized the sale of Krugerrand in Canada, and whether the appointment of a distributing agent required any specific license from Canadian authorities. We never did find out.

Recommendation Six: Code of Conduct

> We ask that the Canadian government reassess the usefulness of its present Code of Conduct for Canadian Companies Operating in South Africa with the view of amending it.

The Taskforce had already proposed a set of amendments to the 1978 Code of Conduct. These would have required the companies to work towards the abolition of the migrant labour system and the abolition of influx controls to allow all workers to live with their families; to press for racial equality in education and equal access to housing and health services. The churches asked that the Code be legally binding and result in penalties for non- or inadequate compliance and that companies follow an identical reporting format, providing employment data as well as a listing of contracts with

South Africa's military and police. The churches had also asked for a public review committee which would include representatives of the Canadian Labour Congress, the churches and other concerned organizations to assess company compliance with the codes.

The ministers replied that the Code of Conduct was under review and that changes would be made after consultations with interested organizations and companies. They promised that the Taskforce's observations and recommendations would be carefully considered. The ministers warned that the Taskforce brief "seem to reflect an unduly optimistic view of what the Code of Conduct may be expected to achieve." The Code's purpose was to avoid discrimination, they wrote, and to improve working conditions for South African employees with regard to employment and training, adequate health care and housing. The hope was that "such measures would have a beneficial 'demonstration effect' outside the companies' actual operations." But the ministers warned the churches that the Canadian Code directly affected "less than one percent" of the total South African work force and that its effect would necessarily be "limited."

The ministers wrote that Canada's policy on extraterritorial jurisdiction ruled out legal enforcement of the Code, but that companies with investment in South Africa had been encouraged to produce public reports. The ministers clearly balked at the idea of the government's involvement in even informal pressure on Canadian companies about their activities in South Africa. They repeated Mark MacGuigan's statement to the House of Commons that the reports could be studied by interested Canadians who could question the companies directly (see p. 55). The churches were invited to do so.

The Taskforce commented on the ministers' complicated reply:

> If such requirements—as contained in Recommendation Six—are deemed to go beyond what can be expected of companies in South Africa, then the argument for liberalization through the presence of Canadian companies collapses. No case can be made that Canadian investment, as one of the vehicles for contact, "strengthens Canada's capacity to encourage the process of change in South Africa" as stated in the ministers' introductory remarks. (cited above, p. 76)

Members of the Taskforce felt justified in asking themselves whether Canada's feeble Code of Conduct could serve any purpose other than justifying continued investment in South Africa.

Recommendation Seven: UN *Security Council Resolution 418*

> We ask that a review of existing legislation and enforcement mechanisms relating to the arms embargo against South Africa take place with all possible speed and that tighter enforcement measures be instituted and published.

Given Canada's narrow interpretation of the letter and the spirit of the UN mandatory arms embargo, the Taskforce had remained sceptical about the rigour with which Canada enforced UNSCR 418. Our unease grew with the revelations in 1980 of the clandestine transactions of the US/Canadian Space Research Corporation (SRC). In March 1980 two senior executives of the company had pleaded guilty in a US court to charges of violating American law by shipping arms to South Africa between April 1976 and September 1978.[28] They were sentenced to six months in jail and fined $45,000. The Canadian dimensions of the case arose from the option that SRC had of making the clandestine shipments from Canada in the hope of staying at arm's length from US law. Indeed the defendants in the American grand jury investigation had pleaded guilty to shipping weapons from the Canadian side of the plant. According to the Canadian government, the RCMP had launched a Canadian investigation in 1977. Following the conviction of the SRC executives in the United States, they were eventually charged and convicted in Canada before a Quebec Court but, in contrast to United States procedures, the time, place and proceedings had been kept secret.[29]

The May 1981 Brief had cited the case of the SRC as evidence that enforcement mechanisms ought to be revised and tightened if Canada was to fulfil its obligation under the mandatory UNSC Resolution 418. The two ministers rejected this recommendation and wrote that Canada had adhered to both the letter and the spirit of Resolution 418. With reference to the SRC, they said:

> Where clear breaches of our regulations have occurred, they have only escaped attention for a time as a result of the deliberate and thorough falsification of records and export permit applications. The investigation, prosecution and conviction of those responsible was a forthright expression of government policy. . . . The action taken has, we have no doubt, strengthened the operation of the system and acted as a deterrent against further malpractice.

The government also rejected as unwarranted the establishment of a parliamentary sub-committee to supervise the enforcement of the embargo. They informed the Taskforce that controls on the export of military strategic equipment were maintained under the legislative authority of the Export and Import Permits Act,[30] where rigorous prescreening of export permit applications was complemented by customs controls at ports, airports and central distribution centres. They told the Taskforce: "There is absolutely no justification for attributing such infractions of the law as do occur, and which are not detected prior to the export of the goods concerned, to a 'lack of enthusiasm' on the part of Canadian enforcement officers." Members of the Taskforce remained unconvinced. They noted that SRC was in fact close to the government and that its representatives frequently conferred with the Canadian and American defence establishments.[31] They could not understand how External Affairs and National Defence, the two departments charged with examining cases "where political or security implications exist," could have failed for two years to detect SRC's falsified export permit applications. The two departments had neglected to pursue the statement made by Joshua Nkomo, a leading Zimbabwean nationalist, to an Ottawa press conference as early as October 1977 that he knew of Canadian guns that were being shipped to South Africa via Antigua. Moreover, on 7 November 1978, the CBC program *The Fifth Estate* had aired "Passage of Arms," a major investigative report that had traced the clandestine delivery of Space Research artillery components from Antigua and from Canada to South Africa.[32]

The churches noted that the controls at ports, airports and central distribution centres remained totally deficient. It had come to light for example, that in 1977 the RCMP had searched crates containing artillery shells on the docks in St. John, New Brunswick, and had let them go, and that at least two more shipments had reached South Africa via Spain in 1978. Suspicions that were clearly aroused in 1977 should have resulted in the kind of "rigorous prescreening" of which the ministers spoke regarding all further SRC export permit applications and shipments from ports, airports and central distribution centres.

A further experience of the Taskforce heightened the churches' scepticism about the reliability of Canada's arms embargo enforcement. On 29 November 1981, the CBC program *Sunday Morning* disclosed allegations that Levy Auto Parts of Toronto had shipped reconstituted Centurion tank engines and parts to South Africa. The export permit, *Sunday Morning* said, had referred only to truck parts shipped from Toronto Harbour on 18 June 1980 on the Norwegian ship *Thorswave* to Durban, South Africa.[33]

On 14 December the Taskforce phoned External Affairs to enquire whether these allegations were being investigated. To our surprise, we were told that it was not the responsibility of External Affairs to launch such an investigation and we were referred to the Department of Justice. There, we were told that this type of investigation would not come under the purview of Justice and we were advised to get in touch with the RCMP. The RCMP legal department explained that they could only investigate if asked to do so by a department of government, and that in this case no request had been made. We then inquired whether the public could request an investigation, but were told that such a public request would be extremely difficult to formulate. The enforcement of the South African arms embargo, the RCMP lawyer said, was based on regulations issued under the Export and Import Permits Act. Thus, if members of the public requested the RCMP to investigate alleged violations, they would have to cite alleged infractions of a specific regulation under the Act. In the view of this RCMP lawyer, such a task without the support of the Canadian government would likely be beyond the means of ordinary Canadians. He added that the issue at hand was of a highly political character and unlikely to receive much official encouragement.[34]

This episode further convinced the churches that their criticism in 1981 of the enforcement mechanism of UNSCR 418 had been justified. Nothing in the ministers' replies nor in their subsequent experience as close observers of the issue had changed their minds.

Recommendation Eight: Dual Purpose Items and Nuclear Collaboration[35]

We ask the Canadian government to reaffirm its commitment and to strengthen its adherence to Security Council Resolution 418 by:

(a) interpreting the terms "arms and related material" as covering the transfer of all technology useful to the military and "dual purpose" equipment, be they transferred through bilateral, third party or through trans-shipment via third county arrangements;

(b) refraining scrupulously from any nuclear collaboration with South Africa.

UNSCR 418 had prohibited the export to South Africa of "arms and related matériel," but had left dual purpose items untouched. The Security Council Committee established by UNSCR 421 to oversee international adherence to 418 had sought to correct this omission. It had argued that modern weapon systems and the technologically sophisticated structures of the military and police often require the same auxiliary parts and technology that are used in civilian application. Such items included computers, telecommunications systems, certain aircraft, aviation and radar equipment, crash indicators, precision instruments and night vision and search-and-rescue equipment among others. In 1979 it therefore asked that states prohibit the export to South Africa of dual-purpose items.[36]

The churches had been reassured by this initiative of the UN Committee and in their 1981 brief had drawn attention to its report. In their response to the Taskforce the ministers made clear that dual-purpose items would receive export permission only if they were destined for bona fide commercial concerns for civilian application: "Where doubts are raised about the end user of such equipment, permit applications are considered by the responsible departments. Should there be any evidence that the equipment in question is to be used for military purposes or against the civilian population, the permit application is denied in keeping with UN Security Council Resolution No. 421." A more careful reading of the Taskforce brief and of the text of the UN 421 Committee would have told the ministers that their policy was not in the least in keeping with the report of the UN Committee. Its recommendation would *not* have permitted the Canadian government to export dual purpose equipment to civilian buyers. The UN Committee had said categorically "states should prohibit the export to South Africa of dual purpose items . . ." For good reasons it had not suggested any exception to this prohibition. There were in South Africa over 500 private companies involved in contracts or sub-contracts for ARMSCOR; few of these would be recognizable by name as serving the state-owned arms manufacturer.[37] It would have been an insurmountable task to search through this intentional labyrinth to identify the "*bona fide* commercial concerns" not linked to South Africa's military-industrial complex, particularly with regard to strategic goods on Canada's Export Control List.

There were other related issues which had troubled the churches. The May 1981 brief had cited a 1979 export permit for three CL-215 amphibian water bombers to the forest department of the South African government. In its promotional brochures, Canadair, the manufacturer, had described the CL-215 not only as ideal for fighting forest fires, but as well as "a long range patrol amphibian; a high capacity spray aircraft; a versatile resource survey platform; a utility emergency transport . . . particularly in internal troop-lift operations." The recipient of these aircraft was certainly not a "*bona fide* commercial concern"; the end user was the South African government, entirely free to employ the CL-215 for whatever purpose it wished.

When we had met with Mark MacGuigan and Ed Lumley on 15 July 1981, MacGuigan had defended the export of the CL-215 aircraft to South Africa, not by citing exemptions to the mandatory arms embargo, but by reference to a different and general set of policy principles governing the export of military and strategic goods and technology. These principles excluded export permits for strategic goods to:

- countries considered to represent a military threat to Canada:
- countries involved in or under imminent threat of hostilities;
- countries to which UN resolutions forbid the export of arms; and
- regimes considered to be wholly repugnant to Canadian values.

MacGuigan stated that the export of the CL-215s had been permitted under these principles since South Africa was not engaged in military hostilities. The grounds of argument were shifting rapidly. We pointed out that South Africa was indeed engaged in military hostilities in Namibia, in Angola and in cross-border raids into neighbouring black states. MacGuigan asked whether we had proof that the CL-215s were employed in these areas. We had no such proof, and MacGuigan coolly observed that Canada's ambassador to South Africa was monitoring the use of the CL-215s there. The Taskforce wrote to Peter Calami, then African correspondent of Southam News, to ask whether he could shed some light on this when next in South Africa. In November 1981 Calami replied that he had been in South Africa and "that the Canadian Ambassador in South Africa was *not* aware that he or anyone on the embassy staff was supposed to be checking on the use of aircraft" (emphasis in the original).[38] The Taskforce reiterated their May 1981 recommendation that the government should interpret UNSC Resolution 418 "as covering the transfer of all technology useful to the military as well as [the export of] all dual purpose equipment."

With regard to nuclear issues, the ministers had reassured the Taskforce that "Canada has no intention of entering into any form of nuclear collaboration with South Africa." The ministers' reply was dated 15 June 1982. Yet less than two weeks previous, from 1–4 June 1982, Canadian officials from the Department of Energy Mines and Resources' Uranium and Nuclear Energy Branch had joined (among others) South African officials, including the director of the South African Atomic Energy Board, in a Symposium on Uranium Exploration Methods.[39] The Symposium, held in Paris, had been organized by the Organization of Economic Cooperation and Development and the International Atomic Energy Agency. Contacted by the Taskforce, an official of Energy, Mines and Resources had stated that this was a purely scientific exchange, as if this was at all reassuring!

Recommendation Nine: Namibia

   (a) We urge the Canadian Government to take immediate action to protect Namibian resources from illegal foreign exploitation by adopting Decree No. 1 of 1974 of the United Nations Council for Namibia.

   (b) We further ask that tax concessions for Canadian companies operating in Namibia be withdrawn. Any expenditure in Namibia for exploration and development should not be recognized as a legitimate cost for calculations in a company's taxable income.

The Taskforce had argued that the extraction of Namibian depletable resources by Canadian and other foreign companies, constituted theft as long as the territory was under illegal South African occupation. In Recommendations Nine (a) and (b) the Taskforce had thus asked for two obvious policy changes which would help to limit these thefts.

The ministers rejected both recommendations. In regard to Decree No.1 they stated that Canada did not "support its [the UN Council for Namibia] creation and we do not consider that it can perform its assigned function or act legally as a sovereign body. Consequently, we do not accept the Council's authority to issue Decree No.1 dealing with the exports of products." They went on:

   Nor do we consider that the commercial operations of Canadian companies in Namibia constitute plunder and theft. We would expect any independent government of Namibia to draw revenues for itself and benefits for its people from the development and economic activity brought about by any Canadian investment. As a matter of public policy, the Government of Canada does not interfere in the activities of Canadian companies in Namibia except where such activities contravene sanctions imposed by the Security Council....

With respect to the tax relief accorded Canadian companies, the rules governing it are of universal application. Moreover, acceptance of the reality of the "fiscal burdens" born by Canadian companies abroad implies no judgement as to the legitimacy of the regime levying the tax.

The reasons for rejecting Recommendation Nine (b) made clear that the Canadian government was entirely out of sympathy with the premise of both recommendations. The Taskforce had been urging the government to withdraw corporate tax concession since 1975. In 1977 Don Jamieson had promised to examine the "implications of possible tax concessions which companies obtain for their operations in Namibia under 'what is essentially an illegal regime.' " Almost the same sentiments were expressed four years later by Mark MacGuigan during the July 1981 meeting with members of the Taskforce. The final response by the ministers to the Taskforce represented a retreat from this earlier albeit soft position to a definite hard one.

Canada's Voting Record at the United Nations[40]

The May 1981 Taskforce Brief had criticized the Canadian government that between 1978 and 1980 it had opposed or abstained from those General Assembly resolutions calling for increased pressure on the apartheid regime in economic, military and nuclear matters.

The ministers rejected this criticism. They explained that Canada, although in sympathy with some of these resolutions, had been unable to support them because they had "grown more strident, inclusive and wide-ranging year by year."

We do not believe that global economic sanctions against South Africa are appropriate, we do not believe they can be effective, and we do not believe that they would promote the changes we desire in South Africa. We are also concerned about the damage they would do to neighbouring countries. The repeated advocacy of global sanctions has been one factor that has forced Canada to oppose or abstain on a number of resolutions. Other propositions we cannot support in the context of our strong advocacy of peaceful change are those which endorse the armed struggle, link Zionism with racism, or condemn friendly countries by name. Such proposals weaken, rather than strengthen international pressure for social and political change in South Africa.

The government insisted that it remained opposed to apartheid and would have supported positive and constructive elements in some resolutions had they not contained propositions it could not condone.

The churches observed that Canada had not availed itself of the option of supporting these resolutions while recording its disagreement with unacceptable clauses, an option it had used in other contexts. They also noted that the Canadian government had not proposed any alternative to those resolutions. Such attempts, even had they failed, would at least have signalled an active concern for increasing peaceful pressures on South Africa to abandon apartheid. The unavoidable conclusion was that Canada at that time voiced no criticism of the apartheid regime.

The ministers, rather than criticizing the Taskforce for cataloguing Canada's evasion of UN votes on South Africa, might have acknowledged that this had actually been a deliberate strategy since 1978. In that year Canada, as a member of the Security Council and of the Contact Group of States, had opposed mandatory sanctions and had promised to negotiate an early independence for Namibia. Since then Canada had used this futile process as an excuse for maintaining official silence on issues that might annoy the apartheid regime. That this was indeed the case was made clear to the United Church of Canada in 1981. In a telegram sent on 27 August to Mark MacGuigan, the United Church had urgently requested that he, as Canada's secretary of state for External Affairs, officially protest the brutal eviction of squatters from Nyanga township, South Africa. Two months later External Affairs replied: "At this time we will not register a formal protest over the incident. . . . In considering public action of this kind, the consequences of the certain resentment of South Africa at what they would regard as interference in their domestic affairs must be weighed against what we are trying to achieve in other areas, notably Namibia."[41] The review of the detailed exchange between the Taskforce and the secretary of state for External Affairs and the minister of Industry, Trade and Commerce between May 1981 and March 1983 makes clear that the Taskforce had not shifted the position of the government on any important issue. Nevertheless External Affairs had recognized the Taskforce as a substantial and knowledgeably non-governmental organization active on the South African issue with an enviable command of the details of Canadian policy and in touch with contemporary South African developments. More than that, the board members of the Taskforce who had been directly involved, and by extension the churches that they represented, had gained confidence in their activities and were more determined than ever to persevere.

No similar major engagement with the Canadian government related to policy changes toward Southern Africa took place again until after the 1984 elections. In the interval there were two important specific issues involving the federal government which the Taskforce addressed. The first concerned Canada's decision to support IMF credits for South Africa in 1982 and the second, renewed evidence of nuclear collaboration with South Africa.

Canadian Support for IMF Credits for South Africa[42]

Early in October 1982 South Africa applied for a major credit of $1.07 billion from the International Monetary Fund (IMF). Alerted about this by the Washington Center for International Policy, the Taskforce wrote at once to the secretary of state for External Affairs and to the minister of Finance. The churches argued that the profound violations of human rights inherent in the apartheid system must be judged an impediment to approval of the credit by the IMF.[43] They therefore urged that the Canadian executive director on the IMF board be instructed to vote against the credit to South Africa.

We also made contact with organizations in Jamaica and Ireland whose governments were represented on the IMF board by the Canadian executive director, to notify them of the upcoming decision. We issued a news release and a Canada-wide alert to all anti-apartheid organizations asking for letters to the government and to their own NGO networks here and abroad to protest the credit. We knew from the copies of protest letters received at the Taskforce that the response to the alert was tremendous and that both the Irish and the Jamaican governments were actively opposing the IMF credit to South Africa. Alas, the Canadian government favoured it.

In explaining why he could not accept the churches' request, Marc Lalonde, then minister of Finance, replied on 8 November: "The IMF must be careful ... not to be accused of meddling in the internal affairs of sovereign states." This was a perplexing reply, given the IMF's routine insistence on substantial economic adjustment measures in most countries as a condition for credit disbursements after the initial tranche due to them. Lalonde also warned that "lack of Fund financing would affect economic partners through debt and payment arrears as well as through the disruption of normal trade and financial flows."[44]

The comment revealed what is often concealed—that protecting the interests of international bankers and international trade took precedence over ensuring that South Africa's minority regime was not further aided in this way.

Allan MacEachen, back again as secretary of state for External Affairs, replied six months later, long after the Fund had approved the credit: "So long as South Africa adheres to the articles of agreement of the IMF, and the loan meets normally applied criteria, Canada would not oppose the loan requested."[45] On 3 November 1982 the IMF executive board made its decision. Canada's executive director, overriding the objections of Ireland and Jamaica, provided the crucial additional 4.19 percent vote needed to reach a bare majority of 52 percent in favour of the credit.

Both Canadian ministers turned out to have been in error. "Lack of Fund financing" would not have put South Africa into payment arrears, as Lalonde had feared. South Africa's presumed need for the loan had already evaporated by year end. South Africa did not collect its credit disbursement due that month, and in late June 1983 it announced that it would repay the entire loan ahead of schedule. This outcome appeared to have been anticipated by South Africa's pro-government press. *Beeld* had written on 6 October 1982, that going to the IMF was "not a matter of weakness ... we could have got along without it" but that the successful outcome of the loan application had demonstrated that "our house is in order."

Allan MacEachen had been as seriously in error by suggesting that Canada could not have opposed the loan because South Africa was meeting "normally applied criteria." At the IMF, Saudi Arabia and India had argued that the IMF's credit criteria had already been violated by South Africa's economic distortions due to its discriminatory labour laws. IMF staff were soon to come to the same conclusion.

In sharp deviation from usual practice an IMF staff team was dispatched to South Africa after—rather than before—the hastily arranged credit. Its report documented that the "labour market regulations in South Africa are clearly not consistent with the realization of the country's full growth potential." It noted "the impediments to the geographic mobility of black workers" and "the system of short term migrant labour contracts whereby black workers have to return to their point of recruitment on the expiration of their contract." "This regulatory system," the report said, "is based on non-economic considerations." It recommended as "essential that the impediments and restrictions in the labour market be eased" to avoid "serious imbalance in the country." Similar technical and economic impediments were attributed to South Africa's unequal and underfinanced education system, said to be "detrimental to the maximum utilization of South Africa's manpower resources."[46]

Although the IMF staff report ignored many other dehumanizing features of the apartheid system, it explicitly noted the economic costs attributable to discrimination against black South Africans—want of freedom of movement and choice of residence, want of free choice of employment and the right to education. Avoidable economic inefficiencies due to legislated interferences in the market economy were (and are) often cited by the IMF as grounds to withhold IMF financing until they are removed. Yet in the case of South Africa—with Canada's support—these "normally applied criteria" had been suspended, MacEachen's exhortations to the contrary notwithstanding.

At the beginning of Part Two, we noted our increasing disillusionment that, despite routine condemnations, the white minority regime of South Africa was still accepted as a collegial member of the economic and political power structures of Western industrialized societies. The hastily arranged IMF credit for South Africa in 1982 and Canada's role therein added to that disillusionment.

Renewed Nuclear Collaboration with South Africa.

Two years after the churches and other NGOs had protested Canadian nuclear collaboration with South Africa (see chap. 3, p. 87) they learned that an international conference on "Electricity and Uranium—A Brighter Future" was to take place in Saskatoon from 3–6 June 1984. It was to be sponsored by the Canadian Nuclear Association, the Canadian Nuclear Society and the Uranium Institute of the UK. The Saskatoon conference was to be addressed by, among others, D. Sinclair Smith, uranium adviser of the South African Chamber of Mines and M. Bates, deputy general manager of Rossing Uranium, Namibia.

The Taskforce wrote to the secretary of state for External Affairs to remind him of the government's 1982 assurance that it would not engage in nuclear collaboration with South Africa. Given South Africa's adamant refusal to sign the Treaty on Non-Proliferation of Nuclear Weapons, the Taskforce argued that no distinction could be made between cooperation with South Africa on the peaceful uses of atomic energy and direct collaboration with its nuclear weapons development. Indeed, South Africa had quite recently refused inspection by the International Atomic Energy Agency (IAEA) of its Valindaba uranium enrichment plant and was widely believed to have detonated a nuclear device in 1979.[47]

The Taskforce also sought a reply to a letter written five months previous enquiring how Canada had voted at the 1983 IAEA General Conference on a resolution that had asked members to "terminate all transfer of fissionable material and technology to South Africa and to refrain from extending to South Africa any facilities which may assist in its nuclear plans and in particular the participation of South Africa in the technical groups of the Agency."[48] In August 1984 Jean Chrétien replied. He was then deputy prime minister and secretary of state for External Affairs. He first assured church members of the government's unequivocal opposition to the abhorrent policy of apartheid. Then in reference to the Saskatoon nuclear conference, he wrote that the government "exercises no control over the proceedings of private, non-governmental conferences held in Canada . . . [they] are therefore at liberty to invite whomever they wish to attend such an international conference."[49]

This explanation ignored the December 1977 policy change that had introduced visa requirements for all South African visitors to Canada. The government therefore could have denied visas to the South African and Namibian uranium experts. Moreover, the proceedings of the Saskatoon conference were not quite as private and non-governmental as Chretién made out. Senior Canadian officials were among the principal speakers.[50]

In the same letter Chretién also informed the Taskforce that Canada had abstained on the IAEA resolution. Although Canada agreed with the general thrust of the resolution, it supported South Africa's continued membership in the IAEA on the principle that all UN member states should enjoy participation in the UN's specialized agencies. The minister stated that South Africa's membership would ensure "continued IAEA safeguard coverage of South Africa's nuclear facilities." Here the minister was referring only to South Africa's two Koeberg nuclear reactors that were permitting IAEA inspectors. He ignored the fact that for the purpose of preventing nuclear weapons proliferation, the crucial South African installations were not the Koeberg reactors but the Valindaba uranium enrichment plant, which was denying access to IAEA. By this oversight, inadvertent or otherwise, Canada turned a blind eye to South Africa's refusal to sign the NPT and its denial of access to IAEA inspection, the very source of South Africa's nuclear weapons development.

The appalling truth about South Africa's nuclear weapons, asserted since 1979 by anti-apartheid activists and nuclear researchers and steadfastly disregarded by the IAEA and Western powers, including the Canadian government, was finally confirmed on 24 March 1993 by F.W. de Klerk, then South Africa's president. He announced that since 1978 South Africa had built six atomic bombs in a clandestine program that ended in 1990. On 19 July 1991 Canada had been able to congratulate him for signing the Non-Proliferation Treaty.[51]

As the October 1984 election drew close, the Taskforce could not but conclude that the Liberal government, on issue after issue, had resolutely maintained a minimalist position despite its avowed abhorrence of apartheid, and had time and again temporized and used misrepresentation to conceal this fact. In consequence the Taskforce had come to see as an important part of its responsibility that it ferret out and make widely known the detailed evidence of such subterfuges.

Notes

1 According to *The Guardian* (UK), 4 April 1979, the League denied reports that it received funds from the South African government, stating that it was financed by business interests.

2 Taskforce on the Churches and Corporate Responsibility, *Annual Report, 1980–1981*, p. 19. Hendrik Verwoerd, regarded as the architect of "grand apartheid," was minister of education and later prime minister of South Africa. He told the South African Senate in 1954, that black education had to be in preparation for certain inferior levels of labour. "Education must train and teach people in accordance with their opportunities in life. ... [N]ative education should be in accordance with the policy of the state (quoted in Bunting, *Rise of the South African Reich*, p. 260).

3 See also "The Riekert Commission," in International Defence and Aid Fund, *Apartheid: The Facts* (London: IDAF Publications, 1991), pp. 45–46.

4 See Taskforce on the Churches and Corporate Responsibility, *Annual Report, 1981–1982*, pp. 2–4, and International Defence and Aid, "Briefing Paper" no. 5 (London, UK, July 1982)

5 National activities included in the total strategy planning and for which expert advice was enlisted, were identified as follows: political, economic and psychological action; scientific and technological action, religious/cultural action; national supplies, resources and production; transport and distribution services; financial services; community services; and telecommunications. For a full discussion see Robert M. Price, "A Total Strategy for Maintaining White Supremacy," in *The Apartheid State in Crisis*, p. 86.

6 Ibid., p. 87.

7 *The Economist*, 15 July 1983.

8 *The Guardian* (UK), 19 December 1982, and *The New York Times*, 25 May 1983.

9 Robert M. Price in a table on the "Imposition of Regional Hegemony" lists eleven South African military attacks against its Southern African neighbours and notes the occupation of Angola's Cunene Province (1979–85) and uncounted intermittent invasions into, and air attacks on, Angola in the decade 1979 to 1989 (*The Apartheid State in Crisis*, p. 93).

10 These are examples of South Africa's destabilization campaigns rather than an exhaustive listing of them.

11 A two-year study financed by the Carnegie Foundation and made public in April 1984 in Cape Town also documented that while South Africa's whites were enjoying the highest standard of living in the world, one third of its black children under the age of fourteen were stunted in their growth for lack of food; infant mortality was thirty-one times higher for blacks than for whites and that in some black areas there was a doctor/patient ratio of 1:174,000.

12 P.W. Botha, prime minister of South Africa, Warrenton, South Africa, 24 July 1982.

13 Ontario, Legislative Assembly, *Debates*, 30 May 1986, p. 1055.

14 *Relocations: The Churches' Report on Forced Removals in South Africa*, published by the South African Council of Churches and the Southern African Catholic Bishops' Conference (Johannesburg, South Africa, 1983), and The Canadian Catholic Organization for Development and Peace (Toronto, 1984).

15 Quoted in Gérard Drainville et al., *No Neutral Ground: Report of the Visit to South Africa and Zambia of the Delegation of the Canadian Catholic Church* (Toronto: Canadian Catholic Organization for Development and Peace, 1986), p. 18.

16 A special tribute is due to E.S. Reddy, an international civil servant who became director of the new UN Centre against Apartheid in the early 1960s. Reddy worked tirelessly as initiator, facilitator, fund raiser and organizer. He understood the United Nations system and used it to the maximum advantage for the struggle against apartheid to which he had dedicated his life.

17 For an analysis of the Canadian Government's response of 15 June 1982 to the Brief of the Taskforce on the Churches and Corporate Responsibility of 5 May 1981, see "Canadian Policy toward Southern Africa" (mimeograph), March 1983 (Taskforce Archives). The quotations in the paragraphs that follow are from the letter of the ministers and the Taskforce's analysis of it. See Cranford Pratt, ed., "Canadian Policies towards South Africa: An Exchange between the Secretary of State for External Affairs and the Taskforce on the Churches and Corporate Responsibility," *Canadian Journal of African Studies*, 16, no. 1 (1982), 497–525, containing the text of the exchange along with the editor's analysis of that exchange.

18 Taskforce on the Churches and Corporate Responsibility, "Canadian Policy towards Southern Africa: An Analysis of the Canadian Government's Response of 15 June 1982 to the Brief of the Taskforce of 5 May 1981" (Toronto: Taskforce on the Churches and Corporate Responsibility, March 1983), p. 3 (photocopy).

19 Export Development Corporation, *Statistical Review*, Ottawa (1981).

20 Taskforce, "Canadian Policy: An Analysis," p. 6.

21 Recommendation 2 involved a dispute with the Canadian Development Corporation. It played no further role in our story and is being dropped from this review.

22 See pp. 38–39 on South Africa's countermeasures to the UN mandatory arms embargo.

23 The UN Security Council can take initiatives such as this under Article 7 of the United Nations Charter only in situations that constitute such a threat to international peace.

24 Clarence Redekop, "Reconciling Canadian Objectives in South Africa, 1976–80: The Search for Balance," prepared for the Study Commission on U.S. Policy toward Southern Africa (mimeograph), July 1980, p. 60.

25 "The $2,772,582.16 . . . represents the value of machinery and parts sold by Massey-Ferguson Industries Limited to its associate company in South Africa" (letter from Peter Collins, vice president, Communications & External Affairs of Massey-Ferguson, to the Taskforce, 18 July 1983.

26 James Travers, *Ottawa Citizen*, 16 November 1982.

27 South African marketing arm for the Kugerrand.

28 In the mid-1970s ARMSCOR made contact with Space Research Corporation (SRC), a US/Canadian company that had developed an advanced 155 artillery system with an extended range shell capable of being modified to take nuclear warheads. Through a highly complicated series of transactions, in which a number of front companies were established and millions of dollars changed hands, ARMSCOR ended up with 20 percent interest in SRC. At least four of the 155mm guns, 60,000 shells and a number of accessories were exported from Canada to South Africa. Patents (including the technology to convert the shells to nuclear use) were also acquired. See Cawthra, *Brutal Force*, p. 94.

29 Taskforce, *Annual Report, 1979–1980*, p. 7.

30 As a result of reorganization, the Department of Industry, Trade and Commerce and the Department of External Affairs were merged on 11 January 1982. Legal authority for the issuance of export permits was henceforth vested in the secretary of state for External Affairs.

31 In May 1980, the Taskforce along with other NGOs protested the participation of SRC representatives in a conference in June sponsored by the American Defence Preparedness Association. Held in the Ottawa Conference Centre, it drew officials from countries and corporations involved in the development of modern weapon systems. The Departments of Defence and Industry, Trade and Commerce were represented, the latter providing the keynote speaker (Taskforce, *Annual Report, 1979–1980*, p. 8).

32 Produced by William Cran, the report was updated for *The Fifth Estate* by producer Gerry Thompson and shown on 22 January 1980.

33 The Toronto Harbour Commission, 18 June 1980, Export Dock Manifest, Item 240, lists Levy Auto Parts as shipper of Contract no. 579; Number of packages: One; Weight: 1630 kg; Description of goods: Auto Transmission, General Components; Destination: Durban.

34 Telephone interviews with the author, 14 December 1981.

35 "Dual purpose items" were defined as strategic items. In the government's terminology they referred to "equipment and technologies of a commercial civilian nature and design that could have military application." Examples would include "computers, telecommunications systems, certain civilian air craft and avionics equipment, sophisticated industrial machinery, etc.

36 UN Security Council Committee, established by UNSCR 421, Report S/14179, had asked that UN member states prohibit the export to South Africa of dual purpose items, i.e., items provided for civilian use but with the potential for diversion or conversion to military use. . . . [T]hey should cease the supply of aircraft, aircraft engines, aircraft parts, electronic and telecommunications equipment, and computers to South Africa.

37 Cawthra, *Brutal Force*, p. 99.

38 Letter from Peter Calami, Southam News, African Bureau, Nairobi, to Renate Pratt, coordinator of the Taskforce on the Churches and Corporate Responsibility, 1 March 1982.

39 It should be noted that the president of the South African Atomic Energy Commission was also a director of the eleven-member board of ARMSCOR, exemplifying the close relationship between the two state agencies. See Cawthra, *Brutal Force*, p. 99.

40 Compiled from "United Nations General Assembly Voting Records," in United Nations, *Notes and Documents* (New York: United Nations Centre against Apartheid, May 1979 and January 1980).

41 Letter from E.J. Bergbusch, director, African Affairs (Anglophone) Division, to Bonnie M. Greene, Committee on the Church and International Affairs, United Church of Canada, 8 October 1981.

42 This section is based on the Taskforce on the Churches and Corporate Responsibility, *Annual Report, 1982–1983*, pp. 29–31, and Renate Pratt, "International Financial Institutions," in Robert O. Matthews and Cranford Pratt, eds., *Human Rights and Canadian Foreign Policy* (Montreal and Kingston: McGill-Queen's University Press, 1988), pp. 175–76.

43 The funds requested almost equalled South Africa's 1981–82 increase in military spending, including the cost of military operations in South Africa-occupied Namibia. The IMF's assessment of South Africa still included Namibian data: it was the only UN agency that continued to treat the two countries as one. See David Gisselquest, "International Monetary Fund Relations with South Africa," submission to the Thirty-Sixth Session, Fourth Committee, United Nations (mimeograph), October 1981.

44 Letter from Marc Lalonde to the Rev. Brian Fraser, chair, Taskforce on the Churches and Corporate Responsibility, 8 November 1982.

45 Letter from the Hon. Allan MacEachen, secretary of state for External Affairs, to the Rev. Brian Fraser, chair, Taskforce on the Churches and Corporate Responsibility, 14 April 1983.

46 International Monetary Fund, "South Africa: Staff Report for the 1983 Article IV Consultation and Review under Stand-By Agreement," 19 May 1983.

47 On the basis of information provided by the Vela satellite and other evidence, the US Defence Intelligence Agency and Central Intelligence Agency (CIA), as well as the Los Alamos Nuclear Laboratory and the Naval Research Laboratory, concluded that a nuclear weapon had been tested on 22 September 1979. The CIA reported to the US National Security Council that the explosion was probably a tactical two or three kiloton weapon detonated by South Africa with Israeli and possibly Taiwanese participation. "... [I]n 1985 the Washington Office on Africa had ... obtained fresh evidence supporting the conclusion that a nuclear test took place in the South Atlantic-Indian Ocean region on the night of 22 September. ... Some analysts believe that the most likely delivery system would have been the G5 nuclear-capable artillery system [produced by SRC and illegally supplied]. The G5 could easily be mounted on a South African warship, and the pattern of the explosion was consistent with that of a nuclear shell fired from such a weapon" (see Cawthra, *Brutal Force*, p. 105).

48 This resolution, 408, had been adopted by the 1983 General Conference of the IAEA.

49 Letter from the Hon. Jean Chrétien, deputy prime minister and secretary of state for External Affairs, to the Rev. Tim Ryan, chair of the Taskforce on the Churches and Corporate Responsibility, 23 August 1984 (Taskforce Archives).

50 According to the conference brochure, senior federal and provincial officials attending the conference included A.R. Hollback, then deputy minister of the Department of Energy Mines and Resources; S.R. Hatcher, R.G. Hart and K.Y. Round, then three vice-presidents of Atomic Energy of Canada Ltd. accountable to the minister of Energy, Mines and Resources; A. Ashbrook, at the time a senior official of the Canadian Crown corporation Eldorado Resources. Other participants included officials from Ontario and Quebec Hydro, the New Brunswick Power Commission and the Saskatchewan Mining Development Corporation.

51 Phillip van Niekerk, "South Africa Secretly Built Atomic Bombs, de Klerk Reveals," *The Globe and Mail*, 25 March 1993, and External Affairs News Release 91/164.

4 From Acceptance to Unease: Canadian Corporate Responses to Apartheid, 1981–84

Banking on Apartheid

Against a background of spiralling oppression in South Africa, Taskforce members continued their efforts to mobilize support for an end to corporate involvement in apartheid. Among the most important activities of the Taskforce was its sustained effort to convince the five major Canadian banks to cease all lending to the South African government and its state agencies and, where relevant, to private enterprises as well. Begun in 1975, the bank campaign continued with undiminished energy in the 1980s.

Each of the churches and most of the religious orders on the board of the Taskforce held shares in one or more of these banks and used their services for their banking needs. A campaign against loans to South Africa therefore involved almost all members of the Taskforce directly and contributed to the emergence of a long-term strategy and immediate tactics which were widely shared within it. Moreover, the Taskforce was persuaded that this particular campaign might indeed succeed. The trust and confidence of ordinary Canadians was central to the image that the banks had long nurtured. They were unsettled by a major challenge to their international lending, especially when that challenge focused on bank loans to a government whose racist policies were profoundly rejected by a substantial number of their individual and institutional clients.

We have already seen that the bankers' common front against the campaign had begun to come apart. In 1978 the Royal Bank of Canada had

Notes for chapter 4 are found on pp. 128–32.

97

attached exacting conditions on new loans to the South African government, while in 1980 the Toronto Dominion Bank had publicly announced
that no new loans would be made to the apartheid government and none
would be renewed. No doubt South Africa's political instability was a factor
in these more cautious approaches. Nevertheless it seemed reasonable
then, as it does now, to see the activities of the churches as reinforcing and
accelerating the banks' decisions to cease lending to South Africa and in
the case of the Royal and the Toronto Dominion banks, to make their decisions public.

These activities contributed to the articulation of general policy guidelines for socially responsible lending that were to assume a far wider significance. The traditional stance of most churches towards corporations of
whose products they disapproved—liquor and tobacco companies, for
example—had been not to invest in them. There was therefore considerable initial support for the proposition that the churches should sell their
holdings in any bank or company whose practices were contrary to their
established policies and Christian social values. An altogether different
strategy gradually emerged out of the deliberations and activities of the
Taskforce. The member churches came to recognize that the withdrawal
of the churches' investments, substantial as they might appear in denominational portfolios, would hardly be sufficient to provide leverage in multinational corporation for a change of policies. Divestment would be a one-
time action that would deprive the churches thereafter of continuing a
variety of shareholder actions. In parentheses it should be said that the
most frequent advice hurled by angry fellow shareholders at Taskforce
members during annual meetings was, "Why don't you just sell your shares
and get out!" Moreover, a serious pursuit of a policy of divestment would
likely result in a continuous and uncertain juggling of the churches' portfolios as yesterday's acceptable investment in a "clean" company revealed
itself as "tainted" today. The members of the Taskforce thus became
increasingly convinced that for their mandate a proactive shareholder policy made the most sense. Accordingly the churches and religious orders
maintained their investments in those corporations and banks whose activities had South African dimensions. They argued in management and
annual meetings for a lessening of these links, reserving divestment as an
ultimate option.[1]

Other organizations with different business relations to international
banking found their own innovative ways to apply pressure. The World
Council of Churches (WCC) and the World YWCA played an important role
in underscoring the international character and vigour of the bank campaign. These large institutions chose publicly to give their business to
banks that had no ties to the apartheid regime. In this way they put material
and moral pressure on persistent lenders. In September 1981 the executive

of the WCC decided to shift its accounts to banks that no longer maintained South African branches or representative offices and had discontinued loans that directly or indirectly benefited either South Africa's military or its nuclear industry. The WCC therefore ended its banking with the Dresdner Bank of Germany, the Union Banque Suisse and Swiss Bank Corporation each of whom had refused to meet the policy criteria of the WCC. By 1983 the WCC decision was fully implemented. In the same year the World YWCA followed its example.

In Canada there were several elements to the bank campaign of the early 1980s; they involved sustained and eventually successful efforts to convince each of the chartered banks to cease lending to the South African government and its agencies; close monitoring of the Royal and the Toronto Dominion Banks to ensure that they remained faithful to their new policies[2] and an ongoing survey of all available research on internationally syndicated loans, bonds and other credits for South Africa's state agencies. Pressure was maintained to halt the sale of Krugerrands, the South African gold coins; and "near banks," such as trust companies, security firms and credit unions were monitored concerning their business with South Africa.

The Five Chartered Banks[3]

In 1981 the Royal Bank bought the London-based Orion Bank and with it some $350 million of syndicated South African loans in which the Orion had participated. The Orion was one of several international banks the Royal had acquired in this period and each one of these acquisitions increased the loans outstanding to the Royal by South African borrowers.[4]

The Taskforce discussed with the Royal Bank the implications of these off-shore loans for the bank's 1978 restrictive lending policy. The foreign banks that the Royal Bank now owned or controlled had had no such policy. The Taskforce pointed out that with these acquisitions the Royal was now a more prominent lender to South African state agencies than any other Canadian bank. Management conceded the point and promised that henceforth its own 1978 policy—not to grant loans where they might help enforce the apartheid system—would apply to all subsidiaries and banks now controlled by the Royal.[5]

At the January 1982 shareholders' meeting, church delegates proposed that the Royal's policy should also specify that no loans should be granted to the South African "homelands" and to Namibia. The chair restated that since 1976 the Royal Bank had made no new loans to South African state agencies and added: "I would suggest that our policy towards the 'homelands' would be similar, let's say, to South Africa, and I repeat that . . . the Royal Bank considers apartheid in all its forms as repugnant as you do . . . and that we would not knowingly make any loans which would directly or indirectly support that policy." His response was probably as helpful as we could have hoped. In December 1984 the Royal reconfirmed that no additional loans had been made since 1976.

The Taskforce confirmed regularly the Toronto Dominion Bank's fidelity to its 1980 policy that under "present conditions" it would not grant new loans or renew existing ones to the South African government or its agencies. Indeed in 1984 the Toronto Dominion was selected as one of several international banks to replace the German and Swiss banks from which the World Council of Churches had withdrawn its accounts.

The public positions of the Royal and the Toronto Dominion banks had thus been firmly in place for several years when in 1985 the Canadian government requested a voluntary ban on new bank loans to the South African government and its state agencies.

In retrospect it appears that the Canadian Imperial Bank of Commerce had abstained as well from new loans to the South African government since the mid-1970s, but this was not at all clear at the time. The CIBC was adamantly opposed to taking a public position on the issue. The inability of senior management to handle with equanimity the legitimate shareholder activities of the churches, and to respond to their enquiries about its South African and other international loan policies, caused the bank much unnecessary aggravation and procrastination.

In 1982 church shareholders of the CIBC reminded the annual meeting that public records still showed CIBC loans outstanding to ISCOR, a major supplier of South Africa's arms industry. They asked the chair for a public commitment not to make any further loans to South Africa. Although the bank had begun to suggest privately that it had ended South African loans, the chair was not about to concede any successes to the churches. He fiercely retorted that any lobbying done by the churches in institutions or congregations would be met with counter-lobbying by the bank.

At the end of 1982 the churches tried a different tack. The United Church of Canada and the Jesuit Fathers of Upper Canada used their combined 100,000 shares to submit a shareholder proposal for more detailed disclosure of the CIBC's foreign loans. An angry CIBC management refused a meeting with the churches to discuss the matter. As this was a time of heightened public interest in the social consequences of massive international lending, this proposal for disclosure of loans amounting to at least 5 percent of the Bank's capital fund tapped into a fairly widely shared concern. The proxy circular contained the churches' proposal along with the bank's own opposing statement urging shareholders to vote against the churches' "political campaign." Despite the bank's admonition, shareholders returning their proxies to the bank must have supported the churches' position in some numbers, for on the day of the annual meeting, a *Globe and Mail* article described last-minute efforts by management to contact those shareholders who had supported the churches' proposal. The article quoted an official of the bank as stating that "a significant number" of shareholders had decided to change their ballots after having been approached.[6]

During an acrimonious debate at the annual meeting, the chair refused to confirm what his senior officers were saying privately, that new South African lending had ceased. Some exasperated shareholders, hoping to support the chair, interjected that the CIBC was making these loans out of "Christian brotherly love." The shareholder proposal lost heavily—a little over 525,000 votes to just under twenty-three million for the CIBC. The end result, however, was that the Bank's 1983 *Annual Report* gave a country breakdown for foreign loans that represented more than one percent of the Bank's total loans. No South African loans were in this category. Following the meeting, senior bank management resolutely refused all contact with the Taskforce. Nevertheless, more specific information was released to selected institutional clients, several of whom in turn told the Taskforce that the bank had not made new loans to the South African government since 1975.

After a change in senior management this "confidential" information was finally publicly confirmed at the annual meeting in early 1985. Thus, when a few months later the Canadian government asked for a voluntary ban on loans to the South African government, the CIBC had already officially joined the Royal Bank and the Toronto Dominion Bank in their position of no new loans to South Africa.

The Bank of Montreal and the Bank of Nova Scotia had remained unmoved by the churches' bank campaign. They only agreed to ban new loans to the South African government when so requested by the Canadian government in September 1985.

From the chair's vigorous defence of South African loans, discussed in chapter 2, it could be surmised that the Bank of Montreal had a special relationship to South Africa, where personal visits of management augmented its business relations. Internationally syndicated long-term loans to South African borrowers in which the BM had taken part amounted to $450 million. The main borrowers were ISCOR, ESCOM and the SARH (now SATS), three state agencies involved respectively in the arms industry, the nuclear sector and in public transportation.[7] Yet the Bank steadfastly refused to discuss its participation in these loans. Seeing the apartheid system through the prism of South Africa's white business community, senior officers of the Bank of Montreal followed South African political developments closely and expressed their unconditional confidence that foreign investment was stimulating change. In the early 1980s they cited South Africa's decision to allow black unionization and to adjust "black influx control" for urban areas as concrete evidence of promising change (see chap. 3, pp. 66–69).

The 1983 annual shareholder meeting of the BM, held in Calgary, faced questions on South African loans from the Calgary church and anti-racism community. Vexed by persistent requests to end loans to South Africa, William Mulholland, chair of the bank declared that he would "possibly never" give such assurances. He dismissed arguments from dissident shareholders that international loans helped sustain South Africa's oppressive system of apartheid: "[S]ome of these judgments are perhaps a little facile in view of the complicated nature of the subject matter and perhaps inclined to be more enduring than events warrant."[8]

Yet the Taskforce knew that, at least internally, BM management had reassessed the wisdom of the bank's South African exposure. In the summer of 1983 the Taskforce received a brown manila envelope containing photocopies of the Bank's internal guidelines for the authorization of international loans. They showed that the Bank had in fact reduced South Africa's credit rating to "D."[9]

Nine years into their discussions with the Bank of Montreal, the churches decided to force the issue with a shareholder proposal. The Jesuit Fathers of Upper Canada, the Pension Fund of the United Church and the White Fathers Missionaries of Africa proposed that the Bank of Montreal agree to cease lending to the South African government and to release figures of these loans made over the last ten years along with aggregate amounts of private loans without identifying its customers. At the meeting on 16 January 1984, Father Jean Lavoie was able to give personal testimony of his time in South Africa where he worked in "single" men's hostels among the black workers from the "homelands." The Church proposal received a respectable 5.8 percent support vote, a sign of an important disagreement between the bank's management and its shareholders on this issue.

The 1984 annual meeting also witnessed a breakthrough of sorts when Mulholland finally disclosed the bank's South African exposure. At the end of 1983, BM loans to South Africa had totalled $59.7 million, of which $40 million had been short-term, interbank loans, while the balance of $19 million constituted an aggregate of various other loans. By January 1985 the Bank of Montreal had reduced its long-term loans to South Africa by $5 million, leaving a total of $54 million outstanding. The reduction suggested that Bank's "D" rating for South African loans had indicated reduced confidence after all.

Three South African issues troubled the Taskforce about the Bank of Nova Scotia. In March 1981 the bank had made a loan to the University of the North in the "homeland" of Lebowa. For the BNS, this loan illustrated the progressive possibilities of international lending. For the Taskforce, in contrast, the loan, small as it was in the larger scheme of things, gave much-coveted legitimacy to the "homeland" system and to the inferior education blacks received under apartheid. Second, church shareholders continued to protest the membership of Cedric Ritchie, the Scotiabank's chair and CEO, on the board of directors of Minorco, controlled by Anglo American Corporation (see chap. 2, p. 33). The churches objected to this close relationship between a senior Canadian banker and South Africa's dominating corporate power structures. Finally, the Taskforce questioned the bank's continued role as the official distributor in Canada of the South African Krugerrands.

In the early 1980s shareholder meetings of the Bank of Nova Scotia took place in Halifax and were annually attended by church shareholders travelling there from Ontario. They received strong support from the Roman Catholic religious community who participated on their own proxies, and other social justice organizations in the Maritimes.[10] At these annual meetings Ritchie sharply rejected all church interventions that questioned the bank's South African involvement. He affirmed his faith in the liberalizing influence of commercial relations[11] and held that, unless the Canadian government said otherwise, the BNS would not change its policies. He refused to disclose amounts and recipients of the BNS's South African loans on the grounds of "client banker confidentiality" and felt that his personal integrity was being questioned over his Minorco directorship.

In the fall of 1983 several members of the Taskforce submitted a shareholder proposal. The Anglican Church of Canada, the Pension Fund of the United Church, the Jesuit Fathers of Upper Canada, the Religious of the Sacred Heart of Jesus of Montreal and the Sisters of Charity of Mount St. Vincent University in Halifax asked the bank to adopt a policy of no further loans to the South African government and its agencies until apartheid was dismantled. At the annual shareholders meeting in January 1984, Sister Thérèse Moore moved acceptance of the proposal. Representing the Sisters of Charity and speaking as well on behalf of the Redemptorist Fathers and the Canadian Conference of Catholic Bishops, she commented on Ritchie's confidence in the liberalizing qualities of international commerce: "The South African government does not need to be loved to retain power; it does need trade and foreign capital, and that is an international link which, despite fine words, has been maintained. If South Africa were to be cut off from foreign loans it would be forced to adapt its policies to become an acceptable candidate once again." Bill Davis, senior finance officer of the United Church of Canada, agreed with the views of management, which had objected that by joining a "no further loans" position, the bank would contribute to a cumulative impact. But that, Davis confirmed, was precisely why the bank was asked to join those who had adopted such a policy.

The proposal received only 3.2 percent of the vote, still considerably more than the number of votes represented by the proposers and evidence that there was a sizable number of other shareholders who disagreed with Scotiabank management.[12]

The churches continued their pressure on the BNS, but had to wait until September 1985 for its loan disclosure. When the bank announced that it would comply with the Canadian government's voluntary ban on loans to the South African government and its agencies, the bank disclosed that it had in fact made no loans to the South African government since 1979 and that its outstanding loans to South Africa were below $10 million. Thus even this seemingly stubborn institution had ceased loans to the South African government six long years before the Canadian government asked that they be halted voluntarily.

There remains a final puzzle associated with the policies not only of the Bank of Nova Scotia but also of the CIBC. Although they had ceased lending to the South African government in the late 1970s, neither of them announced this decision, despite the fact that they could thereby have escaped insistent pressure and public criticism. It is reasonable to infer that they found the shareholder actions and other public activities of the churches so uncongenial and so feared that a precedent might be set for similar issues to be raised by shareholders, that they decided against saying anything that could be interpreted as a success of shareholder activism.

Investment Dealers

In 1984 the United Nations Centre against Apartheid provided data on the involvement in the underwriting of bond placements for the South African government of what were then Dominion Security Ames Ltd. and McLeod Young Weir Ltd., two Canadian investment dealers. Between 1979 and the end of 1984 Dominion Security Ames had been one of a number of participants in the underwriting of bonds valued at $548 million. McLeod Young Weir had joined other firms to underwrite South African bonds for a total of $223.8 million. The bonds were for South African government agencies such as the South African Transport Services and the Electricity Supply Commission. The bonds were maturing between 1987 and 1997.[13]

Correspondence ensued between the United Church of Canada and Dominion Security Pitfield—successor to Dominion Security Ames. It refused absolutely to defer participation in the placement of South African bonds until apartheid was dismantled.

In May 1985, the Taskforce met with Tom Kierans, then president of McLeod Young Weir. He made it clear that the bond placements for South African companies were under consideration. In September, Kierans wrote to the Taskforce: "McLeod has had no policy in the past regarding supporting the bond issues of South Africa or its agencies ... our acceptance of that one past position was more inadvertent than anything else. Presently McLeod Young Weir has no intention of participating in any future

South African bond issue."[14] Thus by 1985 some progress had also been made in convincing Canadian investment dealers that they should eschew South African bond issues until apartheid was dismantled.

Krugerrand Sales

We have seen that the Bank of Nova Scotia had remained the official Canadian distributor of Krugerrands. In November 1984 the Taskforce chalked up a small and belated success when the BNS accepted the terms of a shareholder proposal the churches had prepared. The Bank agreed to de-emphasize Krugerrand marketing and neither list nor advertise the coin. The BNS further agreed to halt the purchase of Krugerrand from the South African Chamber of Mines.[15]

At the end of 1984 this was generally the position of the other large Canadian banks. The Royal and the Bank of Montreal said they were occasional traders in Krugerrand at the level of responding to client demands. Both the CIBC and the TD informed the Taskforce that they had refused an offer to become an official agent for the Krugerrand: "[W]e have never purchased Krugerrands from any South African agencies, and we have declined an invitation to participate in South Africa's distribution network."[16] Consequently on this issue as well, the government was pushing on open doors in July 1985 when it called for a voluntary ban on the trade of Krugerrand by Canada's financial institutions in its first set of sanctions.

There was one further bizarre twist to the Krugerrand issue; it occurred in March 1984. Members of the Taskforce were jolted out of their belief that Canadian public corporations would not actively help to promote the sale of South African products in this country. Yet suddenly this was happening. The CBC had sold television advertising space to Intergold, South Africa's distributing agent of the coins.

We heard of these advertisements from angry viewers in Montreal where they had first appeared, wedged between the *CBC National News* and the *Journal* at prime television time. At the very moment that we were reaching an agreement with the major banks that they would not advertise, display or even list the Krugerrand in their branches, the CBC had acted to rescue Intergold!

Upon enquiring, the Taskforce was told that the advertisement conformed to CBC and CRTC standards. The member churches wrote to Pierre Juneau, president of the CBC, and to Francis Fox, the minister of Communication, to protest acceptance of this South African advertisement. They advised Juneau that in 1982 the secretary of state for External Affairs had written that sales of the Krugerrand would not be promoted by the Canadian government.[17] They suggested that the CBC, as a Crown corporation, should operate within this policy framework and requested that the contract be cancelled. A front page article in *The Globe and Mail* gave welcome publicity to the issue.[18]

In his response Mr. Juneau vigorously contested the Taskforce's complaint. He misread our protest and turned it into a request that the CBC intervene editorially and pronounce judgement about countries with whom Canada should be allowed to trade. Juneau wrote that there were no legal impediments to the ad and rejected the allegation that the CBC was profiting from apartheid through the sale of Krugerrand advertisement.[19] We were genuinely taken aback by Juneau's total lack of sympathy and understanding of both the specific issue and the anti-apartheid struggle more generally. The Canadian public debate about business involvement in the system of apartheid appeared not to have informed either Pierre Juneau or Francis Fox. Despite several reminders Francis Fox never replied.

At the end of June, however, Juneau informed the Taskforce that "the existing contracts have terminated" and that there had not been "any requests for their renewal."[20] Did the CBC or did Intergold terminate the contracts? Had they run their course and had the CBC prevailed on the advertisers that the contracts would not be renewed? We never discovered the answers. It is reasonable to assume that public protests aided by the media helped to get the ads off the air.

Two months after the Krugerrand advertisements had ended, Edward Lumley, the new minister of Communications, informed the Taskforce that although the Canadian government was refraining from South African sales promotion, private and independent interests, which included the CBC, were free to act at their "corporate" discretion.[21]

Municipal and Institutional Challenges to the Banks

The Taskforce and other anti-apartheid organizations had found allies in a number of institutions across the country that began to move their accounts to banks and credit unions not tainted by South African loans. The Taskforce provided information on bank loans, government policies and local anti-apartheid networks, as well as speakers and other support to groups and institutions who were considering such actions.

One such institution was the Toronto City Council, where several city councillors were asking that the city deal only with banks that no longer did business with the South African government. We provided a background paper on South African bank loans to the city's Executive Committee, and in May 1981 church representatives appeared as witnesses, along with other anti-apartheid organizations, on the day set aside for public hearings. On 21 May 1981 Toronto City Council decided "That City Council look with favour on doing business with chartered banks and trust companies that do not have financial dealings with the South African government and further that we instruct the Commissioner of Finance that all things being equal, our banking and investment business be done with companies that do not have dealings with the South African government."[22] There was then a great deal of foot-dragging as various procedural objections were raised, but in the end the Council's decision prevailed and, without doubt, had an impact on the banks and indeed also on other companies vulnerable to consumer boycotts.

Toronto's action sparked other initiatives. The Taskforce furnished background information on the Toronto experience, and in August 1981, Ottawa's City Council adopted an almost identical resolution. Also in the course of the year, the City Councils of Victoria and Nanaimo in British Columbia passed similar resolutions and the Nanaimo School Board restricted its investment portfolio to companies without South African involvement.[23] In 1983 the North York Board of Education of Metropolitan Toronto and the Metropolitan Toronto Board of Education debated how they too could publicly distance themselves from dealing with South Africa. Both Boards voted not to purchase goods and services directly from South Africa and to state this policy in their tender documents.

By 1984 the Taskforce was pleased to note that the initiatives taken by church and other non-governmental organizations to encourage institutions and citizens to favour banks or credit unions with a clear policy position of "no loans to the South African government and its agencies" had captured public attention and had offered to many an opportunity for concrete involvement in an anti-apartheid project.

The Litmus Test

In the story just told there is much evidence that the bank campaign, started in 1975, had gathered sufficient public momentum that Canada's banks had ceased treating South African loans as routine. Instead they had become wary of the cost to their reputation and the potential cost to their commerce if they were to continue their South African lending. Confirmation that this was indeed the case came from an unexpected source. In March 1984 the Jesuit Fathers of Upper Canada, who had been founding members of the Taskforce, were visited in Toronto by two officials of Barclay's National Bank, the largest bank in South Africa and at the time still 40 percent owned by Barclay's Bank (UK). The two South Africans had requested this meeting, they said, because of the increasing difficulty South African banks had in doing business with Canadian banks. They had been told that this reluctance was due to pressure from the Canadian churches, who were distorting political developments in South Africa. The South African bankers were in town to set the record straight. They told Father Jim Webb, S.J., the Jesuits' representative on the Taskforce and Father G.P. Horrigan, S.J., the Jesuits' treasurer, that although the apartheid laws "made South Africa unique" they had lost much of their effectiveness, that they were increasingly ignored and that conditions for blacks were improving steadily.[24] Taskforce members were intrigued by the naivete of these South African businessmen who were either themselves appallingly ill informed about the continued, evident repression of their black fellow citizens or thought that we were. Their propaganda mission confirmed the value of our persistent efforts to influence the Canadian banks and the importance of complementing our actions in Canada with monitoring and exposing political developments in South Africa and Namibia as a counterweight to South African propaganda.

Canadian Companies: Investments, Sales and the Canadian Code

Concurrently with the bank campaign the Taskforce sought to influence the policies and practices of Canadian corporations with investments in South Africa and Namibia. Here as well the churches and religious orders used their investments as proactive shareholders to promote policies within these corporations that would lessen their direct or indirect support of the apartheid system. This section begins with a fairly detailed account of our work with Alcan Aluminium Ltd. and then reviews our efforts to influence the policies and activities of other Canadian companies in South Africa. A major focus throughout is the actual or potential ability of companies to "encourage the process of change," an important part of the government's rationale for supporting such foreign investment (see chap. 3, p. 76).

Alcan Aluminium Ltd.

Alcan's South African story has a special place in this volume. It best illustrates the most common features of Canadian corporate investments in that country. Typically these investments involved a minority interest in a large South African corporation or in groups of companies. Canadian directors, or South African directors representing Canadian minority interests, served in small numbers on the boards of directors of these South African companies. The majority South African partners were comfortably integrated into apartheid's social and political structures and enjoyed a relationship of trust and mutual understanding with the senior executives of the Canadian investor.

Over the years, Alcan's attitude towards apartheid, like that of many other North American corporations, moved from acceptance of apartheid as an internal political reality best left to the South African government, to unease as they began to be challenged about the ugly realities of the apartheid system and their role within it. When these corporations came to acknowledge that apartheid was abhorrent, they settled on the comforting proposition that foreign investment in South Africa was exerting a liberalizing influence for necessary reforms. This rationale provided Alcan and other foreign investors (and their governments) with an ethically acceptable justification for their continued presence in South Africa.

In chapter 2 we examined the reasons that led member churches of the Taskforce to suspect that Alcan's South African partner, Hulett Aluminium Ltd., was making important contributions to military production. The churches therefore pressed Alcan to allay the fear that it was in fact strengthening the arm of the oppressor and to demonstrate that its investment was exercising a liberalizing influence that benefited Hulett's employees in verifiable concrete ways.

Until the Canada Business Corporations Act was revised in 1980, minority shareholders had to be content with raising questions at the end of shareholder meetings. As we saw, tolerance for such questions was often limited, and discussions took place entirely at the discretion of the chair. By 1981 this situation had changed. Minority shareholders of federally incorporated companies were now able formally to place proposals on the agenda of their annual general meetings. A shareholder proposal, once accepted, would be printed in the proxy circular together with all other proxy documentation and would be sent to all shareholders prior to the annual meeting. This had the obvious advantage that minority shareholder concerns reached every shareholder of the company rather than only those who happened to be present at the annual meeting. Shareholders could return their proxy votes to the company for inclusion in the vote counting.

Denominational members of the Taskforce believe that their proposal for consideration at Alcan's 1982 annual meeting was the very first under the new Act. The Taskforce devoted much of its energy to the preparation of the proposal. It was submitted by the United Church of Canada, the General Synod of the Anglican Church, the Canadian Conference of Catholic Bishops and the Redemptorist Fathers. With the help of legal counsel, staff and board members learned the legal and technical formalities required for the submission of shareholder proposals and the rules of proxy solicitations.[25]

The churches' proposal made its case in these terms:

WHEREAS: black resistance to apartheid is increasing, obliging the military to request strategic industries to form industrial security forces for the protection against black unrest;

WHEREAS: ... Hulett Aluminium Ltd. of South Africa, a strategic industry with sales contracts with the South African military ... has formed an industrial security force receiving training and equipment from the South African military;

WHEREAS: Hulett's Chairman serves on the Defence Advisory Board of the South African Prime Minister ...

Given these circumstances, the church shareholders requested that a directors' committee examine the implications for Alcan's South African investment of Hulett's links with the arms industry. They asked that the directors report back to all shareholders before the next annual meeting.

Through its proxy circular Alcan's board and management had recommended that its shareholders vote *against* the churches' proposal. They declared that Alcan, by virtue of having three directors on the board of Hulett Aluminium, was adequately informed about policies and practices of Hulett; that it would be against South African law to disclose defence contracts and that Hulett did "not produce specialized materials or military equipment in any significant quantity." Alcan also contended that the military advisory activities of Christopher Saunders, Hulett's chair, were his personal responsibility and outside of Alcan's purview.[26] Alcan asserted that no added useful, necessary or economic purpose would be served by the proposed review committee. Alcan's 1982 proxy statement illustrates the egregious inability of Canadian corporate investors to see the apartheid state in any other light than as a government that was dealing as best it could with a particularly trying situation. Unabashedly, Alcan accepted the special state security system for its South African premises as a normal precaution.

The Taskforce had been able to attract maximum public attention to the issue through media communiqués and personal contacts, aided no doubt by the novelty value of filing a minority shareholder proposal. Prior to the shareholder meeting, the widely respected Investor Responsibility Research Center (IRRC) in Washington had published an eleven-page analysis of the proponents' and the company's position, together with a lengthy background briefing on South African developments based on IRRC's own information. Many investing institutions in the United States were relying on IRRC analysis to assist them in decisions on shareholder proposals that had social responsibility content. This extensive publicity may well have contributed towards the rewarding support vote the proposal was to receive.

At the shareholder meeting on 25 March 1982, Bishop Leonard Crowley, auxiliary bishop of the Archdiocese of Montreal represented the Canadian Conference of Catholic Bishops. He spoke of the bishops' solidarity with their Southern African sister churches in urging business to use its economic and moral influence to dismantle apartheid. Nathanael Davis, Alcan's chair, developed the thesis that there was hardly any disagreement between Alcan and the churches on the factual description of the company's role in South Africa. But they were worlds apart in the way they looked at these facts. For Nathanael Davis, ceding to the churches' proposal might have a harmful effect upon Alcan's relations with its South African partners. Davis also found entirely normal and indeed inevitable that Alcan products were used by the military—although it seemed to matter that these were rarely finished items. In keeping with the secrecy required by South Africa's law, Nathanael Davis would neither confirm nor deny that Hulett Aluminium had been designated a "National Key Point Industry."

The churches' shareholder proposal received 8.8 percent of the votes cast, a significant result given the newness of the exercise and the overwhelming tendency of shareholders to vote with rather than against management.[27]

During a private discussion following the shareholder meeting, Nathanael Davis told us that he had just been informed of Christopher Saunders'—chair of Hulett Aluminium—resignation from Botha's Defence Advisory Board. As this particular board was officially disbanded in 1982, we do not know whether Saunders' resignation coincided with this circumstance or preceded it. Nor do we know whether our proposal contributed to Saunders' decision to resign.

In late October 1982 Taskforce members met again with senior management to discuss whether there had been changes in Alcan's position. They learned that Anglo American Corporation, South Africa's largest mining and finance house, had meanwhile bought the controlling interest in Tongaat-Hulett. Alcan's own ability to influence Hulett Aluminium's corporate decisions had thereby been significantly diluted. Senior management emphasized that Hulett was primarily a manufacturer of civilian products such as window and door frames and piping, and repeated that its sale of products for military use was insignificant. Members of the Taskforce enquired whether Hulett Aluminium had sales contracts with Pretoria Metal Pressings or with Atlas Aircraft Corporation, both affiliates of ARMSCOR, the state-owned weapons manufacturer.[28] A clear negative response would have strengthened management's contention that Hulett's products were mainly for civilian purposes. Alcan however refused to respond.

The same church shareholders who had submitted the 1982 proposal decided to file a second proposal with Alcan in 1983. The proposal sought a report from Alcan's directors on the income earned by Hulett Aluminium from the sale of specialized products to the South African military. It also asked that Alcan inform its South African partners of its opposition to all sales for the use of South Africa's military.

In its proxy circular and during the annual meeting Alcan repeated its arguments of the previous year, but with an added touch of steely determination. The company, one felt, was no longer responding to the Canadian churches, but rather was seeking to reassure its South African majority partners of Alcan's loyalty. The company's circular argued:

- that disclosure of the detailed information envisaged by the proposal would be contrary to South African law;

- that Hulett could ultimately not refuse to supply its government's [military] requirements; and
- that the adoption of the churches' proposal was "an unjustified and unproductive attempt to interfere in matters of corporate policy in South Africa" that "could impair good relations with the majority shareholders in Hulett who are continuing to work for beneficial change for their black employees."[29]

Denominational representatives were quick to react. They were offended by the suggestion that as shareholders they were not entitled to obtain information about company policies. They questioned Alcan's relations with the majority shareholder in Hulett when this took precedence over Alcan's relations to its Canadian shareholders: "Now, South African law is being invoked in our meeting of Canadian shareholders and we are asked to abdicate our responsibility for what we do in South Africa."[30]

This time other shareholders vigorously defended Alcan's position. One of them nearly got it right when he posed Alcan's dilemma of being asked either to break faith with Hulett or to break South African law. He predicted angrily that eventually shareholders would be asked to divest themselves of their South African holdings in order to maintain their integrity. His prognosis was entirely plausible but for his claim that "most black, coloured and oriental (*sic*) political leaders of South Africa" would not favour disinvestment. Alcan also received some forthright advice from another loyal shareholder. Accusing the churches of favouring Communist organizations, he asked the company not to waste its energies on "these crackpot ideas that are produced on an annual basis."[31]

The final vote was interesting. It was announced as follows:

Total votes cast: 54,701,944
In favour: 3,935,058 =   7.2%
Against: 50,766,886 = 92.8%

These totals represented a slight of hand on the part of the tabulators. The chair also noted that 3,902,886 votes had been "withheld." Since the "withheld" represented actual proxy votes, marked in the column "withheld," they clearly represented registered abstentions. Checking with the office of the corporate secretary after the meeting, it was agreed that had the "withheld" votes not been omitted from the "total votes cast" the result would have been announced as follows:

Total votes cast: 58,604,837
In favour: 3,935,058 =   6.7%
Against: 50,766,886 = 86.6%
Withheld: 3,902,893 =   6.7%

These new totals would not at all have changed the substantial vote in favour of Alcan's position. But they would have shown that 13.4 percent of the voters had not followed management's advice, reflecting substantial unease among the shareholders about management's handling of the South African investment.[32]

By 1984 Hulett Aluminium Ltd. had acquired Hulett Glass and Aluminium and was operating the Hulett Metals' Master and Ferro Alloys Division at Richards Bay. Hulett Aluminium had a workforce of 3,600 of whom 2,880 were black (including mixed race and Asian) and 720 were white. Alcan now had four directors on the board of Hulett Aluminium representing its 25 percent interest, but the ultimate control of the Anglo American conglomerate had further dwarfed Alcan's influence. Taskforce members were aware of the advantages for Alcan of this situation. It could claim credit for any desirable change, but it could also plead impotence due to its minority position whenever Hulett was open to criticism. As a component of its examination of Alcan's entanglement with the South African regime, the Taskforce sought to determine whether Hulett Aluminium had made any verifiable changes in its employment practices for black employees to assess the relative weight that should be accorded to Hulett/Alcan's liberalizing influence.

To have a tangible reference point the Taskforce undertook to analyze the 1982 and 1983 progress reports of Hulett's "Affirmative Action Programme."[33] Alcan distributed these annually in response to the Canadian government's request under its "Code of Conduct for Canadian Companies Operating in South Africa." It was the only such report filed with External Affairs in this period, and it was prepared by a South African corporation.[34] The analyses of Hulett's progress reports were frustrating. Employment figures were given in two racial categories only—white and non-white—the latter category consisting of black, Asian and coloured (mixed race) workers. Thus when benefits were purported to have been accorded to "non-whites," it was not possible to say whether black workers had benefited at least proportionately to their numbers. Even odder was the total absence of information about employment categories, wages, salaries and benefits. The reports contained descriptive narrative on "Trade Unionism and Collective Bargaining," but did not give any information about the company's policy towards black unions nor did they mention grievance procedures and collective bargaining agreements. The Taskforce's analyses of the reports exposed these weaknesses and noted that in the absence of consistent and comparable annual data no conclusion whatsoever could be drawn about conditions for black employment at Hulett Aluminium.

The Taskforce analyses were sent to Alcan and copied to External Affairs. While External Affairs did not react, Alcan arranged two meetings with the

Taskforce, in December 1983 and January 1984. Alcan had sent a copy of our analyses to Hulett Aluminium which, company officers sought to assure us, shared Alcan's philosophical, moral and business outlook. They accepted as justified part of the criticism of the Hulett reports, but were aggrieved that the Taskforce comments had all been negative and expressed confidence that far more progress had been made in black advancement than was being reflected in the Hulett reports.

As in earlier years, just when the Taskforce tried to master the minutiae of possible benefits of Alcan's investment for Hulett's black workers, it was reminded of the sheer magnitude of repression in South Africa. Toward the end of 1984 new and wider security laws were used to subdue popular protests against the new constitution. We became acutely aware of the grotesque asymmetry between our nitpicking over Hulett's trivial "progress reports" and the momentous struggle for liberation under way in South Africa. The central question still to be answered by Alcan was how it could claim that improvements in black employment conditions, even if true, could outweigh in importance the role played by Hulett Aluminium in Botha's total strategy for the defence of white supremacy. Part Three will resume the tale of Alcan in South Africa as the Taskforce presses for its disinvestment.

Bata Ltd.

In June 1982 the National Union of Textile Workers (NUTW) of South Africa had sent the Taskforce a detailed report about employment conditions at the KwaZulu Shoe Company in Loskop. This plant was a subsidiary of Bata Ltd. a privately owned international shoe manufacturer based in Canada. The report alleged that the management of the KwaZulu Shoe Company had refused to meet with its employees, the majority of whom were members of NUTW. It had suppressed all union efforts to obtain company recognition and routinely called in the KwaZulu police who arrested union organizers.

Working conditions at the plant, the Union reported, were intolerable, involving compulsory overtime, suspension of lunch breaks, periodic assaults and intimidation by supervisors, no provision for sick leave and a failure to register a substantial part of the workforce, resulting in the loss of rights to unemployment benefits. The majority of the 700 workers earned monthly wages of rand 117, less than half of the official 1982 poverty line of rand 236 for a family of five in the Durban area, which included Loskop.[35] The union estimated that in 1982 Bata paid its workers in KwaZulu about 35 percent less than it paid its unionized black workers at its Pinetown plant in a "white" industrial area also near Durban.

The Taskforce enquired from External Affairs whether the Canadian embassy had concerned itself with such a blatant disregard of the Canadian

Code. We were told that the embassy was investigating the claims made by the National Union of Textile Workers. However as the Code was voluntary and without consequences for companies not heeding its requirements, External Affairs advised us to write to Thomas Bata directly. This we did in June 1982. Despite several reminders, we received no response. The Taskforce also wrote to Edward G. Lee, Canada's newly appointed ambassador to South Africa and asked him to clarify the situation.[36] He did consult with Bata's South African management, but without manifest results. The Canadian Labour Congress, which had also remonstrated with the Canadian government, eventually learned that Bata was observing KwaZulu union rules and enjoyed the support of KwaZulu officials. In 1985 Michael Valpy, then *The Globe and Mail*'s correspondent in South Africa, reported that Bata refused to account for its employment practices to the Canadian government for fear of offending the South African and KwaZulu authorities.[37]

In August 1984 NUTW had begun organizing at Keate's Drift, also near Durban, where Bata had a second KwaZulu subsidiary. This plant employed about 750 workers, almost all women. According to the union, management followed the same repressive practices as it had done in Loskop. There too it refused to meet with the workers and fired union organizers. By this time Bata had raised the monthly wage rate at the Kwa-Zulu factories to approximately rand 200 still well below the rate it paid its black workers at Pinetown. Valpy calculated that had Bata followed the voluntary guidelines of the Canadian Code of Conduct, it would have paid a monthly wage of rand 450.[38] Chief Gatsha Buthelezi, returning on 7 March 1985 from meeting with the Confederation of Church and Business People in Toronto, called a press conference in Durban and denounced Valpy for his "biased reporting," labelling him the worst journalist in South Africa who should be driven out of the country.[39]

Bata's conduct had attracted the interest of social justice organizations in Natal. They in turn requested detailed information from the Taskforce on the company and its international record of employment practices.[40] With the help of students from Trent University, a portrait was compiled of Bata's considerable international operations and forwarded to Pietermaritzburg. It was much harder to obtain information on Bata's South African operations. Bata company representatives refused to meet church representatives and, as a privately owned company, there was no recourse to shareholder action. However thanks to Michael Valpy's persistent and revelatory articles in *The Globe and Mail*, questions about Bata in South Africa kept circulating and were taken up by his colleagues in Canada. In February 1985 Sergio Cesari, the Bata officer responsible for the company's South African factories, expressed satisfaction that Bata's wages at the two Kwa-Zulu plants did not contravene the Canadian Code of Conduct.[41] Despite evidence to the contrary, Cesari also reported that the KwaZulu plants had remained non-unionized "because workers there rejected a unionizing effort." He said that blacks made up at least half the management teams in both factories and added: "The majority of people in those plants are girls. That follows the tradition—you know, men carry the spears and women do the work." [42]

In June 1985 E.A. Willer of the Canadian embassy (labour affairs) and Roger Southall of the CLC met for two hours with Bata's KwaZulu workers at Keate's Drift to hear their grievances. While the CLC promised to adopt Bata as a target company to help workers establish their union, Willer told *The Globe and Mail* that External "does not play a judgemental role" (on Bata's adherence to the Canadian Code of Conduct). "Basically I was there to listen." [43]

Abruptly, at the end of November 1986, Bata sold its South African investment.

Canada Wire and Cable (International) Ltd.

In May 1984, members of the Taskforce met with senior management of Canada Wire and Cable (CWC) a wholly owned subsidiary of Noranda Inc. Its international division had a complicated relationship with South African interests. It held a 35 percent interest in Transage Cables (Pty) Ltd., a South African-operated manufacturer of magnet wire in Olifantsfontein. The majority interest was held by Canlan, a large diversified South African corporation. CWC appointed two of the eight directors of Transage. While CWC provided capital and technology, it left management to its South African partners. The company had sixty-eight black and twenty white employees.

Transage manufactured special magnet wire which it supplied to electrical installation industries. J.H. Stevens, chair of CWC, speculated that some of the manufacturers supplied by Transage may have military and police contracts, but he could not be certain. Asked whether Canada Wire and Cable was submitting implementation reports on the Code of Conduct for Canadian Companies Operating in South Africa, senior management replied that it was satisfied that the terms of the Canadian Code were observed by Transage—except for those that conflict with South African law—but it did not prepare annual progress reports. CWC said that the workforce had remained steady over eight years and had not taken any initiative to form a union, and that Transage maintained segregated facilities in compliance with South African law. Management saw no problem in providing the Taskforce with detailed employment data from Transage. [44] However, eventually J.H. Stevens informed us that Transage was unable to comply with our request "for reasons of local competition." On 28 November 1985 Noranda Inc. informed the Unit on Public Social

Responsibility of the Anglican Church of Canada that Canada Wire and Cable had disposed of its minority interest in Transage and that the Noranda Group had no other investment in South Africa.[45]

Rio Algom

In April 1982 members of the Taskforce attended the annual meeting of shareholders of Rio Algom. As a rule Taskforce members did not speak at annual meetings unless there had first been discussions with senior management in an attempt to settle an issue in private. Rio Algom, however, had been an exception. For several years, senior management had refused to meet with us and had ignored Taskforce letters enquiring into the company's involvement in the Rossing Uranium mine in Namibia, employment practices at the mine and Rio Algom's relationship to the illegal South African administration.

At the AGM, church shareholders asked George Albino, chair of Rio Algom, why their letters had gone unanswered. Albino apologized to the churches and promised a reply if they were to resubmit their letter. He explained to the shareholder meeting that he was a member of Rossing's board of directors and that he took pride in the accomplishment of the mine. Rio Algom's ten percent interest, he said, represented only "passive participation."

The churches also asked Albino to clarify Rossing's collaboration with the South African military to prepare against possible attacks by SWAPO, Namibia's liberation movement. Albino cut short this question, blaming an overcrowded agenda. He reminded the meeting that as a Canadian company, Rio Algom was operating under Canadian law, which placed no restrictions on investing and operating in Namibia.

Rio Algom's response to our resubmitted letter largely repeated Albino's statement to the shareholders. It also reported that Rossing had completed extensive housing projects, provided amenities and established job training programs, as well as health and medical plans for its employees. Rio Algom believed that "it should not become involved in 'political matters.'" It shied away from defining its relations to the illegal South African administration and did not respond to the questions about the stationing of militia units at Rossing. The Taskforce had also asked Rio Algom to comment on the 1980 findings of a United Nations panel enquiring into uranium mining in Namibia, which had dealt with wage rates, housing, racial policy, medical services and environmental protection measures. In September 1980, that is nineteen months earlier, the United Nations had published the *Report of the Panel for Hearings on Namibian Uranium*, upon which our questions had been based.[46] Rio Algom wrote that it had not had "the opportunity to examine the reports upon which your remarks are based." We had expected Rio Algom to be critical of the evidence presented, but that its CEO as a member of Rossing's board would be ignorant of this UN report seemed incredible—yet it was believable.

Corporate investors in South Africa and Namibia, although aware of the controversy that surrounded their activities, were in fact neither interested nor involved in the many public debates that took place at the time in international and national forums. Their investment decisions depended not on justice considerations but on their ability to predict correctly the political and economic climate and to lobby successfully for government tolerance of, if not assistance for, their enterprises. The government in turn deflected public criticism from the companies. Unless business saw its interests seriously threatened, as did the South African business community in 1985, it saw no cause to join public debates about justice in Southern Africa.

In March 1984 there was a not very constructive meeting between Rio Algom and Taskforce representatives. Rio Algom still insisted that Rossing was a model of social integration, that its participation in the uranium mine was legitimate and did not violate Canadian law and that it took care not to get involved in Namibian politics. Management did not reveal information about Rossing's uranium contracts, reflecting, they said, the secrecy of the uranium industry as a whole. The Taskforce could not convince the company that its very presence in Namibia was a political act, starkly exemplified by Rossing's military cooperation with the South African armed forces[47] and Rio Algom's exploitation of Namibia's non-renewable resources.

In its first brief to the Canadian government in 1975 and in every subsequent brief, members of the Taskforce had urged in vain that United Nations' Decree No.1 for the protection of Namibia's natural resources be enforced and failing that, that Canadian companies harvesting these resources at least not receive tax deductions for taxes paid to Namibia's illegal regime. In 1981, after it was discovered that Canada was importing, processing and reexporting Namibian uranium, the churches tried unsuccessfully to convince the government to halt its own participation in the trade of Namibia's resources. It was little wonder that the churches' contact with Rio Algom had stayed at a sterile level.

Massey-Ferguson

The Taskforce had learned that in addition to the technology transfer contract with Atlantis Diesel Engines (ADE), Massey-Ferguson had retained additional interests from its erstwhile wholly owned South African subsidiary. Like Alcan, it had reduced its South African interest to about 25 percent by selling its majority holdings to Fedmech, a South African manufacturing company. Fedmech itself was owned by a large diversified South African enterprise, Federale Volksbeleggings Beperk.[48] Fedmech had 800 employees in operations on three different sites, producing and assembling farm and industrial machinery, including industrial loaders and transport systems. Massey-Ferguson was represented by one director on Fedmech's board of eleven.

The Taskforce sought to continue their enquiries with Massey-Ferguson on several issues. First they believed front-loaders or bulldozers with the M-F trademark were sold to SATS, the government transport agency that destroyed the homes of black families during forced population removals. Second, the churches were seeking clarification about sales by Perkins Engines, Massey-Ferguson's British subsidiary, of diesel engine technology to ADE, a South African-government company. The Taskforce had been told that the prime objective of Perkins' technology transfer had been to insure that Perkins' engines were available for the agricultural market and that Massey-Ferguson did not believe that ADE was even considering military applications of this technology. On the face of it, this statement had been contradicted by an article appearing in *The Ottawa Citizen*, datelined Pretoria, 16 November 1982, which stated that the technology transfer agreement was valued at $460 million and that it was related to the design and production of all diesel engines required "to meet South Africa's agricultural, commercial and military needs."

Third, as Atlantis, where ADE was located, was a "single race" company town, the Taskforce sought to challenge Massey-Ferguson's cooperation in enforcing the geographical separation of the races on behalf of the apartheid regime. Massey-Ferguson had written to the Taskforce that its technical personnel visiting the plant had not observed any discrimination. Indeed all of the fifty-three companies who had located at Atlantis, among whom ADE was the largest employer, had claimed to have non-racial employment practices. Joseph Lelyveld of *The New York Times* had, however, exposed the lie behind these claims: "But there is a small anomaly in making such a claim here, for in establishing themselves at Atlantis they have implicitly agreed to hire only coloureds and whites. Atlantis Diesel Engines ... is typical in that it hasn't hired a single black of African origin on the grounds that it is legally bound to adhere to the government policy that this is a 'preference area' for coloureds."[49] To clarify these questions the Taskforce asked for a meeting with senior management of Massey-Ferguson; they refused, declaring that they saw no need to meet. Shareholding members of the Taskforce therefore attended Massey-Ferguson's 1983 annual meeting to put their questions to the chair. They cited the passage from *The Ottawa Citizen* and asked about the military implications of Perkins' technology transfer to ADE. Victor Rice, chair of Massey-Ferguson, replied that he had not seen the article, but conceded that in very general terms the statements might be correct. He found that the annual meeting was an unsuitable forum for this type of discussion and offered to deal with the issue at another time. It was an irritating reply, given management's earlier refusal to arrange such a meeting.

Asked about the ADE's one-race employment practices in Atlantis in conformity with apartheid's Group Areas' Act, Rice called on another company officer to explain. This man assured the shareholders that he knew ADE well, and—as predicted by *The New York Times*—could assert that no racial discrimination was practised there. Summing up, Rice insisted that Massey-Ferguson was strictly non-political, that he did not want to discuss South Africa's racial questions and expressed annoyance that South Africa was singled out for criticism.

Massey-Ferguson had experienced major financial difficulties in 1981, which had prompted refinancing assistance from Canadian and international banks and from the federal and Ontario governments. By 1983 these complex financial arrangements, which had kept Massey-Ferguson afloat, had led to the acquisition of substantial numbers of Massey-Ferguson shares by the Ontario government and the Government of Canada—the latter through the Canada Development Investment Corporation (CDIC)—making them part-owners of a corporation with serious South African entanglements.

After renewed but fruitless attempts to meet with Massey-Ferguson's senior management, the Taskforce sought the intervention of Maurice Strong, then chair of the CDIC and a director of Massey-Ferguson. This resulted in the first meeting with senior management in May 1984, a full decade after the first contacts with Massey-Ferguson by the YWCA committee and five years after Conrad Black's letter (see chap. 2, p. 45). The meeting was disappointing. Senior executives said that Fedmech had argued that as a minority shareholder, Massey-Ferguson should not be concerned about union negotiations, black training opportunities and wage policies. Massey-Ferguson thus failed to obtain tabulations of race and work categories of Fedmech employees which might have provided insight into the application of the Canadian Code of Conduct and into Massey-Ferguson's "liberalizing influence" on South African employment practices.[50]

In early May 1985 the Taskforce contacted Massey-Ferguson again to discuss its corporate position in light of the sharply deteriorating South African situation. A meeting did take place, but the new company staff assigned to meet with us claimed to be still too unfamiliar with past correspondence to be able to engage in any detailed discussion. Dissatisfied, representatives of the Jesuits and the Ursulines—both shareholders of Massey-Ferguson—reviewed the unproductive nature of the churches' communications with the company during the annual shareholders meeting on 5 May. Massey-Ferguson, they said, compared unfavourably with many American companies which, by this date, not only disclosed in-plant wages and working conditions but had even pledged to call for the repeal of all apartheid laws. They urged Massy-Ferguson at the very least to cease selling technology that directly aided repression by the police and the military in South Africa.

In reply, Victor Rice insisted that Massey-Ferguson's investment in South Africa was a minuscule part of its operations and declared, in total disdain of the facts, that "we met with the Taskforce lots and lots of times in the last ten years." He promised that he would do his level best to obtain the information the churches had requested and to determine whether company products were being used to destroy black townships. Rice explained Massey-Ferguson's involvement in ADE by citing pressure from the South African government: "either you put your engine into our products or we shall get some one else's engines."[51]

An article in *The Globe and Mail Report on Business* provided candid insight into the company's attitude. It reported that the company had invoked a "letter from the Pretoria Government ruling out release of such data under the Protection of Business Act" to deny pertinent information to the Taskforce. The article quoted a Toronto business executive who recalled a private remark of a senior officer of Massey-Ferguson: "we're too busy fighting for our survival to worry about the churches. To hell with them!"[52]

Control Data Computer Systems

On 13 June 1984 *The Toronto Star* reported that Control Data Canada had won a contract to supply eleven large-scale computer systems to ISCOR, the iron and steel company of the South African government. A month later the SACTU Solidarity Committee (Canada), a particularly effective research NGO, told the Taskforce that External Affairs had informed SACTU that it had granted export permits for this sale. It had done so after Control Data, ISCOR and the South African government had signed end-user certificates that stated that the computers would not be used for military purposes.

Under Canada's restrictive export policies, computer systems had been defined as strategic items which should "not be supplied to countries in or under imminent threat of hostilities." At the time External Affairs allowed strategic equipment sales to South Africa "... only when destined to *bona fide* commercial concerns for civilian application. Where doubts are raised about the end user of such equipment, permit applications are considered by the responsible department. Should there be any evidence that the equipment in question is to be used for military purposes or against the civilian population the permit application is denied."[53] The granting of the export permits for this sale sapped already failing confidence that the Trudeau government was adhering at all to the rules it had set for itself. The export permits should have been denied under its general rule alone: computers as "strategic equipment" should not have been exported to South Africa because of its military engagement in Namibia and Angola. The export permits should also have been excluded under the specific export restrictions applicable to South Africa.

Control Data Canada was to install the systems at ISCOR's plant in Vanderbijlpark which had been built in 1976 (one year before the UN mandatory arms embargo came into force). This plant was to produce special property steel "to make South Africa totally self-sufficient in this highly strategic metal."[54] ISCOR was a major supplier of steel to ARMSCOR, the government's armaments corporation which was under the direct authority of the minister of defence. None of ARMSCOR's production could proceed without steel components.

Members of the Taskforce raised the issue with Joe Clark, the secretary of state for External Affairs in the newly elected Progressive Conservative government of Brian Mulroney. He defended the export permits on the grounds "that although ISCOR is indeed a state-owned corporation, it is a commercial concern and cannot be considered to be a military consignee.... It seems reasonable to accept the written assurances provided by ISCOR that the computer equipment ... is for *bona fide* civilian end-use and will not be used, directly or indirectly, by police or military entities."[55] Although we had become accustomed to the minimalist position of External Affairs, the response from the new government was discouraging. Should we have to make the obvious point that although computers do not shoot and torture people, they make more efficient the delivery of ISCOR's specialized steel to those who were manufacturing weapons and war matériel for use against the black civilian population in South Africa's townships?

The computer sale was finalized at the same time as Canada's ambassador to South Africa declared that his absence from P.W. Botha's inauguration ceremony as South Africa's first state president signified Canada's official protest to South Africa's new constitution. These two acts provided one more example of Canada's contradictory two-track policy: critical diplomatic rhetoric on the one hand and on the other, uncritical support for Canadian trade.

In December 1984 the Taskforce had also outlined its misgivings about the ISCOR computer sales to T.S. Allan, then president of Control Data Canada, and had asked for a meeting with him. The Taskforce had copied this letter to William C. Norris, chair of Control Data Corporation, USA. Allan responded at once and a meeting was arranged for late March 1985.

In early January William Norris wrote a lengthy defence of the corporation's activities as a resident South African investor. He stressed the benefits of its PLATO computer-based education program that was being marketed in South Africa. This, Norris wrote, was an example of the corporation's contribution to business efforts to "dedicate a portion of their business investment to the needs of blacks in South Africa." Norris dismissed as unwarranted the concern about the Canadian supply of minicomputers to ISCOR: "the availability of powerful new microcomputers—

which can be purchased almost anywhere—is so widespread that this simply is no longer an issue." In 1986, as resource person to a Roman Catholic delegation visiting South Africa, I had occasion to visit with the principal and senior students of a Soweto high school. We discussed the benefits of computer technology as a teaching tool. They reported that even if electricity was available—which it was not in most black schools—inadequate training of black teachers within the black education system made the idea of operating such equipment totally unrealistic. The principal offered to show me where their donated equipment was gathering dust. She and her students were well aware that computer companies were citing their contribution to black education as a sign of their generosity and liberalism. If companies were genuinely concerned with the inadequacy of the system, the principal said, they would instead sit down with community organizations to explore ways of supporting their efforts to gain access to a unitary and equal education system.[56]

On 13 March 1985, two weeks before we were to meet with Control Data Canada, the meeting was abruptly cancelled. Mr. D.G. Smith, its Marketing and Communications general manager, wrote that this decision was the result of communications with the Minneapolis head office of the American parent responsible for policy-setting for its worldwide operations. Smith advised the Taskforce to continue its negotiations with Minneapolis.

Members of the Taskforce were unsettled by the unfolding tale that Control Data Canada had obtained Canadian export permits as well as ISCOR's end-user's certificates from Canada's External Affairs at the behest of Control Data Corporation of Minneapolis.[57] They communicated these sentiments to T.S. Allan of Control Data Canada but eventually received a reply from D.G. Smith. He succeeded only in exposing further the cypher-like role of Control Data Canada. He wrote that while Control Data Canada was in the enviable position of having a world product mandate, "to develop, manufacture and export large-scale computer systems around the globe, the policies that dictate where those systems are shipped come from three sources—the Canadian Federal Government, the South African Government, and Control Data Corporation."[58] An article in *The Globe and Mail* gave publicity to this extraordinary exchange between the Taskforce and Control Data Canada. It quoted Smith as saying that he had merely wanted to put the churches in touch "with the people [the Minneapolis head office] ... who can shed the proper corporate light on the subject. We would be trying to deal with something on which we are not really up to speed."[59]

Meanwhile, to inform itself, the Taskforce had made enquiries about the computers destined for ISCOR. The churches attempted one more time to convince Norris of Control Data Corporation that he was mistaken in stating that the systems could be largely discounted as a sign of support for apartheid because powerful new microcomputers were available "almost anywhere":

> our enquiries lead us to believe that in the specific case of the computer series sold to ISCOR, we are dealing not with micro but mini computer systems of a medium to large size variety used in computer-aided design for manufacturing purposes. They are said to assist also in testing, evaluating and improving efficiency and in the monitoring of delivery. . . . One must assume that in choosing Control Data Canada's Cyber 825 and Cyber mini 815 systems, ISCOR was making a considered decision when buying these rather than any other computer systems. That powerful microcomputers are available "almost anywhere" is surely beside the point.

QIT-Fer et Titane Inc.

In 1976, Quebec Iron and Titanium Corporation, now QIT-Fer et Titane Inc., had entered into an agreement with South African enterprises to establish Richards Bay Minerals (RBM) in Natal (see chap. 2, pp. 40–41 above). The role of QIT in this beach sand mining and smelting operation had continued to trouble the members of the Taskforce. Constraints on time and energy had initially precluded further research into the nature of this South African operation. Then in 1985, during a three-month placement with the Taskforce, a Jesuit novice, Conlin Mulvihill, prepared a major research paper on QIT's South African operation.[60]

The parent company had undergone recent changes in its principal ownership. By 1985, QIT had become a wholly owned subsidiary of Standard Oil Company. The majority shareholder in Standard Oil was British Petroleum Company of the UK, an enterprise with significant interests in South Africa. The majority shareholders in Richards Bay Minerals (RBM) included QIT with 42.5 percent, the South African Industrial Development Corporation (IDC), an agency of the South African government with 16.8 percent, as well as three private South African companies with a combined ownership of 40.7 percent. Thus QIT and IDC together had a controlling share in RBM. The presence of IDC co-ownership signalled that the state had a paramount interest in this particular development.[61]

Mulvihill established that QIT's investment in RBM had provided South Africa with QIT's unique ilmenite smelting technology to produce the titanium dioxide slag used in the paint and pigment industry for high-quality white finishes. But there was a difference in the quality of the slag produced in QIT's Quebec operation and the slag produced at Richards Bay. Unlike Quebec's slag, RBM slag was suitable for the production of pigments by the chloride-route as well as by the sulphate-route process. The chloride-route process, but not the sulphate-route, Mulvihill's research showed, was a step in the process for the production of titanium metal, used extensively in military, nuclear and energy applications.[62] Given South Africa's drive for military self-sufficiency since the early 1970s and the importance of titanium metal in modern military and aviation technology, Mulvihill's assumption that the establishment of the QIT mining and smelting operation was linked to South Africa's desire for a long-term domestic source for this important metal seemed eminently plausible.

The Taskforce forwarded Mulvihill's paper to QIT-Fer et Titane Inc. for comment, and several church representatives met with its senior officers in the fall of 1986. The company insisted that there was no producer of chloride-route pigment or of titanium metal in South Africa; that RBM sold titanium products solely in South Africa for conversion to pigment for its ultimate use in paints, plastics and paper; and that neither QIT nor its South African partners sold any titanium products to the South African atomic energy industry or to ARMSCOR, its subsidiaries or suppliers. In order to produce its own titanium metal, QIT suggested, South Africa would need technologies beyond those available within the company. This however was unnecessary because titanium metal was in plentiful supply on world markets. Richards Bay Minerals, QIT assured the Taskforce, had nothing to do with South Africa's strategic needs but only with its promotion of industrial development. Following this exchange with QIT-Fer, and in the absence of evidence to the contrary, the Taskforce removed the section on QIT from its brief on the role of Canadian corporations in South Africa's military and nuclear sectors, which it had prepared for the United Nations Centre on Transnational Corporations. The nagging question could not be answered: would QIT have told the Taskforce if RBM was producing strategic material for Armscor or the Atomic Energy Board? Would not QIT, like Alcan, have been prevented from such disclosure by South African law?

Falconbridge[63]

In November 1984 the Taskforce had asked Falconbridge about employment conditions at Western Platinum Ltd., a mining company in South Africa in which Falconbridge, with a 24 percent interest, had appointed one of Western Platinum's two managing directors.[64] Located at Rustenburg in the Transvaal, with part of its underground complex in the "homeland" of Bophuthatswana, Western Platinum was a major employer of black contract labour. In 1984 the Taskforce designed a questionnaire about employment conditions at the mine to which Western Platinum had responded in full. Alas, the responses showed no evidence of a benevolent influence exerted by Falconbridge's investment in Western Platinum. They only demonstrated that the company clearly participated in the racism that characterized apartheid throughout South Africa (see Table 1).

Table 1: Employees at Western Platinum Mine, 1984, by Category of Work and Race

Category of Work*	Blacks**	Coloureds**	Whites**
Group A (unskilled)	3,543 (r 392)	–	–
Group B Lower (semi-skilled)	609 (r 537)	2 (r 665)	–
Group B Upper (semi-skilled)	–	–	44 (r 1,127)
Group C Lower (skilled)	–	–	151 (r 1,401)
Group C Upper (skilled)	–	–	56 (r 1,994)
Group D Lower (middle management)	–	–	10 (r 2,550)
Group D Upper (senior management)	–	–	7 (r 3,466)
Group E and F (other)	–	–	3 (r 5,133)

* The company noted that Western Platinum practised a job evaluation system whereby the rate for the job category is paid to all races. The statement is difficult to reconcile with the figures given, quite apart from the contradiction of this statement found in the category "Group B Lower (semi-skilled)" which gives the two "Coloureds" a higher wage than blacks for the same job. The Table shows rather that the employment pattern of Western Platinum resembled apartheid in microcosm, a racial pyramid in which blacks form the base and whites the apex.
** Monthly wages in brackets; no benefits are listed (March 1984, 1 rand = \$0.61).

Answers to the questionnaire revealed that the whole of the black workforce of 4,151 were migrant workers housed in company dormitories; that all of these 4,151 black employees were categorized as either unskilled or "lower" semi-skilled, while all of the 272 white employees were listed as either "upper" semi-skilled, skilled or management. There were training programs for black workers, but these served only to increase efficiency in their lowly jobs categories. They were not trained to be promoted into the higher job categories occupied by whites. Finally there were powerful labour unions representing the white workers while there were no black unions.[65] The 1978 Canadian Code of Conduct had not benefited employment conditions of the black workforce.

At the 1985 annual meeting, Father Jim Webb, S.J. speaking on the proxies of the Jesuit Fathers of Upper Canada, the Sisters of St. Joseph of Sault Ste. Marie, the Redemptorist Fathers and the Faithful Companions of Jesus, concluded that Falconbridge should either take remedial action or withdraw: "if you can't do better, why don't you pull out?"

Clearly rankled, William James, chair of Falconbridge, replied that the lowest-paid black workers at Western Platinum were paid a monthly wage of rand 392, and that the value of "room and board" (8–12 per dormitory) provided, amounted to an additional rand 200 a month. This, William James said, was more than the Anglican Church in South Africa paid some of its employees who, he said, did not receive more than rand 300 per month. To the applause of the shareholders he added, "If ours is a disgraceful wage rate, your Anglican confreres are worse. And I don't think it's right for you to come here with your holier-than-thou attitude and say that, when you're paying lower wages than we are. ... our Rand 392 a month is 92 Rand better than yours, and I don't think the Anglican Church is giving them board either."[66] It was effective bravado. However, despite repeated requests in the months that followed, the Taskforce, and particularly its Anglican members, were unable to obtain details from James about the allegations. They momentarily deflected church criticisms and that had been their purpose. James, however, had no intention of being drawn into a discussion of employment practices, not even on the turf that he defined.

On the face of it, these efforts of the churches and religious orders to influence the policies of Falconbridge had but little impact on the company's conduct. Nonetheless, they did broaden the awareness of the shareholders, the press and their own constituents about the realities of the apartheid system and the need to dismantle it.

Concluding Comments

In the years 1980–84, Canadian corporate investors in South Africa and Namibia had not been nearly as responsive to church criticisms as had been the Canadian banks. The Taskforce had probed into the government's putative expectation that its Code of Conduct would prompt Canadian companies in South Africa to effect significant improvements in the employment practices of the companies in which they had investment. These expectations were evidently unfounded, and the Liberal government showed no intention of strengthening the Code. Those companies selling Canadian goods, services and technologies to South Africa had continued and expanded their sales, unmoved even when their sales aided production useful to the police and the military, as the Taskforce had argued in the case of the Ford Motor Company, Massey-Ferguson and the Control Data computer sales. Those engaged in the exploitation of South African and Namibian mineral resources ignored the rise of black opposition. They seemed determined to extract what they could for as long as they could. Nothing in our review of Canadian corporate activity in South Africa indicates that investors were exerting a liberalizing influence for progressive change; indeed, most Canadian investors had been unwilling and at times unable even to produce employment data, let alone show improvement in black employment conditions. One company, Falconbridge, had answered our questionnaire and had produced a typical portrait of black employment conditions under apartheid, without evidence of a leavening Canadian influence.

Notes

1   In 1976 the United Church of Canada did indeed decide to sell its shares in Falconbridge Nickel Mines. Bill Davis, at the time assistant treasurer and later general secretary of the Division of Finance, recalled that "after 2 years of spurious negotiations for information of the company's activities in Namibia with no prospects of meaningful responses from senior management on this as well as other issues important to the Church, there was no point in continuing a relationship" (interview with the author, November 1993).

2   Since the churches remained in touch with these banks concerning loans to dictatorial regimes in Latin America, their position on South African loans and on the sale of Kruger-rand was routinely added to the agenda.

3   During this period the Taskforce had also asked for statements on South African loans from other Canadian banks, trust companies and credit unions. As international research had shown, these did not reveal any lending activity, and most replied that they would not be lending to South Africa at this time. By late 1984 statements had been received from the Royal Trust Company, the Canadian Commercial Bank, the Continental Bank, the Mercantile Bank, the Northland Bank, the Bank of British Columbia, the National Bank of Canada and the Montreal City and Savings Bank, as well as from the Credit Union Central of Ontario, the Canadian Cooperative Credit Society and la Caisse Central Desjardins du Québec.

4   Adding to the Orion's South African loan of $350 million, the Royal Bank's South African involvement grew by $130 million when it bought the Bankhaus Burckardt and Brockelschen of West Germany, and by $21 million through acquisition of 63 percent of the Banque Belgique, for a total of $501 million. As with the Orion most of these loans were in the form of bonds issued by ISCOR, South Africa's state-owned steel corporation (Taskforce, *Annual Report, 1981–1982*, p. 11.

5   Taskforce, *Annual Report, 1982–1983*, p. 16.

6   Martin Mittelsteadt, Report on Business, *The Globe and Mail*, 20 January 1983.

7   Beate Klein, *United States and Canadian Involvement in Loans to South Africa from 1979 to May 1984*, in United Nations, *Notes and Documents* (New York: United Nations Centre against Apartheid, August 1984).

8   Transcript of question period of the 1983 Annual General Meeting of the Bank of Montreal, Calgary, Alberta, quoted in Taskforce, *Annual Report, 1982–1983*, pp. 19–20.

9   Although a system in which "A" and "E" represent the upper and lower limits of credit ratings was (and is) in near universal use, Jake Warren, then vice-chair of the Bank, sought to convince the churches during a meeting in September 1983 that "D" was not necessarily a low rating in the B of M's use of the scale.

10 As was the case with the other major Canadian banks, the BNS was involved in important syndicated loans to Chile and Guatemala. Questions about these loans were persistently raised at the Halifax meetings.

11 He reaffirmed this judgement when responding to letters questioning the bank's international lending policies. See, for example, his letter to Maria Lanthier, directress and secretary, Arrabon House of Toronto, 4 December 1981 (Taskforce Archives).

12 Taskforce on the Churches and Corporate Responsibility, "Report of the 1984 Annual Meeting of the Bank of Nova Scotia" (mimeograph), quoted in *Annual Report, 1983–1984*, pp. 35–36.

13 Klein, *United States and Canadian Involvement in Loans to South Africa*.

14 Taskforce on the Churches and Corporate Responsibility, "Investment Dealers," in *Annual Report, 1984–1985*, p. 39, and Robert Sheppard, "Ontario Probes South African Holdings," *The Globe and Mail*, 21 May 1986.

15 This decision by Canada's fourth-largest bank was important enough to warrant a column in *The Financial Times* of London ("Bank Bows to Church over Sale of Krugerrand," 29 November 1984). The Bank of Nova Scotia thus joined a long line of American dealers who, in 1983, had ceased to sell Krugerrand, including the First National Bank of Chicago, the Continental Bank of Illinois, Dean Witter Reynolds of Sears, the Chemical Bank, Merrill Lynch and other smaller institutions.
16 Letter from Richard Thomson, chair of the Toronto Dominion Bank, to the Taskforce, 10 December 1984.
17 Taskforce, "Canadian Policy: An Analysis," p. 14.
18 Martin Mittelsteadt, "Churches Fault CBC for Krugerrand Ads," *The Globe and Mail*, 19 April 1984.
19 Letter from Pierre Juneau, president of the Canadian Broadcasting Corporation, to the Rev. Tim Ryan, chair, Taskforce on the Churches and Corporate Responsibility, 10 May 1984.
20 Letter from Pierre Juneau, president of the Canadian Broadcasting Corporation, to the Rev. Tim Ryan, chair, Taskforce on the Churches and Corporate Responsibility, 29 June 1984.
21 Lumley offered the view that Canada's policy on South Africa acknowledged merit in maintaining dialogue with South Africa through trade and investment and did not favour economic sanctions since "these would ultimately hurt those people Canada wishes to help" (letter from the Hon. Edward C. Lumley, minister of Communications, to the Rev. Tim Ryan, chair, Taskforce on the Churches and Corporate Responsibility, 28 August 1984).
22 Decision by Toronto City Council of 21 May 1981 (Taskforce, *Annual Report, 1980–1981*, pp. 26–28).
23 The Vancouver City Council had been the first municipal government to take such actions. As early as 27 August 1979 it adopted a resolution that it would no longer deal with financial institutions doing business with the government of South Africa or its agencies and would divest itself of any such investment funds under its care (telephone interview with the Vancouver city clerk, 29 August 1979).
24 Interview in 1994 with Jim Webb, S.J., and G.P. Horrigan, S.J; see also Taskforce, *Annual Report, 1983–1984*, p. 40.
25 We are indebted for the patient, generous and voluntary help given to us by Brian Iler of Iler Campbell & Associates during the first years of submitting shareholder resolutions.
26 Proxy circular, Alcan Aluminum Ltd., Annual General Meeting of Shareholders, 25 March 1982.
27 As already noted in the United States, minority shareholder resolutions receiving a 3 percent support vote were considered significant, enough to allow a re-submission of the same resolution the following year on the grounds that such substantial shareholder unease with management policy warranted a second test.
28 The odd thing was that we knew nothing about these two companies except their names, which had been listed in a book about Armscor. We had guessed they might be the most likely purchasers of aluminum products. In fact, Gavin Cawthra, in *Brutal Force*, published four years later, lists both companies as Armscor subsidiaries (Cawthra, Table XIII, "Major Armaments Producers in South Africa," in *Brutal Force*, p. 275.
29 Proxy circular, Alcan Aluminum Ltd., Annual Meeting of Shareholders, March 1983.
30 Taskforce on the Churches and Corporate Responsibility, "A Report of the 1983 Annual Shareholder Meeting of Alcan Aluminum of Canada" (mimeograph), 6 pages (Taskforce Archives).
31 Ibid.

32 Ibid.

33 In order to remain faithful to Hulett's progress reports, which are examined here, apartheid's terminology of race descriptions are maintained.

34 See Canada's Code of Business Practice, Part One, chapter 2, pp. 32–34.

35 Taskforce, *Annual Report, 1981–1982*, p. 21.

36 Mr. Lee met with the Taskforce before taking up this appointment. We took this as recognition that the Taskforce should not be ignored and that its insights might be helpful.

37 Michael Valpy, "Bata Contravenes Ottawa Code on South Africa," *The Globe and Mail*, 15 February 1985.

38 This monthly wage would have met the official subsistence level of nearly Rand 300 for a black family of five in the Durban area plus the proposed 50 percent above this level.

39 Interview with Michael Valpy, 28 February 1996.

40 One revealing detail of our correspondence is that these organizations were operating under extremely perilous conditions, requiring that our responses to them be despatched in unmarked envelopes and sent to two different South African addresses to obscure their origin and their final destination.

41 Sergio Cesari was right. In 1978 the Taskforce had tried to change Canada's Code on this very point by citing the SACC, the South African Institute of Race Relations, the E.E.C. Code, the British Parliamentary Enquiry and the US State Department, each of whom had advocated wages at the level of South Africa's official "Minimum Living Level" plus 50 percent. External Affairs had refused because "it would be playing numbers." The 1978 Code (still in effect in early 1985) lagged behind the rest of the international codes. Canadian companies were merely advised "to strive" for black wages "significantly above the minimum level required to meet their basic needs" (Taskforce on the Churches and Corporate Responsibility, "Report on Telephone Conference with Officials of the Department of External Affairs" [mimeograph], 14 March 1978 [see Taskforce Archives]).

42 Ross Howard, "South African Workers Treated Well, Bata Says," *The Globe and Mail*, 18 February 1985.

43 Michael Valpy, "Canadians Meet Rural Workers at Bata Plant," *The Globe and Mail*, 18 June 1985.

44 Taskforce on the Churches and Corporate Responsibility, "Notes on the Meeting with Senior Management of Canada Wire and Cable Ltd." (mimeograph), 2 May 1984 (Taskforce Archives).

45 Letter from Alfred Powis, chair and CEO, Noranda Inc., to Ann E. Abraham, chair, Investment Working Group, Unit on Public Social Responsibility, Anglican Church of Canada, 28 November 1985.

46 Report of the Panel for Hearings on Namibian Uranium, Part Two, United Nations Council for Namibia, 30 September 1980, pp. 43–44.

47 In May 1982 at the London annual meeting of Rio Tinto Zinc, Rio Algom's parent company, Sir Anthony Tuke (who had quietly sat through Rio Algom's shareholder meeting earlier in Toronto) confirmed the existence of armed units at the mine: fifteen men of Rossing's security department, thirty auxiliary and twenty-four Swakopmund Commando referred to by Tuke as a "local citizens' vigilante unit." Armaments stored at the mine included automatic rifles, 9-mm pistols, semi-automatic shotguns and tear gas (*The Guardian* (UK), 2 May 1982).

48 There remained also Masfergo Holdings, a holding company and subsidiary of M-F Netherlands.

49 Joseph Lelyveld, "South African Race Policy Begets City for 'Coloured'," *The New York Times*, 2 April 1982.

50 Massey-Ferguson officers told us that since 1979 they had not been able to submit annual implementation reports on Canada's Code of Conduct because of their inability to obtain the relevant information. The Canadian government, by now a part-owner of Massey-Ferguson, had excused the company (and itself) from issuing progress reports (Taskforce, *Annual Report, 1983–1984*, pp. 46–48.

51 Taskforce on the Churches and Corporate Responsibilities, "Report on the Annual General Meeting of Massey-Ferguson, 5 May 1985."

52 Sheldon Gordon, "Pricking Corporate Consciences," Globe and Mail Report on Business (July/August 1985), p. 42.

53 "Canadian Policy toward Southern Africa," response by External Affairs to the 5 May 1981 Brief of the Taskforce of the Churches and Corporate Responsibility, 15 June 1982.

54 *ISCOR Survey*, supplement to *The Financial Mail* (Johannesburg), 7 November 1980.

55 Letter from Joe Clark, Secretary of State for External Affairs, to the Taskforce, 15 January 1985.

56 Drainville et al., *No Neutral Ground*, p. 15.

57 Control Data Corporation's use of international conduits had been in the news before. Since the 1977 mandatory arm embargo, "Most firms have been able to continue sales," said a confidential cable from the American Embassy (quoted by the columnist Jack Anderson in May 1981), "by shifting to non-US sources for components." The American company Control Data had supplied disk-drives to the British ICL, which then supplied computer equipment used by the South African police (quoted in Sampson, *Black and Gold*, p. 187).

58 Letter from D.G. Smith of Control Data Canada to the Rev. Tim Ryan, chair of the Taskforce on the Churches and Corporate Responsibility, 16 April 1985.

59 John Partridge, "Control Data Criticized for Passing Buck to Parent," Report on Business, *The Globe and Mail*, 1 May 1985.

60 Conlin Mulvihill, "The Role of QIT-Fer et Titane in the Development of South Africa's Titanium Industry" (Toronto: Taskforce on the Churches and Corporate Responsibility, 1985), 16 pages (photocopy).

61 The state-owned Industrial Development Corporation (IDC) was involved as well in the development of the SASOL oil from coal project and for SOEKOR, the Southern Oil Exploration Corporation. It was represented on the boards of South Africa's Atomic Energy Corporation; Armscor; and CSIR, the Council for Scientific and Industrial Research, a vast and secret research organization for advancing South Africa's military/industrial complex. IDC also had a 13 percent stake in the Rossing Uranium mine in Namibia. Mulvihill attested: "All of these require titanium and zircon refractory and abrasive products. It is indeed difficult not to see QIT's role as vital in South Africa's quest for self-sufficiency in these strategic areas" (ibid., p. 10).

62 Mulvihill's research also showed that Richards Bay Minerals produced low manganese iron, a raw material for the ductile iron foundry industry; monazite, a radioactive ore containing rare earth compounds; zircon, used in industries such as ceramics and steel as well as refractories and steel foundries; and rutile, which is titanium dioxide in mineral form, with an additional use in welding rods.

63 Based on "Falconbridge," a detailed account of the exchange with Western Platinum Mines in South Africa (Taskforce, *Annual Report, 1984–1985*, pp. 43–47).

64 The majority owner was LONRHO, UK, while Superior Oil, then wholly owned by Mobil Corporation, also held a 24 percent interest. Western Platinum mined platinum, gold, nickel, copper and cobalt.

65 In October 1985 members of the National Union of Mineworkers (NUM) visited the Taskforce. They reported that the mine managers had denied the union permission to

organize on the grounds that Bophuthatswana labour law made organizing by NUM illegal. According to NUM, Western Platinum was located in a "white" enclave in the "homeland." It should therefore be applying South African and not "homeland" law and recognize NUM as the legal union organizer. The Taskforce had sought help for NUM from Canada's ambassador, but he merely restated the problem (letter to the Taskforce from Edward Lee, Canada's ambassador to South Africa, 17 December 1985). In January 1986 members of the Canadian Catholic delegation to South Africa visited the NUM office to receive additional information. The four white unions at Western Platinum operated under a "homeland" exemption clause. NUM, like the Government of Canada, but unlike Western Platinum and its Canadian partner, did not recognize Bophuthatswana's jurisdiction and therefore refused the special dispensation that the "homeland" was offering NUM.

66 Taskforce on the Churches and Corporate Responsibility, "Report of the Question Period of the Annual General Meeting of Falconbridge Ltd., 17 April 1985."

Part Three   1985–87

5 The Struggle Intensifies

The years 1985–86 saw a further escalation of African resistance to apartheid and an intensification of the regime's repression of its black majority. In these years as well, in response to the increasing instability, important sections of the South African business community began to contemplate the need for more significant changes than they had ever before supported. Simultaneously in Canada, the Canadian churches reviewed and strengthened their commitment to aid the struggle for liberation while, following the election of the Mulroney government in 1984, the Canadian government itself initiated discussions, in which the Taskforce was a key player, about how Canada could demonstrate more forthrightly its opposition to apartheid. This chapter deals in turn with each of these several elements of the struggle to end white supremacy rule in South Africa.

The Escalation of South African Resistance

The presentation and acceptance of the new constitution had brought about a totally new situation. The National Forum was convened and soon afterwards the UDF emerged, as a basis for massive resistance against the new constitution, led by students, youth, black trade unions, women's groups, civic organisations and many grassroots people. A new determination to achieve liberation was born; a growing impatience to destroy the present system was emerging; the old sense of resignation on the part of the adult black community was being overtaken by a new determination on the part of young people to stand up and initiate new moves towards liberation. This movement was gaining momentum day after day and I became increasingly aware that nothing would stop it.[1]

This statement by Dr. Beyers Naudé, an astute observer and passionate participant in the struggle against apartheid, captures the mood of South African resistance at the beginning of 1985. Its truth was demonstrated all over

---

Notes for chapter 5 are found on pp. 180–86.

the country. By its radical bans and detentions in 1977, the government had effectively destroyed the major internal anti-apartheid organizations and had silenced their leaders. Other opponents like Stephen Biko had been murdered and yet others had gone into exile, many to join Umkhonto we Sizwe. In the wake of these calamities a myriad of local, community-based organizations began to take root, each involved in the struggle in ways peculiar to its own experience and needs. Prominent among the issues addressed were rent and transportation costs, which had been increased to an unconscionable level by the municipal councils and management committees of the apartheid regime. Other issues focused on trade union and black residential rights and the racially segregated and inferior black education and health services. These grievances were national in scope, but each had their local manifestations and provided the initial targets for the community-based committees.

To begin, the emphasis on local organizing had been a response to the near certainty that any replacement of the national organizations would simply be banned again. It soon proved to be strategically effective. In community-based organizations leadership was shared, and those targeted by the police could rapidly be replaced without loss of momentum. They had the added advantage that informers and agents provocateurs who attempted to infiltrate them were more easily identified than in large organizations.

Eventually alliances were formed to coordinate specific campaigns. By 1984-85 there were large civic organizations such as the Soweto Civic Association, the Port Elizabeth Black Civic Organization and Housing Action Committees in Durban and Cape Town. Each of these, however, still retained its roots—and its strength—in small community organizations as indeed did the United Democratic Front, many of whose over 300 member-organizations had their base in small community action groups.

Protracted national uprisings began in September 1984, initially in South Africa's industrial heartland, the "Vaal triangle" (Pretoria—Witwatersrand—Vereeniging, which also includes Johannesburg). They spread rapidly across the rest of the country. They started as mass protests against rent and bus-fare increases and were soon joined by protests against the system of black education, an issue that had broad support and had been sustained by students, parents and many teachers at an intense level since the 1976 Soweto uprisings.

Under the United Democratic Front and its regional structures, black resistance gathered momentum and became increasingly vocal and determined. The state responded as it had always done, with mass arrests of campaign leaders and prominent members. In October thousands of South African troops and police were deployed to occupy black townships, most heavily in the "Vaal Triangle."[2] These military-style operations reached unprecedented dimensions in Sebokeng where more than 7,000 police and troops were involved in house-to-house combat missions.[3] Black responses came in a show of strength on 5 and 6 November 1984, when a successful stay-away from school was organized, supported by 500,000 workers staying away from work.[4]

For a people with no access to the media, with many of its leaders once more in detention and demonstrations outlawed, such passive measures became effective alternatives to demonstrations. Sixteen stay-aways from work were staged in 1985 in various parts of the country. Their "twin action," black consumer boycotts of white stores, was beginning to seriously alarm South Africa's business community. The cycle of popular unrest and state repression as ever escalated and intensified.[5]

In the fall of 1984, twenty-two leading members of the UDF had been arrested and were eventually charged with high treason. Despite their scrupulous adherence to non-violence, they were also charged with terrorism under the Internal Security Act and—in deference to the enduring power of the ANC outlawed twenty-four years earlier—with promoting the interests of unlawful organizations.

State of Emergency

At midnight on 20 July 1985 P.W. Botha declared a State of Emergency in thirty-six of the most populous areas of South Africa.[6] In August 1985 the Congress of South African Students (COSAS) was banned and over 500 members and officers of the organization detained. In March 1986 during a brief break in the emergency, the minister of Law and Order disclosed that of the 7,700 people detained under the 1985 state of emergency, 2,016 had been under sixteen years of age.[7] Official figures showed that police had killed nearly 500 people since July 1985 and had injured approximately 2000.[8]

Popular resistance nevertheless continued to grow with extra-ordinary resilience. Where organizations were banned others were quickly established to continue the struggle. Thus after the Congress of South African Students (COSAS) was banned, three new movements were formed to deal with aspects of the black education crisis: the National Education Crisis Committee (NECC), largely a successor organization to COSAS; the South African National Students Congress, organizing post-secondary school students; and the South African Youth Congress, addressing the inevitable consequences of inferior black education in the form of unemployment among black youth. These organizations and their leaders were in turn singled out for some of the most severe repression under the emergency rule.

A further dramatic event underscored the emerging black power structures. Toward the end of 1985 the majority of South Africa's black trade unions voted to create a single Congress of South African Trade Unions (COSATU), which strongly advocated national unity in the struggle for liberation. Its prominent role in industrial bargaining made COSATU less vulnerable to state bannings than other anti-apartheid organizations although many of its individual officials and members were victimized by the regime.

The Long Arm of International Bankers

By early summer 1985, black consumer boycotts and workers' stay-aways had reached such proportions that they began to unsettle international investors. They were in turn facing sharp questions from their shareholders at home and had started to sell down their South African interests, with some pulling out altogether. In South Africa young white professional families were emigrating, selling their houses and taking their money out while they could.

International bankers were facing escalating institutional withdrawals of valuable accounts and troubling shareholder questions; they found it impossible to defend further their involvement in South Africa. The Chase Manhattan Bank—South Africa's largest creditor bank and the weather vane of its business climate—had already been reducing its South African exposure. Botha's declaration of the state of emergency precipitated a momentous decision by the bank. On 31 July 1985 the Bank refused to renew its short-term loans and called in its credits as they fell due.[9] The Chase's decision had an electrifying effect on all South African creditor banks, and most North American banks followed the example of the Chase. In contrast, the large German and Swiss banks remained faithful to the apartheid government throughout the emergency. British bankers were slower to react than their American colleagues, but in May 1986 an important decision was made by Barclay's Bank. Having lent in excess of $1 billion to South Africa, Barclay's declared an end to all further loans and refused to be party to any formal debt rescheduling until "there are changes which confirm an end to the bankrupt policy of institutional racial discrimination." In November it sold its 40 percent holdings in its South African subsidiary, "Barclay's National."[10]

In July 1985 the Chase Manhattan had finally reacted to an issue that had exercised the Taskforce for quite some time. Three years earlier international bankers had decided to stay clear of new long-term loans to the South African government and its agencies. However they continued to extend short-term loans to South African private borrowers and in particular to South African banks.[11] These in turn used the short-term loans to make credits available to South African companies. When first the Chase and then other international banks refused to renew their short-term loans and began to call in their credits, the South African banks faced a major crisis for they had loaned these funds on a long-term basis.

Supporters of President Botha were hoping that an important speech to the National Party (dubbed the "Rubicon" speech) on 15 August would contain enough concessions to restore the confidence of the "reform-minded" South African and international business community in his government. In the event, Botha gave a defiant speech designed to unite the "laager." He blamed the foreign media and "barbaric communist agitators" for the unrest and announced that he would not lead white South Africans into abdication and suicide. The speech, partly because it profoundly disappointed unrealistic expectations, caused an instant plunge in business confidence. Money drained out of the country at an alarming rate, totalling an unprecedented rand 7.2 billion in 1985.[12]

On 27 August Reverend Allan Boesak, since 1982 president of the World Alliance of Reformed Churches, had planned a mass protest march on Pollsmoore prison where Nelson Mandela and other political prisoners were then held.[13] Before the march could get under way, Boesak and many other participants were detained and major protests across the country ensued. The rand fell to $(US).35 (where once it had been near-parity). The regime decided to close the foreign exchange markets for four days. On 1 September South Africa declared a moratorium on the repayment of all foreign loans to the end of 1985.

A decade of insisting that their South African loans were "non-political" had now propelled international bankers into the very vortex of South African politics, confirming what the churches and other international critics had consistently maintained: their loans were sustaining the apartheid regime. In the end it took the awesome determination of South Africa's anti-apartheid movements to expose the extent to which the banks had been mortgaged to the political fortunes of the apartheid system.

Initiatives of the South African Business Community

South Africa's business community had already become alarmed and frightened even before the decisions of the international bankers. They had foreseen a rapid decline in business confidence and an accelerated exodus of capital and skills unless South Africa's international reputation was rescued. Prominent business leaders began to distance themselves from the apartheid policies of their government and to advocate reforms.

On 7 January 1985 US Senator Edward Kennedy answered an invitation from Bishop Desmond Tutu and Reverend Allan Boesak to visit South Africa. Kennedy was closely associated with the strong pro-sanction lobby in Washington and his presence in South Africa antagonized his own embassy and the South African government. Yet prominent representatives of the South African business community took advantage of Kennedy's visit to discuss the South African crisis at a private reception in the home of Gavin Relly, chief executive officer of Anglo American Corporation. There Kennedy was presented with a political manifesto signed by six business associations.[14]

In the statement the business associations, representing, they said, 80 percent of South Africa's employment strength, committed themselves to an "on-going programme of legislated reform." Among others, they called for "meaningful political participation for blacks"; "full participation in a private enterprise economy for all South Africans regardless of race, colour, sex or creed"; "universal citizenship"; "development of free and independent trade unions"; and an end to "forced removals of people."

Their advocacy for "meaningful political participation" and "universal citizenship" cannot be read as being synonymous with full democratic rights. If the business associations had meant to include such rights they would have done so, but they had carefully avoided endorsement of black enfranchisement, although its absence was the most glaring feature of white supremacy. Nonetheless, despite its ambivalence and its shortcomings, the business statement was important. It indicated that the business community no longer believed that the prevailing apartheid structures would be able in the long term to maintain the minimum level of law and order needed for sustained investment. More than that, the statement provided the first public indication of the nature of the potential bargain that business hoped would restore stability: limited reforms in exchange for international acceptance of a reformed system and an end to the threat of sanctions.

Meeting with the ANC

As the brutal realities of the July 1985 state of emergency sank in, white South Africa watched in disbelief the return of ANC symbols in the resistance movement. ANC banners and flags, T-shirts and other garments in the gold, black and green ANC colours increasingly made their appearance at political funerals and marches. These symbols of a lasting ANC allegiance confirmed what the anti-apartheid movement had asserted all along: no fundamental change in South Africa's power relationships could be successful without the ANC. It was an astonishing revelation to the white supremacists of the Botha regime. The ANC had been banned twenty-five years earlier, its leaders killed, imprisoned, banned or in exile; they could not be quoted. Yet Nelson Mandela, although imprisoned since 1964, had remained the preeminent leader of black South Africans and the ANC continued to be central to their political aspirations. An increasing number of international power brokers including prominent members of the business community were realizing that major changes were inevitable and that the ANC was bound to play a central role in shaping them.

Indeed, discreet contacts were under way. In January 1985 a meeting had taken place in London between Solly Smith and Seretse Choabe of the ANC and David Willers of the South African Foundation, at the latter's request.[15] Attending United Nations' meetings in March, Oliver Tambo, president of the ANC in exile, had met with bankers, business people and politicians in New York.[16] In South Africa it occurred to a number of business people that in their own lifetime they might have to deal with an ANC government. They were anxious to meet the ANC leaders and to learn first hand—not through a government filter—their visions and policy positions and the perspective they might bring to possible constitutional discussions. It was a curious fact that in the midst of Botha's emergency rule, not only the popular defiance campaigns openly recognized the leadership of the ANC but so also—in their own way—leading members of South Africa's white business community.

On 13 September a small group of prominent South African businessmen and newspaper editors went to Lusaka to meet with the ANC leadership. They included Gavin Relly of Anglo American Corporation; Anthony Bloom, chair of the Premier Group Holdings; Zach de Beer of Anglo American; Peter Sordor of the South African Foundation; Harold Pakendorf, editor of *Die Vaderland*; Tertius Myburg, editor of the (Johannesburg) *Sunday Times*, and Hugh Murray, editor of *Leadership* magazine. They were met by Oliver Tambo, president of the ANC; Thabo Mbeki, director of Information; Chris Hani, commander in chief of Umkhonto we Sizwe (Spear of the Nation) the military wing of the ANC, and his colleague, Mac Maharaj.

According to an ANC summary of the discussions,[17] the South African visitors suggested that the apartheid government was already moving away from apartheid. They wanted the business community to maintain good relations with the regime in order quietly to nudge Botha towards more reforms. The businessmen also seemed to be advocating the creation of a new political grouping somewhere between the National Party and the ANC. They put to their ANC hosts that a takeover of power by the ANC would be too drastic a change, and that since no "middle ground" group would take power without the approval of the ANC, it would be an act of statesmanship on the part of the ANC if it would sanction such a development to ensure that South Africa would not become permanently ungovernable. The visitors also questioned the ANC's commitment to the armed struggle; its alliance with the South African Communist Party (SACP); its acceptance of assistance from the Soviet Union and other socialist bloc states; and the economic policies it proposed for a future South Africa.

ANC representatives disagreed that Botha had the will or the capacity to initiate reforms and to preside over the dismantling of the apartheid system. Nor did they believe that Botha would respond to gentle nudging from the business community. On the contrary, the ANC held that Botha's commitment to white domination was such that he would only initiate change in response to all-round pressure on the regime, pressure that included economic sanctions. It was therefore ANC strategy to escalate rather than reduce the struggle.

Responding to specific concerns, the ANC assured their visitors that the violence of the state and the closing of all constitutional avenues for change left armed resistance as the only alternative. For the ANC unilaterally to abandon armed resistance at this point would be tantamount to abandoning the aspirations of the people. The ANC confirmed that its starting point had always been to strive for a political system in which the will of the majority could be expressed through normal democratic procedures based on one person one vote in a unitary South Africa.

The ANC officials also reaffirmed their adherence to the *Freedom Charter* of 1955, which had promised a redistribution of wealth in a country so severely divided into extremes of wealth for a few and abject mass poverty. Democratic processes would determine the manner of implementation of the policy commitment to redistribute wealth. There would certainly be a role for private enterprise in these economic transformations.

ANC representatives were firm that they could not engage in any negotiations about change until there was an atmosphere conducive to such talks. This required:

- First and foremost, the release of Nelson Mandela and all political prisoners;
- Repeal of the state of emergency, release of all those arrested and detained and suspension of the treason trials;
- Removal of the army and the police from black townships; and
- Unbanning of the ANC and reinstatement of the right to political activity.

The ANC explained the long ANC/SACP relationship to their visitors. The ANC, formed in 1912, had adopted the *Freedom Charter* in 1955 at a Congress of the People in Kliptown. The SACP was formed in 1921 and had later adopted the *Freedom Charter* as a policy guideline for itself "for the present phase of the struggle." Individual communists had always been members of the ANC, some serving in senior executive positions. They were loyally committed to the program and the policies of the ANC.

The ANC urged their visitors to pressure the regime to release Nelson Mandela and all other political prisoners. The ANC advised that corporate management needed to distance itself more resolutely from the apartheid system. Managers should recognize that their workers are engaged in a struggle for liberation and that industrial actions were often politically motivated. Thus business should handle those issues without calling in the army or police and without resorting to measures of racist legislation such as the migrant labour system that authorized the deportation of dismissed workers to their "homelands."

The ANC representatives told their visitors that to date the activities of South Africa's corporations had reinforced the apartheid state, that ARMS-COR—the state armament corporation—gave 60 percent of its production, particularly that with high technology content, to private companies under lucrative contracts. They asked that business leaders detach themselves publicly from such collaboration.

South African Business Goes to the United Nations

On 20 September 1985, *Business Day*, a South African newspaper printed a full-page statement issued by four South African employer organizations and the Urban Foundation.[18] This statement, "The Role of Business in the Reform Process in South Africa," had been presented to the hearings of the United Nations Centre on Transnational Corporations (UNCTC) which took place in New York from 16 to 20 September. The authors stressed the multiracial nature of its "major employer bodies of black and white, English and Afrikaans." "The employers associations and the Urban Foundation 'reaffirmed' support for peaceful accommodation of the political, social and economic aspirations of all South Africans regardless of race, colour and creed."[19] They stressed that there was an urgent need for negotiations for a "new constitutional dispensation," and proposed the inclusion of black leaders "even if some of these are currently in detention." They were concerned about remedial economic development for black South Africans, but not in terms of the ANC's program of "re-distribution of wealth." Rather, in the spirit of Botha's "total strategy," which provided for black urban development under the restrictions recommended by Riekert (see chap. 3, pp. 67–68), they proposed: "An effective economic development strategy aimed at maximum employment and wealth creation in the short and medium term ... regionally orientated programmes to upgrade the quality of life in black towns, and a non-discriminatory and vocation-orientated education policy which will open opportunities for black advancement."[20] They cautioned that blacks might engage in industrial action to achieve political gains—also mentioned by the ANC during the visit of business leaders—and warned of the adverse effects of such actions on the South African business community. The employers' associations and the Urban Foundation argued: "If effective channels of political expressions for blacks up to the highest level are not developed, they will be increasingly forced to employ industrial relations mechanisms to voice grievances.... Such development is unsound and would put the business community in an invidious position."[21] They expressed confidence that organized business was well advanced in the orchestration of an active strategy that would contain the various social elements and lead them to successful reforms.

The assertion that organized business had historically played a benign role in South Africa ran like a red thread through their statement. They told their audience that they had deliberately chosen for themselves "a role as a positive agent for change" and that their organizations were now "in a position to influence significantly the social, political and economic course of events in South Africa." They called for a South African business charter, outlining a set of objectives and principles for "power sharing and black advancement" but did not mention a universal franchise.

Nowhere in their statement to the UNCTC did the business associations acknowledge that they had supported and profited from the system of apartheid for the past forty years, and that during periods of their greatest economic expansion they had countenanced and supported the escalation of the harsh and far-reaching laws that had resulted in the grand design of apartheid. They had not hesitated to take advantage of the deportation to the "homelands" of workers they had dismissed from their mines and factories. Moreover, most of South Africa's business elite had supported Botha's 1983 constitutional reforms, which had confirmed the "homelands" policy and had sought to deny for the foreseeable future any civil and political rights in South Africa to the majority black population.

Nevertheless they offered to put their "negotiating experience and expertise" and their willingness to mediate at the disposal of the "various leaders and groups in the country, both white and black" to speed up the start of negotiations for "a new constitutional dispensation."

Protection of the "market-orientated economy" was at the heart of the concerns that prompted South Africa's business associations to call for "reforms":

> It is the perception of business that if South Africa's people lose control over the process of change ... there will be little room for a substantially market-orientated economic system. ... The demand for change is being supported by the South African business community both in its own enlightened self interest and for reasons of broader pressures of reforms.[22]

They had received the results of surveys showing that "the majority of blacks had not yet fully accepted the capitalist free enterprise system and that they associated it with discrimination."[23] The business organizations were troubled by these findings and even more by what they saw as the increasingly "socialist" leanings of the likely future black leaders who were involved in the powerful and continuing uprisings.

The business community had read correctly the mood of black resistance, but not its cause. It therefore saw as most pressing, the need to check the radicalization of African opinion through early, carefully controlled reforms that would, above all, abolish whatever legislation impeded the free enterprise system and would thereby promote the emergence of a black middle class with a stake in the system. Murray Hofmeyr, chairman in 1989 of Johannesburg Consolidated Investment (JCI), a part of Anglo American Corporation, may fairly be taken to represent the views of concerned business people during the height of popular resistance and state repression. He advocated reforms, not through democratization, but via the promotion of free enterprise:

> the black community is embittered by its exclusion from the central political processes and resentful of what it perceives to be unjust distribution of the benefits of the economy. Many of its leaders believe that apartheid and the free enterprise system are inseparable evils that must be supplanted by some form of centralist social order. ... Businessmen [*sic*] know that a genuinely free enterprise system in South Africa would have the potential for a non-racial engine for growth and general prosperity.[24]

For the majority of black South Africans however, the absolute denial of democratic rights was at the root of all other deprivations. Business would not or could not see that reforms which did not address this central grievance would fail to win black support.

There were some revealing passages in the statements that the business associations made to the UNCTC. They illustrated just how tied into the prevailing framework of apartheid the business organizations still were. Rhetorically they warned, "the real issue is whether the process [of reforms] will be violent or relatively peaceful" as if "violence" was still a matter of choice rather than a daily reality for the populations of the black townships under military siege. Moreover, the business associations supported the recently imposed state of emergency because it accepted the need to restore "law and order." They favoured security actions that were backed by "substantial reforms to recognize black aspirations and to redress legitimate grievances." This, they predicted, was "the key to a return to an orderly South Africa" and to "stability in our townships."[25]

They asked foreign investors to "actively support selective but aggressive engagement" on condition that "at least a majority of blacks" were satisfied that real progress was being made. The business organizations made no attempt to define what they meant by this seeming variant of President Reagan's "constructive engagement" nor what they meant by "real progress," let alone how the "majority of blacks" would be defined and their views identified.

A decade earlier some positive points could have been gained by South Africa's business community had it then sought in some fashion as this to distance itself from the apartheid regime. In the fall of 1985 it was far too late to talk of "reforming" apartheid. All popular movements inside South Africa, including COSATU, the UDF, the various community and students' organizations as well as the churches were united in their opposition to "reforms." They called for the dismantling of the system of apartheid and its replacement by a non-racial, unitary, democratic state. The employer associations did not understand this. Yet the signal they sent abroad was nevertheless important. It confirmed that South Africa was in dire economic straits, that Botha was more than a public relations nightmare and that swift action by the Western industrial states was needed to save South Africa's free enterprise economy.

For the South African churches and their overseas partners, including the member churches of the Taskforce, the dramatic economic consequences that followed the Chase Manhattan's refusal to renew its loans, were instructive. The first round of economic sanctions—suspension of international bank loans—had not been "ineffective"; nor had South African whites "circled their wagons and retreated into the laager" as opponents of sanctions had predicted. Instead, Gerhard de Kock, then governor of the Reserve Bank had gone abroad to search for new lenders. By the end of September he had visited nineteen bank executives, four central banks, the IMF and the US State Department but had returned empty handed.[26] South Africa's business elite now searched on their own for like-minded partners with whom to plan political and economic reforms that would remain congenial to their interests and help reestablish international business confidence. That their attempts were inadequate and self-serving was not as important as the fact that sanctions had proven to be effective.

On 30 September P.W. Botha was to address the National Party congress in Port Elizabeth. The day before ninety-one heads of Afrikaner and English companies as well as representatives of foreign corporations in South Africa placed full-page advertisements in South Africa's newspapers.[27] Under the banner headline "There is a better way," the following text appeared:

> As responsible businessmen committed to South Africa and the welfare of all its people, we are deeply concerned about the current situation. We believe that the reform process should be accelerated by:
>
> - Abolishing statutory race discrimination wherever it exists;
> - Negotiating with acknowledged black leaders about power sharing;
> - Granting full South African citizenship to all our peoples;
> - Restoring and entrenching the rule of law.
>
> We reject violence as a means of achieving change and we support the politics of negotiation. We believe there is a better way for South Africa and support equal opportunity, respect for the individual, freedom of enterprise and freedom of movement.
>
> We believe in the development of the South African economy for the benefit of all of its people and we are, therefore, committed to pursue a role of corporate social responsibility and to play our part in transforming the structures and systems of the country toward fair participation for all.[28]

South Africa's business executives found support for their position among their American counterparts. About 50 prominent business executives had formed the US Corporate Council on South Africa (USCCSA) with W.H. Blumenthal of Burroughs Corporation and Roger B. Smith of General Motors as its joint chairs. On 21 October 1985, they had taken out full-page advertisements in leading newspapers and reproduced "There is a better way." America's business community declared: "Today, we add our voice to theirs . . . to play an active role in peacefully achieving their goals." The advertisement listed the fifty companies that had so far joined the USCCSA.[29]

The business community had worked hard to force Botha's hand prior to the party congress and he had indeed forecast important changes: a common citizenship for all, including the "homelands," and the introduction of a uniform identity document irrespective of race, thereby acceding to the longest-standing black grievances. Alas, the grim state of emergency had generated such repression that it annulled the positive results this change might otherwise have had.[30] Botha had already been piqued by the initiatives of South Africa's industrialists and had called "disloyal" their visit to the ANC. The October statement by American business elite merely confirmed his suspicion that support of the business community for his policies was waning.[31]

The year 1985 had begun with serious international pressure for change and a statement by organized business to Senator Kennedy supporting reforms. Business concern had deepened in July following the banks' embargo on new loans and the partial state of emergency imposed by the Botha regime. The business community had begun to articulate its fear that unless the government was offering reforms, South Africa's economic system itself would be in danger. To Botha's chagrin, South Africa's business and opinion leaders had given public recognition to the continued importance of the ANC by meeting with its leadership in September. Finally in October South Africa's business community had sought and received public support from America's most prominent business leaders. They had also given to Western governments a resonant message that if the white business community in South Africa was calling for reforms then surely Western states should do no less and that the time had come to apply pressure on the Botha government.

Within the wider context of the struggle for black liberation, 1985 had significantly advanced international understanding of the intractable ways that connected South Africa's system of legalized racism with the industrialized West. On their television screens Europe and North America watched the military occupation of black townships in a war which the South African government had unleashed against its black population.

We turn now to examine how the Canadian churches responded to the activities of an intransigent Botha government and to the position of their South African partners who formed part of an increasingly powerful resistance movement.

The Positions on Apartheid of International Church Organizations 1983–86

Following the adoption of South Africa's 1984 constitution, the member churches of the Taskforce reviewed their Southern African policy positions. They were outraged by the attempt to permanently close the door on black political participation and by the ruthless use of force to suppress all opposition to it. They determined to strengthen their policies in response to the new South African situation. Moreover, the hope of finding a serious listener in the new Conservative government, which had come to power in October 1984, sharpened their resolve to look for policies that were sufficiently tough, relevant and practical to make a difference.

In their search the Canadian churches were informed and much influenced by their sister churches and by other anti-apartheid institutions in South Africa with whom they maintained close contacts. Individual personal visits and more formal missions by Canadian church members to South Africa provided recurrent opportunities for extensive consultations with leading anti-apartheid activists. The churches' policy reviews were aided also by the policy positions that were simultaneously being developed by the World Council of Churches and by other international church structures to which member churches were affiliated. Finally the policy reviews of the Canadian churches benefited richly from their participation in the wider anti-apartheid movement, both national and international.[32]

Learning from the South African Churches

The South African churches welcomed and indeed invited missions from foreign churches as these contributed to the effective international mobilization of opinion and to the relevance and effectiveness of church initiatives. One such mission to South Africa was undertaken in January 1986 in response to an invitation from Archbishop Hurley, then president of the Southern African Catholic Bishops' Conference (SACBC) to the Canadian Conference of Catholic Bishops (CCCB) to send a delegation to attend several sessions of the Southern African Bishops' Assembly in January 1986. To convey the value of such visits this particular assignment is described here in some detail.

The Canadian delegation comprised two bishops, two representatives of religious orders, one lay member, one staff member of the Canadian Catholic Organization for Development and Peace and me, seconded by the Taskforce as resource person to the delegation.[33] Although over the years several members of the Taskforce board had visited South Africa, by 1986 most had been denied reentry visas.[34] That it was possible for us to meet a wide range of anti-apartheid organizations and activists despite the severe restrictions of the State of Emergency and to engage immediately in open and meaningful discussions was due entirely to the extensive involvement of the South African churches in the liberation struggle.

Our short stay in South Africa was imaginatively organized by the SACBC's secretariat headed by Father Smangaliso Mkhatschwa and his staff. They provided us with escorts who were themselves members of the black resistance and could take us to individuals and organizations that might otherwise not have talked to us. We travelled to the "independent home-lands" of Bophuthatswana and Ciskei and visited KwaNdebele, a "home-land" whose people were struggling at the time against the imposition of "independence." We saw recent "resettlements" of people still dazed from having been "endorsed out" and dumped in the veld to erect their shacks as best they could from the meagre possessions they were able to bring. We visited people who had been expelled by the Ciskei "homeland" to which the South African government had assigned them. Cast out by both authorities, they now lived in constant fear on "forbidden" (South African) land as internal refugees. Everywhere we met Catholic priests, Protestant ministers and church workers who cooperated in community mobilization and in relief services with local representatives of the United Democratic Front and other community organizers, all constantly at risk of arrest, detention or worse.

We also met church and community organizers during visits to several townships. Here convoys of armoured vehicles, with young soldiers, their guns at the ready, sealed off access roads and were menacing the besieged population. We celebrated mass with the Southern African Bishops' Conference in Mamelodi township to commemorate the recent killings of twenty-six of its residents by the police and soldiers. During the deeply moving service weapons used by the security forces were displayed as symbols of the sufferings inflicted: teargas canisters, rubber bullets,[35] ammunition shells and large leather whips called *sjamboks.*

In Soweto we met with officials of the Soweto Civic Association one of the new democratic structures that had largely replaced the municipal councils of the apartheid administration which the people had boycotted. We visited "street committees" and other small community units and spend several hours with students and teachers in a Soweto Catholic high school.

The Canadian delegation had discussions with several members of the National Executive of the United Democratic Front (UDF). We learned of a resolution adopted at their General Council meeting in April 1985 which rejected the argument that foreign investment benefited the oppressed and exploited of South Africa. UDF officials were pleased with this resolution because they had made their point without explicitly calling for the withdrawal of foreign investment, a demand then still a treasonable offence in South Africa.

Contact was also made with South African trade unions. Chris Dlamini, then first vice-president of the Congress of South African Trade Unions (COSATU) addressed the Bishops' Assembly. Dlamini defended COSATU's commitment to move beyond narrowly defined union matters. COSATU's program included demands for an end to the "homelands" system; the migrant labour system; the pass laws; the state of emergency; the continued imprisonment of Nelson Mandela and all other political prisoners and detainees. Dlamini affirmed that COSATU unreservedly supported international economic sanctions and other measures designed to force the government to abandon apartheid.

Just how trade unions were drawn into the daily community struggles became clear during a meeting with the Pretoria office of the South African Allied Workers Union (SAAWU). Here we discovered fifteen young boys lying prostrate on their stomachs. They had just been released from two days in prison. All had massive wounds crisscrossing their backs, inflicted by lashes from the police *sjamboks*. The SAAWU office was searching for a mission-run clinic that could care for them. The Union had a list of clinics willing to ignore the standard procedure that police be advised of patients with firearm or *sjambok* wounds. Such patients could be charged with "public violence" on the dubious assumption that any victim of gunfire or *sjambok* lashes must have taken part in illegal activities. The deep gashes caused by the *sjamboks* leave permanent scars, which themselves served as future identification marks of "people involved in violence." Through exposures to such concrete, everyday details we became acutely aware of the many dehumanizing dimensions of apartheid and of the resilience of anti-apartheid activists of all races belonging to large networks of organizations who were mobilizing for change. Most of them were supported by either the South African Council of Churches or the Southern African Catholic Bishops' Conference or both.

The Canadian delegation visited the offices of several of these organizations. One was the "Domestic Workers' Association" which helped the predominantly black women working as domestics under conditions of unchecked exploitation and abuse. Also supported by the churches was the Detainees' Parents Support Committee (DPSC), a national organization with a network of local offices. (As the name indicates, the DPSC was initially formed in 1976 in response to police action against the Soweto schoolchildren.) Since 1982 the DPSC had responded to the increased use of solitary confinement and torture and the rising numbers of deaths of political prisoners in police custody. Additional tasks were assumed in 1984 in the wake of mass arrests of black children and youths. Under the internal security laws, amplified by the 1985 State of Emergency, no one but the police was allowed to name persons who had been detained or could say where they were held. The Canadian delegation visited the cramped and crowded offices of the DPSC in Johannesburg where volunteers and staff listened to relatives who had come to describe their children and other missing persons who had been taken away by unknown persons to unknown places. The DPSC then sought to match these descriptions with the information in their files compiled from clandestine reports by persons with access to the detainees such as released detainees, civil rights lawyers checking on other cases or bribed prison officials. Once a missing person had been located, lawyers associated with the DPSC took up the case and pressed the state to lay charges or to release the detainee.[36] Many of the DPSC offices became recurrent casualties of the nation-wide clampdowns, often reemerging—amazingly with copies of their computer files intact—in another place under another name. Before our delegation left South Africa, we learned that the Johannesburg DPSC office that we had visited had been closed by the police.

We also met members of the church-supported "End of Conscription Campaign" (ECC), a mainly white organization run by young South Africans of draft age. They protested the use of the South African army to subdue unarmed compatriots in the townships, and they opposed its deployment in northern Namibia and Angola. The ECC campaigned for legislation that would allow alternative humanitarian services in lieu of military conscription.

In discussions with representatives of the various South African opposition organizations, we were struck by their near unanimous support for increasing economic pressure on the South African government. The support ranged from an uncompromising call for mandatory comprehensive economic sanctions to proposals for a gradual increase of selective sanctions, involving in particular withdrawal of foreign investment that benefitted the police, the military and the nuclear industry. Others asked for a ban on further investments, including a ban on bank loans to South African public or private enterprises. The organizations stressed that international economic sanctions should be recognized as one of the very few effective non-violent means to promote fundamental change causing a minimum of further bloodshed.

Position of the Southern African Catholic Bishops' Conference (SACBC)

The Roman Catholic bishops of South Africa had been among the severest critics of the 1984 constitution. After the 1985 state of emergency had been declared, the SACBC called on the Botha government to open discussions with the recognized leaders of the people. The bishops pointed out the futility of mass arrest, stating that the "real" leaders included "those at present in prison, detention, awaiting trial and in exile." They predicted that "there can be no peace without reconciliation and no reconciliation without justice." Beginning in 1985, the SACBC officially encouraged Roman Catholics to oppose military service because of the deployment of troops against the civilian population in the townships.[37]

The Canadian delegation also discussed international economic sanctions during its meetings with Father Mkhatshwa, Archbishop Hurley and others. It was clear that on this issue the SACBC was divided. While both Mkhatshwa, who had visited the Taskforce in early 1980, and Hurley were sympathetic and even supportive of Canadian church actions, they were unable then or later to count on majority support within the SACBC for economic sanctions. We understood that resistance to sanctions among the bishops was based on fears of more unemployment and increased poverty among the black population. Yet this passage from the closing statement of the January 1986 Assembly of the Southern African Catholic Bishops' Conference made clear in which direction opinion was moving:

> While still open to dialogue, we see no choice but to envisage forms of non-violent action such as passive resistance, boycott and economic pressure, to move our country away from its present state of racial conflict and set it firmly on the road to justice and full participation of all inhabitants in the structures of government. We affirm our total abhorrence of the system of apartheid which is directly opposed to the teaching of Christ and the God-given dignity of every human being and is the greatest single obstacle to peace in our land.

Position of the South African Council of Churches (SACC)

With the exception of the white Nederduitse Gereformeerde Kerk, all of the major and most of the minor Protestant denominations were members of the SACC, with the SACBC enjoying observer status. The SACC had consistently advocated non-violent internal and international measures that would assist the dismantling of the apartheid system. In 1985 the SACC had called for disinvestment and similar economic measures and had requested that their international partner churches promote economic pressure on South Africa in their own countries.

The Canadian delegation had a lengthy discussion with Dr. Beyers Naudé, whose banning order had just been rescinded and who had succeeded the Reverend Desmond Tutu (later Archbishop) as general secretary to the SACC. Naudé told us that the Council was no longer debating whether foreign companies should adopt reforms in the workplace in compliance with the various international codes of conduct. A far more important issue, he said, was the way foreign investment bolstered the system of apartheid. For the SACC the *real* issue was neither fairer treatment for the proportionately few workers employed by foreign companies nor the possible example they might set for others to act likewise. Rather, the SACC saw foreign investors as supporters of apartheid in very fundamental ways; they paid taxes to the regime, they sold their products to the police and the military and engaged in commercial relations with the South African government. Internationally foreign investors had a tendency to become apologists for the policies of the government. The ending of apartheid, Dr. Naudé said, should be a precondition for continued foreign investment. In the same vein he argued that any renegotiations of South Africa's international debt should be conditional on the dismantling of apartheid.

Of particular interest to the Canadian delegation was a visit to the Institute of Contextual Theology. Reverend KeKane on the staff of the Institute, instructed us on the development of Black Theology in Southern Africa. Its teaching was premised on the conviction that unless Christian theology was rooted in the experience of black oppression it would remain inaccessible to the people living under the system of apartheid. Only a theology that placed Jesus' words of "bringing good news to the poor" within the context of their liberation had meaning for the oppressed in Southern Africa.

Meeting with the ANC and SWAPO

On its way home the Canadian delegation had discussions with ANC and SWAPO officials in Lusaka, thanks to the good offices of the Roman Catholic Secretariat there. That this was easily arranged provided yet another illustration of the trust that existed between the Southern African churches and secular anti-apartheid organizations, including the two liberation movements.

During the meeting with senior officials of the ANC, which was chaired by Thabo Mbeki, we learned directly about the discussion in September 1985 between the ANC and South African business and media representatives. The ANC still expressed bitterness about the support given by major industrialists for South Africa's 1984 constitution, and felt that this insensitivity to black repression was evident also in the continued sales by white business to South Africa's arms industries.

ANC officials maintained that they had consistently tried to avoid civilian casualties ("soft targets") in their operations. They explained that for political reasons alone any other approach would be self-defeating and would only alienate potential supporters for their cause. As they must have done many times, they argued once again that after the regime had banned the ANC and had blocked all constitutional means of gaining democratic rights, the armed struggle had become the only option. While the ANC appreciated that not everyone could support the armed struggle, it expected international opponents of apartheid, such as the churches, to put pressure on Western industries not to support the apartheid state and its arms industries.

In early April 1986 the Delegation of the Canadian Catholic Church published a report on their Southern African visit, *No Neutral Ground*.[38]

Our experience had strengthened our view that fundamental change must be achieved with the minimum of further bloodshed. To that end, maximum economic pressure ought to be exerted by the international community to complement the struggle against apartheid already in process in South Africa and Namibia. Such international pressure had been expected and welcomed by most of the people and the organizations we had met. We felt a great responsibility to convey their views to the Canadian Conference of Catholic Bishops, other denominations and to the Canadian public in general.

The mission of the Canadian Roman Catholic delegation in early 1986 had not been unique. It paralleled in many respects the analyses of the major Canadian Protestant churches whose representatives had visited South Africa at other times and had issued similar reports of their missions. Most denominations had also hosted tours in Canada of leaders of their South African partner churches or had otherwise been in contact with members of these churches. These were genuine and successful efforts to remain in solidarity with the struggle for liberation in South Africa and Namibia.

Theological Reflections and Church Initiatives

In September 1985 an important theological document was published under the auspices of the South African Institute of Contextual Theology. Its original title, *Challenge to the Church: A Theological Comment on the Political Crisis in South Africa* had sounded its clarion call. The document was the product of a series of discussions and self-criticisms among a number of prominent Christian laity and theologians from diverse denominations. They had each become profoundly uneasy about traditional Church responses to the intensifying South African crisis. The *Kairos Document*,[39] as it was soon called, was not an official church statement nor was the text considered final by the 150 individuals who had initially signed it. It was offered to the Christian Church in South Africa and to the international Christian community for study, reflection and additional comments.

The Document took its name from the Greek word "kairos" meaning "moment." In the context of the South African crisis, "kairos" denoted a biblical moment of grace in which to reflect on God's plan for the oppressed in South Africa, a moment also to search for alternative theological models equal to the dimension of the crisis that was gripping South Africa and equal to the task of challenging the very legitimacy of the apartheid regime.

The *Kairos Document* was impatient with traditional church statements, even those critical of apartheid. It challenged Christians to reconsider their theology. It demanded a theology of liberation which categorically recognized that the South African regime was tyrannical and that God was on the side of the oppressed. Why, asked the "Kairos theologians," "does 'Church Theology' appeal to the top rather than to the people who are suffering? Why does this theology not demand that the oppressed stand up for their rights and wage a struggle against their oppressors? Why does it not tell them that it is their *duty* to work for justice and to change the unjust structures? (emphasis in the original)[40] Debating these questions, the authors reviewed Church statements that habitually condemned "all violence" even-handedly. "This general abstraction" they argued, wrongly equated "the structural, institutionalized and unrepent violence of the state" with "acts of resistance and self defence" of the oppressed. Thus, "'violence in the townships' comes to mean what the young people are doing and not what the police are doing or what apartheid in general is doing to people."[41] The problem with the Church here, said the *Kairos Document*, is that, "it starts from the premise that the apartheid regime in South Africa is a *legitimate authority* (emphasis in the original). It ignores the fact ... that [the white minority regime] maintains itself by brutality and violent force and that a majority of South Africans regard this regime as illegitimate." The *Kairos Document* warned that those who expressed themselves in favour of "non-violence" within the context of South Africa in 1986 were seeking a neutral position through an "oversimplified and misleading theology of non-violence": "The attempt to remain neutral in this kind of conflict is futile. Neutrality enables the status quo of oppression (and therefore violence) to continue. It is a way of giving tacit support to the oppressor, a support for brutal violence."[42]

The issue of hatred inspired by the state's tyranny was addressed as was the difficult obligation of Christians to love their enemies. For that reconciliation to begin, the Kairos theologians advised, oppression had to end. "The most loving thing we can do for *both* the oppressed *and* for our enemies who are oppressors, is to eliminate the oppression, remove the tyrants from power and establish a just government for the common good of *all people* (emphasis in the original)."[43]

The *Kairos Document* had a profound impact in South Africa. It was immediately recognized in the townships as a statement of what it meant to be truly Christian in a violent society. The preface to the second edition notes that for many "the Gospel became 'Good News' for the first time in their lives." The impact of the *Kairos Document* on the international Christian community was equally clarifying and energizing. It was frequently quoted in Canada and had a significant influence on the reviews of church policy by the member churches of the Taskforce.

The Position and Influence of International Church Affiliations

In 1983 the World Council of Churches Assembly met in Vancouver. Daily news coverage of the event and its debates and decisions on Southern Africa contributed greatly to Canadian awareness of the apartheid system and an appreciation of the important role played by the Christian Church in these troubled lands. The *Statement on Southern Africa* adopted by the Assembly reaffirmed that "apartheid stands condemned by the Gospel." It called for early independence of Namibia; disinvestment of corporate interests in South Africa and Namibia and, for the first time in the history of the World Council of Churches, for international comprehensive and mandatory sanctions against the apartheid state.

A further powerful expression of solidarity resulted from a meeting of church leaders from around the globe in Harare, Zimbabwe, in December 1985 also under the auspices of the World Council of Churches. The meeting issued a joint statement that spoke to the growing Southern African crisis. The authenticity and importance of the *Harare Declaration* was enhanced by the presence at the conference of prominent church representatives from South Africa and Namibia and from the All African Conference of Churches. It is worth quoting at length for it significantly strengthened the resolve of the member churches of the Taskforce to step up their pressure on business and government to loosen their ties with apartheid.

> We have come together to seek God's guidance at this time of profound crisis in South Africa, and have committed ourselves to a continuing theological reflection on the will of God for the Church. WE AFFIRM THAT THE MOMENT OF TRUTH (KAIROS) IS NOW, BOTH FOR SOUTH AFRICA AND THE WORLD COMMUNITY (Emphasis in the original). We heard the cries of anguish of the people of South Africa trapped in the oppressive structures of apartheid. In this moment of immense potentiality, we agree that the apartheid structure is against God's will, and is morally indefensible. The South African Government has no credibility. We call for:
>
> - an end to the state of emergency,
> - the release of Nelson Mandela and all political prisoners,
> - the lifting of the ban on all banned movements,
> - the return of exiles.
>
> The transfer of power to the majority of the people, based on universal suffrage, is the only lasting solution to the present crisis.
>
> We understand and fully support those in South Africa who are calling for the resignation of the Government. We regard this as the most appropriate and least costly process of change and as a contribution towards such a change. As we await a new democratic and representative government in South Africa:
>
> (1) We call on the Church inside and outside South Africa to continue praying for the people of South Africa and to observe June 16th, the Tenth Anniversary of the Soweto uprising, as World Day of Prayer and Fast to end unjust rule in South Africa.
>
> (2) We call on the international community to prevent the extension, the rolling over, or renewal of bank loans to the South African Government, banks, corporations and para-statal institutions.

(3) We call on the international community to apply immediate and comprehensive sanctions on South Africa.

(4) We call on the church inside and outside South Africa to support developments within the trade union movement for a united front against apartheid.

(5) We demand the immediate implementation of the United Nations Resolution 435 on Namibia.

The *Harare Declaration* ended with an expression of confidence that "the liberation of South Africa will bring liberation for all the people in the country, black and white."[44]

Within the international Lutheran family a growing consensus against apartheid had been gaining ground.[45] In 1977 the Sixth Assembly of the Lutheran World Federation (LWF) meeting in Dar es Salaam, voted that a repudiation of apartheid be part of the confessional foundation of the LWF, and bestowed on it the *status confessionis* "to witness actively to their confessional integrity by working for the dismantling of the apartheid system."[46]

In 1983, during a consultation in Harare, representatives of the LWF found that two Lutheran churches, one in South Africa and another in Namibia, had ignored the adoption of the *status confessionis.* The Lutheran World Federation, meeting on 1 August 1984 voted 220 to twenty-three to suspend the membership of the two white Southern African churches—the 6,000 member Evangelical Lutheran Church in South Africa (Cape Province) and the 15,000-member "German Evangelical Lutheran Church in South West Africa" (Namibia) for their failure to be a witness against the policy of apartheid and for impairing the unity of the Church. In addition the 1984 Assembly asked each member church to "urge their own governments [and] business organizations ... to observe strict enforcement of oil embargoes, transfer of nuclear technology, and importation of nuclear material ... and asked each church to take visible and concrete steps including boycotts of goods and withdrawal of investments to end all economic and cultural support of apartheid."[47]

The World Alliance of Reformed Churches (WARC) underwent similar developments. In South Africa the Nederduitse Gereformeerde Kerk (NGK), the traditional Dutch Reformed Church, had divided its membership into four separate churches, one for each of apartheid's population groups. The NGK, closely identified with the apartheid regime and its philosophy, received the first challenges in the mid-1970s. As black clergy began to assume leadership positions in the "black" Nederduitse Gereformeerde Kerk of Africa (NGKA), they also began to question the theological basis for the racial divisions in their Church. The 1975 synod of the NGKA declared apartheid to be unchristian, without scriptural foundations, and rejected it as immoral. The NGKA also called for uniting the Dutch Reformed Churches and for dismantling tribal divisions within NGKA seminaries which the white church had created. The NGKA opened its doors to white ministers of the NGK and asked—but was rebuffed—that this gesture be reciprocated. It also joined the South African Council of Churches.[48]

The historic moment for the World Alliance of Reformed Churches came during its meeting in Ottawa in August 1982. The WARC declared apartheid a heresy and voted to suspend the membership of the NGK until it opened its doors to blacks and supported those suffering from the system of apartheid. Reverend Allan Boesak, moderator of the Sendingkerk of the NGKA who had become a central figure in the struggle against apartheid, was elected president of the WARC.

Eventually in 1986 the "white" NGK issued a policy statement, *Church and Society*, which called upon the white Dutch Reformed Church to open its religious ceremonies to all races. But the new policy left unchanged the NGK's use of apartheid's race classifications in its membership categories. Although the document contained a qualified rejection of apartheid, it failed to meet the conditions set by WARC for readmission.[49]

The readiness of the World Council of Churches and the major international associations of the individual Christian denominations to consult with each other and with key Southern African opponents of apartheid at important junctures in the struggle resulted in profound shared insights and powerful statements. These in turn helped national churches around the world to develop informed positions about events in Southern Africa and to sustain their commitment over the long years of the struggle. Listen for example to Bishop Kleopas Dumeni of the Evangelical Lutheran Church in Namibia who visited Canada in November 1986: "Suffering is our daily bread. We suffer physically, economically, socially and spiritually. I think you hear our voice. It is very important for you to do something freely and motivated by love."[50]

The 1986 Policy Revisions of the Canadian Churches

In the course of 1986, each of the five major denominational members of the Taskforce completed their Southern Africa policy review, each adopting a strengthened set of positions.[51] A brief review will show essential parallels in their concerns, despite some differences in emphases.

Each policy statement expressed love and respect for their Southern African partners and solidarity with South Africa's anti-apartheid organizations. Each asked for God's guidance and strength for those oppressed by the structures of apartheid. There was a unanimous call for the Canadian government to press for the lifting of the state of emergency in South Africa and for the demilitarization of the black townships. The release of Nelson Mandela and all other political prisoners along with the return of political exiles was seen as a necessary precondition for genuine constitutional negotiations. The churches in their separate formulations each reasoned that in order to achieve these goals, the Canadian government—if possible in cooperation with other governments—should impose progressively more severe selective sanctions. Should the South African regime remain obdurate, they pledged support for the imposition of full economic sanctions and asked that these measures remain in force until apartheid was dismantled.

All the new policy positions included statements on Namibia. They were unanimous in demanding an immediate end to Canadian contracts for the processing of Namibian uranium and they agreed that Canada should withdraw from the Contact Group of States. Each denomination advocated Namibian independence under United Nations Security Council Resolution 435, though there was slight divergence in regard to how this might best be achieved. Every denomination also urged Canada to increase development aid to the independent black African states of Southern Africa, known as the "Front Line States" (FLS).

The individual churches dealt differently with the issues raised by the shares they held in industries with continued involvement in South Africa and Namibia. The National Executive Council of the Anglican Church of Canada adopted a resolution in 1985 which stated that if apartheid was still not dismantled at the time of the 1986 General Synod that

(1) no new investments be made in any corporations having investments in South Africa or Namibia; and

(2) that ... investments which directly support the South African Government be terminated until apartheid *is clearly* being dismantled (emphasis in the original).

The Evangelical Lutheran Church in Canada (ELCIC) pledged continuous engagement with the corporate community to press for disinvestment from South Africa and Namibia. If disinvestment was resisted, the ELCIC would urge the companies to declare publicly their opposition to apartheid and to refuse sales to the military, police or the nuclear sector. The Church agreed to divest its shares and to explain publicly the reasons for its divestiture if the companies were not prepared to meet these conditions.

In the 1984–87 General Assembly Recommendations of the Presbyterian Church in Canada, there are no references to the Church's share ownership in companies with South African investment, nor are there specific resolutions enjoining the Church to use shareholder pressure to influence the conduct of corporations and banks in South Africa or Namibia. In 1981, the 107th General Assembly had adopted a "Statement on Racism." Its study and action recommendations explained that "Through actions of the General Assembly our participation in and support of ... the Taskforce on the Churches and Corporate Responsibility, among others, we have continued to speak out against racism and work constructively for the unity of the human family." The serious engagement of successive representatives of the Presbyterian Church in Canada in the agenda of the Taskforce, including its major briefs and actions on corporate and government policies concerning apartheid, bear witness to the faithfulness of the Presbyterian Church to this statement. Nevertheless, there is bound to be a qualitative difference in the sense of ownership experienced by a member denomination of an issue such as shareholder action if that issue has been directly addressed in the senior policymaking body of the denomination rather than being brought to it for decision by its representative on the Taskforce board.

If distance from the decision-making structures by and large characterized the relationship of the Taskforce to the Presbyterian Church in Canada, its relationship to the United Church of Canada was the direct opposite. Often the Taskforce board included several representatives from the United Church of Canada, each from a different division. Before major Taskforce decisions were taken, United Church board members consulted with their divisions and among themselves to seek agreement on the church's responses. Such a hands-on approach was always welcomed by the staff and board of the Taskforce. It helped to ensure that the United Church continued to regard the Taskforce as an important instrument for the implementation of the Church's corporate social responsibility policies.

The United Church was the only member denomination which regularly appointed representatives of the Division of Finance to the board of the Taskforce and to its executive. For the mandate of the Taskforce, the increasingly progressive policy of the Division of Finance regarding proactive share ownership was, and continues to be, of enormous advantage. It has meant that the United Church has involved members of its Investment Committee and Pension Plan Trustees directly in discussions about the social concerns of the Church including their economic implications and international dimensions. Only the United Church involved their financial officers in meetings with corporate management and in annual meetings of shareholders on issues the Taskforce had coordinated.

In 1985 an internal debate in the United Church of Canada developed, which centred on the relative merits of two opposing points of view within the acknowledged "common purpose" of defeating apartheid. The Division of World Outreach held that it was unethical on principle for the Church to gain financially from holding shares in corporations that still had equity investment in apartheid South Africa. It proposed that the Church dispose of these shares without delay.

Others, including the Division of Finance, believed that retaining the Church's shareholdings had the strategic advantage of providing the church with a means of keeping apartheid on the agenda of those corporations in which the church was holding shares and beyond that, on the agenda of the Canadian business community in general. In 1986 South Africa's crushing repression had generated unprecedented pressure for disinvestment from dissident shareholders of North American corporations with investment in South Africa. The publicity generated by this shareholder revolt created immediate publicity in South Africa and, as we have seen, made its foreign investors and its own business community extremely nervous. Those in the United Church who favoured retaining the investment in these companies wanted to do so in order that the voice of the Church could be added to that pressure for disinvestment. They argued for phased and specific actions which "would step up the pressure over a series of stages rather than in a single action that becomes history the day after it occurs."[52] The controversy ended with a majority vote at the 31st General Council in August 1986, in favour of immediate divestment. The motion read: "that this 31st General Council [i]nstruct the Investment Committee through the Division of Finance to divest the UCC portfolio of all investments from corporations and companies having direct equity investment in South Africa until power is shared democratically among all the peoples of South Africa; and urge the Trustees of the Pension Plan to take similar action."[53]

In the summer of 1986 an inter-church brief, *Human Rights in South Africa and the Question of Sanctions*,[54] illustrated the degree to which the Canadian churches were collectively able to offer well integrated and detailed policy recommendations on the basis of their individual policy reviews. They recommended that the new Canadian sanctions announced on 6 July 1985[55] be strengthened, giving highest priority to the suspension of Canadian trade and investment that benefited the South African military and police or the nuclear sector. They asked the government to legislate the withdrawal of Canadian investment from South Africa and Namibia which directly or indirectly supplied these three strategic sectors. Further, the churches recommended legislation to halt all exports to *any* purchaser in South Africa of sensitive high-technology equipment which could be used by the military, the police or the nuclear sector. They called for legislation to end all nuclear cooperation, including private or public scientific exchanges in Canada or elsewhere; and recommended legislation to prohibit participation by Canadian investors in enterprises that depended on the use of contract labour.

Other recommendations sought to discourage Canadian investors from supporting or defending the apartheid system. The churches proposed that the Canadian Code of Conduct be made mandatory for all Canadian investors and that it include a number of additional obligations: they should publicly oppose the laws of apartheid; disclose their sales to the South African government and its agencies; and involve elected representatives of their black workforce in monitoring compliance with the Canadian Code and in signing the company's compliance reports. The churches proposed that companies unwilling to comply with this mandatory code should be asked to disinvest on the grounds that their presence in South Africa exerted no ameliorating influence on the denial of human rights of black South Africans.

To ensure further that the apartheid government was denied international financial support, the Canadian churches proposed legislation to ban all credits or bond placements from Canadian financial institutions for any borrower in South Africa and Namibia, and asked that the Canadian executive director of the International Monetary Fund oppose any South African credit application.

The churches recommended that South Africa's foreign exchange earnings be limited by legislation that would ban Canadian imports of South African agricultural products and other consumer goods, that Canada's oil embargo against South Africa be mandatory and that Canadian shipping companies be required to refrain from carrying oil from third countries to South Africa.[56]

The churches shared a strong conviction that as long as South Africa was illegally occupying Namibia, Canadian legislation should require the withdrawal of all Canadian investment from Namibia and should end tax concessions for companies that continued to operate there. Legislation should also terminate all current contracts for the import and processing of Namibian uranium in Canada.

To complement these proposed economic sanctions against South Africa and Namibia, the Canadian churches called for measures that would increase development assistance for the Front Line States to reduce the impact sanctions might have on their economies. They advocated official Canadian humanitarian aid to the African National Congress and an early consultation between Canada's prime minister and Oliver Tambo, president of the ANC, noting that the ANC had been recognized by the Commonwealth's Eminent Persons Group as the most important political movement for the liberation of South Africa (see below).

These recommendations seem, indeed are, tamer than those advocated by the WCC Assembly meeting in Vancouver and by the *Harare Declaration*. There were many within the Canadian churches and within the Taskforce who supported a policy for comprehensive sanctions against South Africa, but there was no consensus on this important question. Meanwhile there were significant new policies to be recommended which the churches felt would prepare the right political climate for an acceptance of comprehensive mandatory sanctions. Furthermore, the churches' brief was prepared for the members of a legislative committee and spoke to those policy changes that had the potential to be addressed by them, a calculation which turned out to have been correct.[57] In fact, the 1986 brief was part of a much wider engagement of the Canadian churches with the Canadian government over the question of economic sanctions. That engagement had begun with the newly elected Conservative government and its Southern Africa initiative in 1985.

Canada Changes Course on Apartheid: The Contribution of the Taskforce

In the fall of 1984 the Conservative party under Brian Mulroney came to power. The first inkling that major changes were in the offing had come with the appointment of Stephen Lewis as Canada's permanent representative to the United Nations. On 20 November Lewis delivered an unprecedented and impassioned speech in the General Assembly on the evils of the system of apartheid, which the Canadian anti-apartheid community received with great scepticism. It was hard to believe that he was ushering in a significant change in government policy.

But confirmation that Mulroney did indeed intend to change Canada's policy toward the apartheid regime was brought to the churches by a person who had their unqualified trust. In October 1984, to the delight of the anti-apartheid network, Archbishop Desmond Tutu, then secretary general of the South African Council of Churches, had received the Nobel Peace Prize. On 21 December 1984 he met with Canadian church and other anti-apartheid organizations in the Toronto area. Tutu told us of his meeting with Mulroney the previous day and assured us that the new prime minister was likely to make important changes in Canada's South African policy.[58] As we admitted our incredulity that change would originate from this source, Tutu reaffirmed his expectations and expressed in the most gracious terms black South Africa's debt to anti-apartheid activists around the world. He paid tribute to those who in good faith had continued to support the struggle and had ensured that apartheid remained on the international agenda even when there had been little public interest and much hostility. "When the ground is prepared for seeds to take root," he told us, "changes come quickly when the time is right."

Early in 1985 the Canadian NGO and church communities watched with caution as the signals of a forthcoming change in Canadian policy multiplied. The clearest signal came from Joe Clark, the new secretary of state for External Affairs who promised a full review of recent South African developments and of Canadian responses to these developments. A few months later the Taskforce was suddenly thrust into quite a new role.

Round Table on South Africa (April 1985)

On 25 April the Taskforce accepted an invitation from Joe Clark to join a Round Table discussion with representatives from business, labour and academia on possible policy changes toward Southern Africa. Although pleased with the invitation, there were aspects which indicated that External Affairs was determined to minimize the significance of our participation. The invitation came by phone the day before the Round Table meeting and documents for the meeting were delivered by courier later the same evening. This discourtesy, we feared, was not unintentional. Moreover it was made clear that only the chair of the Taskforce would be welcome. As every organization that changes its chair annually knows, the participation of staff, because of their long-term acquaintance with the issues, is essential if the chair is to be adequately briefed on occasions such as this. In this instance the Taskforce board insisted that both the Reverend Tim Ryan, the chair, and I were to attend and External Affairs relented. We thus found ourselves in the unusual role as consultants to the government on policy options for the abolition of apartheid. The shift in the government's approach was slightly unnerving, as we had been accustomed to only minimalist positions on apartheid from both officials and from successive secretaries of state for External Affairs.

The Round Table discussions involved seven senior External Affairs officials, executives from Alcan, Falconbridge, Bata and the Canadian Exporters' Association, as well as Stephen Lewis, Canada's ambassador to the United Nations, and Shirley Carr and Paul Purritt from the Canadian Labour Congress. These last three were friends of the Taskforce with whom we had shared information on South Africa and Namibia. One academic, Heribert Adam, and one university administrator, Colin MacKay, were also present. Although there were many Canadian academics with whom the Taskforce had worked and who had a long record of engagement in the struggle against apartheid, neither Adam nor MacKay were among them. Missing from the Round Table as well were delegates of the many regional Canadian community organizations that had long supported strong anti-apartheid measures. The preponderant presence of External Affairs officials and business executives meant that the Round Table could not convey to Joe Clark a full sense of the appreciation that was expressed across Canada for his government's new openness to taking a more progressive stand.

A Discussion Paper[59] had been prepared by officials of the Africa Bureau of External Affairs. It asked participants to consider a list of Canadian policy options in the light of their effects on South Africa, on the Southern African region and on Canada, and to reflect on measures which might be taken in conjunction with other states. External Affairs also provided a review of policy positions taken by Canada and a comparison of these relative to other countries. In addition, a list of measures proposed by "United Nations bodies" and non-governmental organizations was provided, with External Affairs noting in each case their "possible repercussions, costs and constraints."

A close, though inevitably hasty examination of the Discussion Paper on the eve of the meeting revealed at once that it contained skewed background information, and incomplete and at times misleading comment on measures already taken. Overall it reflected a strong bias against any substantial policy changes. A detailed analysis furnished a depressing insight into the complacency with which External Affairs had responded to Clark's request that it bring forward options on how to strengthen Canadian policy on South Africa. In the course of the meeting it became evident that the Taskforce representatives were the only participants experienced and knowledgable enough to deal in detail with the key issues relating to investment and trade.[60] We therefore provided most of the detailed criticism of the External Affairs' document during the Round Table, criticism which we further developed in a subsequent brief to Clark.

The Discussion Paper first considered "What Canada has done to date."[61] It reported that Canada had

- refused "to recognize the governments or independence of the 'homelands' ";
- issued "political statements";
- "downgraded diplomatic representation in South Africa: closed consulates"; withdrawn trade commissioners;
- applied "an arms and military equipment embargo on South Africa in conformity with Security Council resolutions";
- "suspended active promotion of trade with South Africa: by withdrawing the Trade Commissioners previously assigned to South Africa; suspending EDC export loans and guarantees on Government and Corporate Accounts; ... suspending investment insurance";
- "terminated the Canada-South Africa Trade Agreement and the reciprocal tariff preferences included in it";
- "framed and introduced a government-sponsored Code of Conduct for Canadian companies operating in South Africa"; and
- "adopted a visa requirement for South Africans wishing to visit Canada in order to implement the sports boycott."

It was at once obvious that the authors of this paper were concerned to make Canadian initiatives appear as numerous and as substantial as possible. Thus they included actions such as withholding diplomatic recognition from the "homelands," issuing political statements and formally adhering to the UN arms embargoes which all, or almost all, member states of the UN would have been able to claim. They inserted the termination of the preferential tariff arrangements even though the reason for this was purely commercial and unrelated to any desire to exert pressure on the apartheid regime. They similarly included policy initiatives, such as those relating to the trade commissioners and the code of conduct, which as we have seen, had been minimally implemented and had fallen into disuse, or, as with the suspended EDC facilities, were already obsolete at the time of suspension.[62]

The Taskforce also detected several sleights of hand. On 19 December 1977 Don Jamieson, then secretary of state for External Affairs, had told the House of Commons that "Canada is phasing out *all* its government-sponsored, commercial-support activities in South Africa" (emphasis added), and he forecast additional economic actions.[63] The Discussion Paper for the Round Table omitted any direct mention of Jamieson's House of Commons statement. It presented as single and separate decisions those items from Jamieson's longer list on which the government had acted, but it excluded any mention of those policy decisions that had not been acted upon. External Affairs used the December 1977 terminology when it stated that Canada "[h]as suspended active promotion of trade with South Africa." But was this true? As noted above (chap. 2, p. 54) the Program for Export Marketing Development (PEMD) continued to support commercial activities in South Africa. Statistics available at the time of the Round Table indicated that in the 1978-83 period PEMD grants for companies seeking South African markets had amounted to $226,800.[64] Partly as a result, Canadian companies in South Africa had increased from twenty-one in 1978 to thirty-five in 1982.[65] External Affairs was therefore misleading the participants of the Round Table, the secretary of state for External Affairs included.

Nor was this the only deception employed in the discussion paper. External Affairs provided incomplete information about the EDC. It did not report that the EDC still continued to provide credit insurance and guarantees to Canadian exporters of goods to South Africa, a facility that was highly valued by Canadian exporters. Monitoring the EDC's Annual Reports, the Taskforce found steady increases since 1977 of export insurance granted to Canadian exporters for their sales to South African buyers. These had totalled roughly $184 million between 1978–84, with a peak of $53 million in 1984 alone, ensuring quite literally that trade relations between Canada and South Africa were enhanced rather than phased out.

Finally the discussion paper's review of Canadian measures stated, under the sub-heading "sports" rather than "political," that "a visa requirement" had been introduced for South Africans wishing to visit Canada, and that this was done in order to implement the sports boycott.[66] Don Jamieson, however, had announced the visa restrictions in his December 1977 speech without a single reference to the sports boycott. Instead he had linked the measure to South Africa's outdated Commonwealth privileges. "The fourth measure is related to South Africa's former membership in the Commonwealth which we now propose to change.

From a date to be announced [later determined as 1 April 1978] we will require non-immigrant visas *from all residents of South Africa* coming to Canada" (emphasis added).[67]

Although no public basis existed for External Affairs' notion that the visa requirement was linked exclusively to the sports boycott, the Department certainly implemented it accordingly. Thus the arrival in 1984 of executives from the South African and Namibian uranium industry was unimpeded when they joined Canadian corporate and government officials at a conference in Saskatoon about uranium and nuclear applications (see chap. 3, pp. 92–93) There was a further sleight of hand. It was transparently obvious that almost all the measures noted in April 1985 were those of December 1977. By totally omitting dates in the section "What Canada has done to date," External Affairs had sought to conceal the paucity of policy initiatives since then.

Under "Other Governments," the Discussion Paper first presented "[t]hose which have adopted more limited measures than Canada." Included in this group were Belgium, France, Italy, Japan, the United Kingdom, the United States and West Germany. None of these countries, the Paper noted, "have enacted sports measures as restrictive as Canada's. The majority tend to vote against or abstain more frequently on UN resolutions which oppose *apartheid* than Canada."[68]

No examples were given. We were surprised to find the United States in this list. External's own catalogue of US anti-apartheid positions included a number of measures for which there was no Canadian equivalent. The Discussion Paper, for example, reported that the United States Export-Import Bank did not provide export financing for South African companies unless they could prove that fair employment practices were being followed. No US government credits, export insurance or investment guarantees were available for goods destined for South Africa, and the US had discontinued government-financed trade missions to South Africa. External Affairs also informed the Round Table that the "USA private sector has introduced a voluntary code of conduct (Sullivan Code) for USA companies operating in South Africa. The code is likely to be extended to put further pressure on the companies which do adhere to it. A black list of those who do not adhere to the code is published."[69] The so-called Sullivan Principles (not Code) had invited companies with investment in South Africa to subscribe to six defined principles of employment conditions, and to commit themselves to make annual detailed reports on the implementation of each of these principles to a monitoring agency. Compliance reports were graded from I (highest) to IV (lowest) and were published giving the name of the company and the grade obtained.

In 1984, responding to requests from Bishop Tutu, the Sullivan Principles had been amplified in October and again in December 1984.[70] If codes of conduct were meant to matter at all, the Sullivan Principles were the most serious attempt to be effective. It brooked no comparison with Canada's government code.[71] For these several reasons, the United States should have been listed with those states whose policies on apartheid were more forthright than Canada's.

The second and third clusters of states whose policies the Discussion Paper reviewed were "[C]ountries which have adopted measures similar to those adopted by Canada" and "Countries which have adopted (or propose) more extreme measures than Canada."[72] The Paper placed only the Netherlands and Australia in the second category, but gathered together in the third "more extreme" category the Scandinavian and African countries as well as the Communist states of Eastern Europe. One must question why External Affairs grouped Canada's policies with only those of Australia and the Netherlands, while linking those of the Nordic and African countries with the policies of the East Bloc states. One is bound to conclude that the manner of presentation was designed to encourage a rejection of the position on apartheid held by the Scandinavian and African governments. Furthermore, External's use of the evocative term "more extreme" to characterize the third large cluster of very dissimilar states meant that it was possible to situate Canada in the middle ground between "more limited" and "more extreme," inducing the reader to prefer this, the "reasonable" centre of anti-apartheid measures.

A more useful analysis would have compared only the policies of member states of the Organization of Economic Cooperation and Development (OECD) as these are the states with which Canada normally compares itself. Dividing the OECD members into three categories denoting their South African policies—more limited, more active or similar to Canada—the analysis would have shown Denmark, the Netherlands, Norway, Sweden and the United States more active than Canada. That would have been a more logical classification, but it would not have had the reassuring effect that we hypothesize was the authors' intent.

The Discussion Paper contained other subliminal messages in its summary of the "more extreme" activities. For example, Scandinavian countries, the reader was told, "provide direct humanitarian aid to African liberation movements" and east bloc countries "provide arms to (illegal) African liberation movements."[73] Unaccountably, the African liberation movements had become "(illegal)" in the process.

The Paper commented that Sweden had tried to restrict investment.[74] In fact, Sweden was not trying to restrict investment, it had done so. In 1979 Sweden had enacted *Prohibition of Investment* legislation. By 1985 Sweden's position on South Africa had made it a leader on this issue among Western governments. Increasingly Sweden and other Scandinavian governments took the view that the continued presence of foreign investors in

South Africa could only be tolerated if they refrained from contributing to the maintenance of apartheid and publicly associated themselves with steps necessary to abolish apartheid.

In February 1985 the Taskforce had secured from the Swedish embassy in Ottawa a translation of the pending legislation that would further restrict Sweden's investment in South Africa. The bill had become law three weeks before the Round Table.[75] It was the representatives of the Taskforce rather than External Affairs officials who were able to inform the Round Table about the Swedish law. Indeed, they offered the Swedish initiatives as a model for new Canadian policies. The churches said that Sweden, like Canada, was a middlepower with relatively low levels of South African investment and that it enjoyed, also like Canada, a reputation for fairness and compassion. The new Swedish legislation for example, prohibited new direct and indirect investments as well as bank loans and bond sales for South Africa and Namibia. It obliged Swedish companies in South Africa and Namibia to report annually on their operations, to give details of their wages and benefits and to report as well on the social conditions of their employees and their families. Penalties for non-compliance included fines and up to two years imprisonment. The Swedish government had also barred the importation of uranium from South Africa and from Namibia as long as Namibia was illegally occupied by South Africa. Sweden's policies should not have been linked to those of east bloc states, dismissed as "more extreme" and then ignored.

Other Nordic states were in fact reviewing their policies in the light of the Swedish initiatives. For example, Denmark had joined Sweden to ask the IMF executive director for the Nordic States to review critically any South African application and to stress the negative effects of apartheid on South Africa's economy. Norway had instituted an oil embargo against South Africa. These measures had not been listed in External Affairs' Discussion Paper. It is thus legitimate to conclude that both the minister and the Round Table had been ill served by External Affairs' review of the policies of these other states; it was incomplete, misleading and manipulative.

The Discussion Paper included a section on "Measures proposed by United Nations bodies and non-government organizations."[76] It was organized in two parallel columns. Possible measures were listed on the left, with the right-hand column carrying External Affairs' comments on their "possible repercussions, costs and constraints." There was no column for advantages and benefits. The most that might be surmised was that External Affairs had no adverse reactions to those proposals which were left without negative comment.

Quite a few of the NGO and UN proposals related to trade. In the event that errant minds at the Round Table might be attracted by these, External Affairs had placed an ominous-sounding warning across page 6: "All trade embargoes would be in contravention of the General Agreement of Tariffs and Trade in the absence of an International Agreement or Chapter VII action by the U.N. Security Council (threat to international peace and security). Security Council action unlikely due to veto of permanent members." Soon after the Round Table this warning was effortlessly forgotten in favour of sanctions against South Africa, and for good reasons. History had in fact already provided the requisite precedence in 1977. The United Nations Security Council had invoked Chapter VII of the UN Charter to adopt UNSCR 418, the mandatory arms embargo against South Africa on the grounds that it constituted a threat to international peace and security.

Furthermore, in 1982 Canada had supported the UK in its call for international trade sanctions against Argentina after its invasion of the Falklands (Malvinas). In 1983 the United States—without reference to chapter 7 of the UN Charter—had cut its sugar imports from Nicaragua and in 1985 had expanded its trade war into a virtual trade embargo against Nicaragua. The GATT rules themselves offered the possibility of international trade sanctions against a member of the GATT under Article XXI, which sets out the "security exceptions." These exemptions have been successfully cited by contracting parties of the GATT when they engaged in trade actions, boycotts or embargoes for reasons related to peace and security: "In most cases there seems to have been a tacit acceptance of the right to take such measures, and this may best be represented as deriving from a broad interpretation of Article XXI(b)(iii)—the right to take action considered necessary for the protection of essential security interests in time of war or other emergency international relations."[77] It would have benefited the Round Table discussion had External Affairs mentioned the "security exemptions" of the GATT as an available option.

Further evidence of the Department's manifest antipathy to trade measures was provided by its negative comments on virtually all trade-related proposals. These often cited the danger of South African retaliations as constraints. This comment, for example, was offered on a proposal to embargo the export of high-tech and related capital goods which the Taskforce had made after External Affairs had awarded permits for the export of Control Data computer systems to South Africa's steel industry (see chap. 4, pp. 158–62 above). If such embargoes were adopted, the authors of the Discussion Paper warned, South Africa might restrict the flow of capital goods to neighbouring countries for whom it was a major supplier. Similar forebodings about South Africa's counter moves were voiced in response to a possible oil embargo and to bans on imports of Krugerrand and South African agricultural products.

Other proposals from NGOs (notably the Taskforce) that prompted negative reactions from External Affairs called for the suspension of the PEMD for South Africa and the suspension of EDC's export insurance coverage for

South African exporters. The Paper warned its readers of the obvious intent of such proposals, namely, that the first would reduce the ability of Canadian companies to win South African contracts and that the second would make insurance more costly for exporters who would have to make private insurance arrangements.[78] External Affairs stated flatly that legislated bans on bank loans to the South African government and the private sector and on new corporate investment would be unenforceable if applied only in Canada. They would only be effective, they said, if the banks and corporations agreed to voluntary restraints.[79]

The Discussion Paper also warned that any further downgrading or severing of Canadian diplomatic relations would "reduce Canada's ability to dialogue with South Africa."[80] "Dialogue" is another emotive term. If "more extreme measures" against apartheid had a negative subliminal message, "dialogue" implied positive and constructive problem solving. The reality, however, was that Canadian dialogue with South Africa at that time meant dialogue with "white" South Africa. As a means to secure fundamental change, it had been an exercise in futility over the past four decades. "Dialogue with South Africa" had very nearly become synonymous with collusion.[81]

We have noted that the closest the discussion paper came to endorsing any of the listed UN or NGO proposals, was when it conspicuously offered no objections to a few of them. However, only two proposals received this implicit approval and neither was of any real significance. The first of these called for the termination of the 1956 Double Taxation Agreement with South Africa. By 1985 the Agreement had lost all practical application, for by then, under Canadian tax law, Canadian companies operating abroad were in any case exempted from paying Canadian taxes on earnings taxed by the host government.[82] The second was the proposal to deny refuelling rights to South African aircraft. Given that South Africa had neither overflight nor landing rights in Canada, this item as well was superfluous.

The initiative that External Affairs found most acceptable was a strengthening of Canada's Code of Conduct. Repression in South Africa had reached such dimensions that foreign investors were finding it difficult to defend their continued operations there unless they could simultaneously present themselves as a liberalizing force and as protectors of their workers. With the right formulation and reporting mechanism, a code of conduct might have served this purpose. However, as chapter 6 illustrates, the Taskforce had been forced to conclude that Canada's Code had been of no practical value for black workers in South Africa. Moreover, by 1985, the Canadian Code, even a revamped one, seemed totally unsuited as a response to the racial violence and repression that was going on in South Africa. The churches nevertheless agonized about dismissing the exercise altogether and finally decided that the code could be supported if, but only if, the Code's legal status and requirements were much enhanced.

The Discussion Paper devoted six paragraphs to describing how the Code of Conduct could be strengthened, thereby indicating that the authors favoured this initiative over any other. Suggestions included two items that the churches had recommended in earlier years: a standard reporting format that was applicable as well to minority investors, and the appointment of a monitoring agency that would prepare annual reports to be presented to the secretary of state for External Affairs and tabled in the House of Commons. External Affairs, however, did not agree with the Taskforce that annual reporting be mandatory with certain consequences arising from non-compliance. External Affairs still claimed, as it had in 1982, that mandatory reporting would involve "applying Canadian law extra-territorially" and that it would be of "doubtful legal validity." The Discussion Paper also reported as fact that no other country had made the reporting on code of conduct compliance mandatory, an argument facilitated by ignorance of Sweden's recent legislation which had done just that. Thus even within those proposals that were favoured by External Affairs, the Discussion Paper suggested features that minimized the likely effectiveness of already very timid propositions.

The discussion paper had included the achievement of Namibia's independence as one of the "desirable goals" that Canada should pursue.[83] There was no other comment on Namibia. There was not even a reference to Canada's participation since 1978 in the UN Contact Group of States, created, it was claimed, to secure South Africa's cooperation for Namibia's early independence. In February 1984 I had represented the Taskforce at a meeting between External Affairs, Canadian NGOs and Sam Nujoma, president of SWAPO and after March 1990, president of Namibia. He had suggested that the Contact Group of States had outlived its usefulness. Canada, however, instead of formally ending membership in the Contact Group, was using it as justification to remain silent on Namibian issues in all debates—including those in the United Nations—ostensibly so as not to jeopardize the work of the Group.[84] This fiction, still alive in April 1985, was External Affairs' most likely reason for excluding Namibia from the Discussion Paper's historical review of Canada's actions and for keeping comments on Namibia to the minimum.

At the close of its assessment of possible new policies, the Discussion Paper commented: "Many of our Western partners may not be prepared to adopt punitive measures at this time. There would be difficulty in getting the permanent members of the United Nations Security Council to approve such measures. The effectiveness of punitive measures we take very much depends on collective action."[85] The general tenor and the specific analyses of the paper had clearly been designed to discourage the new secretary of state from any but the most minor initiatives. External Affairs was firmly opposed to trade and other economic sanctions, describing them as "punitive measures" to illustrate that they were unbecoming among countries with unbroken diplomatic relations.[86] Yet eliminating sanctions from their policy options had left External Affairs with little new to propose at the very time when Mulroney and Clark were looking for imaginative and innovative anti-apartheid measures. The South African struggle for liberation was in train, and all signs suggested it would intensify. Arguments in favour of international economic sanctions against South Africa were being advanced with ever greater urgency—not as punishment—but as a means to press the pace for political changes, to shorten the struggle and to minimize the terror and the loss of life that was occurring.[87] In 1985, External Affairs had yet to grasp the seriousness of this issue.

At the close of the Round Table meeting Joe Clark encouraged the participants to submit in writing their own policy recommendations and to explain the reasons given by others in the past for rejecting them. As he shook hands with us he asked that our submission be sent straight to his chief of staff. We took that to mean that he wished to by-pass the Department of External Affairs in order to hear our views without any accompanying annotations from the Department.

Member churches of the Taskforce, sensing that this time their submission might make a real difference to the government's policy decisions, prepared a major brief for the minister.[88] As before, the brief dealt with South Africa and Namibia and covered many of the issues reviewed in Part Two of this volume.

The Taskforce brief sought to interpret the context of Canadian policy towards South Africa in a radically different fashion from that offered by the Discussion Paper. Our brief argued that changes in Canadian policy were overdue, not only because of the intensification of popular resistance in South Africa and the worsening repression by the regime, but also because Canada's stance on apartheid had fallen seriously behind the stances of other Western states. The brief pointed out that even in the United States where President Reagan's policy of "constructive engagement" had opposed all congressional initiatives, a tough anti-apartheid bill had been introduced in March 1985 to both houses of Congress. This anti-apartheid bill would suspend new investments and bank loans to any sector in South Africa; US companies that violated the loan and investment bans would be liable to fines of up to $1 million. The bill would prohibit the import of Krugerrand and the export of all computers to South Africa. The bill stipulated that sanction measures be suspended only if the president and both houses of Congress agreed that Pretoria had taken steps to repeal apartheid.[89]

The Taskforce argued that the earlier contention that foreign investors in South Africa were "agents for change" had been proven wrong. Repression had increased immeasurably and the presence of foreign investors and bankers in South Africa lent legitimacy to the repression. More significant still, businessmen in South Africa had become intensely uncomfortable with the image they presented and were anxious for the first time to distance themselves from Botha's apartheid regime. As evidence for this the brief referred to the statement presented in January 1985 to Senator Edward Kennedy by six South African employers' associations.

The Taskforce's brief reflected two important political judgments which the Taskforce members had made by this time. First, the churches' assessment of the South African situation suggested that white opinion was beginning to contemplate the need for substantial reforms in order to avert international economic isolation. They therefore felt that tactically this was the moment to maximize international pressure on the Botha regime. In this, the Canadian churches' brief reflected the explicit position of their South African partners. In April 1985 a telex had communicated the first important decision on foreign investments by the Executive of the South African Council of Churches (SACC): "The Executive, in the full awareness of the emotional tensions, as well as the divisions aroused by the issue of disinvestment, nevertheless believes that a growing percentage of blacks, including organizations and trade unions with great influence, increasingly support the call to disinvestment as one of the few remaining methods to achieve justice without violence."

Equally important to the content of this brief was the second political assessment the members of the Taskforce had made. During its first years of operations they had assumed, despite clear differences of opinion, that External Affairs was essentially an ally in the fight to end apartheid. The 1981–83 exchange between the churches and the Department had changed this view.[90] The Taskforce had learned from this exchange that government policies regarding South Africa and Namibia, even when forcefully stated, were consistently interpreted as narrowly as possible and minimally implemented. Since then the Taskforce had come to view External Affairs, as it had viewed the private sector, as immobilized by its long historical ties to South Africa's white power structures and its unshakable faith in the beneficent consequences of foreign investment. However, following Mulroney's 1985 statements and Clark's Round Table consultation on policy changes, members of the Taskforce thought of the new Minister as an ally. They judged that it might be possible to offset very significantly the influence of External Affairs by providing Clark with proposals for policy initiatives that would be much closer to the role the churches wished Canada to play than any that had been suggested so far by External Affairs.

Acting on these two political judgments, members of the Taskforce prepared a brief that proposed a series of very specific changes in Canadian policy towards South Africa and Namibia, many of them advocated by the churches for the past decade. These were accompanied by careful exposi- tions of their context to show that the proposed initiatives were entirely feasible and appropriate, thus probing the readiness of the Mulroney gov- ernment to move ahead as promised. This brief, like previous ones, became an instrument of public education and was made available to an increasingly receptive news media and through the churches' own educa- tional networks. The brief made five main recommendations.

(1) The immediate termination of the Program for Export Market Devel- opment for South African business and the suspension of the Export Development Corporation's coverage of export insurance and guar- antees for exports to South Africa.

These two initiatives should have resulted from the Jamieson announce- ments seven years earlier, but had been stalled within the bureaucracy.

(2) A review of Canada's enforcement instruments for the mandatory arms embargo under UN Security Council Resolution 418.

Although External Affairs had always argued that the Export and Import Permits Act was sufficient for the full implementation of UNSC 418, the churches had remained unconvinced and wanted the embargo to be sub- ject to an Act of Parliament, setting out legal parameters, regulations and penalties for infractions that would include, but go beyond, the present provisions under the Export and Import Permits Act.

(3) Tighter export controls on high technology items.

The churches had become convinced that the restrictions imposed on the export of equipment that could be converted or diverted for the use of South Africa's military and police were insufficient. They argued that by 1985 South Africa was less dependent on the import of weapons and ammunition than it was on the import of high technology items which, although in themselves non-military, nevertheless served South Africa's increasingly sophisticated military and police apparatus. The churches were troubled that the government had not taken into account this qualitative change in South Africa's military needs and had continued to issue export permits for "non-strategic" high technology items.

A related recommendation called for the suspension of scientific, nuclear or military exchanges between South African and Canadian experts and for the suspension of South Africa's right to participate in ongoing committee work within the International Atomic Energy Agency. The churches insisted that these suspensions be observed as long as apart- heid was maintained and South Africa refused to sign the Nuclear Non- proliferation Treaty.

(4) Major revisions to the Canadian Code of Conduct for Canadian Companies operating in South Africa.

The wealth of relevant data that the Taskforce had collected since 1978 had made its members very sceptical about the value of this, or indeed any Canadian, code. Most Canadian investors held minority interests in large South African enterprises and had surrendered control or even influence on the day-to-day business operations. It therefore could not be claimed that these investments exerted a liberalizing influence. Time and again Canadian investors had told the Taskforce that they had no management responsibilities in companies in which they had invested, that they had no access to information about wages and working conditions, but that they had faith in their senior partner's enlightened employment policies. These peculiarities of Canadian minority investment alone should have shaken any remaining faith in the ability of the Canadian Code to improve employment conditions, let alone bring liberalizing influences to bear on the structures of apartheid, whatever that might mean.[91]

Moreover, in 1978 South Africa had adopted the Protection of Business Act in order to stifle just such influences. The Act restricted the enforcement by South African companies of foreign requests, orders or instructions.[92] Subsequently some companies, when withholding information from their shareholders, cited this Act.[93]

The 1985 brief recommended that a Canadian Code of any consequence would have to include the following elements: compliance with the Code would be mandatory; companies would disclose all supplies and sales to the South African military or police and to industries that supplied them; companies would make annual reports to an established monitoring agency according to a standard reporting formula and there would be a penalty for non-compliance. The monitoring agency would annually publish its findings including non-compliance data, listing each company by name. In addition, the churches recommended that companies should report on their efforts to promote:

- the right of all workers to live with their families near their place of work;

- the abolition of the migrant labour system and South Africa's "homeland" policy;

- the right of all South Africans to an equal, integrated and universal education system; and

- the repeal of all apartheid laws, including provisions of the Internal Security Act that permit arbitrary arrests, detention without trial, bans and house-arrests for reasons of political dissent.

(5) Divestment of Canadian companies directly or indirectly supplying the South African military and police.

Although South Africa's 1980 Key Points Act had drawn attention to the involvement of foreign investors in its strategic industries, Western governments had remained mute.[94] In a world obsessed with the threat of Communism, there was an implicit acceptance by Western countries and by companies directly or indirectly involved in military production, that South Africa, although nominally ostracized by a mandatory arms embargo, was entitled to keep secret the details of its defence arrangements. South Africa's Key Points Act therefore found understanding and acceptance.[95] Organizations such as the Taskforce, however, felt that the secrecy imposed by the Act concealed the very information the Canadian government ought to be seeking, namely the identity of the companies producing and supplying items for South Africa's military or police and the nature of these products. The Canadian churches had repeatedly pointed out the untenable contradiction in the activities of Canadian investors who directly or indirectly supplied South Africa's security forces. They were aiding the defence of the very system which they were putatively expected to liberalize by complying with the Canadian Code of Conduct. Such companies, the churches argued, should disinvest from South Africa.

The brief also included recommendations with regard to Canada's policy on Namibia. These were a reiteration of the points that the Taskforce had been making unsuccessfully for the last decade. They were, alas, no less pertinent in 1985 than they had been in 1975. Once again the Taskforce asked for compliance with United Nations Decree Nr. 1 of 1974 to halt the exploitation of Namibia's non-renewable resources while it was under the illegal occupation of South Africa, and the withdrawal of tax concessions from Canadian companies operating in Namibia under license and concessions from South Africa.

The churches used the occasion to acquaint the new secretary of state for External Affairs with the tangled history of Canada's most unacceptable import. Although Canada did not recognize South Africa's jurisdiction over Namibia, the government had continued to allow the importation and processing of Namibian uranium by Eldorado Nuclear Ltd.,[96] a Crown corporation. In April 1985 seven import certificates for the years 1985 and 1986 were in force. Until 1984 import permits of Namibian uranium had listed South Africa as the country of origin of the Namibian uranium. After the Taskforce had enquired whether this description indicated that Canada regarded Namibia as an integral part of South Africa, an official of the Atomic Energy Control Board informed us that import permits no longer required the name of the country of origin. Instead the permit now required the name of the "exporting country," which in the case of Namibian uranium would still be South Africa. With this little bureaucratic trick, Canada could no longer be accused of recognizing as legal South Africa's occupation of the territory. All the same, it remained unseemly and wrong that Canada, as a member of the UN Contact Group that was nominally dedicated to restoring to Namibians their birthright, would simultaneously grant itself rights to their depletable resources.

The brief urged the government to convene a meeting of the de facto defunct Contact Group and to propose a final report to the UN Security Council in order that this fictitious association be removed "from the books," and that consideration be given to mandatory measures to force South Africa's withdrawal from Namibia.

The Taskforce brief was dispatched on 16 May 1985. A short week later church representatives[97] met with the secretary of state, his spokesperson Sean Brady and senior officials of the department's special "Task Force on Southern Africa," which was assembled for the policy review.[98]

In welcoming the representatives of the churches, Clark said that the Conservative Party had a partisan history on the issue of South Africa, which it intended to pursue on a non-partisan basis if possible.[99] He was anxious to define a Canadian position on South Africa by the time of the Nassau Commonwealth meetings later in the year, but made it clear that Mulroney was pressing for some more immediate action, hence the "quick policy review" by the newly appointed External Affairs' Task Force. Clark expressed his personal scepticism about the effectiveness of sanctions, but asked the churches for examples of possible sanctions that might be proposed. The Taskforce representatives held to the strategy they had followed when preparing their brief for Clark. They pressed for measures that they thought would be easiest for Clark to adopt and hardest for External Affairs to oppose. They suggested for a start that the government should implement fully the policies announced in December 1977 which were intended to phase out all government-supported commercial activities in South Africa. To these should logically be added a ban on the export to South Africa of dual purpose or strategic items. Church representatives became alarmed when Eric Bergbusch, then chair of the Department's Task Force on South Africa, protested at once that the inclusion of strategic items would amount to "an economic embargo in disguise."[100]

Reviewing this consultation a decade later, and in the light of subsequent developments, one is struck by the intriguing position—or rather positions—that Clark revealed in the course of the meeting. He did not explain the need for a new policy on apartheid on the grounds of heightened repression in South Africa and black resistance to it. Rather, he alluded to an enlightened tradition within the Conservative party which he was following. Yet Clark expressed a personal scepticism about the wisdom and effectiveness of sanctions, and announced that he would make effec-

tiveness his criteria for any decision in regard to them. He stated bluntly
that he would not be influenced by what other countries had done. This,
church representatives felt, was a deliberate bid to distance himself from
their position, for they had cited numerous examples of more forthright
policies of other middle powers, notably the Scandinavians; as well they
had noted the strong proposals then pending in the US Congress. Clark's
rather strident pronouncements strangely contradicted the urgency with
which he had asked for a brief from the Taskforce and the speed with which
he had scheduled this meeting.

Clark also made a point of praising the viewpoints expressed by the companies at the Round Table and told the churches that he intended to consult the South African ambassador. This too sounded as if Clark was
putting the churches in their place. From letters and briefs, including the
one under discussion, External Affairs already knew that for many years the
churches had called on Alcan, Falconbridge and Bata (all three had been
represented at the Round Table) to modify or to halt their involvement in
South Africa. To praise their views on South Africa was to cast doubt on
the legitimacy of the Taskforce's position.

Had these blunt and uncompromising statements ended the exchange,
the Taskforce representatives would have been disheartened. They would
have seen that their expectations for a new policy on South Africa had been
misplaced since Clark's perspective did not seem to differ from the opin-
ions expressed by the Department's Discussion Paper at the April Round
Table. Why, then, had the Taskforce been summoned so urgently? The
answer to this riddle was surely that Clark, having made his official and his
personal position vigorously clear, also had an immediate job to do. Mulroney was determined to have new policy recommendations on his desk for
an early announcement and was, as well, looking for policy initiatives that
he could take to the October Commonwealth meeting. In May 1985 neither Clark's own position on sanctions nor those of the Department of
External Affairs were at all helpful. Thus Clark had summoned to Ottawa
the one organization that had available at short notice detailed policy recommendations of the sort the prime minister seemed to want. Clark badly
needed a first draft of a set of such recommendations which he and External
Affairs could then reshape and modify for an early policy announcement.
This appears to be the only plausible explanation for the extraordinary dis-
sonant nature of Clark's positions: his brusque reception of the churches'
representatives and their brief on the one hand, and on the other his apparent total dependency on the very policy proposals which he scorned and
which the Taskforce had to offer.

This would account for two further requests to which the churches
responded. Clark asked for names of South Africans who would be able to
help Canadian diplomats to interpret what was happening in South Africa

and who might suggest additional effective actions. Clark also asked for a concise tabulation of those church policy recommendations which, in our view, had been disregarded or insufficiently implemented by the previous government. He wanted these to be accompanied by the rationale that underlay the recommendations.

After ten years of anti-apartheid activities, the Taskforce earned appreciation from two uncommon sources. The secretary of state for External Affairs wrote to thank the Taskforce for

> the very sound and well enunciated advice which has been offered. The opinions expressed have always been, in my view, based on solid research and genuine desire to help the suffering people of South Africa. Your letter has once again served to contribute to our knowledge and to increase our contacts among knowledgeable and informed observers on South Africa. ... I thank you for all the work the Taskforce has done on this topic.[101]

The Globe and Mail in an editorial entitled "The Clerical Solution," gave rare praise to the churches. It disagreed that by isolating South Africa "pressure can be effectively applied upon apartheid," but found the "well researched brief . . . a useful contribution to the policy debate." The Taskforce appreciated the publicity for its main arguments and recommendations.[102] As will become clear, the Mulroney/Clark initiatives that followed in July and September of 1985 included many of the churches' recommendations, but their impact had been blunted by weak and vague formulation and, in important cases, by a reliance on voluntary compliance alone. It had been much more a case of the Taskforce being used as a resource by the Department of External Affairs than a conversion of External Affairs to positions long held by the churches.

Notes

1 From Beyers Naudé's reflections on 16 September 1984 just before his seven-year banning order was lifted, quoted in Ryan, Beyers Naudé: Pilgrimage of Faith, p. 203. Naudé, a prominent minister of the Nederduitse Gereformeerde Kerk, had been ostracized by his community and persecuted for his beliefs. He had been director of the ecumenical Christian Institute of South Africa until it too was outlawed in 1977 and Naudé was banned.
2 By the early 1980s the apartheid state was increasingly using the army in the repression of political resistance. In 1981 the *Defence Act* had been amended specifically to allow the mobilization and deployment of the South African Defence Forces to contain major popular uprisings (International Defence and Aid Fund, *Apartheid's Violence against Children* [London: IDAF Publications, 1988], p. 33).
3 International Defence and Aid Fund, *Apartheid: The Facts*, p. 108.
4 Ibid.
5 Ibid.

6 Wider powers under the state of emergency included the sealing off of black townships while search-and-arrest operations took place. The police and the army were empowered to: make arrests without a warrant and detain for up to two weeks, to be extended indefinitely or ordered released with conditions by order of the minister for law and order; bar media publication of the identities of detainees; bar contact with legal counsel except for express permission from the responsible minister or commissioner of police; search any building or vehicle; and issue orders on any matter in the interest of maintaining public order (*The Globe and Mail*, 22 July 1985).

7 International Defence and Aid Fund, *Apartheid's Violence against Children*, p. 25.

8 International Defence and Aid Fund, *Apartheid: The Facts*, p. 108.

9 For details see Sampson, *Black and Gold*, pp. 38–48. According to Anthony Sampson, Willard Butcher, chair of the Chase and soon nicknamed "the Butcher of the Rand," took the decision on technical grounds alone "with no indication of moral motives." But "soon afterwards he received a letter written on tattered toilet paper by a black political prisoner in South Africa, thanking the Chase. The sheets were carefully pieced together and xeroxed, to be circulated around the bank."

10 Ibid., pp. 57 and 337.

11 At the time Canadian banks had cited client/banker confidentiality for refusing to divulge the extent of their South African interbank lending.

12 This contrasts with an inflow of capital in 1984 of Rand 1.3 billion ("Flow of Capital from South Africa," *Weekly Mail*, 2–8 December 1988, p. 19, quoted in Price, *The Apartheid State in Crisis*, Figure 7.2, p. 228.

13 Boesak was a minister and moderator in the "coloured" Sendingkerk, the Dutch Reformed Mission Church. At a meeting in Ottawa in 1982 he had been elected president of the World Alliance of Reformed Churches, which denounced apartheid as heresy. In 1983 he was a co-founder and was elected a vice-president of the United Democratic Front.

14 Michael Valpy, "Kennedy's Visit Widens the Gaps in Already Divided South Africa," *The Globe and Mail*, 25 January 1985. The manifesto was submitted by Die Afrikaanse Handelsinstituut, The Association of Chambers of Commerce of South Africa, South Africa's Federated Chamber of Industries, National African Federation of Chamber of Commerce, Steel and Engineering Industries Federation (signatories and text of "Statement of the National Employer Groups of South Africa of January 7, 1985," reproduced by Prophets and Profits, New York, March 1985).

15 See chap. 2, p. 58, note 18 for the original role of the South African Foundation as a business lobby for "improving South Africa's image abroad" and as South Africa's host for all-expenses-paid visits to the country of "reliable supporters in key positions in the power structures of the world."

16 See Sampson, *Black and Gold*, pp. 254–55.

17 "Summary of Discussions between Certain Representatives of Big Business and Opinion-Makers in South Africa and the ANC, Held on 13th September 1985 in Zambia" (mimeograph), Lusaka, 14 September 1985. We have not been able to confirm the full accuracy of this Summary by cross-reference to any minutes kept by the visiting South Africans. However the Summary to which we had access had not been prepared for publicity but as a record for the internal use of the ANC. It can therefore be assumed that the ANC had made every effort to ensure accuracy.

18 Die Afrikaanse Handelsinstitut; the Association of Chambers of Commerce; the National African Federation of Chambers of Commerce; the Federated Chamber of Industries and the Urban Foundation.

19 *Business Day* (South Africa), 20 September 1985.

20 Ibid.

21 Ibid.
22 Ibid.
23 Michael Chester, "Rosholt Wants Clarity on Black Participation," *Johannesburg Star*, 4 December 1984.
24 Auret van Heerden, "Inside South Africa: Business Fights Sanctions," in Joseph Hanlon, ed., *South Africa: The Sanctions Report—Documents and Statistics* (London: Commonwealth Secretariat, 1990), p. 196.
25 All quotations in this paragraph are from *Business Day*, 20 September 1985.
26 Sampson, *Black and Gold*, p. 45.
27 One of the ninety-one signatories was Christopher Saunders, chair of the Tongaat Group of companies, Alcan's senior partner in South Africa and formerly a member of Botha's Defence Advisory Board. See chap. 2, p. 39 above.
28 *Johannesburg Sunday Times*, 29 September 1985.
29 *The New York Times*, 21 October 1985. A year to the day later, on 21 October 1986, Roger Smith announced that GM was pulling out of South Africa. "We have been disappointed in the pace of ending apartheid," he said (Sampson, *Black and Gold*, p. 334).
30 The abolition of the hated "pass laws" had been one of many issues demanded year in and year out by Helen Suzman, the intrepid member for the Progressive Federal Party in South Africa's legislature, who told the author that "when they were finally abolished, the situation was so bad that nobody paid any attention to this victory."
31 At the same time a row erupted at Stellenbosch University, of which Botha was chancellor. In October, he had confiscated the passports of nine students to prevent their meeting abroad with the ANC Youth League. The students mobilized impressive support for protest action from staff and fellow students and gave the row national and international prominence. It confirmed the ANC's resilience and growing popularity, even among South Africa's white youth. Tension had already been high following the judicial execution of one of South Africa's famous young poets, twenty-eight-year old Benjamin Moloise.
32 Organizations that were particularly helpful to the work of the Taskforce in this period included the ANC's Canada office; the Calgary Committee on Racism; CUSO; the Canadian SACTU Solidarity Committee and the Toronto Committee for the Liberation of Southern African Colonies (TCLSAC). Internationally the Taskforce's anti-apartheid network included the Interfaith Centre for Corporate Responsibility in New York, the End Loans to South Africa Committee in Britain, the World Campaign against Military and Nuclear Cooperation with South Africa in Norway, the Shipping Research Bureau of the Netherlands and the German Bank Aktion. From the beginning the Taskforce also relied on the wealth of factual information on developments in South Africa and Namibia provided by publications of the International Defence and Aid Fund for Southern Africa (IDAF), located in London, England, since being banned in South Africa in 1966.
33 The visit took place between 21 January and 2 February 1986 and included meetings with the ANC and SWAPO in Lusaka, Zambia. Members of the delegation were: the Most Rev. Gérard Drainville and the Most Rev. Faber MacDonald of the Canadian Catholic Conference of Bishops; Sister Thérèse Benguerel and the Rev. Alvin Gervais of the Canadian Religious Conference (respectively of Quebec and Manitoba); Professor Martin Mujica of the University of New Brunswick; and Thomas Johnston, Associate Executive Director of the Canadian Catholic Organization for Development and Peace.
34 My own visa request was closely questioned by the South African embassy. My passport with the visa was delivered two hours before my departure and granted only because the Canadian Bishops insisted that unless I could accompany them they would forego the visit themselves and publicize South Africa's conduct.

35 We learned here that rubber bullets, despite their reassuringly non-lethal connotation, were hard rubber projectiles, about five inches long and one inch in diameter. Fired at short distance from a high-velocity shotgun, they could both maim and kill.

36 Although there were no official figures for the scale of violence against children, a good estimate can be gleaned from material prepared by groups monitoring police actions. This indicates that for the years 1984 to 1986, 312 children were killed by police gunfire. Others were killed when run down by police vehicles and some were killed in police custody. Eleven thousand were detained without trial; 18,000 were arrested on charges arising out of protests; 173,000 were held awaiting trial in police cells. The estimates exclude children killed in the "homelands" by the South African army or by security forces (International Defence and Aid Fund, *Apartheid's Violence against Children*, Figure 1, pp. 13–14).

37 Drainville et al., *No Neutral Ground*, p. 18.

38 Ibid.

39 *The Kairos Document: A Theological Comment on the Political Crisis in South Africa*, Third World Theology Series (London: Catholic Institute for International Relations, 1986).

40 Ibid., p. 12.

41 Ibid., p. 13.

42 The two quotations relating to the question of "violence" are from ibid., pp. 14–15.

43 Ibid., pp. 24–25.

44 Church leaders came from Western Europe, North America, South Africa and other parts of Africa. They comprised representatives of the World Council of Churches, the World Alliance of Reformed Churches, the Lutheran World Federation and the All-Africa Council of Churches. They met in Harare from 4–6 December 1985 on the invitation of the World Council of Churches.

45 For references to decisions of the Lutheran World Federation and the Evangelical Lutheran Church in Canada, see David Pfrimmer, *The Evangelical Lutheran Church in Canada: Position on South Africa and Namibia*, edited by Pat Simonson (Winnipeg: The Division for Church and Society of the Evangelical Lutheran Church in Canada, 1987).

46 Ibid., p. 9.

47 Ibid., pp. 10–11.

48 Ryan, *Beyers Naudé: Pilgrimage of Faith*, p. 174.

49 International Defence and Aid Fund, *Apartheid: The Facts*, p. 35.

50 Pfrimmer, *The Evangelical Lutheran Church in Canada*, p. 15.

51 Dates of decisions and decision-making structures: The Anglican Church of Canada—The Executive Council (October 1985) and General Synod (June 1986); Canadian Conference of Catholic Bishops (no formal policy)—expressed through a letter from CCCB to the Prime Minister (15 October 1985); CCBC and Catholic Religious Orders—policy recommendations in Drainville et al., *No Neutral Ground* (April 1986), and participation in the preparation of Taskforce briefs to the Canadian government; Evangelical Lutheran Church in Canada—Church Council (October 1986); Presbyterian Church in Canada—107th, 110th and 112th General Assembly Recommendations (1981–87); and United Church of Canada—General Council Resolutions (August 1986).

52 South African Investment, Briefing for the Executive of General Council, November 1985.

53 As a postscript we note that the 31st General Council specified eight corporations whose shares ought to be sold forthwith. Of these IBM and General Motors decided to withdraw from South Africa in October 1986; Moore Corporation, Cominco, International Thomson and Xerox did so in 1987, leaving Minnesota Mining and Merck still in South Africa after 1987.

54 "Human Rights in South Africa and the Question of Sanctions. Comments prepared for the Parliamentary Standing Committee on Human Rights and presented by the Consultative Committee on Human Rights of the Canadian Council of Churches, the Inter-Church Coalition on Africa and the Taskforce on the Churches and Corporate Responsibility" (mimeograph), 14 July 1986, pp. 8–9 (Taskforce Archives).

55 These sanctions are fully discussed below chap. 6, pp. 188–92.

56 Mindful of the possible adverse impact of these trade embargoes on Canadian entrepreneurs, the churches requested financial assistance for such firms to enable them to find alternative suppliers and markets.

57 At the end of its hearings the Standing Committee resolved that unless by 30 September 1986 South Africa had agreed to take steps to dismantle apartheid and to transfer power in Namibia under UNSCR 435, "we call upon the Parliament of Canada to immediately enact legislation to prohibit economic trade and investment activity by Canadian companies and/or individuals with the Republic of South Africa, its government and its people" (Canada, House of Commons, Standing Committee on Human Rights, *Minutes of Proceedings and Evidence*, 17 July 1986, pp. 10, 118–19).

58 The United Church of Canada and the Inter-Church Committee on Africa had asked and the Department of External Affairs had refused to arrange a meeting between Tutu and Prime Minister Mulroney during Tutu's visit to Canada. That the two men nevertheless met in private on 20 December 1984 was due entirely to the determined efforts of Mary Anglin, a United Church activist in Ottawa, who set in motion an ad hoc group of parliamentarians, officials and herself which secured a date for this important meeting (interview with Mary Anglin, 15 June 1995).

59 Africa Bureau, Department of External Affairs, "Roundtable on South Africa," Discussion Paper, 22 April 1985 (mimeograph), unclassified, for official use only, 9 pages.

60 We were not competent to comment on those portions of the Discussion Paper which dealt with the international sports boycott and with government funding of NGO- or United Nations-administered projects in South Africa or Namibia.

61 Africa Bureau, Department of External Affairs, "Roundtable," pp. 1–2.

62 See chap. 2, pp. 53–56, for a detailed review of the inadequate implementation of the Canadian government 1977 policy changes.

63 Canada, House of Commons, *Debates*, 19 December 1977, p. 2000.

64 Calculated from tabulated Canadian PEMD dispersements 1972–83 in T.A. Keenleyside and Patricia Taylor, "The Impact of Human Rights Violations: A Contemporary Dilemma," *Behind the Headlines* (November 1984), p. 10.

65 Statistics Canada, August 1985.

66 Africa Bureau, Department of External Affairs, "Roundtable," 22 April 1985, p. 2.

67 Canada, House of Commons, *Debates*, 19 December 1977, p. 2000.

68 Africa Bureau, Department of External Affairs, "Roundtable," p. 4.

69 Ibid., p. 3.

70 The amplifications had asked signatory companies to campaign in South Africa for the right of black business to locate in urban areas, for complete freedom of mobility for black workers and for a unitary education system.

71 See chap. 2, pp. 54–56 for discussion of the 1978 Canadian Code of Conduct for companies operating in South Africa.

72 Africa Bureau, Department of External Affairs, "Roundtable," p. 5.

73 Ibid.

74 Ibid.

75 *Prohibition of Investments in South Africa and Namibia and Other Measures against Apartheid—An Unofficial Translation of the Swedish Government's New Bill on Prohibition of Investments in South Africa and Namibia* (Stockholm: Ministry of Foreign Affairs, February 1985). It had been signed into law on 1 April 1985.

76 Africa Bureau, Department of External Affairs, "Roundtable," pp. 5–8.

77 Edmond McGovern, *International Trade Regulation: GATT, The United States and the European Community* (Exeter: Globefield Press, 1986), pp. 423–24. I am indebted to Ann Weston of the North-South Institute who referred me to this volume.

78 Africa Bureau, Department of External Affairs, "Roundtable," p. 6.

79 Paradoxically External Affairs had come closer to the mark than it could have predicted. Only three months later the Chase Manhattan Bank refused to renew short-term South African loans, starting the largest "voluntary" ban ever by international bankers on loans to South Africa.

80 Africa Bureau, Department of External Affairs, "Roundtable," p. 7.

81 Writing about this particular period, Adam and Moodley captured well External Affairs' idea of dialogue with South Africa: "The South African Embassy in Ottawa and individual Canadian bureaucrats kept each other well abreast of minute manoeuvres. For example, the Embassy was informed about all the arguments of each participant of the roundtable sessions the next morning, although the meetings were supposed to be confidential" (Heribert Adam and Kogila Moodley, *Democratizing Southern Africa: Challenges for Canadian Policy* [Ottawa and Toronto: Canadian Institute for International Peace and Security, 1992], p. 104).

82 "Canada terminated the Canada-South Africa Trade Agreement in January 1980, and withdrew its tariff preferences to South Africa the following June. . . . Canada does allow Canadian companies to claim a deduction . . . for taxes paid to a foreign government on dividends repatriated to Canada by their overseas subsidiaries. . . . The rules [governing the tax relief] are of universal application" (letter to the Taskforce from the Hon. Mark MacGuigan and the Hon. Ed Lumley, 15 June 1982, pp. 4, 6, 12).

83 Africa Bureau, Department of External Affairs, "Roundtable," p. 1.

84 By 1985, the Contact Group had practically ceased to exist. Since 1981 the Reagan administration was involved in "constructive engagement"; its "Cuban linkage" had suspended attempts to achieve Namibian independence and justified US military support for South Africa's occupation of parts of Angola. In 1983 France formally announced that it had suspended its participation in the Contact Group. The British were training the Mozambiquan army and were no longer contributing to discussions of the Contact Group. The West Germans had abandoned Resolution 435 and were assisting the illegal South African administration by hosting constitutional conferences to promote permanent tribal structures for Namibia's "internal leaders."

85 Africa Bureau, Department of External Affairs, "Roundtable," p. 8.

86 Note the two occasions when the Canadian government vigorously and successfully intervened in the United Nations Security Council to avert resolutions on mandatory economic sanctions against South Africa to force its departure from Namibia: in 1977 by promising that the Contact Group of States would win South Africa's cooperation without sanctions, and in 1981 when Canada's ambassador announced the failure of the Contact Group and immediately lectured the Security Council that at this point sanctions against South Africa would likely be the worst course of action to follow.

87 This point was effectively made by a report commissioned in February 1988 for the Commonwealth Foreign Ministers' on Southern Africa at their first meeting in Lusaka: "Opponents of sanctions often describe them as 'punitive'—as punishment for South Africa because it maintains apartheid. This is wholly erroneous and a wilful misunderstanding. Sanctions should be seen as 'persuasive'—as a means of bringing pressure to bear and so persuading the white government of the necessity of entering into genuine negotiations. . . . This is why sanctions are an essential component of negotiations and not an alternative to them" (*South Africa: The Sanctions Report. Prepared for the Commonwealth Committee of Foreign Ministers on Southern Africa* [London: Penguin Group, 1989], p. 11).

88 Taskforce on the Churches and Corporate Responsibility, "Canadian Policy toward Southern Africa: A Brief Presented to the Rt. Hon. Joe Clark, Secretary of State for External Affairs (Toronto: Taskforce on the Churches and Corporate Responsibility, May 1985), 52 pages (photocopy).

89 This would include the de-nationalization of black South Africans; freedom for black work seekers to seek employment where they could find it; the end to forced removals; the abolition of the Group Areas' Act; negotiations with the true representatives of the black population; release of all political prisoners; implementation of UN Security Council Resolution 435 on Namibia (ibid., pp. 33–34).

90 See chap. 3, "The 1981–83 Exchange Between the Government and the Taskforce," pp. 75–89.

91 Such claims were also made for the American "Sullivan Principles" but with greater justification. US investment in South Africa had involved over 350 substantial and mainly wholly owned subsidiaries that had been able indeed to yield considerable influence for whatever cause they chose to further.

92 The adoption of the Act coincided with the publication of the first reports on the implementation by US companies in South Africa of the newly established Sullivan Principles.

93 Massey-Ferguson had reportedly invoked this Act to deny the members of the Taskforce employment data of South African companies in which M-F had investment. See chap. 4, p. 121.

94 Hulett Aluminum, Alcan's South African majority partner, was a Key Point Industry. See chap. 4, pp. 112–13.

95 See chap. 3, p. 78–79, for the 1982 response from the secretary of state for External Affairs to the Taskforce concerning South Africa's Key Points Act.

96 CAMECO Corporation since 1990.

97 The Rev. Clarke Raymond, executive director of Programs, General Synod, Anglican Church of Canada; Dr. Tony Clarke, director of (Anglophone) Social Action, Canadian Conference of Catholic Bishops; the Rev. David Pfrimmer, executive director, Lutheran Church of America, Canada Section; Moira Hutchinson, associate coordinator, Research of the Taskforce.

98 External Affairs' Taskforce on Southern Africa was headed by Eric J. Bergbusch until mid-1986, by John Schoiler until November 1989 and by Lucie Edwards until the External Affairs' Taskforce was dismantled in February 1992.

99 His reference was presumably to the fact that at the 1961 Commonwealth meeting, John Diefenbaker, then Canada's prime minister, had been the only "white" head of state to side with the Afro-Asian members of the Commonwealth and, ignoring External Affairs' advice, had opposed the readmittance of South Africa into the Commonwealth after it had changed its status to republic.

100 Taskforce on the Churches and Corporate Responsibility, Notes on Meeting with the Rt. Hon. Joe Clark, secretary of state for External Affairs, 22 May 1985 (photocopy), 3 pages.

101 Letter to W.R. Davis, chair of the Taskforce, 10 July 1985.

102 *The Globe and Mail*, 24 May 1985.

6 Canada's Anti-Apartheid Initiatives, 1985–86

For nearly eight years after Jamieson had announced the elements of a new Canadian policy towards South Africa, and despite overwhelming evidence of its ineffectiveness and minimal character, no efforts had been made to give firmer policy expression to the official rhetoric of hostility to apartheid. Then with the defeat of the Liberals and the election of a Conservative government under Brian Mulroney, Canada suddenly emerged to assume a leadership role, particularly in the Commonwealth, in the mobilization of greater international pressure on South Africa.

This new Canadian activism was not sustained beyond 1987 at the latest; it was not as consistent and strong as the government at times pretended it to be; it was mainly the result of prime ministerial insistence and implemented reluctantly and minimally in all areas that touched commercial interests. Nevertheless, in the early years, Canadian initiatives contributed in important ways to widen and deepen international pressures to end apartheid.

As the new Canadian policies were announced members of the Taskforce observed closely the various Commonwealth initiatives and Canada's role in regard to them. The Taskforce's usefulness to External Affairs ended as swiftly as it had begun and the churches were not consulted again as the Department and the Privy Council Office shaped the details of the new Canadian initiatives. The Taskforce thus resumed its role as an informed critic of government policy and as an active participant in the expanding network of Canadian anti-apartheid organizations.

This chapter will trace the learning process of the churches as they came to understand the political and bureaucratic dynamics that were moulding

---

Notes for chapter 6 are found on pp. 214–18.

official policies. The Taskforce's perception of these was greatly aided by the occasional internal government document that arrived anonymously, sent presumably by an official who shared the Taskforce's concerns. This chapter will review important Commonwealth initiatives that led to the introduction of economic sanctions more extensive than any that External Affairs had ever supported and that were therefore none too secure as they were minimized, at times softened, reinterpreted and inadequately implemented.

The Development of Canadian Policies, July to October 1985

Statement of 6 July 1985

The resolve of the Mulroney government to challenge the apartheid policies of the South African government found its first public articulation in Joe Clark's "Statement on South Africa" on 6 July 1985 at Baie Comeau, Quebec. The choice of Brian Mulroney's riding for this announcement in the middle of summer added political savvy and drama to the event. It suggested urgent consultations between the secretary of state for External Affairs and the prime minister resulting in resolute Canadian responses.

Clark prefaced his policy announcements with a strong and competent comment on the situation in South Africa, which satisfied prevailing public sentiments:

> Canada cannot tolerate a course which means continued repression within South Africa, and lawless raids outside—on countries which are our friends and our partners in the Commonwealth. There is a rising tide of revulsion in Canada—and elsewhere—at the injustices of *apartheid*. We cannot accept that the majority of South Africans should remain on the outside, deprived of dignity and basic human rights, harassed by police, arbitrarily held in detention, denied citizenship, some separated from their families, all deprived of a true voice in their own country's affairs. ... And the suffering is too great. It must not continue.[1]

Clark announced twelve anti-apartheid measures; ten of these paralleled policy recommendations that the Taskforce had presented to Clark eight weeks previously. While it was evident that the churches' proposals had provided the framework for the government measures, a detailed comparison between the two revealed a determined effort by Clark and External Affairs to lessen the practical impact and long-term effectiveness of the new initiatives. That minimizing process was immediately apparent, for topping the list of new measures that followed his grim portrait of apartheid were revisions to Canada's business Code of Conduct:

> (1) The government has decided to strengthen the voluntary "Code of Conduct Concerning the Employment Practices of Canadian Companies Operating in South Africa."[2]

The churches had long regarded the Code at best as ineffective and secondary. Nevertheless they had conceded that with certain, quite major amendments, the Code might bring some benefits to black workers and encourage Canadian companies to show their opposition to apartheid. Clark ignored these proposed amendments, but had borrowed the churches' terminology by announcing that the government had "decided to strengthen" the voluntary Code. Yet his changes to the Code amounted to no more than equipping it with an overdue monitoring and reporting structure.

> (2) The government will tighten its application of the United Nations arms embargo by restricting exports of sensitive equipment such as computers to the police, the armed forces, and other South African departments and agencies involved in the enforcement of apartheid.

This measure sounded similar to one of the recommendations made by the churches, but actually fell far short of it. They had advocated a prohibition of such exports to South Africa altogether rather than merely to "South African agencies involved in the enforcement of apartheid." The churches had also stressed that this prohibition should include all items that could be diverted or converted for the use of the military and police, such as aircraft, electronic and telecommunications equipment, computer systems and parts of each of these. The announced measure did not in fact change current practice but simply confirmed it. As we saw in the case of the Control Data computer sales to the iron and steel company of South Africa, although export permits were required, they were readily issued for sensitive high technology equipment as long as the sale was not directly to South Africa's police and military agencies. The Clark announcement thus in no way lessened the risk that high technology items would end up in the hands of the police, the military "and other agencies involved in the enforcement of apartheid."

> (3) The government has accepted the voluntary United Nations arms embargo on the <u>importation</u> of arms manufactured in South Africa. This measure was recommended by the UN Security Council late last year. It will now be in force in Canada.(underlining in the original)

This voluntary measure had not been part of the churches' recommendations. Neither they nor indeed anyone else had anticipated that Canada might import South African arms. This measure must reflect an intent to inflate the significance of Canada's new policy position.

> (4) The Canada-South Africa Double Taxation Agreements will be abrogated.

The abrogation of the Agreement had been recommended by the churches as a welcome though symbolic action. However it had no real direct consequence. Canadian tax law permitted Canadian investors abroad to deduct from their Canadian taxes, taxes paid to host governments anywhere; South Africa and Namibia were not exempted.

(5) The Programme for Export Market Development (PEMD) will no longer be available to Canadian exporters for market development in South Africa.

The churches wholeheartedly welcomed this measure, which they had recommended.

(6) We are terminating the applicability to South Africa of global insurance policies issued by the Export Development Corporation under Section 24 of its Act.

This measure as well corresponded to the churches' proposal. With it, Clark had brought Canada into line with the practices of the USA, Sweden, Denmark, Norway and Holland, who had already suspended their state-financed export insurance for exports to South Africa.

(7) Canada has been a faithful adherent of the sports boycott first agreed at the Commonwealth Meeting in 1977. We are now reaffirming our backing of the boycott on sporting contacts between nationally-representative Canadian and South African athletes.

The Taskforce recognized the importance of the international boycott of sports with South Africa, but had never itself directly addressed it.

(8) As a further voluntary measure, under Security Council Resolution 283, which recommended that countries end commercial activities related to Namibia by agencies under government control, the government has decided to terminate all toll-processing of Namibian uranium imported from South Africa.[3] Such processing, has been carried out under contracts between Eldorado Nuclear, a crown corporation, and parties in third countries. Existing contracts will be honoured but no new contracts for the processing of Namibian uranium imported from South Africa will be entered into. Should South Africa set a date for the implementation of the UN Plan for Namibian independence, we shall consider rescinding this measure.

Suspending the pillage of Namibia's depletable resources had been a standing recommendation of the Taskforce since 1975. It therefore welcomed Clark's announcement, but with profound reservations. The Taskforce learned that current contracts for the processing of Namibian uranium were scheduled to run until at least 1988. That no new contracts would be signed was applauded, but the Taskforce was dismayed that present contracts continued. The churches argued that if it was wrong after 1988 to import and process Namibian uranium, it was wrong in 1985 and had indeed been wrong since 1966, when the United Nations General Assembly had voted with Canada's support to terminate South Africa's rule over Namibia. Clark made clear, as had the Trudeau government before him, that Security Council Resolution 283 of 1970 had *recommended,* but had not made mandatory, an end to "commercial activities related to Namibia by agencies under government control" to underscore that Canada had been under no legal obligation to implement resolution 283.[4] Neither in July 1985 nor at any subsequent date did Clark terminate tax concessions for taxes paid to the illegal regime by Canadian companies operating in Namibia.

(9) The Security Council recently recommended that governments prohibit the sale of Krugerrands in their jurisdiction. Because that may involve problems with GATT, we have decided to discourage their sale by drawing that resolution to the attention of all Canadians and by conveying it to the financial institutions which deal in gold coins.[5] I would emphasize that the Security Council's resolution is not binding. There is therefore no coercion in this matter but our consultations made us confident that the recommendation will be respected.

The churches had recommended a *ban* on the import of Krugerrand. They were discouraged by the faint-hearted formulation of the measure. Just how faint-hearted was underlined by the fact that the government was not planning any further "discouragement" beyond this announcement. Clark was probably right in his assumption that there was little need for further government pressure. But he was wrong to claim success for himself in this measure. Without the international campaign against the trade in Krugerrand and popular pressure on Canada's financial institutions, his Krugerrand measure would hardly have passed any "effectiveness test."[6]

Clark had in fact singled out the call to prohibit the sale of Krugerrand from a multifaceted UN Security Council resolution which he failed to identify. UNSC Resolution 566 of 19 June 1985 had also urged UN member states to take voluntary measures against South Africa, including suspension of new investments and the application of disincentives to achieve this goal; reexamination of maritime and aerial relations with South Africa; and restrictions on sport and cultural relations. Clark referred to none of these additional recommendations.

(10) Because cooperation between government departments and agencies may directly or indirectly lend support to the enforcement of apartheid, the government has decided to monitor more closely contacts between federal departments and agencies and departments and agencies of the South African government, particularly in sensitive areas.

Clark's tenth measure did not explain the meaning of "monitor more closely" nor what were the "sensitive areas" to which he referred. The churches could only hope that this vague commitment would include the halt that they had recommended in scientific exchanges between Canadian and South African uranium experts, which had taken place in previous years.

The churches had made the point that Canada should be at least as scrupulous about such scientific exchanges as it was about the sports boycott.

In sum, the first Canadian sanctions were most modest. Of the ten measures, only three, the government's suspension of the PEMD for South Africa, the termination of the EDC's insurance coverage for exports to South Africa and the strengthening of the sports boycott were significant. In contrast, the remaining seven measures were in turn either insignificant, symbolic, postponed, imaginary or unclear. The voluntary Code of Conduct, the voluntary embargo on the importation of arms manufactured in South Africa and the official discouragement of the sale of Krugerrand were insignificant. The abrogation of the Canada-South Africa Double Taxation Agreement was purely symbolic. The termination of Namibian uranium processing was postponed for ongoing contracts and the decision to restrict the exports of sensitive and high technology equipment represented no change at all. Finally, the decision to "monitor more closely contacts" between Canadian and South African public servants, "particularly in sensitive areas," was cloaked in such vague terms that its meaning seemed to be deliberately obscured.

Clark did hold out hope for additional measures. He did this on 6 July and again on 14 August 1985, when he announced the recall of Canada's Ambassador to South Africa: "The measures announced . . . were a first step in the review of policy towards South Africa . . . we are looking to the South African government to take real and practical steps to dismantle apartheid. Unless we see concrete actions not just vague intentions, further measures to oppose apartheid will be adopted."[7] Clark also encouraged interested organizations to submit their views to a joint House of Commons-Senate committee which was conducting hearings on Canadian foreign policy at this time.

Statement of 13 September 1985

In a lengthy statement to the House of Commons on 13 September, Clark announced a number of new measures and restated those announced on 6 July. He stressed the timeliness of government actions, given the emergence of opposition to the Botha regime in South Africa's business community. He invited "as part of our duty" expressions of Canadian anti-apartheid outrage "to show the South African government how deeply [Canadians] are offended by their racist practices." Simultaneously he admonished those who advocated that Canada sever all diplomatic and commercial relations with South Africa. Had the government done so, he argued "we would have been in no position . . . to add to the pressure being felt by the South African government." Nevertheless, Clark told the House that "Canada is prepared to invoke total sanctions if there is no change . . . [and that] the

Government of South Africa should have no doubt that we will invoke full sanctions unless there is tangible movement away from apartheid."[8]

Clark called for the release from prison of "all those whose offence is simply to oppose apartheid" and urged that Nelson Mandela as well as Desmond Tutu and Allan Boesak be included "among those who should be invited for dialogue, not rebuffed or relegated to silence, or dismissed with contempt."[9] However he made no reference to the African National Congress, the United Democratic Front and other black opposition organizations whose struggle against apartheid had spanned several decades. Rather Clark went out of his way to give disproportionate weight to the belated reformism of prominent business leaders whose recent statements had raised expectations that their activities would soon transform apartheid.[10] This is not surprising. The Canadian government's decision to increase pressure on the apartheid government was centrally motivated by a desire to support the call for reform that was coming from within the white business elite.[11]

Clark told the House:

> Bishop Tutu can no doubt bear his rebuff from President Botha. Both Nelson Mandela and Allan Boesak may bear their imprisonment. But can South Africa bear the result? It is clear that one community in South Africa, the business community, is beginning to have its doubts.
>
> Their confidence shaken, business and investors within and outside South Africa have fostered a wave of disinvestment—without the prompting of governments, but surely reflecting both the events on the ground in South Africa and the signals many governments have sent.
>
> If some South African entrepreneurs have, for too long, lent support to apartheid, the consequence of their movement now cannot be overstated. Canada's contribution to bringing about those new realities recognized by South African business has been significant. Our policy, through several administrations, has been one of consistent opposition to apartheid.[12]

This was an extravagant reading of recent South African history. It was of course true that South Africa's business associations were exasperated by Botha's stubbornness, which they held responsible for much of the loss of business confidence. But had they "fostered a wave of disinvestment"? By September 1985 international banks had ceased lending to South Africa and some foreign companies were disinvesting. These developments had however been deplored—not fostered—by South Africa's business associations and had prompted their call for reforms. They had in fact explicitly and emphatically counselled against disinvestment often on the grounds that reforms could only take place in an atmosphere of increased investment and business confidence. As Clark moved closer to a more serious consideration of economic sanctions he sought, deliberately but inaccurately, to generate the impression that he was responding not to long-standing demands from South African black leaders, the churches and other anti-apartheid organizations in Canada, but to the advice of South African business.

The disinvestment that had taken place was not due to "signals many governments have sent" and least of all to any signals from the Canadian government prior to 6 July 1985. Disinvestment had taken place because black resistance was making apartheid a bad risk and because persistent hard work on the part of the churches and non-governmental organizations in many countries had made continued business in South Africa a public embarrassment. Clark's remarks on disinvestment were disingenuous. His statement, that Canada through its consistent opposition to apartheid over several administrations had significantly contributed to "bringing about those new realities recognized by South Africa's business" was wrong to the point of being preposterous.

In his 13 September statement to the House of Commons, Clark announced a number of additional measures "as part of our continuing pressure on apartheid."[13]

> (1) A voluntary ban on loans to the Government of South Africa and all its agencies. We are asking all Canadian banks to apply such a ban and we have reason to believe that they will do so. Some have already acted on their own and we welcome that. The ban will not affect any outstanding credits nor prevent loans that would clearly be to the benefit of blacks.[14]

By the end of 1984, as we have seen, Canadian banks had themselves decided to extend no new, direct loans to the South African government and its agencies. The call for a voluntary ban on loans therefore requested nothing that was not already bank policy. However Clark had not made any mention of two further bank activities that would be of help to South Africa—their participation in bond issues, which had already been addressed by the Taskforce, and their participation in interbank lending to South African banks.[15]

> (2) [T]he appointment of Mr. Albert Hart as Administrator of the [voluntary] Canadian Code of Conduct ... We are issuing today a Standard Reporting Format for the annual public reports which have been requested under the Code of Conduct.

> (3) [A] voluntary ban on the sale of crude oil and refined [petroleum] products to South Africa ... Our sales in this area have been limited in the past. This measure is being taken now to ensure that Canada does not become an alternative source of supply in the future.

> (4) [A]n embargo on air transport between Canada and South Africa ... [for] both cargo and passenger flights. As we have no bilateral air agreement ... the effect of this measure is therefore to stop charter flights and reciprocal air service.

The appointment of a Code administrator had been included in the 6 July statement, and the air transport embargo was largely symbolic. However, the ban on the export of crude oil and petroleum products to South Africa was, potentially at least, an important sanction measure. This initiative was nevertheless weaker than it ought to have been. Crude oil and petroleum products were correctly classified by oil-starved South Africa as military commodities. Therefore oil exploration and conversion services and equipment should have been included in the Canadian measure. Malcolm Fraser, when chair of the United Nations Panel on the Activities of Transnational Corporations in South Africa had recommended "that the existing oil embargo be made mandatory, and that there should be no supplies of equipment, services or technology to this sector ... because of the instrumental role of military and police power in the enforcement of apartheid and ... the importance of energy in sustaining these activities."[16] We will return to this issue in a subsequent section; it transpired later that External Affairs was trying to redefine petroleum products in order to lessen the coverage of even this voluntary commitment.[17]

Clark told the House that the government was engaged in several high level consultations in preparation for the meeting of the Commonwealth Heads of Government in mid-October and for the opening session of the United Nations General Assembly which would follow shortly after. Included in these consultations were President Julius Nyerere of Tanzania, who had paid an official visit to Canada in July, and Sir Shridath Ramphal, secretary general of the Commonwealth, who was expected in early October. In addition, there were to be consultations with the Front Line States and, though not mentioned by Clark, a visit from Sir Geoffrey Howe, the British foreign secretary. Clark ended his comments with this stern warning:

> As the world speaks, the unusual phenomenon of growing pressure on the South African government from within that country will be given an opportunity to bear fruit. Our actions today; those taken by other governments and those which will be taken will, collectively, keep the pressure on. If the Government of South Africa remains unbending to that pressure, then *Canada will be left with no resort but to end our relations absolutely.* (Emphasis added)[18]

External Affairs Bypassed

By late September 1985 Mulroney had become impatient for reliable and imaginative advice on Southern Africa policy options and looked for help beyond the Department of External Affairs and its newly formed Southern Africa Task Force. On 27 September Mulroney asked Bernard Wood, then executive director of the North-South Institute, to be his personal representative to the Southern African Front Line States (FLS).[19] Wood was to visit the FLS to convey to them the sincerity of the prime minister's commitment to fundamental change in South Africa and to seek a consensus on how best to proceed cooperatively at the upcoming Commonwealth Heads of Government Meeting (CHOGM). These were tasks that would normally be carried out by a senior official of the Department of External Affairs or by someone from the Privy Council Office. Wood's own writing about this period delicately suggests that senior officials in External Affairs were out of sympathy with the activist turn of Canadian policy. "South Africa's odious character, and the torrent of unrest, resistance and repression ... were fully accepted by the middle of 1985 as grounds for priority by the Canadian political leadership, although somewhat less fully at the senior official level."[20]

Wood met with the heads of government of Zambia, Botswana, Zimbabwe and Tanzania. He met as well with the secretary general of the ANC, this itself constituting an advance since Canada until then had shunned all official contact.[21] Wood reported that a broad consensus existed among the FLS for a strong stand by the Commonwealth on Southern Africa. "The Commonwealth must pass the test of advancing the cause," Wood wrote, "... it should seek consensus but it must be consensus with movement."[22] He explained why economic sanctions were required and that Canada need not fear that past inaction would impede its leadership in 1985:

> Acceptance ... of the principle of sanctions, or measures outside of economic pressure, will be essential, especially since selective sanctions and the threat of more have already been working in fact, together with internal pressures and the worsening financial and business climate.... The Front Line States are encouraged, if some a little surprised by the vigorous and sustained Canadian measures of recent months ... Canada does not need to prove anything about its recent performance on Southern Africa ... although scepticism can always re-emerge.[23]

Indeed Wood noted that Mulroney was regarded as "having the greatest potential moderating influence" in persuading Prime Minister Thatcher to abandon her adamant opposition to sanctions. Wood was confident that the FLS would not call for comprehensive economic sanctions, providing the Commonwealth agreed on a core list of selective sanctions and resolved to maintain the pressure on South Africa, and assuming that no new South African provocation occurred.

Wood reported that the minimum package of measures that would be acceptable to the FLS at CHOGM would include:

- fullest enforcement and penalties on the arms embargo and tougher penalties for violations;
- fullest implementation of the oil embargo;
- ending of all official assistance for export and investment promotion; and
- discouragement of South African tourist promotion.

In addition, a further tightening of the sports boycott and an increase in humanitarian assistance would represent the "minimum package." This could be augmented, Wood noted, by various action-oriented studies on, for example, the feasibility of restricting new investment in and agricultural imports from South Africa, of cutting air links altogether or on the possible damage to the FLS of increased sanctions. Wood reported that the FLS who were the most exposed to South Africa's military and economic aggression were "prepared to accept this, in order to help pressure South Africa," but would need to be exempted from certain kind of sanctions.[24]

Wood also reported great scepticism among the FLS about the usefulness of continuing the Contact Group of States which seven years earlier had undertaken to end South Africa's rule in Namibia. Since Reagan had in 1981 linked consideration of Namibia's independence to the departure of Cubans from Angola, the Contact Group had ceased to function. Wood found the leaders of the FLS deeply frustrated over the Group's failure to shift the US position and to prevent South Africa's military incursions deep into Angola. Wood admitted to Canada's own discomfort in the Contact Group and hoped that "perhaps Canada can help, even in this morass." Wood offered Robert Mugabe's suggestion that Canada reopen discussion of Namibian independence when the Group of Seven next met, the rationale being that the Group of Seven was more representative of the members of the Contact Group than was the Commonwealth. As an alternative, Wood noted that the French had received international approval for their withdrawal from the Contact Group and pondered whether "Canada could at least send a public signal of diminishing patience by following suit."[25]

In the fall of 1985, Cranford Pratt, a political scientist at the University of Toronto, was visited on very short notice by Bob Fowler, then a senior official in the Privy Council Office (PCO). He told Pratt that Mulroney had turned from External Affairs to the PCO for advice on the next round of sanctions and asked Pratt for his suggestions. Fowler, as Clark had done in his consultation with the Taskforce, also requested detailed justifications for Pratt's proposals and a rehearsal of critical comments that might be advanced against them. Drawing on easily arranged briefings (!) with the staff of the Taskforce, Pratt stressed that it was necessary for the government to introduce for the first time economic sanctions on normal trading relationships that would have real bite. He advised Fowler to focus on Canada's military relationships to the apartheid government and to propose a ban on Canadian loans to or investment in South African enterprises with sales—direct or indirect—to South Africa's military and police. Pratt reasoned that these measures were imperative in order to give integrity to Ottawa's insistence that changes in South Africa be achieved by peaceful means.

Official Policy Review

Sometime in late 1985, the Taskforce received anonymously a copy of a document, *South Africa Policy Review—Commonwealth Heads of Government Meeting*, which had been prepared by officials of External Affairs and the Privy Council for the 8 October meeting of the Cabinet Committee on Priorities and Planning. It contained an eight-page proposal and Wood's telegraphed report from which we have already quoted.[26] It contributed greatly to our understanding of the objectives being pursued by the government and will be explained here in some detail.

The Policy Review was concerned to define for Canada a position that might reconcile Margaret Thatcher's adamant anti-sanctions position with the impatience for sanctions of the FLS, supported by Australia and by Third World members of the Commonwealth. The review noted, "Our moderate stance gives us more influence with the British than, say, Australia whose position is eccentric."[27] It advised Cabinet that the recent extensive consultations had attuned Canada better "than most Commonwealth members" to find common ground for positive decisions at the CHOGM. It stressed that the Front Line States "want *selective action* but are not in private pressing for extreme measures" (emphasis in the original). Importantly, the Cabinet Committee was assured of "general domestic support for the Government's current stance."[28]

In the section headed "Canadian Strategy," ministers were assured that Mulroney would try to avoid isolating Britain without, however, forfeiting the trust of the FLS and other Commonwealth members in Canada's seriousness: "For Canada, the inclusion of the measures we have already adopted possibly augmented by a commitment *to consider* some [additional] measures . . . (e.g. government procurement, measures re Namibia, or even something on investment) should suffice" (emphasis in the original).[29] The ministers were advised that the measures Canada had already taken should be of advantage when "drawing a distinction between *agreed* measures and steps *recommended* for consideration . . ." (emphasis in the original).[30] Most of Canada's new commitments would therefore be minimal and most could take the form of studies, missions or seminars.

Under the heading "For Defensive Use," the *Policy Review* offered suggestions in the defence of the recommendations. It argued that stepping up the pressure on South Africa was opportune because it would reinforce internal trends in South Africa which the PCO attributed to "business pressure"—making no reference to black resistance.[31]

The Cabinet Committee was cautioned that it would be unwise to introduce more stringent sanctions such as bans on agricultural products or trade and financial boycotts. Britain would "not go along with such measures" nor would they "be endorsed by the *USA* in the [UN] Security Council" (emphasis in the original). Moreover, "Recent studies by Canadian officials ... demonstrate that such measures would have severe consequences for some Canadian firms and on South Africa's neighbours."[32]

The conclusion is inescapable that the authors of the PCO *Policy Review*, like those of External Affairs' *Round Table Discussion Paper* in April, were hostile to economic sanctions and sought to minimize Canada's commitment to them while striving nevertheless to preserve Canada's new international image as a leading participant in the fight against apartheid.

The *Policy Review* had referred to studies by Canadian officials that projected the adverse effects of stronger trade and financial sanctions on Canadian enterprises and on South Africa's neighbouring states. However, the data (summarized in an annex to the cabinet paper) would hardly suggest to most observers though they did to the authors of the review, that these adverse effects were significant.[33] It reported that banning exports would lose Canada 0.2 percent of her export market, while South African exports would be cut by 1 percent. Even for the two major industries exporting to South Africa, sulphur and pulp, banning exports would provide only "short-term" difficulties until they found substitute markets. Banning imports would affect "Canada's iron and steel industry and certain manufacturers would be hurt, at least in the short term, by an embargo on the import of strategic minerals and metals from South Africa."

The studies showed that a ban on further investment [in South Africa] "should not cause any significant hardship to that country's economy." Direct Canadian investment in October 1985 was estimated to be about 1 percent of South Africa's total foreign investment with only 0.6 percent of its foreign debt owed to Canada. Yet despite this evidence, the study did not conclude that Canada could therefore tighten its sanctions without too great a sacrifice. Instead it concluded that "tightening sanctions would be useless as they would have little impact on its [South African] economy." But—and here we discover the fundamental reason behind this line of argument—the annex reported:

> While neither country's economy as a whole would be significantly affected by comprehensive Canadian sanctions, *specific Canadian firms* with substantial interests in South Africa could be harmed. In particular, those with a titanium mine near Richards Bay, or with a significant part interest in the Rossing uranium mine in Namibia, could be affected, depending on the scope and breadth of the Canadian government actions. (Emphasis in the original)

The two companies in question were identified as Quebec Iron and Titanium and Rio Algom.[34]

Had the Taskforce needed it, this paragraph would have been an eye-opener. On many occasions the churches had turned in good faith to External Affairs to ask for a change of policy that would halt Rio Algom's untenable involvement in Namibia. As part owner of the Rossing uranium mine, it was exploiting Namibia's non-renewable resources under license of South Africa's illegal administration. For this activity Canadian taxpayers underwrote deductions allowed by Revenue Canada for taxes paid by Rio Algom to the illegal occupying power. Yet in this cabinet paper senior officials of the government went out of their way to warn that "comprehensive Canadian sanctions" could harm Rio Algom's 10 percent interest in the Namibian uranium mine.[35]

The reference to Quebec Iron and Titanium was no more reassuring. In 1976, the Montreal-based Quebec Iron and Titanium Corporation (QIT-Fer et Titane inc.) had entered into an agreement with South African enterprises to establish Richards Bay Heavy Metals, a titanium sand mining and smelting operation in Natal.[36] From 1982 on, the second largest shareholder (after QIT) was the South African state-owned Industrial Development Corporation (IDC).[37] Although the government felt that there would be general support by the people of Canada for strong government action against the apartheid regime, these questionable investments by the two companies, one in South Africa and one in Namibia, were enough to sway senior advisors to recommend against comprehensive or even stronger selective sanctions.

Finally, in the spirit of "every cloud has a silver lining," the Policy Review assured the Cabinet Committee, that the very presence of the British at the CHOGM would have a constraining effect: "Given the British position, we do not anticipate Canada will be confronted at Nassau with serious proposals for mandatory or comprehensive measures."[38]

Nassau Commonwealth Meeting[39]

On 20 October 1985 the heads of governments of the Commonwealth met in Lyford Cay, Nassau. They successfully negotiated there the "Commonwealth Accord on Southern Africa." It called on the South African government to take these five steps toward ending apartheid:

(1) Declare that the system of apartheid will be dismantled and specific and meaningful action taken in fulfilment of that intent;

(2) Terminate the state of emergency;

(3) Release immediately and unconditionally Nelson Mandela and all others imprisoned and detained for their opposition to apartheid;

(4) Establish political freedom and specifically lift the existing ban on the African National Congress and other political parties; and

(5) Initiate, in the context of a suspension of violence on all sides, a process of dialogue across lines of colour, politics and religion, with a view to establishing a non-racial and representative government.

Nassau's most prominent decision was to appoint seven persons from Commonwealth countries—The Eminent Persons Group—with a mandate to facilitate the processes of change along these lines. The heads of governments also proposed that the member states of the Commonwealth proceed to implement a new set of sanctions. The majority of these initiatives, just as the privy council officials had predicted, were identical with the Canadian sanctions already announced by Clark on 6 July and 13 September. The Commonwealth declared its support for "the strictest enforcement of the mandatory arms embargo against South Africa"; Canada had announced this measure on 6 July. The Commonwealth recommended a ban on "all new government loans to the Government of South Africa and its agencies"; on 13 September Canada had disclosed an agreement with the Canadian banks to observe a "voluntary ban on new commercial loans to the South African government and its agencies" (except for loans "to the benefit of blacks," a gratuitous qualification which was omitted from the Commonwealth text). The Commonwealth proposed a unilateral ban on the import of Krugerrands; Clark had reported that Canada's financial institutions had agreed voluntarily to stop selling the coins. The Commonwealth also recommended an embargo on "all military cooperation with South Africa and discouraged joint participation in "all cultural and scientific events" except those that contributed to the ending of apartheid; Clark, on 6 July, had announced that Canada would monitor more closely such contacts "particularly in sensitive areas." Finally, the Nassau Accord's recommendation that members ban "the sale and export of oil to South Africa" had been anticipated in Clark's 13 September announcement.

There were, however, a few important differences between the Nassau recommendations and the positions already taken by the Mulroney government. In particular, Canada's commitment to restrict high technology exports remained crucially at variance with the wording of the Commonwealth communiqué. Commonwealth heads of governments had agreed to ban "the sale and export of computer equipment *capable of use* by South African military forces, police or security forces" (emphasis added).[40] In contrast, on 6 July Joe Clark had announced that Canada was restricting "exports of sensitive equipment such as computers *to* the police, the armed forces, and other South African department and agencies involved in the enforcement of apartheid" (emphasis added).[41] Canada did not then adjust its policy after the Nassau meeting to match that of the Commonwealth agreement. The difference in the wording was not simply a matter of semantics. The Nassau Accord was based on a recognition that most high-technology items could be used for civilian as well as for military purposes. For that reason it called for a ban on the export to South Africa of all such items that could be diverted or converted for military purposes. It was not until 27 September 1988 that Canada caught up with the 1985 Commonwealth sanction measure and announced that it would ban Canadian export of high-technology items "*to any end-user in South Africa.*" Canadian high-technology exports to South Africa—excluding those directly to the police, military and related agencies—were thus permitted until late in 1988, in contravention of the Nassau Accord.

The very considerable overlap of the measures recommended by the Nassau CHOGM with those already taken by Canada suggests that Canada had substantially shaped the Commonwealth's agenda of action. It is reasonable to suggest that the FLS, anxious to keep Canada firmly in the vocal anti-apartheid camp, were ready to permit Canada to identify the initiatives to be endorsed. Canada's influence can also be discerned in a further set of measures which the meeting agreed would be invoked in six months if no adequate progress had been made in dismantling apartheid. These measures included a ban on air links with South Africa, which had been announced by Clark in his 13 September statement; the abrogation of double taxation agreements with South Africa, which had been announced by Clark on 6 July; and the termination of all government assistance to investment in and trade with South Africa, a recommendation that corresponded to Canada's 6 July suspension of EDC and PEMD coverage for South Africa. Canada, however, also accepted new measures to be held in reserve. They included four that Canada itself had not proposed or anticipated:

• a ban on new investment or reinvestment of profits earned in South Africa;

• a ban on all government procurement in South Africa;

• a ban on government contracts with majority-owned South African companies; and

• a ban on the promotion of tourism to South Africa.

Mulroney did not hesitate to accept their addition to the list and Canada was thereby committed to a set of sanctions that was stronger than those advocated by External Affairs (and the PCO).

Mulroney's Address to the United Nations

No other Canadian remarks on South Africa have been received with as much public enthusiasm, or remembered for as long by anti-apartheid organizations everywhere, as those delivered to the General Assembly of the United Nations by Brian Mulroney on 23 October 1985. Although these remarks filled but one page of his address, they earned him a standing ovation. They raised hopes in Canada, as well as in South Africa's resistance movement, that at long last Canada was taking its place alongside the Nordic states and Third World nations in a firm commitment to freedom and democracy in South Africa. Echoing Joe Clark's remarks to the House of Commons a month earlier, Mulroney referred to the unprecedented opposition to apartheid by South Africa's business community and suggested that internal dissent and external condemnation were already taking their toll on the government. But the words that brought the UN to its feet were these: "My Government has said to Canadians that if there are not fundamental changes in South Africa, we are prepared to invoke total sanctions against that country and its repressive regime. If there is no progress in the dismantling of apartheid, our relations with South Africa may have to be severed absolutely."[42] Mulroney had gone straight to the United Nations from his first Commonwealth Heads of Government meeting. No doubt this recent immersion in a major debate of heads of government dealing with international actions against apartheid had contributed to the vigour and resoluteness of the prime minister's statement at the United Nations. But it would be wrong, as some commentators have done, to attribute Mulroney's UN remarks to a momentary enthusiasm rather than to a clear Canadian policy position that had already been enunciated and would be repeated. This was not the Prime Minister's "high-wire-act . . . in which he *unilaterally* threatened the potential total break with South Africa" (emphasis added).[43] Mulroney's speech at the UN in fact mirrored in all respects Clark's statement to the House of Commons a month earlier.[44] Like Clark, Mulroney identified Mandela, Tutu and Boesak as representative of the struggle but forbore any reference to liberation movements or internal resistance organizations; like Clark, he paid tribute to South Africa's business community, which he credited with "unprecedented opposition to apartheid"; and like Clark, Mulroney assured his audience that Canada was prepared to invoke total sanctions and sever its diplomatic relations with South Africa.

The significance that ought to be attached to the Prime Minister's statement to the UN General Assembly became a public issue two years later when, despite greatly increased repression in South Africa, the Canadian government neither imposed total sanctions nor severed diplomatic relations. Adam and Moodley, in a study sponsored by the Canadian Institute for International Peace and Security, and Bernard Wood, then its director, tried to explain away this major retreat. Adam and Moodley, when commenting on criticism from NGOs and academics that the government was stalling on sanctions, suggested that these critics had misread the government's earlier policy positions: "The accusations stemmed more from disappointment that Ottawa had not met certain NGO expectations than from an accurate perception of the policy."[45] Bernard Wood acknowledged Mulroney's UN speech but dismissed its importance, seeing it rather as a "deviation" from a "fairly carefully calibrated strategy."[46]

Their effort to marginalize the importance of Mulroney's UN speech cannot be sustained. Not only had Joe Clark anticipated in an earlier speech the main components of Mulroney's UN remarks, he also reaffirmed on later occasions the same set of policies. This is how Clark, in February 1987, prefaced a major address on Canada's evolving position on apartheid: "let me repeat *the position of this Government of Canada.* It was stated, clearly and early, by the Prime Minister in the General Assembly of the United Nations on October 23, 1985. Let me quote the two key sentences" (emphasis added).[47]

Clark then repeated the passage from that speech which we quoted above. Again in November 1987 Clark confirmed this same basic position of the government in a statement to the House of Commons: "South Africa should be in no doubt that, if other measures fail, all of Canada's economic and diplomatic contacts will be terminated."[48] The record is thus incontrovertible. Mulroney's UN speech in October 1985 was in no way an eccentric self -indulgence. It was a considered statement of policy that Clark had articulated as well, before and after the prime minister's UN speech. NGOs and academics had not been deluded; they had perceived this policy correctly and had supported it. They were to react strongly when the government abandoned this position in 1987 at a time of much greater repression in South Africa.

The Circumstances of Economic Sanctions in 1986

Hopes were high late in 1985 that the manifold pressures on the apartheid regime would lead to positive change. These pressures came from the undiminished black uprisings, the collapse of confidence of foreign business, the flight of capital and insistence on reforms on the part of the South African business elite. To provide added point and focus to these pressures, the Commonwealth late in 1985 had created the Eminent Persons Group (EPG) with the specific mandate to facilitate a process of change in South Africa.

Mission to South Africa

The EPG went to work almost at once.[49] After preliminary meetings in London it spent February and March 1986 in Southern Africa. The group consulted members of the government, representatives of parliamentary parties and of the business community, members of the resistance movements and the South African churches.

The EPG accepted, but only partially, that business leaders had great potential to assert effective pressure on the Botha regime. Their leverage, the EPG suggested, was based on the calculation that "the prosperity of the country depended upon achieving improvements in black purchasing power and the creation of more skilled jobs for blacks."[50]

The EPG noted that business leaders had "a clear preference for dealing with 'moderate' blacks' " who, in their view, "held out the best hope for a peaceful and prosperous future." After consultations with majority black organizations, the EPG commented diplomatically: "Our clear impression was that the business community was seeking peaceful reform along the middle-ground but was, to some extent, out of touch with black opinion. We expressed the view that they could and should exert greater pressure on the Government."[51] The EPG also consulted with member churches of the South African Council of Churches and the Southern African Catholic Bishops Conference. The EPG reported fully on the circumstances that made

> the church with its extensive grassroots contacts and intimate knowledge of the problems and difficulties of ordinary people, ... an accurate barometer of the popular mood. ... We found the church a force for change. This applied both to the leadership and the laity, to the cities and townships as well as the rural areas. At the parish level we spoke with clergy who in normal circumstances would have been content to pursue their pastoral duties, but now found themselves compelled to speak out against injustice and racism because of their pastoral concern for people—detention and trial, misrepresentation and harassment, threats and injury. Church buildings have become almost the only sure refuge for freedom of expression and interracial association, and even their sanctity is at times periodically violated.[52]

The EPG noted the important distinction made by the churches between "reforms," which were the objective of the government and the business community, and the replacement of the system of apartheid with a unified, non-racial and democratic South Africa, which was the objective of the progressive churches in South Africa. The churches observed that people's patience was wearing thin and violent resistance to a violent system was increasingly being seen as the only alternative. Failure to dismantle apartheid, they warned, would increase violence and bloodshed.

Before returning to London in late April 1986, members of the EPG also met with government leaders of the Front Line States and with exiled leaders of the liberation movements. The Group then drafted its "Possible Negotiating Concept," a set of proposals which they hoped would lead to a negotiated phasing-out of apartheid. It outlined concrete steps which the EPG had concluded must be taken by the apartheid government and its opponents to create the preconditions for serious negotiations about constitutional change. For the South African government these involved:

(1) Removal of the military from the townships, providing for freedom of assembly and discussion and suspension of detention without trial;

(2) The release of Nelson Mandela and other political prisoners and detainees; and

(3) The unbanning of the ANC and PAC and the permitting of normal political activity.

The EPG proposal also required of the ANC, other liberation movements in exile and of the internal resistance movement, to agree to enter into serious negotiations and to suspend violence.[53] The EPG communicated these proposals first to the South African government, which manifested far greater reluctance to negotiate than the EPG had been led to believe. The EPG also presented its proposals to the ANC in Zambia and met with representatives of the UDF, COSATU and AZAPO in South Africa. The EPG reported that "each of these groups responded with keen interest."[54]

As the EPG was preparing for a meeting with the South African Cabinet Constitutional Committee on the morning of 19 May 1986, the South African Broadcasting Corporation announced that South African commandos had attacked Harare, Gaberone and Lusaka, allegedly targeting "ANC bases." The Group was affronted by this wanton action: "It was all too plain that, while talking to the Group about negotiations and peaceful solutions, the government had been planning these armed attacks."[55]

It was convinced that the timing of the raids had been designed to force it to abandon its mission. It therefore decided to hold its ground and to meet the Cabinet committee. There it faced a myriad of further objections that indicated a determination to stall. The government, for example, made the impossible demand that the ANC unilaterally not just suspend, but renounce violence for all time, regardless of the outcome of negotiations. The EPG had to concede that it saw confirmed the forebodings of the many who had warned it not to put faith in the South African government.

The EPG then cut short its mission[56] and released its report on 12 June 1986. The Group wrote that its inability to fulfil the terms of the Nassau Commonwealth Accord was due entirely to the South African government's unwillingness to pursue a realistic negotiation process. The EPG reminded the Commonwealth of its commitment to adopt further economic measures in the event that adequate progress towards ending apartheid had not been made within a period of six months and urged the adoption of them immediately.[57] It warned that in the absence of a concerted effort to demonstrate that the Commonwealth was serious, the South African government could easily conclude

> that it would always remain protected from such measures, ... [In that case] the process of change in South Africa is unlikely to increase in momentum and the descent into violence would be accelerated. In these circumstances, the cost in lives may have to be counted in millions.... [The question] is not whether such measures will compel change; it is already the case that their absence and Pretoria's belief that they need not be feared, defers change.[58]

Increasing Pressure for Economic Sanctions

The deliberately insulting rejection of the mediation efforts of the EPG and the imposition of the second, and even harsher, state of emergency generated mounting pressure on the Canadian government that it make good its promise to step up economic sanctions commensurate with the rise in South Africa's repression. That pressure had indeed begun even before the collapse of the EPG initiative. On 2 April 1986 Bishop Desmond Tutu, by then a major voice for black liberation, called a press conference in South Africa.[59] He encapsulated with typical succinctness the agony of South Africa and the challenge to the international community presented by the near civil war conditions in his country. In public defiance of South Africa's security laws he pleaded: "Our children are dying. Our land is burning and bleeding and so I call upon the international community to apply punitive sanctions against this Government to help us establish a new South Africa that is non-racial, democratic, participatory and just. This is a non-violent strategy to help us do so."[60] Tutu's courage to call for economic sanctions from within South Africa inspired the Taskforce to become even more insistent and to seize every opportunity to propose actions that would complement the struggle for justice going on that country. The Taskforce wrote to the prime minister on 8 April asking him to respond to Tutu by strengthening existing economic sanctions and adding new measures. As a priority, the churches proposed legislation to block all possible venues of supplies to South Africa's security forces and nuclear industries. They asked that the voluntary ban on new loans include as well bond placements and cover any borrower—public or private—in South Africa or Namibia. The churches sought termination of the use of contract labour by Canadian investors and the extension of Canada's oil embargo to include a ban on the transport of oil and oil products by Canadian vessels to South Africa from a third country. Referring to the prime minister's statement to the United Nations that he was prepared to invoke total sanctions, the churches asked that a date be determined by which comprehensive sanctions would be adopted if there were no major change for the better.[61]

In his reply, the prime minister did not respond to the request for a timetable, but he did reiterate that "if there are not fundamental changes in South Africa, we are prepared to invoke total sanctions against that country." Without any comment on the churches' specific recommendations, the prime minister expressed confidence in the efficacy of the pressure on South Africa that was being exerted by the international community.[62]

In July 1985 Joe Clark had pledged that the conclusions of the two parliamentary bodies, the Special Joint Committee on Canada's International Relations and the House of Commons Standing Committee on Human Rights, would be an additional basis for the government's policy decisions on Southern Africa. The Taskforce had been among many Canadian organizations that had appeared before both committees.[63]

The Special Joint Committee on Canada's International Relations released its findings at the end of June 1986. On Canada's relations with

South Africa, the Committee unanimously recommended: "Now that the Group of Eminent Persons has reported—as we feared it would—that no significant progress is occurring in dismantling apartheid, Canada should move immediately to impose full economic sanctions, seek their adoption by the greatest number of Commonwealth members, and promote similar action by non-Commonwealth countries."[64] It also recommended that contacts be expanded with the highest levels of black political organizations in South Africa and that assistance to black neighbouring countries be increased.

Soon after, the House of Commons Standing Committee on Human Rights specified in similar forthright language that if the South African government had not agreed by 30 September 1986 to the negotiating process set out in the Nassau Accord and if it continued to refuse Namibia's independence under UN Security Council Resolution 435, the Parliament of Canada should "enact legislation to prohibit economic trade and investment activity by Canadian companies and / or individuals with the Republic of South Africa, its government or people."[65]

The Canadian government did not then nor later implement the considered recommendations of either of these parliamentary committees, leaving disillusioned the many organizations who had devoted time and energy to presenting well-argued briefs.

An early public indication of the onset of government ambivalence regarding further economic sanctions came with the official responses to South Africa's murderous air and commando raids against Zambia, Zimbabwe and Botswana on 19 May 1986. To be sure, Clark expressed Canada's "outrage at this inexplicable and arbitrary act of violence" and strongly condemned South Africa's military attacks on the three Front Line States. He also extended sympathy to the governments and condolences to the victims of the raids.[66] But he made no mention of additional economic sanctions or any other concrete measure against South Africa nor did he offer immediate assistance to the affected states.

On 12 June 1986, the date of the release in London of the report of the Eminent Persons Group, Joe Clark made a further statement to the House of Commons. His reference to South Africa's military raids on Commonwealth allies was limited to these remarks: "Twenty-three days ago, while the Eminent Persons Group was still in Capetown, the Government of South Africa launched bombs and raids on Zambia, Zimbabwe and Botswana."[67]

Clark warned the House that "the temptation" was great to conclude that South Africa would never respond to "our entreaties." But that was not the view of the EPG which, he said, believed that "steady pressure is essential to any prospect of peaceful change."[68] Clark's paraphrasing of the EPG's conclusions entirely failed to convey the impatience and sense of urgency of the closing paragraph of the EPG's report: "The question in front of the Heads of Government is in our view clear. . . . Is the Commonwealth to stand by and allow the cycle of violence to continue? Or will it take concerted action of an effective kind? Such action may offer the last opportunity to avert what could be the worst bloodbath since the Second World War."[69] Clark did announce several measures, two of them economic sanctions from the list of additional actions in the Nassau Commonwealth Accord. He ended government procurement of South African products and urged provincial governments to do the same. Clark also asked for a voluntary ban on the promotion of tourism in South Africa. He cancelled accreditation to Canada of four South African attachés of the South African mission in Washington for Science, Mining, Labour and Agriculture. He announced additional funding for educational projects in South Africa and told the House that the Canadian Embassy would remain closed on 16 July, the tenth anniversary of the Soweto uprisings.

Clark assured the House that Canada would remain in the "forefront of those who oppose apartheid" and warned: "These measures do not rule out further steps in the future. On the contrary, they portend more severe measures, if the South African Government continues to refuse to enter a dialogue except on its own terms."[70] Few within the Canadian churches felt that these limited additions to existing government sanctions were in any way an adequate response to South Africa's wilful termination of the EPG's mission and to its military raids against the Front Line States. The leaders of the Anglican, Catholic, Lutheran, Presbyterian and United Churches decided to issue a "Church Leaders' Letter" to the Prime Minister. In preparation for this, members of the Taskforce met with senior External Affairs officials on 18 June 1986. Taskforce members were given copies of two sets of sanctions from the Nassau Commonwealth Accord. The first set were sanctions under paragraph 6, which had already been adopted. The second set, under paragraph 7, were sanctions proposed for adoption if South Africa failed to make progress in dismantling apartheid. Since the regime had wilfully aborted the EPG mission, there was no doubt that the Commonwealth Review Committee would seek adoption of this reserve list of sanctions.[71]

External Affairs told the members of the Taskforce that Canada was ready to adopt the final four additional measures proposed under paragraph 7, although at least two of these had not been favoured by the government. In contrast to earlier opposition to all trade embargoes because they would violate GATT rules, External Affairs no longer objected to "a ban on the import of agricultural products" and "a ban on all government procurement in South Africa." However, although Canada would go along with the remaining two measures, External Affairs had strong reservations about each of them. A "ban on new investment or reinvestment of profits earned in South Africa," officials felt, was far more difficult to implement than the proposed ban implied. Its effect would simply pressure foreign companies to withdraw from South Africa altogether, an observation which they saw as an argument against, rather than in favour of, a ban on new investments.

External Affairs officials were also unhappy about "a ban on government contracts with majority-owned South African companies." They worried that this measure would create problems for Canadian industry. They reported that Clark had met with negative reactions on an open-line radio program in Flin Flon, Manitoba, to any move toward comprehensive sanctions against South Africa. The main employer in Flin Flon was Hudson Bay Mining and Smelting (HBMS) a company in which Anglo American Corporation of South Africa held the majority interest.

The Nassau Accord was silent on how the new economic sanctions should be implemented. Church representatives commented that voluntary Canadian sanctions, such as applied to corporate and bank involvement, were more difficult to monitor and to enforce than legislated and mandatory sanctions. External Affairs however offered the argument—rejected as absurd by the Taskforce—that voluntary commitments were superior to legislated measures since they showed that a wider section of the Canadian public concurred with sanctions. Officials added—as a new twist—that legislated sanctions might also conflict with the Canadian Charter of Rights and Freedoms.[72]

Reminded by the churches that the prime minister had promised total sanctions if there was no progress in the dismantling of apartheid, officials suggested that it was entirely hypothetical to speculate about how long certain conditions would need to prevail before Canada would impose comprehensive economic sanctions. Presaging what was soon to become one of Clark's main argument against comprehensive sanctions, External Affairs cautioned that Canada was not a "major player" and primary efforts ought to be made to bring those with a larger stake in South Africa "on side." Canada was not interested in moral purity, the churches were instructed, but in effectiveness. and it was therefore consulting with the USA, Germany, France, Ireland, Switzerland and the Nordic states to find common ground for concerted international pressure on South Africa.

Taskforce members were troubled. They feared that Canada's avowed preoccupation with diplomatic efforts to coordinate states with larger stakes in South Africa to impose economic sanctions, was furnishing Canada with an excuse to retard its own economic sanctions. Church representatives gained the distinct impression that even after the Nassau Commonwealth Accord, External Affairs' great caution against any strong anti-apartheid initiatives had changed little from the days of the Liberal government. The dramatic change in Canadian policy announced with passion by the prime minister and with vigour by the secretary of state for External Affairs, had left their officials unmoved. In the meeting with the Taskforce they had maintained their minimalist approach and a pugnacious resistance to suggestions that economic sanctions be tightened.

By the time Canada's church leaders came to write to the prime minister, the South African government had imposed its second state of emergency. At midnight on 12 June 1986 a nationwide state of emergency had blanketed the whole country, outstripping in severity previous clamp-downs. It brought to an end the ability of the national and international news media to report events anywhere in South Africa. Indeed, a twelve-hour blackout had been declared on the news of the emergency itself to safeguard an element of surprise as South Africa's security forces swept the country arresting undisclosed numbers of opponents.[73] In many ways this state of emergency was aimed at the media, particularly the international media. Under cover of censorship, the regime could reach deep into the townships and smash the networks of the local structures and civic organizations. The unprecedented harsh censorship brought down the curtain on the daily television, radio and newspaper reports of armed repression and resistance, which had kept alive, before the international public, the realities of apartheid. The regime had calculated that the pervasive censorship would simply dry up the flow of daily information on repression and resistance in South Africa and thereby check international outrage. Although this ploy was obvious to the established news media, it was at least partially effective, since most were reluctant to use the many alternative news services that had begun reporting clandestinely from South Africa, because their reports could not be verified.[74] The apartheid government at once stepped in with its version of events and in particular with a campaign that blamed the continuing uprisings against it on foreign—mainly communist elements associated with the ANC—which the government said, needed to be weeded out before reforms could begin.[75]

As a result of these developments the "Church Leaders' Letter" to the prime minister of 10 July 1986 took on a particular urgency. The Canadian churches regarded the forthcoming meeting of the Commonwealth Review Committee in August 1986[76] as a decisive moment to take concrete steps against apartheid in the light of Botha's manifest unyielding position. The Church leaders therefore proposed Canadian legislation to:

- ban South African agricultural imports;

- ban exports to South Africa of all high-technology equipment useful to the military, police or nuclear sectors;

- require withdrawal of Canadian investment involved in supplies to South Africa's police, military or nuclear sectors; require the withdrawal of companies employing contract labour and of companies from South Africa-occupied Namibia; and

• end all nuclear cooperation with South Africa, including all private or public sector scientific exchanges.

Canada's church leaders urged direct contact between the Government of Canada and the ANC and SWAPO, as well as increased support for the front line states and for South African refugees and political prisoners.

London Commonwealth Review Committee, August 1986

Margaret Thatcher's continuing antagonism to economic sanctions made unanimous agreements among the seven heads of state who constituted this committee impossible.[77] Thus the six heads of state of Australia, Bahamas, Canada, India, Zambia and Zimbabwe, but not Britain, adopted those sanctions that had been earmarked under paragraph 7 of the Nassau Accord. They added several measures which they agreed to commend for adoption to the rest of the Commonwealth and the wider international community. Canada, having already adopted the majority of the items on this list, thus agreed to the following additional measures which Joe Clark introduced during the remainder of 1986:

• a [voluntary] ban on new investment and reinvestment of profits earned in South Africa (confirmed 19 November 1986);[78]

• a ban on government contracts with majority-owned South African companies;

• a ban on the import of agricultural products, uranium, coal, iron and steel (effective 1 October 1986);[79]

• a tightening of the [voluntary] ban on new bank loans to any borrower in South Africa, public or private; and

• the withdrawal of all consular facilities in South Africa except for Canadian nationals and nationals of third countries to whom Canada rendered consular services (effective 7 November 1986).[80]

The year thus closed with a good start on economic sanctions by Commonwealth members. As well, in September, the European Economic Community had adopted its various sanction measures and the Scandinavian countries were poised to tighten theirs further. Significantly the United States, one of the largest trading partners of South Africa, had ratified strong economic sanctions. During the summer of 1986 a major sanctions bill had been passed in the US House of Representatives. President Reagan countered with anti-sanction arguments that so exasperated the Senate that it too adopted a strong bipartisan bill for economic sanctions. When Reagan vetoed this, he prompted a major historical debate in Congress during which Pik Botha, South Africa's foreign minister, telephoned senators warning them of South African retaliation and Buthelezi called to say that sanctions would hurt blacks. Nonetheless, on 2 October 1986, Congress mustered a two-thirds majority to override the president's veto and in a complete foreign policy reversal passed The Comprehensive Anti-Apartheid Act by a vote of 78 to 21.[81] In its scope it resembled the economic measures taken thus far by the majority members of the Commonwealth. Indeed in 1987 Joe Clark rather grandiosely expressed the belief that the Commonwealth measures of August 1986 "may have helped anti-apartheid activists to push the US Congress to override a presidential veto and to enact sanctions a short time later."[82] But there was an important qualitative difference. Under the Act, none of the US measures was voluntary. The legislation included bans on the import of gold coins, steel, coal, textiles and unprocessed Namibian uranium. The Act banned air links with South Africa which, because of established landing rights, was of far greater importance than the Canadian ban on non-existent air links; and it disallowed new corporate investments and government support for any trade with South Africa.[83]

Finally, also in 1986, the United Nations Security Council adopted Resolution 591, designed to strengthen the 1977 arms embargo against South Africa.[84] It urged member states to ensure that military equipment did not reach South Africa through third countries and asked members to ban the export of spare parts for embargoed aircraft and items which *might be destined for South Africa's security forces such as electronics, telecommunications equipment, computers* and four-wheel drive vehicles (emphasis added).

Having been thrust into a leadership role by Mulroney, Canada's part in all of this had been significant. Although Canadian anti-apartheid organizations were now pressing for additional economic sanctions, they did acknowledge that the government had shifted to proactive involvement from a past position of idle rhetoric. The expectations of the anti-apartheid community remained high. Both Mulroney and Clark had declared repeatedly that Canada was prepared to invoke total sanctions if there was "no progress in the dismantling of apartheid." By the end of 1986, there had not only been "no progress," but instead a brutal reassertion of white supremacy. Canadian anticipation of additional and tough economic sanctions was justified, yet in the end unfulfilled. In chapter 8 we examine the government's slow and deliberate disengagement from its public commitment to introduce comprehensive sanctions.

First, however, we return to the ongoing work of the Taskforce to convince Canadian corporations either to challenge directly the structures of apartheid in South Africa and Namibia or to withdraw their investments.

Notes

1 "Statement on South Africa by the Right Honourable Joe Clark, Secretary of State for External Affairs," Baie Comeau, 6 July 1985 (Statement 85/37), p. 2.

2 Each indented paragraph (1–10) denoting new Canadian policies is a direct quotation from Clark's statement (ibid.).

3 Anyone reading the statement without a detailed knowledge of the history of neglect which Namibia had experienced at the hands of the industrialized powers in the United Nations would have assumed that Security Council Resolution 283 to which Clark referred was a recent UN decision. Few would remember that 283 had been adopted in 1970 and ignored for fifteen years by Canada and other industrialized states.

4 For further details see "Canada and Namibian Uranium" (Toronto: Taskforce on the Churches and Corporate Responsibility, 1982) (photocopy). The churches met with External Affairs in June 1988 and learned that the contracts in force in 1985 had in fact not yet expired. Thus Canada, through its Crown corporation, continued to profit from the extraction of Namibia's depletable resource at the very least right up to the year before the start of the final independence negotiations for Namibia.

5 Here Clark echoed External Affairs' Roundtable discussion paper of 22 April, warning that "all trade embargoes would be in contravention of the General Agreement of Tariffs and Trade (GATT) in the absence of an International Agreement. . . . In this instance it had been the Security Council which had called for the prohibition of the sale of Kruger-rand and it had been the Canadian government which had weakened the wording (Africa Bureau, Department of External Affairs, "Roundtable"). See p. 170 for applicability of Article XXI of the GATT to international sanction measures.

6 The measure soon became obsolete. On 9 September 1985 the USA banned the import of Krugerrand; two months later South Africa suspended production of the coins (Alan Cowell, "South Africans Suspend Krugerrand Production," *New York Times*, 14 November 1985).

7 "Statement by the Right Honourable Joe Clark, Secretary of State for External Affairs, Concerning South Africa," Ottawa, 14 August 1985 (Statement 85/47), p. 2.

8 "Statement in the House of Commons by the Secretary of State for External Affairs, the Right Honourable Joe Clark, on South Africa," 13 September 1985 (Statement 85/50), pp. 1–2.

9 Ibid., p. 6.

10 The first statement of South African employers' associations was issued on 7 January 1985 on the occasion of the visit by Senator Edward Kennedy to South Africa. See chap. 5, p. 139.

11 Joe Clark's statement to the House of Commons by design or coincidence took place on the very day that a party of senior South African business leaders and media executives flew to Lusaka for the historical meeting with the ANC. See chap. 5, p. 140–43.

12 "Statement in the House of Commons" (Statement 85/50), p. 7.

13 All indented paragraphs in this section are direct quotations from "Statement in the House of Commons," 13 September 1985 (Statement 85/50).

14 Ibid., p. 11.

15 These were estimated to total US$400 million in 1985. See John Lind, "Northern California Interfaith Committee on Corporate Responsibility: Bank Lending in South Africa," March 1985 (mimeograph).

16 Malcolm Fraser, "Statement on the Report and Recommendations of the Panel of Eminent Persons on the Activities of Transnational Corporations in South Africa and Namibia to the Second Committee of the General Assembly of the United Nations" (New York: United Nations Centre on Transnational Corporations, 1985) (photocopy).

17 Clark's "Statement" of 13 September also contained several non-economic measures beyond our purview. They deal with the opening of a Register inviting public and private institutions to record the voluntary measures they have taken against apartheid and the announcement of major government funding for humanitarian aid to organizations such as the International Defence and Aid Fund for Southern Africa ("Statement in the House of Commons" (Statement 85/50), pp. 13–14.

18 Ibid., p. 30.

19 Bernard Wood, "Canada and Southern Africa: A Return to Middle Power Activism," *The Round Table*, 315 (1990), 286.

20 Ibid.

21 "Report of the Prime Minister's Personal Representative to the Front-line States, September 27-October 17, 1985" (dated: Dar es Salaam, 7 October 1985), appendix to "South Africa Policy Review—Commonwealth Heads of Government Meeting," prepared for the Cabinet Committee on Priorities and Planning, 8 October 1985 (Taskforce Archives).

22 Ibid., pp. 3and 6.

23 Ibid., pp. 7 and 12.

24 Ibid., p. 4.

25 Ibid., p. 17.

26 "South Africa Policy Review—Commonwealth Heads of Government Meeting," 8 October 1985.

27 Ibid., p. 1. This contradicts External Affairs' Roundtable discussion paper of 22 April 1985 which had identified Australia as a country which held similar positions as Canada on South Africa (Africa Bureau, Department of External Affairs, "Roundtable").

28 Ibid., p. 3.

29 Ibid., p. 4.

30 Ibid., p. 3.

31 Ibid., p. 5.

32 Ibid.

33 Ibid., Annex, pp. 1–3.

34 Ibid., Annex, p. 4.

35 Clark's concern in announcing the end of processing of Namibian uranium that existing contracts for the Canadian processing of Namibian uranium be honoured left little doubt about the identity of the company whose interests were thus protected. See "Statement on South Africa" (Statement 85/37), p. 6.

36 For details on QIT-Fer et Titane Inc. and its South African investment, see chap. 4, pp. 124–25.

37 The state-owned IDC had responsibility as well for other state enterprises such as SASOL, the gas from coal conversion project, and for SOEKOR, the Southern Oil Exploration Corporation. It was represented on the board of South Africa's Atomic Energy Board, on the board of ARMSCOR, South Africa's Armaments Corporation, and on the board of CSIR, the Council for Scientific and Industrial Research, the vast and secret research organization serving South Africa's military industrial complex (*McGregor's Who Owns Whom, 1980* [Sommerset West, RSA: Purdy Publishing, 1980], p. 164, quoted in Taskforce, *Annual Report, 1984–1985*, p. 52.
    Policy Review—Commonwealth Heads of Government Meeting," 8 October 1985.

38 P.C.O. "South Africa Policy Review—Commonwealth Heads of Government Meeting," 8 October 1985, p. 5.

39 For references to the Commonwealth Accord, see "Commonwealth Accord, Nassau, The Bahamas 1985," in *Racism in Southern Africa: The Commonwealth Stand* (London: Commonwealth Secretariat, 1989), pp. 61–64.

40   Ibid., p. 63.

41   "Statement on South Africa" (Statement 85/37), p. 3.

42   Canada, Office of the Prime Minister, *Notes for an Address by the Right Honourable Brian Mulroney, Prime Minister of Canada, United Nations General Assembly, New York, October 23rd 1985*, p. 4.

43   Adam and Moodley, *Democratization of South Africa*, p. 98.

44   Cf. ibid., p. 11, with "Statement in the House of Commons" (Statement 85/50), pp. 1–2.

45   Adam and Moodley, *Democratization of South Africa*, p. 106.

46   Wood, "Canada and Southern Africa," pp. 287–88.

47   "Canada's Role in Southern Africa," notes for a speech by the Rt. Hon. Joe Clark, secretary of state for External Affairs, to the Canadian Council for International Cooperation, Montreal, 28 February 1987 (no. 87/11), p. 1.

48   "Statement in the House of Commons by the Right Honourable Joe Clark, Secretary of State for External Affairs," Ottawa (Statement 87/64), p. 3.

49   Members of the Commonwealth Group of Eminent Persons were: Malcolm Fraser, prime minister of Australia (1975–83), co-chair; General Olusegun Obasanjo, head of the Military Government of Nigeria (1976–79), co-chair; Lord Barber of Wentbridge (UK), past chair of the Standard Chartered Bank; Nita Barrow (Barbados), past president of the World YWCA (1975–83) and the World Council of Churches; John Malecela, foreign minister of Tanzania (1972–75) and member of Cabinet (to the end of 1985); Sardar Swaran Singh, Indian minister of External Affairs and other government positions (1964–66 and 1970–74) and on the Executive Board of UNESCO (1985); and the Most Rev. Edward Scott, primate of the Anglican Church of Canada (1971–85) and moderator of the Executive and Central Committees of the World Council of Churches (1975–83) (*Mission to South Africa: The Commonwealth Report—The Findings of the Commonwealth Eminent Persons Group on Southern Africa* [Harmondsworth: Penguin Books, 1986], pp. 7–9).

50   Ibid., p. 94.

51   Ibid,. p. 97.

52   Ibid.

53   Ibid., pp. 103–4.

54   Ibid., p. 117. The EPG had already received Chief Buthelezi's endorsement of the Nassau Accord as the minimum the South African government should do to encourage dialogue. Buthelezi had predicted that violence would subside with the release of Mandela and that he would be willing to serve under Mandela should the latter be elected by a majority in a democratic South Africa (ibid., p. 94).

55   Ibid., p. 120.

56   EPG members speculated about the reasons behind South Africa's blunt methods to discourage their continued stay in the country. Fraser and Obasanjo held that the regime could not allow the EPG to build on common ground it had found between Tambo, Mandela and Buthelezi which would have led to a powerful political alliance threatening Pretoria's "homelands" policies (Sampson, *Black and Gold*, p. 294). The Most Rev. E.W. Scott agreed with this judgment in an interview in 1994.

57   The EPG noted that South Africa well understood that sanctions were an effective tool to achieve political change. In January 1986, South Africa had imposed a complete embargo against Lesotho, a country entirely surrounded by South African territory, and had toppled the government which it had considered hostile after only two weeks of sanctions (*Mission to South Africa*, p. 140).

58   Ibid., p. 140.

59 On 7 September 1986 Tutu was enthroned as archbishop of Cape Town, formally: The Church of the Province of Southern Africa.

60 United Nations, *Notes and Documents* (April 1986).

61 Letter to the Rt. Hon. Brian Mulroney, prime minister of Canada, from W.R. Davis, chair, Taskforce on the Churches and Corporate Responsibility, 8 April 1986.

62 Letter to W.R. Davis, chair of the Taskforce on the Churches and Corporate Responsibility, from the Rt. Hon. Brian Mulroney, prime minister of Canada, 25 April 1986.

63 The Taskforce tabled the text of its letter of 8 April to the prime minister and presented a detailed brief on specific Canadian investments and loans which directly or indirectly benefited the South African military, police or nuclear sector already reviewed in this volume.

64 Canada, Secretary of State for External Affairs, *Independence and Internationalism: Report of the Special Joint Committee on Canada's International Relations* (Ottawa: Queen's Printer, 1986), p. 110.

65 Canada, House of Commons, Standing Committee on Human Rights, *Minutes of Proceedings and Evidence*, 17 July 1986, p. 10:3.

66 Department of External Affairs, Communiqué no. 95, 19 May 1986.

67 "Commonwealth Group of Eminent Persons on South Africa," notes for a statement by the Rt. Hon. Joe Clark, secretary of state for External Affairs in the House of Commons, Ottawa, 12 June 1986 (Statement 86/35), p. 1.

68 Ibid.

69 *Mission to South Africa*, p. 140.

70 "Commonwealth Group of Eminent Persons" (Statement 86/35), p. 3.

71 We have already noted that the sanctions under Nassau's paragraph 6, and quite a few under paragraph 7, had been formulated by Canada before the Nassau meeting in October 1985, including the ban on government procurement and promotion of tourism just announced. Canada, however, had still not adapted the wording on its ban of export of sensitive equipment, such as computers, to the wording of paragraph 7(d) of the Nassau Accord. Nassau asked that all exports of sensitive equipment which were for use by the military and police be halted. Canada was restricting such exports only if they were destined *directly to the police, the armed forces and agencies involved in the enforcement of apartheid*. ("Statement on South Africa," 6 July 1985 [Statement 85/37], p. 3).

72 Taskforce, meeting with External Affairs officials, 18 June 1986, mimeo, Taskforce Archives.

73 *Save Robert McBride: No Apartheid Executions* (London: Southern Africa, The Imprisoned Society, 1988), p. 10.

74 To its credit, throughout the years of severe censorship, the *New York Times* advised its readers that its South African reports had passed "South African censorship review," making clear that its reporting was restricted.

75 For the members of the Taskforce, as for other national and international anti-apartheid organizations, the networks which had been built over the past decade, through the United Nations Centre against Apartheid and the World Council of Churches, as well as the churches and other progressive organizations in South Africa itself, became critically important as sources of reliable information about events in that country.

76 The decision for a Commonwealth Review had been taken at the October 1985 Nassau Commonwealth Heads of Government meeting: "... the President of Zambia, and the Prime Ministers of Australia, the Bahamas, Britain and Canada, India and Zimbabwe should review the position after six months and, in the absence of sufficient progress, leaders would consider further measures of economic pressure" (*Racism in Southern Africa*, p. 39).

77 Britain agreed to voluntary bans on new investment in South Africa and on the promotion of tourism to South Africa. It also declared that it would accept and implement a decision by the European Economic Community to ban the import of coal, iron, steel and gold coins from South Africa. See "Communiqué of the London Review Meeting 1986," in ibid., p. 68.

78 Department of External Affairs, Communiqué no. 201, 19 November 1986.

79 Department of External Affairs, Communiqué no. 164, 26 September 1986. The items were placed on the Import Control List, requiring potential importers to obtain an import permit, which "will normally not be granted."

80 Department of External Affairs, Communiqué no. 193, 6 November 1986.

81 See Sampson, *Black and Gold*, pp. 331–32.

82 Jeff Sallot, "Clark to Lead Public Relations Drive," *The Globe and Mail*, 19 October 1987.

83 Sampson, *Black and Gold*, pp. 20 and 330.

84 UNSCR 591, adopted 28 November 1986, quoted in *Apartheid: The Facts* (London: IDAF Publications), p. 116.

Part Four 1987–90

7 The Taskforce and Continuing Canadian Corporate Involvement in South Africa

The last two chapters may have created the impression that the Taskforce had become so preoccupied with public policy issues that it had abandoned its direct pressure on Canadian investors to modify their conduct in South Africa and Namibia or to withdraw their investment altogether. This was not the case. Indeed, as the impact of the State of Emergency spread across South Africa and the war against the people of Namibia continued, the member churches saw their corporate mandate affirmed by their South African and international partners. This chapter recounts the activities of Canadian corporations that continued their South African investments. It also reviews the efforts to win compliance with an international campaign to enforce an oil embargo against South Africa from the Canadian petroleum industry, in particular from Shell Canada. It begins however with an anecdote that reveals how uncritical—if not supportive—of South Africa's racism had remained Canada's ruling elite.

In July 1985 the Taskforce had received a request from Linda Diebel of the Ottawa Bureau of *The Gazette* (Montreal) for information on pro-apartheid organizations in Canada. Although we did not actually pursue research in this area, we did assemble a fair number of press clippings and documents that allowed us to gauge the power and influence of the pro-apartheid lobbies in Canada. One of the most influential of these was the Canadian—South Africa Society. In 1980 the president, James M. McAvity, had replied to our enquiry that the Society was "privately financed through members' dues together with grants as needed from the South African Foundation" a South African lobby for international business interests[1] (see chap. 2, footnote 18, p. 58 for details of the South African Foundation). The Taskforce continued to receive information about the Society's meetings and membership from anonymous sources.

The documents showed that the Society had secured from Allan MacEachen, then secretary of state for External Affairs, a meeting on 26 January 1983 with officials of External Affairs and with Senator Keith Davey. Later that day there had been a dinner with senators, members of Parliament and officials who were addressed by John Chettle, the North American director of the South African Foundation.[2] The "Report on the Fifth Annual General Meeting" of the Society held on 23 October 1984 in the St. James Club in Montreal announced inter alia, the reelection as Vice-Chair of "His Excellency Hon. Maurice Sauvé," husband of Canada's Governor General Jeanne Sauvé. The Taskforce copied these records to Diebel and *The Gazette* published a major article by her the following day. It included intemperate remarks by James McAvity criticizing the Mulroney government for its anti-apartheid policies and announced that the Society had private plans to use its "influence and connections with Barclay's Bank and others, to round up business on our own for our people in South Africa."[3]

The following day, Maurice Sauvé, on the board of directors of Barclay's Bank of Canada, wrote to McAvity that he felt obliged to resign from the Society "in the face of your recent statements."[4] Two other directors also resigned: Canon Malcolm Hughes of Christ Church Cathedral in Montreal and Quebec Superior Court Judge Kenneth Mackay.

The preponderance of prominent businessmen among board members of the Canadian-South Africa Society confirmed the power behind the government's reluctance to press for stronger anti-apartheid measures, particularly where these affected the business sector. In 1985 they included Paul Leman, former president and still at the time a director of Alcan Aluminium Ltd., of Bell Canada Enterprises Ltd. and CIP Inc.; David Beatty of Beatinvest of Toronto and a director of Goldcorp Investment, Gold Fund and Spar Aerospace; the Society's chair Denis Jotcham, a communications consultant and past president of the Montreal Board of Trade; John E. Wood, secretary of Redpath Industries and the president, James McAvity, former chair of the House of Seagram and former president of the Canadian Export Association.[5]

The Taskforce and Canadian Corporate Investors

Alcan's South African Investment

Member churches of the Taskforce had been arguing with Alcan for more than a decade over its 24 percent investment in Hulett Aluminium, a major South African aluminum fabricator. The churches had been troubled by

Hulett's role as supplier of the arms industry, and for good reason. Hulett Aluminium had been designated a Key Point Industry by South Africa's minister of defence, a reliable indicator of the company's strategic importance. We have reviewed the churches' earlier shareholder initiatives and Alcan's acknowledgment that Hulett Aluminium did produce specialized material for South Africa's military, but that these did not represent a significant part of Hulett's total sales.[6]

South Africa's July 1985 State of Emergency prominently featured the repressive role of the police and the military in black townships. In light of this, the churches reviewed Alcan's South African operation in September 1985 and concluded that Alcan's continued South African involvement had become untenable. Church shareholders drafted a proposal calling on the company to withdraw its investment. In their supporting statement they wrote: "The Canadian government placed a ban on equipment sales to South African industries that serve the military and police. Alcan should do the same and ban sales of specialized materials for military equipment. Since this can apparently not be done as long as Alcan continues its partnership with Hulett Aluminium, Alcan should dispose of its investment."[7] The shareholders offered to withdraw the proposal if an agreement on disinvestment could be reached before the December deadline for the submission of shareholder proposals for the March annual meeting. Alcan's response was prompt. A meeting was quickly arranged and four company officers arrived at the Taskforce offices on 9 December 1985. They were headed by Alcan's chief legal officer, a senior vice-president, and included one of Alcan's directors on the board of Hulett Aluminium (appointed from Alcan's European division), as well as two senior officers from the Montreal office. They met with representatives of the Anglican and United Churches, the Jesuit Fathers of Upper Canada and the Ursulines of Chatham Union, four of the six institutions submitting the draft proposal.

The discussion that followed exposed the gulf that continued to separate the perception of this major Canadian investor in South Africa from that of the Canadian churches. Heedless of South Africa's state of emergency, Alcan still appealed for help to bring about "non-violent" change. At the same time its executives expressed exasperation over the churches' insistence that Alcan should oppose Hulett's sales to the South African military. In a lengthy discussion concerning the Key Point legislation, it became clear that Alcan officials were not familiar with the Act and the Taskforce provided copies to advance the discussion.[8] Company officials contended nonetheless that given the insignificance of the sales to the military, Alcan's enduring contribution in South Africa—improvement in black employment conditions and better standards of education—should be regarded as more important.

Alcan's director on the board of Hulett Aluminium had returned from South Africa the previous month and assured the Canadian churches that he had spoken to trade union representatives and Roman Catholic clergy, including Archbishop Hurley, who had confirmed the director's belief that from the point of view of the black population disinvestment by foreign companies would be immoral. Alcan officials warned, as had their South African business colleagues, that social and political reforms could not take place in times of economic uncertainties.

The churches however remained firm in their view that the sales by Alcan's South African partner to the South African military outweighed in importance whatever influence Alcan might have on improving the employment conditions for Hulett Aluminium's black workforce. The churches maintained that the issue was of general concern in Canada and in the USA and that all shareholders, not only those who attended the annual meeting, should be given a chance to express their views on the churches' shareholder proposal.

The parties agreed that the churches' proposal go forward as formulated and that Alcan would mail it with its proxy material to all shareholders in time for the 27 March annual meeting. For the first time the churches used the time-consuming and costly full range of techniques permitted under the law to engage in concentrated proxy solicitation. They canvassed Alcan's institutional investors throughout Canada and the United States. Although the response of other investors to proxy solicitations is generally not known, on this issue the Taskforce had received sufficient indications from individual and institutional investors from both sides of the border to have a fair idea that the churches could expect substantive—though still minority-shareholder support—for their disinvestment proposal.

The proxy solicitation was under way during the time of the visit to South Africa by the delegation of the Canadian Catholic Church. In a private interview with Archbishop Hurley, we asked him about the visit from Alcan's director on the board of Hulett Aluminium. Hurley had no recollection of ever having spoken to this man. In Durban I was able to get in touch with a researcher and community organizer in the Pietermaritzburg area where Hulett Aluminium was located. At short notice a meeting was arranged with him and a union representative from the company.[9] They confirmed what had long been suspected, that the company was manufacturing a variety of specialized components for military production under contract from ARMSCOR and its subsidiaries. These included rocket shell casings, bomb stabilizer fins and specialized sheet metal for armoured vehicles. These disclosures were clearly incompatible with Alcan's assertions that Hulett Aluminium sales of specialized material for military use were "insignificant." In fact the visitors from Pietermaritzburg indicated that another subsidiary of Hulett produced aluminium powder for both mine blasting and for explosives in missile heads.

Upon our return to Canada in February 1986, the Taskforce released this information to the media. The churches expanded its proxy solicitation on the basis of this new and damaging disclosure. On 20 March, just days before Alcan's annual shareholder meeting, the company phoned the Taskforce and announced that it had disposed of its South Africa investment, "for business reasons." Church shareholders agreed to withdraw their proposal provided their representatives could address the shareholders at the annual meeting.[10]

On 27 March 1986, Bill Davis, then general secretary of the Division of Finance of the United Church, told the shareholders: "The action the company has now taken is consistent with our firm belief that good corporate citizenship and sound business judgement are compatible. The Company's decision to sell can be seen as one further signal to the Government of South Africa that its apartheid policy does not sit well on any grounds, moral or business." Bishop Gérard Drainville, Bishop of Amos, Quebec, informed the meeting that he had been part of the Catholic delegation visiting South Africa in January. He reported:

> We found an overwhelming consensus in favour of international economic pressure on the South African government in support of the internal efforts to work toward the abolition of apartheid. Very specifically, black South Africans asked that industries should not supply the military and the police. This is hardly surprising given the brutality with which the army and the police, these agents of the state, terrorize, injure and kill people in the black townships, far away from white habitation. We are very glad indeed that Alcan has decided to put a distance between itself and this repression. We hope that Alcan's decision will provide an example for other Canadian companies with investment in this inhumane system of apartheid.

Falconbridge and Western Platinum

Earlier Taskforce actions regarding Western Platinum Ltd., a mine in which Falconbridge had almost 25 percent ownership were discussed in chapter four.[11] That chapter reviewed the difficulties experienced in 1985 by the National Union of Mine Workers (NUM) in organizing workers at Western Platinum. Parts of the mine were located in South Africa proper where NUM was recognized, while other parts were in the Bophuthatswana "homeland" ruled by the dictator Lucas Mangope who ran his own union.

The Taskforce had analyzed Western Platinum responses to its questionnaire on employment conditions at the mine, and urged Falconbridge to correct the manifest discriminatory features in Western Platinum's employment policies. At the annual meeting in early 1985, they requested that Bill James, chair of Falconbridge, ask the two Falconbridge directors on the board of Western Platinum to initiate a policy review that would have as its objectives the suspension of the contract labour system for its employees and the elimination of all company collaboration with the apartheid regime, particularly in the military, police and security operations at the mine. In October 1985 Bill James informed the Taskforce that the review was being considered and in March 1986, at a meeting with Falconbridge senior management, James reported that Western Platinum had retained a management consultant. The consultant was scheduled to report in August on how Western Platinum's employment record compared to other companies in the mining industry. Members of the Taskforce questioned the leisurely pace of the study and the relevance of the comparison with other mining companies which had largely the same pattern of racial employment categories camouflaged as graduated job descriptions. Western Platinum statistics obtained through the Taskforce questionnaire in 1984 had already established the fact that black mineworkers who constituted 4,151 out of a workforce of 4,425 were confined to the two lowest of nine job categories. Comparison with other mines was not at issue. The Canadian partners of Western Platinum were either unable or unwilling to advocate the end of contract labour at the mine nor would they insist that the police be challenged when they came to look for apartheid's political opponents in the single-sex dormitories of the company. Falconbridge, like Alcan and other Canadian minority investors, placed great faith in the liberalizing effects of their investments, but when faced with evidence of specific instances where this was clearly not the case, it conceded that it deferred to its South African majority partner. The best Falconbridge could offer was the paltry assurance that Western Platinum was planning to provide more married quarters for black workers—that is to say, up to the 3 percent permitted under the apartheid laws![12]

At the April 1986 annual meeting, church shareholders were promised by the chair that Falconbridge would insist that NUM's efforts to unionize black mineworkers throughout the mine should not be impeded. Meanwhile new evidence emerged which was embarrassing for Falconbridge. Its report on Western Platinum's compliance with the Canadian Code of Conduct did not satisfy the Code's wage requirements. The report disclosed that wages for the lowest paid black mine workers were only 20 percent above the "Minimum Living Level" (MLL), a theoretical subsistence budget established by the Bureau of Market Research of the University of South Africa for a family of five.[13] These wages fell well below the minimum wage stipulated for the lowest category of black workers by the voluntary Canadian Code, suggesting that it exceed the MLL by at least 50 percent.[14]

By August 1986 rumours began to circulate that Falconbridge was anxious to sell its South African investment. Yet the company made a calculated purchase of Mobil's 24.5 percent share in Western Platinum in November 1986, increasing its ownership to 49 percent. As the purchase contravened Canadian policy of a voluntary ban on all new Canadian investment, it temporarily discomfited the Canadian government, which had made much of the efficacy of voluntary compliance by Canada's business community. The secretary of state for External Affairs issued this statement:

> I regret Falconbridge's decision to increase its investment in Western Platinum Ltd. of South Africa. The decision contravenes Canadian Government policy.... Voluntarism remains our preference, although that approach will naturally be affected by the degree of compliance shown by Canadian companies. In the wake of Falconbridge's decision we will review closely the mechanism for implementing the policy on investment.[15]

However, Falconbridge withdrew from South Africa altogether in February 1987. It had bought Mobil's interest only to obtain a better deal for the sale of its share in Western Platinum.[16]

Massey-Ferguson/Varity 1986–89[17]

At the 1985 shareholder meeting, Victor Rice, Massey-Ferguson's chair, had promised the churches that he would obtain from Fedmech, his South African partners, information on wages and employment conditions. He had also agreed to verify whether front-end loaders produced by the company (still with M-F markings) were used by the South African Transport Services (SATS) for the destruction of black dwellings during forced population removals.[18] After repeated and unsuccessful attempts to elicit this information from Massey-Ferguson, a consultation with senior management took place just prior to the 1986 annual meeting.

Massey-Ferguson officials had returned from South Africa, where they had completed compliance reports for Fedmech and Atlantis Diesel for the administrator of the Canadian Code of Conduct. They offered copies to the Taskforce. Massey-Ferguson was one of four companies identified by the administrator of the Canadian Code in his 1986 report as paying a minimum wage in 1985 at or below the level of a subsistence budget, and therefore lower by at least 50 percent than recommended by the voluntary Code of Conduct. Senior executives at Massey-Ferguson explained that the very low wages for the lowest paid black workers were due to a temporary recession in the agricultural equipment sector. They were confident that wage levels would meet Canadian guidelines in the future.[19]

Massey-Ferguson officials echoed executives of other Canadian minority investors when they advised the churches that their company's influence for change was narrowly confined to occasional discussions with their South African partners. To show its willingness to work for change, for example, Massey-Ferguson had supported Fedmech's contributions to the South African Urban Foundation, which was funded by a number of South African firms and which reportedly had supported changes to the Group Areas Act. But the 1982 recession had obliged Fedmech to stop these contributions. This seemed to have exhausted the extent of Massey-Ferguson's proactive anti-apartheid stance.

Massey-Ferguson was unable to guarantee that its earth-moving equipment was not used during forced population removals by South African government departments. Company officers also conceded that as a consequence of their licensee agreement with ADE, Perkins Diesel engines might be installed in trucks purchased by the South African government for police operations.[20]

It will be remembered that major multilateral refinancing of Massey-Ferguson in 1981 had led to the federal and the Ontario governments respectively acquiring 2.5 and 1.5 percent of Massey-Ferguson shares. In 1981 the Taskforce had sought but failed to convince the federal government to tighten its enforcement of the mandatory arms embargo against South Africa by including equipment of use to the police and military that was produced by Canadian investors and their affiliates. In 1985 the churches had returned to the government and had asked for a review of its relationship to the company in the light of Massey-Ferguson's activities in South Africa.

On 10 October 1985 the Taskforce approached David Peterson, the premier of Ontario. He had been one of the first provincial premiers to announce a ban on South African wine imports and in August 1985 he had stopped the purchase of South African products by the government of Ontario. The churches reminded Peterson of the province's status as shareholder of Massey-Ferguson and outlined the issues of the company's South African investment. They expressed the hope that the province's anti-apartheid position would extend to a willingness to join the Jesuit Fathers of Upper Canada in a shareholder proposal asking Massey-Ferguson to withdraw from South Africa. As an alternative to joint shareholder action, the churches proposed that the province simply vote its proxy in favour of the Jesuit proposal.

Peterson's discouraging reply informed the Taskforce that he had had consultations with federal government officials and had been told that the shares held by the two governments were "preferred shares" which "in principle have no voting rights." He concurred with the federal point of view that co-sponsoring a shareholder proposal "would be interpreted by the Board of Directors as an exercise in undue influence on the management of the company." Peterson wrote that Ontario supported federal initiatives to seek compliance with the Canadian Code of Conduct of companies such as Massey-Ferguson.[21]

This retreat from a principled position was disappointing, and Bill Davis, then chair of the Taskforce and senior financial officer of the United Church of Canada, responded to Peterson. He expressed the view that in 1986 calls for the abolition of apartheid would have to be met by means stronger than voluntary compliance of an extremely limited Code of Conduct and that demands for disinvestment were likely more meaningful.

Davis also corrected the premier's impression that the province owned non-voting shares. In April 1984, after the company had failed to pay dividends, the preferred shares had by law become voting shares. Finally he informed the premier that the churches, as minority shareholders, did not regard the submission of or support for shareholder proposals "as an exercise in undue influence" on management, but as a legal right and responsibility.[22]

The premier replied to the Taskforce on 16 June and included a copy of a letter of the same date which he had written to Massey-Ferguson. The text of both letters indicated that they were to have been delivered in time for the annual meeting on 17 June, enabling the recipients to refer to them if they wished during the discussion. But inexplicably the letters had not been signed until after the annual meeting and were not delivered until 18 June. The premier expressed the province's concern about the company's South African investment. He referred to Archbishop Tutu's recent visit and his "eloquent appeal" that had brought "the challenge most strongly home to us" and to the "no less forceful" report of the Commonwealth Eminent Persons Group which had just been released.[23] Although in his letter to Massey-Ferguson Peterson talked of "these steps that are needed," he did not say that Tutu as well as the EPG had called for increased economic sanctions and carefully avoided being identified with these positions. He concluded, therefore, rather meekly: "In view of such compelling evidence that these steps are needed, the Government of Ontario, as a shareholder in Massey-Ferguson Limited, would ask that the company give urgent consideration to its policy with regard to its investments in South Africa and its role in helping to oppose the system of apartheid in that country."[24]

The annual meeting of shareholders took place on 17 June. Representatives of the church shareholders received perfunctory responses to their request that Massey-Ferguson ensure that its activities in South Africa did not contribute to the enforcement capability of the apartheid regime. Victor Rice, the chair, told the shareholders that Massey-Ferguson took the view that its purpose was to make money for its shareholders and that politics should be left to the politicians. He said that the production of its equipment could generally be regarded as a benefit to the black population, but that he could not guarantee that some of it would not end up in the hands of the government of South Africa.[25]

In July 1986 officers of the company, by now renamed Varity Corporation, appeared before the Parliamentary Standing Committee on Human Rights. They sought to convince the Committee that Atlantis Diesel Engines (ADE), the state-owned corporation with whom Perkins Diesel, Varity's wholly owned British subsidiary, had a licensee agreement, was "completely non-discriminatory" in its racial employment policies.[26] This, of course, was an equivocation since Atlantis, where the plant was located, was designated a "coloured area" and blacks, by virtue of their race, were excluded.[27] Thus ADE and Varity fully complied with the Group Areas Act, one of the most contentious cornerstones of the apartheid regime.

In early 1987 two member institutions of the Taskforce, who held shares in Varity Corporation, decided that the matter of the company's South African investments should be brought to the attention of all shareholders through a formal shareholder proposal. This decision of the Jesuit Fathers of Upper Canada and the Ursulines of Chatham Union was supported by the other denominational members of the Taskforce. The episode is worth recounting in detail for the profile that emerged of Varity Corporation and of the tenacity of the churches.

The story began with a meeting on 21 January 1987 with Varity management to discuss the draft proposal.[28] It asked Varity's board of directors:

- to take immediate steps to terminate Varity's investments in South Africa;
- to take immediate steps to terminate Varity's license agreement with Atlantis Diesel Engines, and if there were legal obstacles, provide a report and a plan of action to shareholders within ninety days; and
- to announce publicly to the South African government Varity's plans to leave South Africa as soon as possible.

There was a clause-by-clause discussion at this meeting, but in the end it was understood that the proposal would go forward pretty much as drafted. Varity management advised that if the proposal was to be included in the proxy material sent to all shareholders before the annual meeting, it should reach Varity head office before the 20 March deadline. There was not the slightest indication that serious difficulties were afoot.

At the end of January, Varity contacted the Taskforce to ask that church shareholders delay filing the proposal until after a further meeting with a Varity executive who had returned from a visit to South Africa. The churches agreed to this. When they met with management on 23 February they learned that Varity planned not to circulate their proposal with its proxy material. A discussion ensued regarding section 131 (5) (b) of the Canada Business Corporations Act (CBCA). This section allows companies to omit the circulation of shareholder proposals if they had been "submitted ... primarily for the purpose of promoting general economic, political, racial, religious, social or similar causes." Members of the Taskforce denied that their initiative should be so characterized. Moreover, they noted that since Varity shares were traded in the United States, the regulatory rules of the Securities Exchange Commission (SEC) might yet require Varity to circulate the proposal. Varity had evidently looked into this possibility and pointed out that the SEC required a longer lead period than the CBCA and that the churches had already missed the SEC deadline of 23 January—two days following the previous meeting between the Taskforce and Varity. Varity sought to convince church shareholders to forget the formal proposal and instead to raise questions from the floor of the annual meeting. The churches reasoned that as most shareholders did not attend annual meetings they would remain uninformed about the issues under discussion. Formal shareholder proposals, on the other hand, accompanied by an explanatory statement of the proponents and by a written opinion of management, reached all shareholders and afforded them an opportunity to express their own judgement by proxy vote.

Varity management then offered to include with its proxy material a statement about the company's South African investment and pledged to refer discussion about it to the board of directors. Varity officials, however, insisted that they, rather than church shareholders, formulate this statement. This the churches could not accept. They were perplexed that despite Varity's conviction—in time argued in court—that the churches were "wrongfully" promoting "general economic, political, racial, religious, social or similar causes" the company was prepared to debate these "causes" in the annual meeting and even circulate a statement of its own about them, but would not let the shareholders vote on them. The Jesuits and the Ursulines filed their shareholder proposal on 9 March 1987, having obliged Varity by notifying it in advance of the filing date. Such courtesy was not reciprocated by Varity.

Ten days later, without further communication, Varity dispatched a lawyer to serve legal notices on the two proponents, informing them that an application had been made to the Supreme Court of Ontario asking it to confirm Varity's right under section 131 (5) (b) of the CBCA to refuse circulation of their shareholders' proposal, and that the motion would be heard on 7 April.[29] This legal action took the churches by surprise. Although they knew that in Canada the courts settled disputes of this nature, the Taskforce had assumed that it was up to the shareholders whose proposal had been refused circulation to choose between abandoning the action or seeking redress in a court of law. Varity's move left the churches little option but to respond, despite the drain on their time and resources.

Four days later Varity wrote to the Jesuits and the Ursulines. The letter was clearly designed to discourage any action on the part of the churches to seek a favourable ruling for their proposal from the SEC, the American regulator. Varity wrote:

> we hereby inform you that the Company [Varity] deems the omission of the proposal from the proxy materials to be proper under the United States Securities Exchange Act.... Under Rule 14a-B (a) (1) [*sic*] ... a proposal must be submitted by a record or beneficial owner [*sic*] of at least 1% or U.S. $1,000 in market value of securities.... Our records indicate that ... your

holdings constitute less than 1% of the Company's outstanding Common Shares and less than U.S. $1,000 in market value. As a result your proposal does not qualify for inclusion in the Company's 1987 proxy materials under U.S. securities laws.[30]

The letter was signed by R.D. Garland, director of Legal Services of Varity. It turned out to attempt an "end run." Garland did not mention that the company itself was unsure of its obligations and that it had on the same day written to the SEC requesting to be exempted from circulating the shareholder proposal.

Varity had told the Taskforce on 23 February that the shareholder proposal had missed the SEC's 23 January deadline, with the implication that the SEC's more liberal rules on proxy circulation were now out of reach for the churches. Yet copies of correspondence show that on 23 March Varity's New York lawyers were still arguing with the SEC, hoping to convince it that the shareholder proposal need not be circulated because, they wrote, "the final proposal was not received until March 10, 1987, which was later than the allowable time under the Exchange Act, but within CBCA limits" and because neither the Jesuits nor the Ursulines owned enough shares to qualify under SEC rule 14a-8 (a) (1).[31]

The Jesuits, filing under the Canada Business Corporations Act, which required no minimum value of share ownership, had submitted its proposal on the basis of only five shares held in their own name although they had beneficial ownership of additional shares. Varity had not requested documentary evidence showing the total of Varity voting shares held by them, and there had thus been no reason to disclose this additional fact.

On 2 April the Jesuits and the Ursulines, with the support of all the member churches of the Taskforce, announced their decision to oppose Varity's court application. On 3 April the Jesuits of Upper Canada filed an affidavit with the Ontario Supreme Court showing that they were beneficial owners of more than $10,000 worth of Varity shares. This was done without awareness of the implications of this disclosure, but to forestall arguments that the proponents did not have a genuine economic interest in Varity. Information contained in the affidavit was received by Varity on 3 April—four days before the initial court hearing—and was reported the same day in *The Globe and Mail.* These facts were important for they contradicted Varity's later statement that it had only learned of the Jesuits' total holdings *during* litigation and declared that "if we had been advised, we wouldn't have gone to court."[32]

On 7 April 1987 Mr. Justice Austin of the Supreme Court of Ontario heard the case, and on 10 April ruled in favour of Varity's request that it did not need to include the shareholders' proposal "in its mailing to shareholders for its annual general meeting." Because the issue was of great importance to future shareholder action of the Taskforce, the proponents appealed the decision, once more with the financial and moral support of all members of the Taskforce. Claude Thomson, Q.C., of Campbell, Godfrey and Lewtas represented the churches. It was his contention that the operative word in Section 131 (5) (b) was "general" and that the section was designed to prevent shareholders from advocating "general economic, political, racial, religious, social or similar causes." In contrast, Thomson argued, the proponents called for specific action. Considering that business decisions may properly take into account the social and economic consequences of corporate activity, the specific issue addressed by the minority shareholders, Thomson held, met the criteria of Section 131 (5) (b) of the CBCA. Thus a proposal asking the co-owners whether they wished to have their assets used in a manner which the proponents believed to be economically and socially responsible, should not be prevented from reaching all shareholders.

Two out of three judges of the Court of Appeal nevertheless accepted Varity's argument that eliminating apartheid was clearly the "general" cause of the churches' shareholder proposal, and on 21 April 1987 upheld the trial judge's decision and ruled in favour of Varity. The late Mr. Justice Tarnopolsky dissented and wrote, "what could be more specific than a proposal to divest your property in South Africa whatever the motive?"[33]

For the moment, the churches believed that they had been soundly defeated by legal provisions which favoured the interests of corporate management. In this respect the United States processes differed markedly from the Canadian system. There the Securities Exchange Commission rather than the courts acted as first line arbiter concerning the interpretation of statutory shareholder rights. In addition, the United States Security Exchange Act had been amended to delete a clause identical to section 131 (5) (b) of the Canada Business Corporations Act. This amendment resulted in routine filing of hundreds of shareholder-initiated proposals each year to the benefit of informed discussion at annual meetings. This was essential background for the next twist in this complicated story.

On 30 April Varity hand-delivered a letter to the Jesuits. The company wrote that if they provided evidence of ownership for at least one year of Varity voting shares valued in excess of US $1,000, the corporation would be required by the SEC to include the Jesuits' shareholder proposal in its proxy statement. Varity lamented that "this turn of events has imposed a severe strain on the timetable of our annual meeting" and asked the Jesuits to respond at once rather than sometime within the fourteen days allowed them by the SEC.[34] The Jesuits obliged, not wishing to be the cause of delaying the annual meeting of shareholders. At Varity's request there was a further meeting on 1 May to apprise the members of the Taskforce of the new situation.

However, the unabridged version of behind-the-scenes negotiations reached the Taskforce on 6 May, when the Jesuits and the Ursulines received from the American Security Exchange Commission copies of lengthy submissions from Varity to the SEC. Varity had, through Cahill Gordon & Reindel of New York (23 March) and on its own (21 April), sought to convince the SEC that it could omit circulation of the shareholder proposal by citing first rule 14a-8 (a) (2), failure to produce evidence of sufficient share ownership; and then adding rule 14a-8 (a) (1), failure to observe the SEC submission deadline. Addressing Varity (the "Company") on 6 May 1987, the SEC however decided that:

> In the absence of a representation that the Company requested the documentary support required by Rule 14a-8 (a) (2) and that the JFC [Jesuits of Upper Canada] did not respond by furnishing appropriate documentation within 14 calendar days after receiving the request, the [SEC] Division is unable to concur with your view that the proposal may be omitted pursuant to Rules 14a-8 (a) (1) and (a) 2. Accordingly, we do not believe that the Company may rely upon Rules 14a-8 (a) 1 and (a) (2) as bases for omitting the proposal.[35]

In December 1986 the Taskforce had again invited the Ontario and federal governments to join the two religious orders as co-filers in the shareholder proposal for the 1987 annual meeting or, alternatively, to commit their shareholder vote in support of it. David Peterson replied on 4 March 1987 that the circumstances of Ontario's acquisition of shares precluded its participation "as a normal shareholder." The province would, however, continue privately to dialogue with Varity to make its concerns clear. A week later, when the proposal was submitted to Varity, the Taskforce issued a press release. The particular significance of Varity's presence in South Africa, the statement said, lay in the fact that it represented investments by Canadian taxpayers through federal and Ontario holdings. Commenting on Peterson's unusual logic, the Taskforce restated its commitment to shareholder democracy: "regardless of how or why shares in a company are acquired, a shareholder must exercise the responsibility of ownership. The governments of Canada and Ontario must make a decision in the near future ... as to whether they will support or oppose the shareholder proposal requesting Varity to disinvest from South Africa."[36] The federal government did not reply until 10 April 1987, the day the Supreme Court of Ontario had found in favour of Varity and well past the legal deadline for submitting the shareholder proposal. Joe Clark wrote on behalf of the prime minister that government policy did not promote disinvestment of Canadian companies operating in South Africa, but urged instead compliance by companies of the Canadian Code of Conduct.[37] He confirmed that the federal government controlled 2.7 percent of Varity's voting shares, a control that Clark described as having been "brought about by special circumstances." Clark wrote that "it would be inappropriate for the Government to exercise undue influence on the management of an essentially private sector company."

Varity had attracted a great deal of news coverage by its successful court challenges against circulation of the churches' shareholder proposal and by the peculiar reasons for its unexpected reinstatement. After all the advance drama, the carefully structured annual meeting on 10 June provided for yet more tension. Varity told the churches of its discovery at the last minute that several lines from the shareholder support statement had "erroneously" been omitted. Varity asked to be allowed to provide the complete version at the annual meeting rather than mailing it out, to avoid postponing the annual meeting until all shareholders had had the opportunity to respond. Again the Jesuits and the Ursulines obliged. They were angered however when, at the annual meeting, the chair made no reference to the error in the circulated proposal.

Father Michael Czerny, S.J., spoke on behalf of the Jesuit Fathers of Upper Canada. Sheila Kappler, O.S.U., of the Ursulines of Chatham Union, represented her own order and the proxies of several other religious orders. They reviewed critically the nature of Varity's involvement in South Africa, and proposed that the company terminate its investment there. Ann Abraham, vice-chair of the Taskforce, spoke on her personal proxy, calling the presence of Varity in South Africa "a social statement of support for apartheid."[38]

Victor Rice, Varity's chair, challenged the right of people who have not personally visited South Africa to speak on the issue and called on two black South Africans whom Varity had brought from South Africa to give "expert testimony": Jonas Chaka, a machine operator and training instructor employed by Fedmech, Varity's South African affiliate, and Dr. C.L. Bikitsha, a seventy-one-year-old medical doctor introduced as chief of the Amazizi Tribal Authority of Butterworth, Transkei. Predictably they both spoke in favour of Varity's position to continue its South African operations. According to press reports, after their statements they "dashed out a back door before reporters could corner them" and were not seen again.[39]

The vote count at the close of the meeting introduced two more curious elements. Rice announced that of the shares voted, 14.7 percent (10.7 million common shares) had been voted in favour of the churches' proposal and 85 percent (62.5 million shares) had been in opposition to it. Considering that Varity's legal manoeuvres over the proxy circulation had prevented the churches from proxy solicitation, the vote represented a considerable victory for their proposal. Note, for example, that in October 1986 General Motors Corporation decided to withdraw from South Africa on the day that 9 percent of its shareholders voted for disinvestment.[40] Victor Rice, however, downgraded the importance of the vote. He told the shareholders that the results were "misleading" because "for obvious political reasons" the federal and provincial governments had supported the proposal! Figures later supplied by Varity management on the exact distribution of votes were even more dramatic than anticipated:

Total shares voted: 98.5 million

In favour: 10.7 million   or   10.9%

Against: 62.5 million   or   63.2%

Abstained or withheld: 25.3 million   or   25.7%

These figures show that a total of 36.6 percent of the shareholders had not supported the position of Varity management.[41]

The governments' support vote, improperly revealed by Victor Rice, remained a puzzle. Clark and Peterson's replies to the request from the churches that they join their shareholder action for disinvestment had been unequivocally negative. Yet the Ontario and federal governments had evidently decided that voting the shares in support of disinvestment was compatible with the governments' policy, but that co-sponsoring a shareholder proposal for disinvestment was not.[42]

That the federal and Ontario governments indeed held this view was confirmed toward the end of 1987, when the two religious orders were preparing for a second shareholder proposal asking Varity to disinvest its South African assets. The Taskforce had written to Premier Peterson and to Prime Minister Mulroney thanking them for their vote in support of the 1987 action, and expressed the hope that they would co-sponsor a 1988 shareholder proposal containing similar arguments. Joe Clark replied for the prime minister: "If there is a further shareholder's proposal to the effect that Varity should disinvest itself of its South African holdings, the federal government's position will be the same as it was last June—namely support for the proposal. We are not, however, in favour of government sponsorship of such a proposal. Nor are we now considering legislation on the subject."[43] David Peterson wrote that while the government did not think it appropriate "for the Province of Ontario to co-file a proposal with your organization for consideration at this year's shareholder's meeting ... I can assure you that the Government fully supports the Churches' position on divestment by Varity and will once again vote in support of your Resolution."[44]

The Jesuit Fathers of Upper Canada and the Ursuline Religious of London prepared a new shareholder proposal for Varity, which reiterated the request that Varity terminate all business relationships in South Africa. A meeting with management prior to submission did not resolve the fundamental differences between the churches and the company and the proposal was submitted without changes. This time it was circulated to all shareholders with Varity's proxy materials without any further challenge.

Early in 1988 Varity had divested its small holdings in Atlantis Diesel Engines, but had retained its technology transfer agreement and its investment in Fedmech.[45] On 3 March 1988 the Taskforce received a copy of an interesting telex that Varity had sent to South Africa's foreign minister after the apartheid government had yet again tightened its repression by outlawing a wide range of anti-apartheid organizations and imprisoning their leaders. The telex of 3 March expressed exasperation with the conduct of the regime because of the problems it created for foreign investors at home:

> the recent repressive actions ... can only bring comfort to those who are demanding divestment and withdrawal of Western business interests, while creating onerous complications for those companies, such as Varity Corporation, which are attempting to remain productive participants in the South African economy. ... We urge the Government of South Africa to reconsider its policy of suppression of basic human rights, and to pay urgent heed to world public opinion seeking a peaceful end to forced racial separation.[46]

The annual meeting took place on 1 June 1988. Varity's proxy statement urged shareholders to oppose the churches motion on the grounds that the company complied satisfactorily with the Canadian Code of Conduct. The company's carefully worded statement that 40,000 tractors bearing the Massey-Ferguson trade mark were owned or operated by black farmers and farm workers was possibly not wrong, but the intended message was grossly misleading. Black farm workers, often dispossessed of their land through "black spot removals," were the lowest-paid and least-protected workers in South Africa. They eked out a minimal existence on prosperous white farms. To use for Varity's propaganda purposes the fact that these black workers used Massey-Ferguson tractors—owned, of course, by their white employers—was in the worst possible taste.

Father Edward Sheridan, S.J, introduced the motion and Father Daniel Genneralli of the Scarborough Foreign Mission Society seconded it. They garnered a respectable 14.4 percent vote in favour of their disinvestment proposal which, as promised, had again been supported by the federal and Ontario governments.

Although the Taskforce continued to press Varity to withdraw from South Africa and included the company on its postcard campaign for particularly recalcitrant South African investors, no progress was made. In 1990 Varity Corporation decided to move its head office to Buffalo, New York, where it became a US incorporated company, answering to American sanction laws.

Postscript

We recall that in 1977 a young South African from Crossroads had visited the Taskforce and described how African squatter camps were levelled by bulldozers from the South African Department of Railways and Harbours during forced removals of black families to the "homelands." She had told the churches that these bulldozers or front-end loaders carried the M-F trade mark—still used by producing companies under an agreement with Varity.

For over a decade the Taskforce had attempted to find independent or company confirmation of this allegation. Varity had been able to count the numbers of M-F tractors operated by South African black farmers and farm workers, but had claimed to be unable to establish whether its equipment was sold to the South African government and was used in forced population removals. Confirmation that the young woman had been right and the Taskforce entirely justified in its suspicion came too late for action. On 9 September 1990 a brief item on a South African squatter camp in Calfontaine, near Johannesburg, was aired during the CBC national television news. It dealt with black population removals and featured a yellow frontloader with the familiar M-F trademark.

*Rio Algom*⁴⁷

In its May 1985 brief to Joe Clark the Taskforce had asked for the termination of Canadian processing of Namibian uranium and the discontinuation of tax relief to Canadian businesses for taxes paid to South Africa's illegal administration in Namibia. The government had decided to end Namibian uranium processing but not until the contracts in force in 1985 had run out. It had not, however, withdrawn the tax allowance for Canadian investors in Namibia. In 1986 the churches renewed their attempts to have the company's tax deductions removed by the government and to convince Rio Algom to leave Namibia. The Taskforce's ability to deal knowledgeably with Rio Algom and its Namibian investment benefited from the work of the Ecumenical Contact Group. Its members were the ecumenical Christian councils of Britain, Canada, France, West Germany and the USA, the same states that constituted the Contact Group of States which, in 1977, had promised but ultimately failed to negotiate early independence for Namibia under Resolution 435 of the United Nations Security Council. Canadian church organizations participating in the Ecumenical Contact Group included the Canadian Council of Churches, the Roman Catholic Episcopal Commission for Social Affairs and the Canadian Catholic Organization for Development and Peace. The Ecumenical Contact Group worked closely with the Council of Churches in Namibia (CCN) representing approximately 70 percent of Namibia's population.

Since its inception in 1982 the Ecumenical Contact Group monitored the activities of the Contact Group of States and its effect—or want of it— on South Africa. Each of the five international church organizations also sought to persuade their own governments to live up to the international expectations they had created when they established the Contact Group. By 1985 the Ecumenical Contact Group was deeply disillusioned with the seven-year-old exercise, agreeing with its Namibian colleagues that there had been no progress in the implementation of Resolution 435.[48]

In November 1986 Namibian church leaders visited Ottawa. Thanks to arrangements made by the Inter-Church Coalition on Africa, members of the Taskforce participated in a consultation between the Namibian delegates and the Parliamentary Standing Committee on Human Rights. The Namibians expressed their profound discouragement over the failure of the Contact Group of States to achieve its promised objectives. In an officially prepared document they appealed to the Canadian government not to waste more time on these moribund diplomatic initiatives and to concentrate instead on Namibia-specific sanctions against South Africa. The Namibian representatives asked the Canadian government to "implement UNSCR 238 (1970) and 301 (1971) calling for a trade embargo against South Africa's illegal occupation of Namibia ... [and] adopt a policy in which your country is no longer complicit in the suffering of the Namibian people."[49] In discussion with the Namibian church leaders the Taskforce was able to confirm that the Namibian churches continued to support Decree No.1 of the UN Council for Namibia designed to protect Namibia's resources from foreign exploitation, and that they considered UNSCR 435 the most meaningful UN resolution for Namibian independence. They urged that Canada withdraw from the Contact Group of States and join with other countries in the search for new international initiatives for the implementation of UNSCR 435. A second delegation of the Council of Churches in Namibia visited Canada in May 1987 and several of its members participated in board meetings of the Taskforce reinforcing the commitment of the Canadian churches to their cause.

Following its contact in late 1986 with the Namibian delegates, the Taskforce was anxious to renew its discussion with Rio Algom. It met with its senior officers on 16 April 1987. While the Taskforce gave detailed information about the increasing repression in Namibia as presented to them by the Namibian churches, Rio Algom's senior management reported that their information did not suggest that conditions had worsened. The company was satisfied that Rossing was a model employer, that Rio Algom's interest was in any case passive and that the issues which concerned the churches needed to be settled politically but did not involve Rio Algom's investment position.

Two weeks later, during the annual shareholder meeting, church shareholders told Rio Algom's chair that his role as investor and director of Rossing was indefensible: "The participation of a Canadian company in a strategic industry located in Namibia indicates, at the very least, recognition of and compliance with the laws of the illegal regime and thus lends credibility to its rights to govern, a right not recognized by the government of Canada."[50] In the course of the annual meeting Rio Algom's senior management agreed to receive representatives of the Namibian churches to hear their account of conditions in Namibia and their views on foreign investment in general and on the Rossing Uranium mine in particular. This meeting took place on 26 May 1987. Accompanied by members of the Taskforce, Daniel Tjongarero and Skinny Hilundwa of the Council of Churches of Namibia told Rio Algom's senior officers that companies like Rossing were delaying the independence process. Foreign investors, they argued, legitimized South Africa's illegal occupation and sustained it financially. Their exchange with company officers was frank but irreconcilable. There was no agreement about the situation in Namibia nor about the choice of policies that would benefit the people of Namibia.[51]

Two years after the Canadian government had announced termination of the "toll processing" of Namibian uranium, it nevertheless continued, ostensibly because contracts in force in 1985 had not yet run out. Rio Algom had repeatedly insisted that its uranium investments in Namibia were without question lawful in the eyes of the Canadian government while the government, for its part, continued to allow tax deductions for companies with Namibian investment. These facts had led the Taskforce to speculate about the relationship between Rio Algom and the Canadian government even before it had evidence of External Affairs' predilection for Rio Algom's Namibian investment.[52] Reinforced by its recent exchanges with its Namibian partners, the Taskforce was determined to at least keep the Canadian pillage of Namibia's non-renewable resources on the public agenda. To this end a formal proposal for public disclosure of the details of Rio Algom's Namibian investment was submitted for discussion at the 1988 annual meeting by the Anglican Synod of the Diocese of Ottawa and the Ursuline Religious of London, Ontario.

Philip Creighton, F.C.A., represented the proxy of the Anglican Diocese of Ottawa together with his own shares and moved adoption of the proposal. Creighton told the chair that the Diocese of Ottawa had ethical guidelines against which it evaluated its investments. Reviewing Rio Algom, he explained, the Diocese had been troubled to learn of the company's activities in Namibia. The Diocese understood that Rio Algom had a 10 percent interest in Rossing Uranium Ltd. with RTZ, Rio Algom's parent, holding a further 35-40 percent; and further, that George Albino, Rio Algom's past chair had a seat on the board of Rossing but did not attend meetings. Creighton recalled that the churches had been told that Rio Algom's interest in the Namibian uranium mine constituted only a "passive" investment. When pressed to account for its seeming inaction in the matter, management had replied "it was 'passive' enough to have no information about or responsibility for the Rossing operation, but not 'passive' enough to be considered unprofessional!"[53] Creighton said that he had carefully examined Rio Algom's and RTZ's annual reports from 1983 onward, but had been unable to find any hard information on Rossing other than that required by financial auditors and expressed frustration on behalf of socially concerned shareholders. He proposed that Rio Algom's board of directors drop its "passivity," take an active role in the operation of Rossing, and "look searchingly at our highly profitable investment in Namibia." Creighton assured Rio Algom that he did not question the company's financial accounts, but asked that additional information be provided by a report to the shareholders within ninety days. This report should contain:

- a full financial disclosure of Rossing Uranium Ltd., including payments made to the South African administration as profit participation, royalties, rents, fees, taxes etc.;

- an assessment of the legal and ethical implications of Rossing's continued operation in defiance of United Nations Decree No. 1 of 1974 and a sober consideration and exposition of the reasons for the investment in that troubled land;

- a justification for the company's continued profit derived from the Namibian operation in light of the Canadian government's 1985 decision to deny Eldorado Nuclear new contracts for the processing of Namibian uranium; and

- disclosure of basic production and marketing data, such as reserves, production levels and end use of uranium shipments.[54]

Ross Turner the new chair of Rio Algom replied that he had been present at several meetings with the churches to discuss their request that Rio Algom withdraw from Namibia. He considered the current shareholder proposal to have the same underlying purpose—the withdrawal of the investment. The board, he said, was of the view that the Namibian investment was neither illegal nor immoral. Adoption of the churches' motion, he said, would not assist the achievement of independence. The process leading to Namibia's independence was a political matter and inappropriate for Rio Algom's involvement. The last statement was at once contested by Ann Abraham, who represented the proxy of the General Synod of the Anglican Church and told the chair that investing in Namibia was in itself a political act.

The shareholder vote presented an unexpected result for the churches' proposal. It received support from 3,523,364 or 11.72 percent of the total shares voted. As Rio Algom's proxy circular had stated that 51.46 percent of its voting shares, the block of 22,506,672 shares owned by RTZ, were being voted against the shareholder proposal, the following calculation presents an insight into Rio Algom's own dissident shareholder vote:

Shares voted for the churches: 3,523,364

Shares voted in opposition: 26,525,996

Total shares voted: 30,049,360

Minus RTZ block: (22,506,672)

Total shares voted minus RTZ block: 7,542,688

The Canadian church shareholders, thus, received an amazing 46.7 percent support vote from the balance of Rio Algom shareholders.[55]

By 1989 negotiations for Namibia's independence had progressed. The United Nations Transitional Assistance Group were moving into the country and Namibians were gearing up for their first-ever democratic elections. On 23 March members of the Taskforce were able to introduce two senior SWAPO officials to Rio Algom's executives. It must have been an exceptional event for Colin Macaulay, the former managing director of Rossing Uranium who had become Rio Algom's president, to meet Andimba Toivo ja Toivo one of SWAPO's legendary founders. Active since 1957, Toivo ja Toivo had been charged in 1968 under the notorious Terrorism Act and convicted in a South African court. He had been imprisoned for twenty years on Robben Island. Toivo ja Toivo was accompanied by Hinyangerwa Asheeke, deputy representative of SWAPO's observer mission to the United Nations.

Toivo ja Toivo told management that while Rio Algom may have believed that the Canadian churches had been too far removed from the Namibian struggle to carry any kind of weight, they had in fact been SWAPO's ambassadors and had spoken for the people of Namibia. Rio Algom maintained that it had been at all times operating within Canadian law. Company executives thought that once independence had been achieved, Namibians would view history from a different perspective. They would then appreciate that mining the ore at Rossing had presented extremely difficult technical problems which would unlikely have been solved at a later date. Asheeke brushed aside such rationalization. He reminded Rio Algom that concrete plans for the uranium mine had been formulated in 1966 by an international business consortium together with the South African government, at the very time that the United Nations had voted to end South African rule in Namibia. Rossing's opening in 1974 had coincided with the creation of the United Nations Council for Namibia and the adoption of Decree No. 1 for the protection of Namibia's natural resources. Asheeke put it to Rio Algom that such blatant contempt for the people of Namibia and their internationally recognized rights had left deep scars of mistrust of companies such as Rio Algom.[56]

There was fine symbolism in the fact that such prominent SWAPO members accompanied the Taskforce to its last meeting with Rio Algom. Within a year they would serve in the first democratically elected government of Namibia.

Campaign to Enforce the Oil Embargo

Oil as Munition of War

Although rich in mineral resources, South Africa had no natural sources of oil and, despite expensive oil from coal conversion plants (SASOL), its dependence on imported oil left it very vulnerable. Oil was so indispensable to South Africa that it had long been designated "a munition of war" by the government.[57] No statistics on oil imports had been published since 1973, and since 1979 strict security-related regulations governed oil companies operating in South Africa. One analyst summarized the regime's control as follows:

> The South African government has tightened its control over oil supplies by a series of regulations.... Companies are obliged to stockpile reserves, to sell a certain percentage to the state (including to SADF), to produce specified products ... and to liaise closely with the regime.... In June 1979 an amendment to the Petroleum Products Act made it a criminal offence to publish information on "the source, manufacture, transportation, destination, storage, quality or stock levels of any petroleum, acquired or manufactured for or in the Republic."[58]

Want of oil was South Africa's Achilles' heel; an effective oil embargo would have greatly contributed to an early end of the apartheid regime.[59]

The member churches of the Taskforce had long recognized this fact. They had protested Canada's decision in December 1979 to oppose a UN General Assembly resolution for an international oil embargo against South Africa.[60] In September 1985, when the Canadian government finally acknowledged the strategic importance to the apartheid regime of oil and oil products, it nevertheless had placed only a voluntary ban on such exports to South Africa. As Canada did not export oil to Southern Africa, this voluntary ban affected only petroleum products and, as we shall see, it had been singularly ineffective. Most anti-apartheid organizations, including the Taskforce, took a far more serious view of the issue and attempted on their own to pressure the oil companies directly.

Internationally, a loose network of organizations had begun to monitor the relations of their resident oil companies to the apartheid regime.[61] The aim was to force these companies to withdraw from South Africa and to secure a total ban on the supply of oil and oil-related products and services to the apartheid regime. Royal Dutch/Shell in particular had been targeted

244 In Good Faith

for increased pressure by the US churches and anti-apartheid organizations in Britain, Holland, Scandinavia and Australia. The Taskforce and other Canadian organizations followed this lead and focused on Shell Canada.

Shell's Importance to South Africa

Shell South Africa, a wholly owned subsidiary of Royal Dutch/Shell, had long been one of the largest foreign investors in South Africa and Namibia.[62] At the time the Royal Dutch/Shell group had 280 operating companies in over 100 countries.[63] It was therefore able to avoid delivering crude oil directly to South Africa yet could ensure its continued supplies. In January 1987 the Shipping Research Bureau (SRB) documented for example, that since mid-1981 Shell made no direct crude oil deliveries to South Africa from any country that had joined the oil embargo against it. However the SRB had also discovered that: "In the period 1979–1981 at least 23 tankers owned, managed or chartered by Shell delivered oil to South Africa, and that at least 9 sailed from Brunei. The total number of tankers identified as having sailed from Brunei to South Africa from 1979 until September 1986 is 56 with a total volume of Brunei crude oil delivered in this period of about 6.7 million tons."[64] In 1982 the Brunei government adopted an oil embargo containing clauses in contracts for oil sales which specified that South Africa was to be excluded. Shortly after, in 1983, the Brunei Shell Petroleum Company began selling crude oil to Marubeni, a Japanese trading company, ostensively destined for the USA. Marubeni however resold the oil to Marc Rich & Co. A.G. based in Zug, Switzerland, which sold the oil to South Africa.[65] Similarly, when Shell was exposed in 1981 as a transporter of Omani oil to South Africa, Transworld Oil, another company also operating in Oman, began buying large quantities of Shell-produced Omani oil, which in turn found their way to South Africa.[66] Since 1979 all OPEC countries had embargoed oil sales to South Africa, Shell was the most important oil company able to circumvent this international embargo and to ensure the supply of oil on a large scale to South Africa. It profited handsomely from the premium price it could demand.[67] Shell South Africa, along with other resident oil companies, fuelled apartheid's military operations in the townships and its wars in Namibia, Angola and other neighbouring black states. Royal Dutch/Shell's relationship to apartheid made an appropriate target for international pressure.

Shell South Africa was also subject to strong domestic censure. In 1987 Beyers Naudé, then general secretary of the South African Council of Churches joined the ANC and SWAPO in support of international pressure on Shell to disinvest: "The action of the world community to force Shell to withdraw from South Africa and to sever all economic links is a logical consequence of the resolution of the SACC ... it reminds Black and White in South Africa of the world's determination to bring an end to apartheid."[68]

Such statements contrasted sharply with the image the company culti-
vated for itself. In June 1986 the Taskforce approached Shell Canada Ltd.[69]
J.M. MacLeod, the company's president and chief executive officer, replied
that while Shell Canada had no influence on either Shell South Africa nor
on the shareholders of the Royal Dutch/Shell Group, he wished to note
that the latter had been and continued to be "direct and outspokenly critical of apartheid" and that it was Royal Dutch/Shell's belief that "Shell
South Africa, by working inside that country to combat apartheid, can do
more to bring about change and benefit to that country's black population
than can be achieved by withdrawing and becoming a mere spectator."[70]
Shell Canada also provided the churches with a copy of the *Shell South
Africa Social Report, 1985–86*, published by Shell South Africa as well as
other documents supportive of Shell's position. These documents suggested that there was no international oil embargo in effect against South
Africa, but only restrictions imposed by a number of individual countries
on the destinations of their oil exports. The Shell Group companies were
observing these restrictions, including those imposed on South Africa. The
documents stated categorically, "in fact no [Royal/Dutch Shell] Group
company is selling or shipping oil to South Africa."

In 1986 documents justifying Shell South Africa's continued presence
in South Africa had begun to proliferate and were distributed to the growing number of Shell's international critics. In fact in 1986, Shell Oil Company, the US subsidiary of Royal Dutch/Shell, engaged a Washington
consulting firm to help the oil giant check an expanding boycott of Shell
products and shareholder protests. This move coincided with a call by
major US organizations, including the churches for a nation-wide consumer boycott of Shell. Similar campaigns were under way in Europe,
Scandinavia, Canada and Australia.

The consulting firm employed by Shell Oil to produce an effective
counter strategy was "Pagan International." It recommended a variety of
techniques, each tailored to influence specific critics.[71] Pagan saw church
organizations and academics as requiring a two-pronged approach. First, a
new "religious" body was formed of disaffected clergy and laity and named
the Coalition on Southern Africa. It was clearly a creation of Pagan; indeed
its address was Pagan's office in Washington. The new Coalition was to
"work" with US and international church leaders to deflect them from the
boycott campaign. The second prong was aimed at church as well as academic critics. They were to be engaged in organized discussions dealing
with "post-apartheid society" for which speakers, documents and seminars
were being provided. A year after its launch, a copy of the 266-page strategy report found its way to the Interfaith Center on Corporate Responsibility (ICCR) in New York. Publicity given by ICCR to this costly and
surreptitious campaign blunted much of the intended impact.[72]

Shell Canada's Place in the Royal Dutch/Shell Group

In May 1987 the Canadian Labour Congress decided to back a national consumer boycott of Shell Canada products. While individual member churches and religious orders made independent decisions on their support for the boycott, the Taskforce began to prepare for possible shareholder action.

Late in 1986 it had written to Shell Canada, detailing Shell South Africa's strategic involvement at every level of South Africa's energy industry.[73] The Taskforce noted that Shell South Africa held a 50 percent interest in SAPREF, the country's largest oil refinery, and operated an oil pipeline in conjunction with the apartheid government. Shell South Africa had important interests in coal mining and was involved in South Africa's oil from coal conversion projects. The company held a 50 percent interest in the Rietspruit colliery and co-owned the largest coal-exporting terminal in South Africa.[74] The Taskforce letter concluded that the nature of Shell South Africa's interests appeared to support the status quo. The churches urged Shell Canada to persuade its parent Royal Dutch/Shell, as well as Shell South Africa, to disinvest as the most effective way to fight apartheid.

Correspondence with Shell Canada continued for the better part of 1987.[75] On 5 February 1988 members of the Taskforce met with Shell Canada executives along with a senior public affairs officer of Shell Transport and Trading Company, the British partner of the Royal Dutch/Shell, and a representative of Shell South Africa's public affairs and legal department. The ease with which Shell Canada could produce these partners is worth noting in the light of Shell Canada's later claim that it was difficult for it to communicate the wishes of Canadian shareholders to these companies.

The meeting went over familiar ground.[76] Shell executives praised Shell South Africa's constructive role in the black community and its progressive labour relations. They noted that John Wilson, then chair of Shell South Africa, had called for the unbanning of the ANC. Shell, they said, wished a future in post-apartheid South Africa and was not prepared to jeopardize this chance by courting the regime's displeasure. The company conceded that South African laws prevented it from disclosing energy needs and supplies. Shell could state, however, that no Shell company outside South Africa supplied any oil to South Africa. The world crude oil market was so fragmented, Shell executives explained, that shipments of oil changed hands many times and no hard evidence had ever been found to show that international Shell or its subsidiaries were shipping oil to South Africa. This was hardly a confirmation that Shell respected the oil embargo. Rather it was an argument of the "you'll never prove it" variety. Church representatives made the point that a company wishing to conceal its identity as an oil supplier would also find these same factors expedient, for crude oil was obviously reaching South Africa from abroad.

The Canadian churches told Shell that they agreed with their own partners in South Africa that Shell's disinvestment from South Africa would
be a powerful and non-violent contribution to ending apartheid. The
Taskforce was convinced that Shell's presence in South Africa, far from
making it an effective force for change, greatly contributed to the defence
of the regime. It proposed that Shell's preoccupation with planning its
role in a post-apartheid society should follow rather than precede all
efforts to dismantle apartheid. Thus were the classic positions of those col-
laborating with the regime and those pursuing proactive anti-apartheid
policies once more defined, this time with the Royal Dutch Shell family of
subordinate firms.

On 27 April 1988 members of the Taskforce attended the Calgary
annual general meeting as shareholders of Shell Canada.[77] They pressed
hard that Shell Canada use its influence to convince Royal Dutch/Shell to
disinvest its South African interests. J. M. MacLeod, chair of Shell Canada,
assured the shareholders that like most Canadians he abhorred apartheid
but that, contrary to the churches' belief, Shell Canada had no influence
outside of Canada. He offered to continue discussions with the churches
in private meetings, and warned that the specific issues were unsuited for
annual meetings of shareholders. A questioner, not related to the churches,
enquired whether it would not indeed be sensible for one Shell company
to exert some influence on another as had been proposed. At that point
Lo C. van Wachem intervened. He was managing director of the Royal
Dutch Petroleum Company, Shell Canada's majority shareholder
(71.4 percent) and one of its directors. He put an end to the discussion
and affirmed that each national company was autonomous and none
should try to influence the other.[78] After the shareholder meeting, the
Taskforce added Shell Canada to its postcard campaign directed against
particularly inflexible companies.[79]

Shell Canada Resists Shareholder Vote

Discounting the predictable vote of Royal Dutch/Shell with its ownership
of 71.4 percent of Shell Canada shares, an attempt was made to test the
level of support for a church shareholder proposal among the remaining
public shareholders of Shell Canada. On 23 January 1989 the churches
proposed to Shell Canada's management that it support a shareholder proposal which they planned to present. The proposal would ask the board of
directors to communicate to Royal Dutch/Shell the wishes of its Canadian
shareholders that Shell withdraw its operations from South Africa. Shell
Canada management resolutely rejected support for the proposal.

Three days later the Sisters of Charity of Mount St. Vincent, Halifax, the
Presbyterian Church in Canada and the United Church of Canada—all
shareholders of Shell Canada—formally submitted this proposal under the

provisions of the Canada Business Corporations Act (CBCA). They anticipated that Shell Canada would circulate their proposal in the company's
proxy circular for consideration and vote by their fellow shareholders at the
1989 annual general meeting. The proposal addressed Shell's preoccupation with post-apartheid South Africa:

> The process of negotiations leading to the creation of a multiracial democratic
> South Africa will only begin ... when economic pressures force all parties to
> the bargaining table. As part of this economic pressure church and labour
> leaders in South Africa have called on Shell to disinvest its holdings, and anti-
> apartheid organizations around the world have united in a campaign in sup-
> port of this call to Royal Dutch/Shell.

The churches' proposal asked Shell Canada's board of directors to convey
to Royal Dutch/Shell the wish of its Canadian public shareholders that it
withdrew its South African investments and terminate all license and franchise agreements with South African entities.[80]

Shell Canada, however, elected, as had Varity Corporation two years earlier, to rely on Section 131 (5) (b) of the CBCA to justify its refusal to
include the churches' shareholder proposal in the proxy circular, and
thereby to deny a vote on the issue at the annual meeting. Shell Canada
successfully applied to the Court of Queen's Bench of Alberta to be permitted not to circulate the proposal.[81] As it had done in the case of Varity,
however, the US Security Exchange Commission (SEC) told Shell Canada
to circulate the churches' proposal. Unlike Varity, Shell Canada then defied
the SEC. It requested that the SEC review of its ruling. Without waiting for
a reply, however, Shell Canada mailed its proxy materials to its shareholders, excluding the churches' proposal. When the SEC finally confirmed its
earlier ruling on 19 April, Shell Canada would have been obliged to postpone the annual meeting until the churches' proposal had been mailed to
all shareholders, and time had been allowed for the return of proxy votes
by those not planning to attend the meeting. Church shareholders, rather
than inconveniencing company and shareholders, waived the legal requirements and entered into a dialogue with Shell Canada about a compromise
solution. Shell Canada abruptly broke off the negotiations two days before
the annual general meeting.

The shareholder meeting on 26 April 1989 was an unpleasant affair. In
a needlessly discourteous attempt at intimidation, the chair, Jack MacLeod,
warned church representatives that they would be "cut off" if they used
inflammatory language during the meeting. He banned the distribution of
the churches' proposal even to those shareholders present, and limited to
a total of twelve minutes the remarks of two proponents of the churches'
proposal. MacLeod put them on notice "that discussion must be relevant
to the subject, impersonal and directed to the chair, or it will be ruled out
of order."[82]

Reverend Bill Phipps, executive secretary of the Alberta and North West Conference of the United Church of Canada, explained that by virtue of Shell's interests in South Africa it was contributing to the staying power of the apartheid regime. He spoke to the essence of Shell Canada's avowed concern: "Our resolution was carefully worded so that it did not ask Shell Canada to do something which is outside its power. This resolution simply calls on the directors of the company to pass on to the management of the Royal Dutch/Shell Group the desire of the Canadian public shareholders that Shell begin the process of disinvesting from South Africa."[83] Reverend Dr. Ray Hodgson, on the proxy of the Presbyterian Church in Canada, reviewed Shell Canada's determination to prevent its shareholders from voting on the churches' shareholder proposal. Hodgson noted that Shell Canada, having asked the SEC for its ruling and being told twice to circulate the churches' proposal, had disregarded the SEC, showing "itself willing to play by the rules only as long as the rules were in its favour."[84] He referred to the time, money and energy Shell Canada had devoted to deflect this issue, all for the sole purpose of disenfranchising its shareholders.[85]

MacLeod, for his part, reiterated that the Shell Group of companies believed that Shell's withdrawal from South Africa would worsen rather than improve conditions there and that Shell Canada therefore did not intend to persuade Royal Dutch/Shell to adopt a disinvestment policy. Having successfully prevented the majority of its public shareholders from expressing their view on the issue, MacLeod eschewed discussion of shareholder rights.

By denying its public shareholders a vote on Shell's South African investment, Shell Canada was likely trying to avoid an outcome similar to the one achieved by the Taskforce at the Rio Algom 1988 annual general meeting. There, 46.7 percent of Rio Algom's public shareholders had supported the churches' shareholder proposal in favour of withdrawal. In 1989 public pressure for disinvestment would have been even stronger than it had been the previous year. At the Shell Canada meeting, the result of a shareholder vote might have exposed an embarrassing discrepancy in the policies followed by the management of Shell Canada and Royal Dutch/Shell and the wishes of its public shareholders.

Shell Canada's treatment of its shareholders was not an isolated incident. It paralleled in every aspect the manner in which Shell companies in other countries dealt with similar shareholder pressures and suggested that the approach had been dictated by Royal Dutch/Shell directives. US shareholder rights organizations had sought since 1988 to overcome the refusal by Shell Oil to let shareholders vote on the issue. Shareholders in England and Holland were similarly treated. In 1988 Shell even took the Lewisham council (UK) to court and was able to overturn a decision to exclude Shell from tendering for council contracts.[86]

In 1986 Shell South Africa had fired striking miners at its Rietspruit coal mine, disabusing perceptions of the company's progressive labour policies. Cyril Ramaphosa, then secretary general of the National Union of Mine Workers (NUM), an affiliate of COSATU, expressed the mood of an angry union, which henceforth prevailed: "If it is up to us, Shell may go tomorrow not only because we feel that all foreign companies should pull out, but also because this company is treating its workers as if they are nothing, as air ... in the field of the apartheid and of union-busting practices Shell has built up a bad record. Yes we want this company to leave the country."[87]

Following Nelson Mandela's release from prison in February 1990, two union representatives of the Chemical Workers Industrial Union (CWIU) also a member of COSATU, visited the Taskforce. They were concerned that sanctions be maintained until the cornerstones of the apartheid system were removed.[88] The CWIU had called on all petroleum companies in South Africa to negotiate with the union the terms of their possible withdrawal. This was done in order to safeguard jobs and working conditions under new management which would follow disinvestment. While other oil companies had agreed to negotiate such terms with the CWIU, Shell South Africa had refused to do so on the grounds that it had no intention of withdrawing.

During their meeting with the Taskforce, CWIU representatives were also anxious to correct the image of Shell South Africa as a progressive employer and promoter of social change in South Africa. The CWIU reported that unlike other petroleum companies, Shell South Africa refused to conduct union negotiations on a national basis, with the result that working conditions, while good in the major plants, were much worse in many smaller locations. The union also told the Taskforce that Shell South Africa's community programs were more designed to counter international criticism then to be effective. For example, Shell South Africa had rejected CWIU's request to negotiate its educational and social programs. The union would have preferred that Shell South Africa's educational funds were used to assist with their children's primary and secondary school fees, rather than fund the comparatively few, high-profile students who reached university level. As well, the CWIU had unsuccessfully asked that community funding be more widely distributed in areas of maximum need rather than in a few ostentatious and well-publicized projects.

At the end of March 1990, well past the year's deadline for submitting formal shareholder proposals, but just shortly after Mandela's release from prison, Shell Canada telephoned the Taskforce to say that it would now consider a shareholder proposal from the churches such as the one it had rejected the previous year. It is surely not too cynical to link this change of mind to Mandela's release and the need to repair Royal Dutch/Shell's international image as it faced "post-apartheid" South Africa in earnest.[89]

Position of Texaco, Mobil Oil and BP in Canada

The Taskforce addressed three additional Canadian subsidiaries whose parent companies had operations in South Africa: Texaco Canada, Mobil Oil Canada and BP Canada Inc. In January 1989 Imperial Oil Ltd., which had no investments in South Africa bought Texaco Canada, while Mobil Oil Canada's parent, Mobil Corporation, disinvested its South African holdings in April of the same year.[90] The relationship with the third, BP Canada, developed in an interesting fashion.

In early December 1988 the Taskforce had written to Donald Harvie, chair of BP Canada, whose parent company, the British Petroleum Co. PLC., with an investment of approximately US$300 million, was the largest British investor in South Africa and paralleled in significance and diversification the South African operations of Royal Dutch/Shell. Harvie then forwarded to the Taskforce a letter from Gordon Smith, the regional coordinator, Southern Africa, of BP in London, to whom Harvie had sent a copy of the Taskforce letter.[91]

Smith wrote that BP would remain in South Africa as long as it could contribute to social change and conduct its businesses profitably there. He rejected the suggestion that by its presence BP supported apartheid. BP's presence was neutral, Smith held, "after all, blacks drive cars and rely on B.P. products as much as whites." Explaining BP's oil supplies in South Africa, Smith indicated that BP had found a way to work around the international embargo: "All BP companies strictly observe the oil embargo, and BP Southern Africa is independent of the Group [of BP companies] for its supplies except for small quantities of non-embargoed products."[92]

In his letter Smith claimed that a recent statement of the Synod of Anglican Bishops in South Africa showed a shift of position away "from calls by some for comprehensive mandatory sanctions." Smith's comment was more than a little vague. Still, the Taskforce consulted the record on this issue of the 1988 Lambeth Conference, the largest communion of Anglican bishops and compared this with *The Statement of 4 December 1988 of the Synod of Bishops of the Church of the Province of Southern Africa*, the Synod's most recent statement. The two statements were entirely compatible. Lambeth called upon the Churches to press their governments to "3(a) bring maximum pressure to bear on the South African regime in order to promote a genuine process of change towards the establishment of democratic political structures in a unified state";[93] The Synod of Anglican Bishops in Southern Africa concurred word for word with this statement.[94] Where Lambeth called for pressure to "3(b) institute forms of sanctions calculated to have the maximum effect in bringing an end to the evil dispensation, and in establishing a just peace among all citizens,"[95] the Synod of Anglican Bishops in Southern Africa stated that "We believe that the imposition of carefully selected and specifically targeted forms of pressure, including economic and diplomatic pressure, hold the potential to bring about relatively rapid change."[96] The Taskforce saw no contradiction between the two Anglican statements and the Taskforce's policy of targeted sanctions, which placed particular emphasis on the disinvestment of companies in strategic industries.

BP's Gordon Smith set great store in the benevolent contributions of business associated with the "greater economic empowerment of black people, which has given them an added assurance and confidence in their rightful demands for equality": "Business development generally has made the major contribution to this process and enlightened and progressive companies [among them BP Southern Africa] have gone further by taking a lead in trying to hasten it—evolution at revolutionary speed."[97] Like Royal Dutch/Shell, BP stressed its importance to "post-apartheid society." It viewed as "counterproductive to the achievement of post-apartheid society" the call for "disinvestment by responsible multi-national corporations." BP, Smith wrote, was working for peaceful change and added adroitly that its very corporate power served as an asset to this endeavour: "I very much doubt it would have been able to take such a prominent role were it not for the encouragement, support and I suggest, 'protection' of a multi national organization like BP."[98]

Not since the 1970s had the Taskforce encountered such extraordinary claims. In its many years of experience with corporate activity in South Africa, the Taskforce had been able to illustrate that companies, particularly those in the strategic sector such as the petroleum industry, were so integrated in the maintenance and defence of apartheid that any beneficial role they might otherwise have played could not offset this central fact.

Victory over apartheid was finally achieved, not because companies such as Royal Dutch/Shell and BP had remained in South Africa, but despite their presence. Had they not fuelled the regime's war against the democratic forces, liberation would not have come so late nor cost as much in deaths and blighted lives.

Summary of Canadian Corporate Withdrawals from South Africa, 1990–91

The annual report of the administrator for the Canadian government's Code of Conduct recorded that by 1991 the following Canadian companies had disinvested from South Africa.[99]

1986   Alcan Aluminium Ltd.
        Bata Ltd.
        Dominion Textiles Inc.
        Jarvis Clark Co. (CIL)

1987   AMCA International
       Champion Road Machinery Ltd.
       Chempharm Ltd.
       Cobra Metals & Minerals Inc.
       Cominco Ltd.
       DelCan Ltd.
       Falconbridge Ltd.
       International Thomson Org. Ltd.
       Jos. E. Seagram & Sons Ltd.
       Moore Corporation

1988   JKS Boyles International Inc.
       National Business Systems Inc.
       Ford Motor Co. of Canada Ltd.

1989   QIT-Fer et Titane Inc.
       [transfer of ownership to RTZ Corporation (UK)]

1990   Nil

1991   Varity Corporation

There were still some puzzles related to the status of QIT-Fer et Titane even at this late date. As the administrator's report pointed out, in February 1988 QIT's equity holding in Richards Bay Minerals was acquired by BP International Ltd. In June 1989 RTZ Corporation acquired BP International's mineral holdings, including its interest in RBM. A letter from B. J. Grierson, chair of QIT-Fer et Titane of 31 March 1994 told the Taskforce that "[A]lthough QIT has no ownership interest in RBM, it continues to operate in the same business group because of the common ownership.... QIT continued to file reports under the Code of Conduct for Canadian Companies for as long as the code was monitored by Government." In other words, QIT continued to operate as Canadian management of RBM regardless of change in the ultimate ownership. Grierson's statement is in conflict with a letter of 6 June 1990 from Joe Clark to the Taskforce in which he declared that "Management of RBM, and the application of national sanctions, has passed to the United Kingdom from Canada.... Richards Bay Minerals is no longer subject to any direct influence by the Canadian Government." Indeed, contrary to Mr. Grierson's assumption, the 1989 *Annual Report* on Canadian Code of Conduct was the last to carry an entry for QIT-Fer et Titane. It is puzzling why, despite QIT's apparent willingness to report, the Canadian government would have ignored reports on the management function of the company, the very structure responsible for employment practices at RBM.

The administrator confirmed that generally Canadian investment had been in affiliated South African enterprises, and that most of the large investors had withdrawn from South Africa by the end of 1987. He noted that in 1985, 20,000 "non-whites" had been employed in companies with Canadian investment, by 31 March 1987 that number had fallen to 3,084 "non-whites."[100] By 30 June 1991 that figure was sixty-nine (it included 12 South African "non-whites" employed in the Canadian Embassy!)[101] The 1991 Annual Report finally conceded what the Taskforce had been reporting all along: "where equity participation is less than 50%, Canadian management reports no involvement in the management or operation of the affiliate and suggests little or no influence over the issues at stake."[102]

The decision of the Canadian banks to withhold new loans from South Africa and these withdrawals by Canadian investors likely constituted Canada's most important contributions to the struggle against apartheid. Companies withdrawing from South Africa did not at the time appreciate such an association, and preferred to cite "business reasons" for their decisions without quite realizing that at this late stage in the struggle that was all that counted. Their disinvestment added to the international loss of business confidence and helped to isolate the apartheid government until it finally had no choice but to engage in constitutional negotiations. In the early 1970s B.J. Vorster, then prime minister of South Africa, had proclaimed that every new loan and every new foreign investment was a brick in the wall of apartheid. In the late 1980s the reverse showed itself to be as true: as each brick removed from that wall eventually helped to bring it down.

Notes

1 Letter from J.M. McAvity to the author, 3 October 1980.
2 The Canada-South Africa Society, Suite 100, 1434 St. Catherine Street West, Montreal, Quebec H3G 1R4, "Memorandum" to all members of the Society from J.M. McAvity, president, February 1983.
3 Linda Diebel, "Opposes Sanctions, Sauvé's Husband Director of Group Backing S. Africa," *The Gazette*, 26 July 1985.
4 "Maurice Sauvé Quits S. Africa Lobby Group," *The Toronto Star*, 27 July 1985.
5 Diebel, "Opposes Sanctions"; Laurie Monsebraaten and Paula Todd, "Sauvé's S. Africa Link Angers Rights Groups," *The Toronto Star*, 28 July 1985; and "Quebec Judge to Quit as S. Africa Lobbyist," Montreal (CP), 7 August 1985.
6 See chap. 4, pp. 108–14. At one point a senior Alcan executive even suggested that Hulett was likely to produce no more than lunch buckets for the South African army!
7 Shareholders submitting the proposal were: The General Synod of the Anglican Church of Canada; the Canadian Conference of Catholic Bishops; the United Church of Canada; the Jesuit Fathers of Upper Canada; the Sisters of Charity of Mount St. Vincent, Halifax; and the Ursulines of Chatham Union. The shareholder proposal was included in the proxy material and sent to all shareholders prior to Alcan's annual meeting on 27 March 1986.

8 Taskforce on the Churches and Corporate Responsibility, "Summary Notes of the Meeting with Senior Management of Alcan Aluminum Ltd., 9 December 1985," 15 January 1986 (mimeograph), p. 2.

9 This meeting took place in the garden of Archbishop Hurley's residence where we had been staying. Hurley had stayed in Pretoria but had warned me that his phone and his house were "bugged."

10 Taskforce on the Churches and Corporate Responsibility, News Release, 20 March 1986.

11 See chap. 4, pp. 125–27. Western Platinum mined platinum, gold, nickel, copper and cobalt. In 1985 Falconbridge was represented by three directors on the board of Western Platinum, and appointed one of two managing directors of the mine. Ownership was distributed as follows: Falconbridge, 24.5 percent; Lonrho PLC (UK), 51 percent; Mobil Corporation, 24.5 percent.

12 Taskforce, *Annual Report, 1985–1985*, p. 34.

13 Falconbridge Ltd. and Western Platinum Ltd., "Code of Conduct Concerning the Employment Practices of Canadian Companies Operating in South Africa, Standard Reporting Format," completed by Falconbridge Ltd. for the period 1 October 1984 to 30 September 1985, p. 13.

14 "(3) Wages: ... the minimum wage should initially exceed this minimum [living] level by at least 50 percent" ("Code of Conduct ... Canadian Companies in South Africa," Annex B, in *Annual Report on the Administration and Observance of the Code of Conduct Concerning the Employment Practices of Canadian Companies Operating in South Africa*, submitted to the Rt. Hon. Joe Clark, P.C., M.P., by Albert F. Hart, administrator [mimeograph], p. 3).

15 Department of External Affairs, "South Africa: Falconbridge Investment," Communiqué no. 201, 19 November 1986.

16 John Spears, "Falconbridge Doubles Stake in Pretoria Firm," *The Toronto Star*, 18 November 1986, cited in Taskforce on the Churches and Corporate Responsibility, *Annual Report, 1986–1987*, p. 23.

17 Massey-Ferguson changed its name to Varity Corporation in June 1986.

18 For an earlier discussion of Massey-Ferguson, see chap. 2, pp. 44–46 and chap. 4, pp. 118–21. In 1985 Massey-Ferguson held an 18.95 percent interest in Fedmech, a company producing heavy machinery for the agricultural, industrial and transportation equipment. Massey-Ferguson had two directors on the board of Fedmech, which in turn was part of Federale Volksbeleggings Beperk, a large South African group of companies. Massey-Ferguson through its wholly-owned subsidiary, Perkins Diesel (UK), also had a licensee agreement and a small interest in the state-owned Atlantis Diesel Engine Co. (ADE), a Key Point Industry located in Atlantis, a "coloured only" area in the Cape. ADE products were to assure South Africa's self-sufficiency in diesel engines for, inter alia, the military and police.

19 Massey-Ferguson and Fedmech Holdings Ltd., "Code of Conduct Concerning the Employment Practices of Canadian Companies Operating in South Africa, Standard Reporting Format," 25 May 1986, p. 9.

20 "Another technique to by-pass sanctions is to increase the portion of apparently civilian items in military equipment. The Ratel armoured personnel carrier is a good example. It is based entirely on European designs and uses standard automotive components, *including a locally made diesel engine—itself based on foreign technology*" (emphasis added) (quoted from "Sales to South Africa," in *Independent Expert Study on the Evaluation of the Application and Impact of Sanctions, Final Report to the Commonwealth Committee on Southern Africa* [London: Commonwealth Secretariat, 1989] [photocopy], p. 34.

21 Letter from the Rt. Hon. David Peterson, premier of the Province of Ontario, to Bill Davis, chair, Taskforce on the Churches and Corporate Responsibility, 23 January 1986.

22 Letter to Premier David Peterson, from W.R. Davis, chair, Taskforce on the Churches and Corporate Responsibility, 9 April 1986, cited in Taskforce, *Annual Report, 1985–1986*, pp. 40–41.

23 Archbishop Tutu had addressed the Legislative Assembly of Ontario on 30 May 1986; the Eminent Persons Group had reported on 12 June 1986.

24 Letter from David Peterson, premier of Ontario, to J.P. McCarter, secretary, Massey-Ferguson Ltd., 16 June 1986. A copy was sent to W.R. Davis, chair of the Taskforce. A cover letter of 18 June from Joy Gordon, International Relations Branch, Ministry of Intergovernmental Affairs, noted that the premier's letter was not signed until late afternoon of 17 June and could not be delivered to Massey-Ferguson earlier.

25 Taskforce, *Annual Report, 1985–1986*, p. 42

26 Canada, House of Commons, Standing Committee on Human Rights, *Minutes of Proceedings and Evidence*, 17 July 1986, p. 10:77.

27 The company's report on the ADE's compliance of the Canadian Code made this very clear. Under item 1.6 (Workforce), the report states: "Atlantis Diesel is located in a coloured development area, [and] to date, blacks cannot be employed. ADE employs Whites, coloured, Indians but not black [*sic*] (i.e., Africans). Within that context all employees are treated equally" (Massey-Ferguson Ltd. and Atlantis Diesel Engines Ltd., "Code of Conduct Concerning the Employment Practices of Canadian Companies Operating in South Africa, Standard Reporting Format," 7 April 1986, p. 13).

28 A record of the sequence of events between January and June 1987 is contained in Taskforce on the Churches and Corporate Responsibility, "1987 Church Shareholder Proposal to Varity Corporation, Record of Events," 1 September 1987 (mimeograph), which was sent to the board of directors of Varity Corporation and its corporate secretary. See also Taskforce, *Annual Report, 1986–1987*, pp. 24–30.

29 Later Varity management apologized for the fact that a lawyer arrived on the doorstep of the Ursulines and Jesuits to serve the papers without Varity having extended the courtesy of phoning or writing beforehand to explain the steps it was taking (Taskforce, "1987 Church Shareholder Proposal to Varity Corporation, Record of Events," p. 2.

30 The two errors noted are that the SEC rule should have read "14a–8(a)(1)" and "a record or beneficial owner" should have read "a record of beneficial ownership. . . ."

31 Letter from Cahill Gordon & Reindel, New York, to the Securities Exchange Commission, Washington, DC, re: Varity Corporation, Rule 14a–8 under *Securities Exchange Act* of 1934, 23 March 1987, p. 2.

32 Company communications director Jack Nowling, quoted in Patricia Lush, "SEC Ruling Forces Vote by Varity Shareholders on South Africa Pullout," *The Globe and Mail*, 9 May 1987.

33 John Spears, "Church Groups Fail to Sway Court on Varity Vote over South Africa," *The Toronto Star*, 22 April 1987.

34 Letter from R.D. Garland, director, Legal Services, Varity Corporation, to Father J.P. Horrigan, S.J., Jesuit Fathers of Upper Canada, 30 April 1987 (by hand).

35 Issued by Cecilia D. Blye, special counsel, and communicated to Varity via Cahill Gordon & Reindel by William E. Morley, chief counsel of the SEC, 6 May 1987. Copies of the correspondence were included to avoid summarizing the arguments. Copies of the documents were provided to the Canadian proponents.

36 Taskforce on the Churches and Corporate Responsibility, Media Release, 12 March 1987.

37 The report for 1986 of a revised Canadian Code of Conduct was prepared by John Small, the new administrator. He established new rating categories, from I (best) to IV (worst), based on criteria that included non-discriminatory employment conditions. Small rated Varity's affiliate Atlantis Diesel Engines (ADE) category I for employment practices,

unmoved that ADE's decision to locate in an area for "coloureds" only, involved it in discrimination against black South Africans in compliance with apartheid's *Group Areas Act*. Small simply explained: "As ADE is in a designated coloured development area most of its employees are Coloured. ADE did not differentiate among its employees on the ground that doing so would counter its policy of non-discrimination" (*Code of Conduct: Canadian Companies in South Africa, Second Annual Report for the Year 1986*, Ottawa, 29 May 1987 [mimeograph)], p. 10.

38 David Climenhaga, "Varity Shareholders Vote to Stay in South Africa," *The Globe and Mail*, 11 June 1987.

39 Ibid.

40 In a statement on GM's withdrawal from South Africa, Roger Smith, its chair, commented on the increasing *seize* of shareholder votes in favour of disinvestment: "Where it used to be that a vote of 3–6 percent for disinvestment was considered significant, current tallies are coming in at 10–25 percent in favour. ... Since most banks and large shareholders will back management and management gets not only its own shares but also all unmarked ballots, 'the cards are stacked' heavily in favour of the status quo. The size of the votes lately ... represents a 'minor shareholders' revolt'" ("Auto Maker's Statement," *New York Times*, 21 October 1987.

41 Taskforce on the Churches and Corporate Responsibility, "Report on Debate of Proposal, Annual Meeting of Shareholders of Varity Corporation, 10 June 1987" (mimeograph). The figures do not add up to 100% due to rounding.

42 The shares were held by the (federal) Canada Development Investment Corporation and the Ontario Development Corporation.

43 Letter to Ann Abraham, chair of the Taskforce on the Churches and Corporate Responsibility, from the Rt. Hon. Joe Clark, secretary of state for External Affairs, 14 December 1987.

44 Letter to Ann Abraham, chair, Taskforce on the Churches and Corporate Responsibility, from the Rt. Hon. David Peterson, premier of the Province of Ontario, 5 January 1988.

45 *Administration and Observance of the Code of Conduct Concerning the Employment Practices of Canadian Companies Operating in South Africa* (Ottawa, 1988), quoted in Taskforce on the Churches and Corporate Responsibility, *Annual Report, 1987–1988*, p. 16.

46 Quoted in Taskforce, *Annual Report, 1987–1988*, p. 26.

47 See chap. 4, pp. 117–18.

48 This was also the judgment of the UN secretary general: "There has been no progress in my recent discussions with the Government of South Africa concerning the implementation of Security Council resolution 435 (1978)" (UN Secretary-General Javier Perez de Cuellar, Report to the United Nations Security Council, UN Document S/17442, 6 September 1985.

49 "An Open Appeal to the Canadian Government from the Churches in Namibia, 27–28 November 1986," Ottawa (mimeograph). It was signed by the Rt. Rev. Bonifatius Haushiku, bishop of the Roman Catholic Diocese of Windhoek; the Rev. Kleopas Dumeni, bishop, Evangelical Lutheran Church in Namibia; W. Hamutenya, laymember of the Roman Catholic Diocese of Windhoek; Salmi Shivute, nursing sister, Evangelical Lutheran Church in Namibia; the Rev. Dr. Abisai Shejavali, general secretary, Council of Churches in Namibia. The group was supported by the Rev. Brien Grieves, presiding bishop, Episcopal Church, USA, and the Rev. Massey Gentry, Anglican Communion and Episcopal Church, USA. The church leaders were visiting church, government and media representatives in Bonn, Rome, the Vatican, Copenhagen, Oslo, Helsinki, Stockholm, Canterbury, London, Paris and Washington.

50 Statement by Ann Abraham during the annual meeting of shareholders of Rio Algom Ltd., 29 April 1987, quoted in Taskforce, *Annual Report, 1986–1987*, p. 32.

51 On 18 August 1987 South African security forces arrested Daniel Tjongarero and charged him under Section 6 of the *Terrorism Act*. The Taskforce turned, among others, to Rio Algom, asking the company to make inquiries about the circumstances of his arrest. Rio Algom did not respond to this request. Tjongarero was released later that year.

52 See "PCO Policy Review," chap. 6, pp. 198–99.

53 Taskforce on the Churches and Corporate Responsibility, "Report on the Debate on the Proposal of Church Shareholders at the Annual Meeting of Rio Algom Limited, 27 April 1988," (mimeograph), p. 1.

54 Ibid., p. 2.

55 Ibid., p. 3.

56 The meeting between SWAPO officials and Rio Algom is described in Taskforce on the Churches and Corporate Responsibility, *Annual Report, 1988–1989*, pp. 60–61.

57 Cawthra, *Brutal Force*, p. 87.

58 *The Financial Times* (SA), 23 June 1979, and *Government Gazette*, 22 June 1979, cited in Cawthra, *Brutal Force*, p. 89.

59 "In 1983 a Pretoria Cabinet Minister admitted that 'the acquisition of oil was more difficult than arms' and that the oil embargo 'could have destroyed' the apartheid regime" (*London Observer*, 3 June 1984, cited in Cawthra, *Brutal Force*, p. 88.

60 In December 1979 Canada had voted to oppose a UN General Assembly resolution calling for an international oil embargo against South Africa. The churches had told the Canadian government that "Support for the oil embargo would place pressure upon the South African police and the military in much the same way as does the arms embargo. It is surprising and regrettable that Canada opposed this resolution." See Taskforce on the Churches and Corporate Responsibility, "Canadian Policy towards Southern Africa: A Brief Presented to the Hon. Mark MacGuigan, Secretary of State for External Affairs, and Herbert Gray, Minister of Industry, Trade and Commerce," 5 May 1981, p. 14.

61 While anti-apartheid organizations in industrialized countries would be able to identify international oil companies operating within their borders and address them directly about their activities in South Africa, a major service was offered by the Shipping Research Bureau (SRB) of Amsterdam which tracked oil deliveries to South Africa and reported on oil company operations within South Africa. It published its findings in an occasional *Newsletter on the Oil Embargo against South Africa* (Amsterdam: Shipping Research Bureau). The Taskforce drew extensively on the SRB *Newsletter*.

62 It had extensive operations in petroleum, chemical and mining industries in the two countries. See *The Financial Mail* (SA), 22 April 1988.

63 Royal Dutch Petroleum Company, *Annual Report, 1987*, p. 10, quoted in Jean Sindab, *Shell Shock: The Churches and the Oil Embargo* (Geneva: World Council of Churches Programme to Combat Racism, 1989), p. 13. The Royal Dutch/Shell Group is composed of the London-based Shell Transport and Trading Company and the Royal Dutch Petroleum Company based in the Netherlands.

64 "Brunei Shell: How Brunei Oil Ends Up in South Africa," *Newsletter on the Oil Embargo against South Africa* (Amsterdam: Shipping Research Bureau, January 1987). The SRB refers to *The Observer* (UK), 2 November 1986; a joint press release by the Holland Committee on Southern Africa and Working Group Kairos, Amsterdam/Utrecht, of 14 November 1986; *De Volkskrant* (Netherlands), 15 November 1986; *The Borneo Bulletin* (Brunei), 15 November 1986.

65 "Brunei Shell: How Brunei Oil Ends Up in South Africa."

66 *The London Observer*, 12 August 1986, quoted in Catherine M. Kovak, "Fuelling the Machines of Apartheid: Shell in South Africa," *ICCR Brief*, 15, no. 5 (1986).

67 *The Multinational Monitor* of 15 April 1986 wrote: "During the first three years of the embargo, Shell delivered 4.5 million tons of crude—nearly one third of South Africa's

annual needs." *The London Observer* of 5 August 1984 stated that in 1980 Shell had received $8 a barrel in "incentives" from the South African government to import the oil (cited in Kovak, "Fuelling the Machines of Apartheid," p. 3A.

68 Statement by Dr. Beyers Naudé, 9 May 1987 (see Sindab, *Shell Shock*, p. 27). On 10 September 1986 SWAPO and the ANC had issued a statement that the two liberation movements supported the call for Royal Dutch/Shell to break all economic and other links with apartheid (ibid., p. 28).

69 Shell Canada and Shell South Africa were two of over one hundred national companies within the "Shell Group." At the time of the events described here, ownership of Shell Canada Ltd. was divided between Shell Investments Ltd. (SIL) and public shareholders. SIL held about 71 percent of the voting interest (but 78 percent of ownership) of Shell Canada Ltd. SIL was wholly owned by Shell Petroleum N.V. of the Netherlands, which in turn was 40 percent owned by Shell Transport and Trading, the UK parent, and 60 percent owned by Royal Dutch of the Netherlands, its Dutch parent.

70 Letter from J.M. MacLeod, president and CEO of Shell Canada Ltd., to Bill Davis, chair of the Taskforce, 3 July 1986.

71 See David E. Anderson, UPI News, 30 September 1987, cited in "Shell against International Campaign 'The Neptune Strategy': Secret Formula by Shell to Counter Boycotts," *Newsletter on the Oil Embargo against South Africa* (Amsterdam: Shipping Research Bureau, January 1987). Pagan International was led by Rafael Pagan, Jr., who several years previously had advised Nestlé on how to combat the international campaign against its promotion of infant formula in Third World countries. Pagan had also been consultant to Union Carbide after the Bophal disaster in India.

72 Diane Bratcher, "The Neptune Strategy: SHELL in South Africa," *ICCR Brief*, 16, no. 7 (1987). Responsibility (New York). "The Neptune Strategy" was the code name Pagan had given to its campaign.

73 Letter from Sheila Kappler, chair of the Taskforce, to J.M. Macleod, president and CEO of Shell Canada Ltd., 14 November 1986.

74 For further details see Kovak, "Fuelling the Machines of Apartheid." In 1988 researchers of "Kairos," a Dutch Christian anti-apartheid organization, found that the port of Rotterdam was used to tranship as "Dutch Coal" South African coal for British and European destinations, boosting South African coal imports to the Netherlands from 200,000 tonnes in 1982 to 2.2 million tonnes in 1987. On 17 October 1988 *The London Observer* wrote: "Royal Dutch/Shell plays a key role in disguising South African coal as Dutch coal to contravene the current coal boycott. Ships owned or chartered by Shell bring coal from the South African terminal which it co-owns to the Netherlands" (cited in Sindab, *Shell Shock*, p. 17).

75 One of these was a four-page letter "TO EXECUTIVES" from Lo C. van Wachem, managing director, Senior Group, Royal Dutch/Shell Group of Companies, datelined The Hague, 23 September 1986. During a fifty-minute television documentary, Mr. Pagan of Pagan International's "Neptune Strategy" was interviewed. It transpired that Pagan had met van Wachem in the summer of 1986 in Houston, Texas, to sign a contract with Royal Dutch/Shell. This would explain the global similarity of approach of Royal Dutch/Shell companies when dealing with their critics (VPRO Television, 1200 JC Hilversum, Netherlands, 11 October 1987, cited in *Newsletter on the Oil Embargo against South Africa* [October 1987]).

76 The summary of the exchange that follows is drawn from Taskforce, *Annual Report, 1987–1988*, pp. 20–21.

77 Representing the United Church of Canada was the Rev. Fred Bayliss, general secretary of the Division of World Outreach, while the Rev. Dr. Ray Hodgson represented the Pension Board of the Presbyterian Church in Canada and as well the proxies of the Sisters of

Charity of St. Vincent de Paul of Halifax. This account of the meeting is taken from Taskforce on the Churches and Corporate Responsibility, "Notes on the Question Period of
Shell Canada Annual Meeting, 27 April 1988" (mimeograph), 3 pages.

78 Kimberly Noble, "Church Groups Threaten Boycott of Shell Stations," *The Globe and
Mail*, 28 April 1988.

79 The other two companies were Varity Corporation and Rio Algom. Their cases are discussed above.

80 Taskforce on the Churches and Corporate Responsibility, Press Release, 26 January
1989.

81 The churches did not contest. Costs were too prohibitive and chances of winning remote
after Varity's successful challenge in 1987.

82 Taskforce on the Churches and Corporate Responsibility, "Report on the Annual General Meeting of Shell Canada Ltd., 26 April 1989—Calgary, Alberta" (mimeograph),
5 pages.

83 Taskforce on the Churches and Corporate Responsibility, "Report on the Annual General Meeting of Shell Canada Ltd.," in *Shell Canada—The Shell Group's Investment in
South Africa Becomes an Issue of Shareholder Rights*, Taskforce mailing, May 1989, (mimeograph, pp. A–I), p. G.

84 Ibid., p. G. It is worth noting that in 1992 the SEC adopted new regulations that reduced
the protection enjoyed by Canadian shareholders under SEC rules in regard to shareholder proposals submitted to Canadian corporations whose shares were listed on American exchanges. Under the new "Multijurisdictional Disclosure System" of the SEC,
Canadian disclosure obligations set out in Section 131-5-b of the Canadian *Business Corporation Act* were henceforth the predominant basis of SEC decisions with regard to
Canadian corporations.

85 Ibid.

86 See *Southscan: A Bulletin of South African Affairs* (London), 11 May 1988, p. 6.

87 *FNV Magazine* (Netherlands), 8 November–6 December 1986, quoted in *Newsletter on
the Oil Embargo against South Africa* (January 1987).

88 At this point in South Africa's historic change, De Klerk had ended the ban on most political organizations and had suspended political executions. However, troops were still
occupying black townships; the state of emergency was still in effect; the majority of political detainees had not yet been released; the apparatus of repressive legislation of the
apartheid system was still in place.

89 As late as 19 January 1990 Shell Canada asked the Supreme Court of British Columbia
to set aside a Vancouver City Council decision of 12 September 1989 that declared Vancouver "Shell Free." The court ruled in favour of Shell Canada on 24 May 1990. See
Minutes of Vancouver City Council, Regular Council Meeting, 12 September 1989,
"Shell Boycott," pp. 10–12.

90 "Mobil Quits South Africa after 90 years," *The Globe and Mail*, 1 May 1989; see also
Taskforce, *Annual Report, 1987–1988*, pp. 53–54.

91 Letters from Donald Harvie, chair, BP Canada, to Ann Abraham, chair of the Taskforce,
14 December 1988 and 5 January 1989.

92 Ibid.

93 *The Truth Shall Make You Free: The Lambeth Conference, 1988. The Reports, Resolutions
and Pastoral Letters from the Bishops* (London: Anglican Church, 1989), p. 228.

94 "3. How to Eradicate Apartheid," in "Statement by the Synod of Bishops of the
Church of the Province of Southern Africa," News Release from the Church of the
Province of Southern Africa, Cape Town, 4 December 1988, Archives, Anglican
Church of Canada, p. 3.

95 *The Truth Shall Make You Free*, p. 228.

96 "4. Types of Pressure," in "Statement by the Synod of Bishops of the Church of the Province of South Africa," p. 4.

97 Letter from Gordon Smith, regional coordinator, Southern Africa, British Petroleum Company PCL, to Ann Abraham, chair, Taskforce on the Churches and Corporate Responsibility, 16 December 1988.

98 Ibid.

99 Robert McLaren, "[T]he 1990–91 and Sixth Report on the Administration and Observance of the Code of Conduct Concerning Employment Practices of Canadian Companies Operating in South Africa," Victoria, 1 December 1991 (mimeograph), p. 4. On p. 6, Figure 1, McLaren also noted the steep decline in the value of direct Canadian investments from over $250 million in 1981 to less than $10 million in 1991.

100 John Small, code administrator, "The Administration and Observance of the Code of Conduct Concerning the Employment Practices of Canadian Companies Operating in South Africa," in *Third Annual Report for the Year 1987*, Ottawa, 31 May 1988 (mimeograph), p. 9.

101 Robert McLaren, "[T]he 1990–91 and Sixth Report on the Administration and Observance of the Code of Conduct Concerning Employment Practices of Canadian Companies Operating in South Africa," p. 9.

102 Ibid., p. 7.

8 The Long Road Back from Sanctions, 1987

The Widening Gap between the Canadian Government and the Churches over Sanctions

In December 1986 Denmark became the first Western country to impose a comprehensive economic embargo against Pretoria. In February 1987 a UN Security Council resolution on selected mandatory economic sanctions modeled on the Comprehensive Anti-apartheid Act of the United States had won majority support, though it was vetoed by Britain and by the Reagan administration, still bruised from its defeat at the hand of the Congress. Sweden, which would have preferred to work within the United Nations, then followed Denmark's example. On Commonwealth Day, 9 March, Sweden's foreign minister announced at a meeting with Commonwealth ambassadors that it was bringing in legislation for a unilateral trade embargo against South Africa. Completing the common positions of the Nordic states, Norway imposed—also in March—a comprehensive trade embargo, followed by Finland in July 1987.[1]

Thus by mid-summer 1987, Western states seriously committed to economic sanctions against South Africa included the members of the Commonwealth (although on important issues it excluded Britain), the Nordic states and the US. With regard to anti-apartheid measures, Canada was in good company, but in terms of legislated economic sanctions it was beginning to lag behind the Nordic states and the US. It was at this very time that the Taskforce began to worry that the Canadian government was retreating from the anti-apartheid strategy that Mulroney had pioneered.

Notes for chapter 8 are found on pp. 286–89.

In the fall of 1986 the Taskforce had initiated a detailed review of the various economic sanctions that the Canadian government had announced since 1985 and in October the churches wrote to enquire about the scope of the government's implementation of sanctions and its means of monitoring compliance. External Affairs' reply—five months later—illustrated the widening gulf between the government and the churches on this issue.[2]

The first set of items in this exchange related to a number of quite specific details of sanction measures. According to the government, the new voluntary ban on commercial loans to South Africa's private sector included interbank lending. As Canadian law left it to the individual banks whether to disclose the amount of outstanding South African loans, independent monitoring of bank compliance was practically ruled out. The government, however, confirmed that the voluntary ban on private-sector loans excluded bond placements by Canadian banks and security companies. Unhappy about this omission, the Taskforce pointed out that even the (voluntary) British ban on new bank loans applied to new acquisition of share and loan capital by South African enterprises, thus including bonds. Moreover, in 1985 the Province of Ontario had reviewed its relations to those domestic and international commercial enterprises that continued business with the South African government. The provincial treasurer made it clear that Ontario would give preference in its business dealings to those companies no longer involved with South African state agencies and invited written statements to this effect from potential business partners. In response, the securities firm of McLeod Young Weir had told the press that it would not participate in any future South African bond issues.[3] Such business reaction suggested that the federal government would have been supported had it adopted an approach similar to that of the Ontario government and had included bond purchases in its ban on new loans to South Africa.

In response to other questions, External Affairs confirmed that companies were expected to comply voluntarily with the ban on new investment and reinvestment of profits earned in South Africa. As with the ban on new bank loans, it was thus well-nigh impossible for the public to probe the rate of compliance in this area. The Taskforce had also proposed legislation to effect the withdrawal from South Africa of specific types of Canadian investments. In particular such legislation was intended to target companies that directly or indirectly supplied South Africa's military, police or nuclear sector, and that continued to use South Africa's contract labour system. The churches also expressed concern that the government had not examined the role of Canadian consulting firms in South Africa. Some of these were providing strategic assistance to the South African government in the area of oil exploration, safe oil storage and development of alternative energy sources—thereby undermining the Canadian and international the oil embargo. The government's response ignored the issues on monitoring corporate compliance and on consultancy services. It responded, however, unequivocally to rule out any legislation that would affect the activities of companies in South Africa, citing once again the principle of extraterritoriality and referring the Taskforce to an earlier, 1982, exchange on this question. In the view of the churches, however, there was a difference between the issue they had now raised and that of 1981-83. In 1981 the Taskforce had asked the government to instruct Ford South Africa and Massey-Ferguson to refuse to comply with South Africa's Key Point laws. In 1986 the churches did not ask the government to regulate the activities of Canadian companies in South Africa or South African companies with Canadian investment. Instead they proposed that Canadian law require the withdrawal from South Africa of Canadian companies or investors who were involved directly or indirectly in the assistance to apartheid's strategic industries. Such a requirement would have been the equivalent of prosecuting sanctions violators in Canada.[4]

The Taskforce had been researching the participation of Westar Mining, a Canadian coal-producer, in the establishment of the International Coal Institute formed to help its members increase their international coal markets. Three large South African Companies—Apex Mines, Douglas Colliery and Trans-Natal Coal—were also founding members.[5] The Taskforce had written to Westar Mining that South Africa's participation in the International Coal Institute could be interpreted as a sanction-breaking activity. The government dismissed the argument and responded that Canadian producers were in competition with South African companies and would have no interest in helping South Africa to circumvent sanctions. This dismissive response did not concede that the Coal Institute promoted the interest of both the Canadian and the South African coal exporters. A government concerned with seeking to broaden the international commitment to economic sanctions against South Africa might have wanted to communicate with the International Coal Institute.

The Taskforce also addressed the difference in language between Canada's restrictions on the export of sensitive electronic equipment to South Africa and the restrictions that had been placed on such items under the Nassau Commonwealth Accord on Southern Africa and under UN Security Council Resolution 591 of 1986. Canada had banned such sales to the South African military, police and government departments. In contrast, the Nassau Accord called for a ban of all high technology exports *capable of use* by the military, police or security forces. The Security Council resolution had enjoined member states to ban the export of all items that *might be destined for South Africa's security forces such as electronics, telecommunications equipment and computers* (emphasis added). The Taskforce argued that because Canada permitted sales of such equipment to private South

African companies, it was in fact not complying fully with the either Commonwealth Accord nor with UNSCR 591.

The issue had been further confused by a new "Export Controls Policy" that Clark announced on 10 September 1986. It stated boldly: "Canadian policy will continue to prohibit the export of military and strategic goods to the Republic of South Africa."[6] This suggested that Canada was now in harmony with both the Nassau Commonwealth Accord [5 (d) and (e)] of 1985 and with UNSCR 591 of 1986. However another section of the policy statement explained that Canada had agreed "to limit exports of all military goods to military end-users, in accordance with UN Security Council Resolution 418 (1977), and more recently, . . . to refuse to export strategic and military goods to all RSA departments and agencies."[7] This phrasing clearly meant that such items could, indeed, still be sold to South Africa's private sector. It seems that the government was simply presenting Canadian policy as stronger than it actually was.

One might want to argue that the distinction between the two statements was too trivial to worry about. But that was not the view of External Affairs. In February 1987 the Taskforce and Project Ploughshares, an ecumenical sister coalition, had considered Canadian exports to South Africa as part of a larger brief, which they had submitted to the secretary of state for External Affairs. The brief, "Canadian Government Policy on Military Exports," addressed, inter alia, the question of military exports to human rights violator governments and—given Canada's public commitment to sanctions—particularly its military exports to South Africa. The brief had attracted considerable news coverage and drew responses from Joe Clark and his officials at External Affairs.[8]

On 10 April 1987 Clark made a short and courteous reply to this joint brief, promising a detailed written response and a meeting later in the year. However, the Taskforce and Project Ploughshares never did receive a reply. They therefore themselves organized a meeting in November to which were invited Joe Clark and External Affairs officials as well as defence critics from the opposition parties. Neither Clark nor his officials found time for this meeting and in the end it was attended only by the churches and opposition defence critics.

On 25 April *The Globe and Mail* published excerpts of Clark's 10 April letter, which the Taskforce had released to elicit meaningful responses. Clark had rejected the contention that Canadian exports of military-related goods could still end up in the hands of South Africa's military because, he said, each export application for military-related goods for South Africa was examined separately by his department "to ensure that sensitive equipment is not sold to the police, the armed forces and other South African departments and agencies involved in the enforcement of apartheid. . . . Export permits will be denied for goods that are to be used for military purposes." External Affairs told *The Globe and Mail* that it required certificates to prove that the end-user of such sensitive equipment was not, after all, the South African military or police. Asked whether such certificates could be trusted to prevent the equipment from reaching the military, and whether Canada could verify the ultimate end-user of its equipment, Denys Tessier, spokesman for External Affairs was quoted as saying: "Canada relies on the certificates and does not have inspectors in South Africa to check on who is using the equipment. Similarly, Canada would not allow inspectors from foreign countries to carry out inspections here."[9]

Eight years earlier, a senior External Affairs official had commented that using end-user certificates for exports of "dual-purpose" (strategic and civilian) equipment to South Africa "would not be helpful. Canadian firm A could sell to South African firm B, which could make minor changes and sell to the military or police anyway."[10] In 1987 however, Canadian sanctions notwithstanding, the reliance on such useless pieces of paper provided Canada with the justification to continue the export of high-technology equipment to South Africa.[11] All this was being decided at the same time as Canada was condemning South Africa for its domestic repression and for its repeated cross-border military raids.[12]

Taking Sides in Southern Africa

This was the title of a three-day conference in which the Taskforce participated. It took place in Montreal in late February 1987 and was organized by the Canadian Council for International Cooperation. Joe Clark, as secretary of state for External Affairs, delivered the opening address. Moira Hutchinson, coordinator of the Taskforce since May 1986, reflected on the experience of the Taskforce.

Hutchinson's paper "Taking Sides in Southern Africa—Disinvestment, Divestment and Sanctions" detailed the diverse areas of Canadian involvement in Southern Africa that had prompted continued church pressure on corporations, banks and on the Canadian government. She illustrated that given the government's aversion—at least so far—to comprehensive and mandatory sanctions, a multifaceted approach to selective economic sanctions could also be an empowering form of ongoing pressure for NGOs. Companies could be challenged, for example, to defy apartheid by converting temporary contract labour into a permanent labour force, by providing housing to the families and by building schools for the children. They could be pressured into refusing to cooperate with the security forces and into helping prevent political persecution of their workers by donating funds for their legal defence in political trials. At the same time, she added, pressure should of course continue on the Canadian government to introduce additional sanctions and to implement more effectively those economic sanctions that were in place. Hutchinson showed the difficulty of monitoring the implementation of Canadian sanctions even for an experienced organization such as the Taskforce. The ban on new bank loans to any South African borrower, she pointed out, remained voluntary. The Bank of Canada and the Department of Finance refused to assist the Taskforce with monitoring this ban. They would disclose neither compliance rates nor composite figures for outstanding Canadian loans to South Africa, which might permit rough estimates. It was therefore not at all certain whether the Canadian government even assured itself that the voluntary ban was observed by the banks.

Hutchinson also discussed the churches' reservations about the usefulness of the Canadian Code of Conduct for companies operating in South Africa. Given its existence, however, Hutchinson reported that the Taskforce had sought to strengthen it by suggesting additional proactive features such as mandatory compliance; inclusion of elected black workers in the monitoring and signing of company annual reports; and disclosure of sales by Canadian investors to the military, police and nuclear sectors. The Canadian government had rejected each of these proposals.

Neither had the government accepted the churches' recommendation that it legislate the withdrawal of Canadian investment from those South African enterprises that supplied the police, the military and the nuclear sector. She encouraged her audience to put pressure on the government and on these investors "if the government believes that such investment is wrong, it is apparently relying on public pressure to bring about their withdrawal."[13]

Hutchinson feared, however, that the government's decision not to match the Nassau Accord's more inclusive wording on the ban of high-technology exports was indicative of its disinclination to tighten sanctions in this respect. She asked anti-apartheid organizations to pressure the government to halt such exports. Hutchinson recognized the usefulness of keeping all options open in the pursuit of ending apartheid. The government had promised total sanctions and the moment certainly justified a challenge to the government to make good its 1985 promise. Hutchinson joined in this frustration, but she also urged that in the absence of total sanctions there was a need to press for incremental sanctions and for exposing failures within the private sector and in the Canadian government to fully implement existing sanctions.

Clark's Speech to the Montreal Conference

Hutchinson's contribution to the conference focused on tightening and fully implementing existing Canadian economic sanctions while keeping up the pressure for comprehensive ones. Clark's contribution, in contrast, rolled back the process. He introduced a debate that might have been more appropriately held prior to the October 1985 Nassau Common-wealth Accord. Gone was the crisp and vigorous sense of a mission for change in South Africa that had characterized Clark's 1985 and 1986 announcements of sanctions. Instead, Clark indulged in ponderous philos-ophizing about the burden of Canada's responsibilities as leader in the cause against apartheid.

Clark prefaced his speech with the assurance that Canada was prepared to invoke total sanctions and declared that Canada had "acted on all Com-monwealth sanctions drawn up in Nassau and London."[14] The govern-ment, Clark said, had made two strategic decisions. It had decided that its bottom line position had to be clear that if nothing else worked, Canada would end its diplomatic and economic relations with South Africa.[15] Sec-ondly the government had decided that "Canada's influence against apart-heid could be better employed by building steady international pressure than by suddenly and dramatically ending our relations."[16]

This, he held, was appropriate because Canada's influence with others was greater than its own trade with South Africa and that only those with greater economic clout could force the dismantling of apartheid. He returned several times to the catalytic task Canada was performing, a task which, as he portrayed it, seemed to present insurmountable odds. In the course of arguing that the Canadian government had come to the conclu-sion that a policy based on sanctions alone would not put enough pressure on South Africa, he discouraged all optimism about an early success in Can-ada's efforts of influencing its powerful allies: "For one thing, we see little likelihood of the governments of major economies applying sanctions on the scale that would be required to force Pretoria to change. That result may come in time, and certainly Canada will use our influence to build the weight of sanctions, but it is not realistic to expect an impenetrable wall to be set up suddenly or even quickly."[17] It is not clear what Clark meant by "sanctions on the scale that would be required to force Pretoria to change." That statement would seem to imply that only an imminent collapse of South Africa's economy would force such change. Yet a few pages later Clark announced: "[T]he world's purpose is to bring South Africa to its senses, not its knees. We are seeking to change an evil social system, not cripple a strong economy."[18] Clark went on to express the wish to resume trade in a South Africa free of apartheid and the hope that "the prejudice ends before violence disrupts all over in the sub-continent." What a curious choice of words. Surely to describe as "prejudice" a state system of legalized racism was to downplay the deliberate effort to dehumanize black South Africans. It also implied that the sub-continent had so far been spared "vio-lence," when for at least thirty years the region had been involved in liber-ation struggles. Clark concluded with this puzzling reflection:

With that in view, we must all seek means to keep lines open to all parts of South Africa—black and Botha, Buthelezi and Tambo, Mandela and Afrikaner. The worst result would be for us to cause the Botha Government to change its view, and then not have the channels to effect change.... The dilemma is that, as we isolate a repugnant regime, as we must, we also reduce the opportunities for that regime to change.[19]

An important section of Clark's remarks was devoted to the application of this muddled perspective to the question of economic sanctions. He said that Canadians had asked him why South Africa should be singled out for sanctions from among many other human-rights violator regimes; whether sanctions were effective and whether Canadians should have anything to do with the African National Congress. Clark felt that the issues must be addressed in the interest of building a consensus against apartheid. He referred to reservations about sanctions which he felt were held by many opponents to apartheid and by other "serious people everywhere" who were concerned about the distortion they caused in international trade and payment systems and the price exacted on countries that impose them. Clark did not then explain that those states, Canada included, which had committed themselves to sanctions as a means to end apartheid, must have been aware of the consequences and must have been prepared to deal with them. Neither did Clark offer a response to the most shopworn of all the arguments against sanctions that he felt had to be aired, namely that sanctions would "harm the victims of apartheid." He could have, but did not remind Canadians that the overwhelming majority of black South Africans, their leaders and his Commonwealth colleagues of the Front Line States had been among the most determined in urging the international community to impose economic sanctions.

Clark's speech illustrates a strange dynamic that had evolved during this period of increasing demands for comprehensive Canadian sanctions. Clark's previous sanction announcements had frequently repeated the government's policy—made famous by Mulroney's speech to the United Nations—that Canada was "prepared to invoke total sanctions." This had gradually turned into a sort of incantation in Clark's public statements, always reminding Canadians of this ultimate possibility. Eventually the very elevation of the idea of comprehensive sanctions as "the final recourse" served the government as a rationale for delaying them. Clark's remarks at the Montreal conference were a classic example of this technique. He did not at all invite a discussion on the next round of Canadian sanctions. Instead he revisited the arguments against sanctions that had been offered as far back as 1961, when black leaders had rejected them. In May of that year, Nelson Mandela, as secretary general of the ANC and still at liberty in South Africa, had called on international friends to isolate the government of South Africa "diplomatically and economically."[20] Three years later, on

12 June 1964, after Mandela and his colleagues had been sentenced to life imprisonment, Nobel Peace Laureate Chief Albert Luthuli, president of the ANC, appealed "to all governments throughout the world, to people everywhere, to organizations and institutions in every land and at every level, to act now to impose sanctions on South Africa that would precipitate the end of the hateful system of apartheid . . . and bring about the vital necessary change and avert what can become the greatest African tragedy of our times."[21] It was discouraging to say the least that two years into Canada's own economic sanctions, a quarter century after Mandela and Luthuli's brave statements, which had been matched so recently by the conclusions reached in the EPG's report, Clark was articulating doubts about sanctions without himself providing vigorous rebuttal.

The secretary of state for External Affairs noted a further issue that he said "must be faced." This concerned Canadian critics who shared an "apprehension about the methods and the motives of the African National Congress." He recognized the validity of these "genuine concerns, which limit seriously the ability of ANC spokesmen (*sic*) to reach Canadians who profoundly oppose apartheid . . . Canadian critics of the ANC condemn both its resort to violence, and the association of some of its leaders with the Soviet Union."[22] Clark's own political record in this respect is consistent with his evident sympathy with this position. In 1973 the Trudeau government had recognized the "legitimacy" of the struggle of the liberation movements in Southern Africa "to win full human rights and self determination." Canadian NGOs had been able to receive modest matching grants from CIDA for humanitarian development projects benefiting the ANC. In 1979, under Flora MacDonald as secretary of state for External Affairs and Joe Clark as prime minister this policy was rescinded. It was important enough in their view to constitute one of the few changes they could make during their brief period in power. The new position ruled out any further government assistance to the ANC.[23] With insignificant modifications this policy remained in force under Joe Clark's long tenure as secretary of state for External Affairs until Nelson Mandela's release in February 1990, when the policy became more convoluted but only marginally more helpful to the ANC as a liberation movement.

It is much to be regretted that in February 1987, as the apartheid regime prepared for its white-only elections in May and cranked up its own scare campaign about Communist influences in the ANC, Clark did not attempt to dispel the cold-war crusade of the ANC's Canadian critics. He did not mention that the Nordic states, not known as Communist satellites, had supported the ANC almost since the time it was banned in 1960. He did acknowledge that the ANC had had fifty years of non-violent history before it was banned and added awkwardly that its leadership included "moderate members and those who are not." Clark sermonized: "If countries like

Canada turn away from the ANC, that would make everyone immoderate, and not only add to the prospect of violence, but give credence to the Marxist component. Soviet influence grows in violence and in vacuums, and it is profoundly in the interest of the West to seek to stop that violence, and fill those vacuums."[24] He added that he would meet with Oliver Tambo later in the year because Canada would be more likely to "achieve both peace and freedom by dealing with the ANC than by leaving them to extremes."[25]

It does seem clear that Clark's speech signalled that a major policy retreat was in train. Only a month previous, Mulroney, travelling in Southern Africa, had given a far more nuanced statement regarding the ANC's commitment to the armed liberation struggle than Clark did. Eschewing insinuations about Communism, Mulroney echoed the EPG's conviction that in the absence of a bilateral truce it was unrealistic to ask the ANC to suspend the armed struggle and face an "apartheid state that is armed to the teeth." The prime minister recognized that there can be compelling reasons for armed resistance:

> As a Canadian, I can speak only from a Canadian perspective. I have not, in my background in Canada, had any cause to use or advocate the use of violence. I was born and raised in a fully democratic egalitarian state. ... I cannot speak for Robert Mugabe [first prime minister of Zimbabwe after successfully leading the armed struggle for majority rule] whose life has been entirely different, who was raised in an entirely different society and who has known repression and the lack of freedom and liberty.[26]

Clark's speech to the Montreal conference disappointed the NGOs assembled there. They had been given to understand that cabinet had approved new sanctions and had hoped for an announcement at the conference to mark the occasion and to infuse new energy into a collaborative NGO/government effort against apartheid. Indeed, shortly after the conference a *Globe and Mail* column reported that in January Joe Clark had received Cabinet approval for further unspecified economic sanctions to adopt as he saw fit.[27] In Montreal, however, Clark said that "Canada still wants to see apartheid dismantled but there may be other avenues [than additional economic sanctions] to explore." It was, he felt, an open question as to "what further sanctions will be effective, at what pace, in the company of what other measures."[28] He listed a second order of soft policy measures which included (once again) Canada's Code of Conduct for Canadian Companies Operating in South Africa; scholarships for black South Africans; and government support for NGO assistance to the "victims of apartheid."

Given the ideological makeup of the Progressive Conservative government and its great reluctance to legislate convincing economic sanctions and to sever or even just downgrade its diplomatic relations with South Africa, government funding for NGO projects that were imaginative and credible may have been the most helpful contribution that could have been expected of it. This, however, could have been done without the grand-standing and without the pretence that Canada was a leader in the drive for international sanctions.

Still, along with many NGOs and academic commentators, the Canadian churches regarded the policy shift as a major setback. They questioned the rationale of substituting humanitarian funding to private agencies for new government sanctions when they should both have been pursued. Being attuned to the twists and turns of corporate and government phraseology and listening to Joe Clark at the Montreal conference, the churches under-stood earlier than most Canadians that they were witnessing in February 1987 the start of an orchestrated strategic retreat from the 1985-86 policy of economic sanctions against South Africa.

South Africa's "Darkest Age"

On 15 April 1987 Ronald MacLean, Canada's ambassador to South Africa, confronted senior South African officials with a stiff diplomatic protest against another turn of the screw of government restrictions. Since the sec-ond state of emergency in June 1986, over 25,000 people had been detained without charge or trial, including 1,424 children between the ages twelve and eighteen.[29] The new emergency powers threatened, with jail for up to ten years, any form of petition against detentions without trial, from public meetings and letter-writing campaigns to slogans on T-shirts and coffee mugs. MacLean also objected to being summoned along with other diplomats for a lecture by South Africa's foreign minister on the threat of an ANC attack in the 6 May elections. He said Canada did not believe Pretoria's claim that "150 terrorists were already on their way through neighbouring countries" to launch such attacks. MacLean urged the Botha regime to refrain from cross-border raids, ostensibly billed as "preemptive military strikes."[30]

Botha's anti-ANC scare campaign had been effective—too effective. It was meant to placate voters who were tempted to desert to the "right" and to frighten others from straying to the more liberal Progressive Federal Party. Having put out this fictitious story, however, Botha was now in dan-ger of appearing weak unless he struck down "the ANC plotters." He warned black neighbouring states that ANC "terrorists" were infiltrating across their borders, and on 25 April 1987 launched an airborne com-mando raid on Livingstone, Zambia, a resort town near the Victoria Falls where four Zambian border guards lost their lives. In South Africa the "right-wing" opposition praised South Africa's military, while white liberals dared not criticize the attack. Canada and other Western states issued strong communiqués but, although Clark had approval for new sanctions to use "if the time was right," South Africa's renewed attack on a Commonwealth ally was evidently not sufficient to warrant more than a diplomatic rebuke.

274 In Good Faith

In fighting the 1987 election, Botha abandoned all reform pretensions. His emphasis on the need for security to ward off a black revolution won the National Party an increased majority on 6 May, but resulted also in increased votes for the "extreme right" parties. To them belonged the more important success as they replaced the decimated liberals as the official opposition.

Returned to power, Botha immediately curbed once more what was left of opportunities for dissent. On 10 June 1987, just before Soweto Day, he renewed the state of emergency, giving the police still wider powers of detention. He increased their control over movement and media restrictions, and ordered stringent regulations of attendance and duration at ever-increasing numbers of political funerals henceforth conducted under the eyes of gun-toting security forces. Towards the volatile black student population the police and army were given free rein for intrusive and intimidating interventions. They checked strict adherence to the syllabus in black schools, enforced the ban against political slogans on students' clothing, curbed meetings on school property and arrested schoolchildren and teachers under the slightest pretext. Archbishop Tutu called this South Africa's "darkest age."

How had South Africa's business community reacted, first to the more onerous and nation-wide state of emergency of June 1986 and then to Botha's hard-line electioneering and the general lurch to the right evident in the white election results? The short answer is that, although discomfited, the majority of South Africa's business elite returned to the fold.[31] They had backed the imposition of the tough state of emergency in June 1986 and had accepted Botha's warning that the ANC posed an immediate revolutionary threat.

During the 1987 election campaign the business community had swung behind Botha's "law and order" platform. Anthony Sampson quotes an unnamed director of Anglo American as saying: "faced with the choice between chaos and injustice, it may sometimes be necessary to choose injustice."[32] By and large South African business agreed. Botha's tough stand had restored their confidence and the effective media censorship would, they hoped, not only stifle international criticism but would gain time for appeals to rally South Africa's international friends. The business leaders blamed sanctions and disinvestment for their failure to achieve change, and once again insisted that liberalizing reforms could only be achieved with renewed investment and the recovery of economic prosperity.[33]

Yet, as if to mock the steadfast increase in Botha's repression, a remarkable change was taking place. The initiatives for political action had slipped from the apartheid regime into the hands of the resistance movements. Notwithstanding the state's massive command of the instruments of power and control and the suffering it was inflicting on its opponents, the politics of the white minority government began to be defined by the initiatives of the black resistance.

A few historical snapshots will illustrate this change. Since the beginning of the uprisings in September 1984, the internal resistance, lead largely by the UDF, had convinced black South Africans of the hitherto unimaginable, namely that the system of apartheid was not invincible. The severe state of emergency of June 1986 had cracked down hard on the UDF; it had netted thousands of political prisoners and had banned the UDF. Although forced underground it continued to gain new affiliates. The latest had been the newly formed South African Youth Congress, which had been able to meet in total secrecy in March 1987. As astonishing was the secret meeting in Durban on 29 May 1987 of 200 delegates from the UDF's nine regions. It was the third national meeting since its launch in 1983, and its resolutions were announced in early June by Murphy Morobe, the UDF's publicity secretary who had emerged from a year in hiding. The UDF had called for international aid to the Front Line States in recognition of their solidarity, at great cost to themselves, with the resistance in South Africa; the UDF had also agreed on guidelines for foreign funding of South African organizations. Too often, Morobe said, international funds were used to gain influence in opposition groups, or were offered as unacceptable substitutes for international economic sanctions. He announced that the UDF would seek agreement from its affiliated organizations for the adoption of the ANC's June 1955 *Freedom Charter*.[34] The government promptly launched investigations into the activities and funding of the UDF and other anti-apartheid organizations. In October it declared the UDF to be an "affected organization" and proscribed receipt of all overseas' funding.

Since the formation of the Congress of South African Trade Unions (COSATU) in December 1985, black trade unions had moved resolutely to the front of South African politics. In addition to the churches, COSATU and its affiliated unions were among the few organizations still at liberty to give voice to black aspirations and outrage. Although many individual members and union leaders were detained and maltreated, and its programs, political rallies and specific campaigns constantly hampered by the state, COSATU as a trade union federation remained unbanned because of its importance to the business sector. The regime had clearly calculated that if it could not ban COSATU outright, it would instead subject it to the kind of smear campaign it so successfully employed against the ANC. By calling COSATU a stalking horse for the ANC and the Communist Party, it sought to sabotage the unions' "living-wage" campaign as "Marxist-inspired." In the ensuing years of "South Africa's darkest age" many prominent union leaders along with other members in the resistance movement were murdered in state-condoned atrocities.[35]

Although the states of emergency had outlawed strikes, through "stay-aways" and boycotts of white-owned stores the unions were able to continue these activities to the great irritation of business, whose profits depended on the consumer power of the black majority and on the skills of black labour on their shop floors. After the imposition of the June 1986 emergency, union leaders in large numbers had been swept into detention, leaving employers without negotiators for the annual wage settlements. Business contacted the unions and offered assistance to obtain the release of the detained trade unionists. These offers were rejected. The unions were not prepared to accept self-serving favours from the very constituency that had supported the state of emergency, which in turn had led to the incarceration of their leaders.[36]

Despite the state of emergency, the capacity of the resistance to mobilize only grew. On 6 May 1987, the day of the election, a successful two-day "stay-at-home" organized by COSATU, the UDF and the National Education Crisis Committee denied all services to white communities. It was the largest general strike in South Africa's history involving an estimated 700,000 industrial and mine workers and tens of thousands of schoolchildren. The stay-at-home was total in Soweto, Tembisa and New Brighton and was supported by sympathy boycotts at several white English speaking universities.[37]

Also in 1987 workers of the South African Railway and Harbour Workers' Union (SARHWU) went on a crippling six-week strike which had started over the arbitrary dismissal of a worker. The South African Transport Services (SATS) refused to recognize SARHWU because it was affiliated with COSATU. The government arrested over 300 railway workers. When the union ignored SATS' deadline for ending the strike, the agency called out the police and dismissed—illegally as it turned out—1,800 workers on the Witwatersrand. Eight strikers were shot dead by the police. The number of striking workers rose to 22,000 as the strike spread to other parts of Transvaal and to the Orange Free State. Once more South Africa's private sector had to intervene, pressing for the resumption of rail services to avert further financial losses. SATS was compelled to acknowledge that it had been wrong to dismiss the workers and agreed to an out-of-court settlement including the reinstatement of the dismissed workers.

COSATU's effective political involvement caused a spate of bombings and vandalism of COSATU-affiliated union offices. In the early morning of 7 May 1987, two powerful bombs exploded in the basement of COSATU House, wrecking the Johannesburg multi-storey headquarters of the federation. The building was declared "unsafe," and COSATU was denied access to its equipment or documents. Temporary buildings used by COSATU after the bombing were targeted by arsonists.[38]

On 16 June, Soweto Day, a second stay-at-home in Soweto, sponsored by the South African Youth Congress, saw an estimated one and a half million workers refusing to work. The regime, which had been unable to collect township rent since 1984, made a renewed attempt to break the rent strike. New legislation sought to make companies responsible for deducting the rent from the workers' payroll. But foreign as well as domestic business emphatically opposed any role in enforcing such legislation.[39]

Finally, in September 1987, the world's attention focused on the child prisoners of the apartheid regime. "Children, Repression and the Law in South Africa," a major international conference in Harare, brought together children and youths from South Africa, their lawyers and representatives of the Detainees' Parents Support Committee and other South African social agencies working for change. Their sad and appalling experiences of incarceration and torture testified to the regime's political and moral bankruptcy.

Response of the Canadian Government

The Canadian government now had to assume that it would face at least four years and maybe more of a renewed and unexpectedly strengthened regime in South Africa of hard-core defenders of the apartheid system. In 1985 Mulroney and Clark had lavishly praised the leadership role of South African business in initiating meaningful changes and had used its example as a compelling reason for Canada's own more intense involvement. Canada now had to decide whether to shift its long-term support to the black resistance movement or to follow the example of South Africa's white business community and tone down its involvement.

The Canadian government, far from responding to the mounting South African repression by realizing its commitment to invoke total sanctions, decided to abandon it. It was a particularly complex manoeuvre. The prime minister had been its strongest champion and had gained for Canada prestige and influence in the Commonwealth and in the United Nations which the government did not wish to forfeit.

Mulroney had visited Southern Africa in late January 1987 and consulted with his Commonwealth colleagues. He agreed that South Africa's situation was rapidly deteriorating and had promised additional Canadian sanctions. He had assured them that Canada would stand with its Southern African friends in the struggle against apartheid "until freedom and representative government will prevail." He had met with ANC representatives and had told them that although Canada could not endorse the armed struggle, he understood the ANC's reasons for it. He had promised to seek agreement from the Group of Seven at the next summit meeting to strengthen economic sanctions against South Africa.[40]

To his credit, Mulroney did attempt to raise the issue during the June Group of Seven summit in Venice. However, after the recent electoral triumph of South Africa's right, there was no inclination to indulge the Canadian prime minister on this issue. Thatcher and Kohl led the opposition to Mulroney's proposal for a formal declaration on the need for change in South Africa. They disagreed with Mulroney's argument that "the failure to say anything would be the most powerful message—of encouragement—that could be sent to Pretoria." Mulroney's pleading gained the issue only a brief mention in the listing of "other" political topics the Group had "worried about." Asked whether his intervention did not amount to "tokenism," Mulroney replied: "It's not going to change anything tomorrow, I agree. But it may do something for young blacks in South Africa who are sitting listening to some radio somewhere and hear that this group coming together in Venice took the time at least to acknowledge that the concepts of freedom and democracy did not escape our attention. At the very least, it sent the right sort of signal out."[41] Senior Canadian officials did not hide their disagreement with the prime minister's initiative and registered their own view that it was "a misunderstanding of the summit process" to expect "a regional issue like South Africa" to be included in the final communiqué.[42]

For Mulroney, the inability to move the Group of Seven on an issue to which he had been personally committed since 1984 must have been hard to accept. He valued his political association with the Group of Seven and was ideologically in tune with its members. Their rejection of his proposal amounted to a personal snub from his international peers. At home it strengthened the right wing in his cabinet and caucus, which had become restive over Mulroney's South African stance. The way was thus clear for Canadian policy to shift in the direction long preferred by the Department of External Affairs and by Joe Clark himself.

In August 1987 Joe Clark had gone on a four-day, four-country tour to Southern Africa. During an injudicious eight-hour visit to South Africa, he sought to make good his promise to "keep lines open to all parts of South Africa." Pik Botha, South Africa's foreign minister, whom Clark had described as "a member of the reform group in his government," barred him from visiting Mandela in prison and announced that Clark was "not welcome to come and run a circus here."[43] Clark's attempts to convince Pretoria to initiate reforms were peremptorily rebuffed during a meeting with Pik Botha, whose parting shot was tailor-made for Joe Clark's sensitivity to Marxist ideology: "I don't understand why the West expects negotiations that will inevitably lead to a Marxist regime in this country."[44] Clark had prided himself in his ability to talk to both sides of the racial divide, yet had returned without evidence that white South Africa was willing to listen to him.

Meanwhile, the image of the ANC as a violent, Marxist-dominated movement, which Pik Botha had pressed upon Clark was being confounded by increasing evidence of the ANC's openness to dialogue with white South Africans. Since 1985 it had responded with interest to such initiatives for dialogue without compromising its position that apartheid had to be dismantled. The latest meeting had taken place in Dakar, Senegal, in early July 1987. During a four day conference arranged with the help of Danielle Mitterand, wife of the French president, some fifty Afrikaner intellectuals and writers met with the ANC to explore possible paths to a joint political future.[45]

Clark as well as Mulroney, alas, soon demonstrated that they were still much influenced by the negative stereotype of the ANC offered by the Botha regime. Oliver Tambo, president of the ANC, had accepted an official invitation to Ottawa. It was the first meeting of Mulroney and Clark with the ANC leader. Tambo arrived on 26 August at Toronto's international airport to an enthusiastic welcome of resident ANC officials and a large group of members of the Toronto anti-apartheid NGOs. Tambo's welcome by his official hosts in Ottawa, however, was anything but cordial or even respectful. Analyzing Tambo's visit *The Globe and Mail*'s Hugh Winsor described Tambo's visit as a "tip-off to a softening of the Canadian government policy against apartheid": "The emphasis during Tambo's visit was not on the consolidation of a police state in Pretoria, on the detention of 10- and 12-year-old children, or on massive and brutal oppression, now systematically hidden from the outside world by censorship." Rather, Winsor wrote, it was "a victory of sorts for the South African regime's propaganda campaign," which was having its impact on Tory backbenchers.[46] He was referring to a large advertisement that the South Africa's embassy had placed in *The Globe and Mail* on the day of Tambo's meeting with Mulroney. It was a rerun of Botha's successful propaganda during his May election campaign, depicting the ANC as a Communist-dominated terrorist organization.

Tambo had come to thank Canada for its support in the struggle against apartheid and in particular to explore with Mulroney and Clark ways of escalating this pressure. He asked for tougher economic sanctions and the isolation of the regime. But despite cabinet clearance for new sanctions since January, Clark pointedly told reporters that Canada was not necessarily committed to new sanctions: "I wouldn't want to limit the possibility of finding means of pressure to the instrument of sanctions as traditionally defined."[47]

What actually took place in meetings on 28 August between Tambo and Mulroney and Tambo and Clark was pieced together the following day in Toronto, when Oliver Tambo met with anti-apartheid activists from church, labour and NGO support organizations. Tambo was careful not to offend diplomatic etiquette. Nevertheless, he told of his disappointment on several levels. One was Mulroney's suggestion that the ANC unilaterally "suspend violence" in return for further economic sanctions and in particular for renewed attempts to bring Margaret Thatcher on side. This was a complete reversal from Mulroney's January statement in Southern Africa cited above. It showed a total lack of appreciation that, at best, the toughest sanctions could complement but never replace the popular struggle in South Africa or the armed struggle of the ANC. Tambo had not come to ask Canada to support the armed struggle; he had wanted Canada through sanctions to weaken the hand of the oppressor. Sanctions, Tambo had said in Ottawa, "would have the effect of limiting the scale, scope and duration of the armed struggle.... We would reach the desired result without too much damage and without too much sacrifice."[48]

Instead Mulroney had confronted Tambo with a copy of an odious South African advertisement. Tambo told the meeting in the Anglican Church House, "with all due respect, I do not think Canadians should look to what the South African government is saying about the ANC to determine its own strategy." Joe Clark had treated his invited guest at least as roughly as had Mulroney. He virtually blamed the ANC for hindering Canada's attempts at anti-apartheid mobilization by being *open to the accusation* of "violent marxism" (emphasis added). Clark complained: "We are a country that has been seeking to mobilize public opinion, not only in our own country, but elsewhere in the Western world, against apartheid, and the accusations that the ANC is a violent Marxist organization don't make the job any easier."[49] Tambo was astonished that Canada would borrow so liberally from the regime's propaganda. He noted that in his experience the majority of the world did not care what the apartheid regime was saying about the ANC. Most governments concentrated instead on the central reality of apartheid's violent repression. The fixation with Communism, he said, had dominated his Ottawa visit. He did not apologize for the presence of Communists in the ranks and on the executive of the ANC. "We are all fighting the same enemy," he said, "there is not a tittle of evidence" that the ANC was controlled by Moscow. He noted that although the West had fought with Stalin against Hitler, it failed to understand that the ANC was fighting another Hitler in South Africa. Canada's intimation that the ANC rid itself of its Communist members—some had joined the ANC as early as the 1920s—would be ignored. Why he asked, was Pretoria tacitly being defended by this kind of argument?[50]

The tenor of Oliver Tambo's reception in Ottawa further signalled the encroaching mood in External Affairs. It was as if his very visit had served this purpose. Tambo's presence in Ottawa had provided the occasion to "return" Mulroney to a reading of South African events more congenial to External Affairs and to the Conservative party. Both Mulroney and Clark indulged in strong anti-communist polemic and pronouncements about the violent nature of the ANC. It bears repeating that both the presence of South African Communists in the ANC and the decision to engage in armed resistance were issues rooted deeply in the long history of the liberation movement. They were eloquently addressed by Nelson Mandela in his famous "Statement from the Dock" on 20 April 1964.[51] If Canada had been bothered by them, it should have raised objections in 1985 before the government's decision to assume a leadership role at the Nassau Common-wealth meeting. One must ask, therefore, what political judgement led to the decision in 1987 to tone down public expectations of additional economic sanctions and to reorient Canadians toward softer options.

An extended discussion at the end of August 1987 with a source close to the Privy Council provided this persuasive interpretation: the rationale for economic sanctions had been the belief that one could nudge a reluctant South African government into change. This assumption was no longer tenable by the electoral victory in May 1987 of the right and the extreme right in South Africa. There was now no likelihood that a white liberal wing would move toward reforms and a dismantling of apartheid. Instead Canada's Privy Council officials foresaw a long struggle ahead for South Africa's black population resulting in much bloodshed and violence. Although comprehensive economic sanctions and the severing of diplomatic relations would be the logical next step, officials argued that such a step would be interpreted as a Canadian decision to support unreservedly the black struggle for full democratic rights. Such a decision would separate Canada from the other Group of Seven states, for none was expected to come to the same conclusion. Privy Council officials had therefore advised Cabinet to avoid any further initiatives that would deviate from the positions of Canada's allies, and in particular, to reduce Canadian involvement in economic sanctions.

There is much in our review of Canadian policy decisions and South African developments since 1985 that supports this interpretation. Originally the government had expected that the adoption of an outspoken anti-apartheid stance would align the Conservative government of Canada with the white South African business elite and other high-profile liberals who had come to prominence there since 1985 and who had received high praise from Canada for their reform-minded initiatives.

In the fall of 1987, however, Mulroney and Clark had to grapple with a new reality. In Venice Mulroney had failed to move his more powerful allies to support new anti-apartheid initiatives. In his brief visit to South Africa Clark had tasted the arrogance of power of the newly confirmed Botha regime. Both men now felt that the time for an enlightened capitalist's approach had passed. They calculated that Canada and like-minded allies could no longer hope that by exerting economic pressure they would obtain from the South African government an agreement for reforms that would safeguard a free market economy there. Canadian policymakers now feared that a long and intensifying liberation struggle lay ahead, led by an ANC which they believed to be heavily influenced by its Communist members. With remarkable speed, history was to demonstrate that these calculations were fundamentally flawed, trapped as they were in ideological preconceptions. Canada's policymakers were unwilling or unable to credit the strength and determination of the ANC and its central unifying force in the struggle. They failed to recognize the powerful role of the many composite parts of the resistance movement inside South Africa, which were soon to merge into the Mass Democratic Movement in support of the ANC. Given the flawed calculations of the government, however, support for economic sanctions had evaporated. Henceforth Mulroney largely left to his secretary of state for External Affairs the management of Canadian policy toward Southern Africa.

Clark's most urgent need now was to prepare for the Vancouver Commonwealth Heads of Government Meeting (CHOGM) scheduled for October 1987, the first since the momentous meeting in Nassau in 1985. His task was to scale down public expectations of additional Canadian sanctions and at the same time to keep intact Canada's image as a leading champion of international pressures on South Africa In mid-September Clark met with the British foreign secretary to discuss how Britain's anti-sanctions position could complement Clark's inclination to move toward alternative "measures." Between them they proposed a Commonwealth Committee to study possibilities of assistance to the Front Line States, which would reduce their vulnerable dependency on South Africa and offer protection from Botha's commando raids. Such a committee was indeed formed, and was chaired by Roy McMurtry, Canada's high commissioner to London. Clark also suggested creation of a group of experts to study sanction compliance by Western states, an initiative that would direct attention away from any consideration of new sanctions. The two men seemed to have reached a broad consensus in favour of alternatives to sanctions.[52]

Also in September, in a long interview with Carol Goar in *The Toronto Star*, Joe Clark contended that Canada had wanted to press its Commonwealth partners to adopt a new package of economic sanctions at the Vancouver Commonwealth meeting, but cautioned that discussions with western leaders had convinced him of "a temporary sanctions fatigue."[53] This was clearly the case in Ottawa and probably also among the other governments of the Group of Seven. However the Nordic states maintained their total trade embargo against South Africa while the European Economic Community held to its various import restrictions. Clark must also have been aware that the tough Anti-Apartheid Act of the US, in force for nearly a year, was about to be augmented by a decisive escalation of US sanctions. In June 1987 Leon Sullivan, author of the Sullivan Principles, had become so disillusioned with the failure of business to exert a liberalizing impact on the structures of apartheid that he had called for total disinvestment of US companies from South Africa. As if to underscore Sullivan's summons, Congress passed the Double Taxation Law, which came into effect on 1 January 1988. It denied corporations and individuals tax deductions on income earned in South Africa and Namibia.[54] In addition, members of the Commonwealth were committed to selective economic sanctions, most with the potential to be tightened, and the FLS were pressing hard for additional sanctions. In none of these circles was "sanctions fatigue" conspicuous.

Yet Clark persisted with this theme: "I think we're going to be able to come back to the question of sanctions again. But through this period, we've got to find other ways to sustain the opponents of apartheid. That requires some imagination."[55]

Trying out some of these other ideas, Clark spoke of "reaching into South Africa" to assist endangered opponents of apartheid and to engage in public education to raise Canadian awareness of apartheid, thus moving, he said, "beyond the simple sanctions-or-no-sanctions debate." These ideas presaged the position he successfully advocated at the Vancouver meeting.

The sobering aspect of the Goar interview was not only that Clark worked hard to move public anticipation away from economic sanctions. He displayed as well a depressing lack of interest in the South African events which, since 1984, had broken the bounds of Canadian and international tolerance. When Goar asked why the issue of apartheid had become so prominent, Clark speculated that it might have been due to "a spontaneous focusing of world opinion" three years ago. In April 1985, during the Round Table meeting, Clark had himself asked this very question and was told that P.W. Botha's 1984 constitution must be held responsible, entrenching as it had, for all times, the exclusion of black South Africans from democratic participation. That had been the spark in September 1984 that ignited sustained black popular uprisings, answered by the regime's punitive states of emergency. It was that which had caused Canadian and international revulsion and had stiffened the resolve to end apartheid. It is not really credible that Canada's secretary of state for External Affairs could have remained ignorant of the reasons behind the great increase in Canadian and international concern. Yet Clark had replied to Goar's question: "I don't know why it happened, it's partly the media. A lot of people became aware of the greater possibility of change in southern Africa."[56]

Before the Vancouver meeting some tension surfaced over possible nonlethal military aid to the FLS, which had been given tentative currency by Canadian officials in early September. Indeed, Roy McMurtry described such possible Canadian aid as including "anything from boots to Jeeps, any equipment that is not actually used to kill people."[57] But on the eve of the

Commonwealth conference, Mulroney categorically dismissed the notion: "We are not going to be offering military aid," he said in a television interview. Sir Shridath Ramphal, secretary general of the Commonwealth, held his ground when he told a news conference the following day that the defence of these countries remained very much before the Commonwealth, regardless of Mulroney's remarks. Although the issue appeared in the final Commonwealth statement, Mulroney did not address it again until he was seeking support for Canada's election to the UN Security Council in 1988.

At the end of their closed-door deliberations, the Commonwealth heads of government agreed on "The Okanagan Statement on Southern Africa and Programme of Action."[58] The statement outlined events since their Nassau meeting and noted that no progress had been made in the dismantling of apartheid. It added: "With the exception of Britain we believe that economic and other sanctions have had a significant effect on South Africa and that their wider, tighter, and more intensified application must remain an essential part of the international community's response to apartheid." But what followed were not additional sanctions. There was a shift of emphasis in the international community's response to existing sanctions and away from Commonwealth-generated new measures. The Okanagan Statement committed the Commonwealth to secure adoption by the balance of the international community of the measures adopted so far by Commonwealth members, as well as the measures adopted by "the United States and the Nordic countries." No provisional list of new Commonwealth sanctions was drawn up, as had been done at Nassau, to be implemented in the event of further South African intransigence. There was no effort to correlate existing sanctions of the Commonwealth to those of the United States and the Nordic countries, though in important aspects this would have strengthened international sanctions generally. Commonwealth leaders simply stated the obvious that each country could on its own or in concert with others take actions—including sanctions—as deemed appropriate to the evolving situation in South Africa. It is fair to suggest that the Okanagan Statement reflected Canada's delaying tactics in the commissioning of two studies, one an ongoing evaluation of the impact of existing sanctions and the second an expert study on South Africa's relations with the international financial system (see advice of the PCO to cabinet above, p. 197).

Commonwealth leaders did not collectively agree to come to the aid of the security needs of their Southern African colleagues. On this issue the Okanagan Statement adopted the embarrassing language that bureaucrats reserve for moments of equivocation. It noted that the Commonwealth might, "if requested," "embark upon a process of consultations with a view to enabling those of our members in a position to do so to make appropriate contributions to the security needs of Mozambique and the other Front-Line States requiring such help."[59] In fact we recognize Canada's "signature" in much of the Statement. The projects in South Africa were to involve "assistance to the victims of apartheid"; funding for black education; support for South Africa's trade unions; and promotion of "real internal dialogue" to increase "contacts with South Africans of differing viewpoints." Another Canadian proposal that in view of "draconian curbs imposed on the press" the Commonwealth "should give high priority to counteracting South African propaganda and censorship," also became part of the "Okanagan Statement."[60] Unlike economic sanctions, these general propositions were not necessarily made more effective by being endorsed by the full Commonwealth meeting.[61] Finally, under "The Way Forward," the heads of government—except for Britain—agreed to establish a Commonwealth Committee of Foreign Ministers for Southern Africa (CCFMSA) "to provide high-level impetus and guidance" on Southern African issues. It comprised the foreign ministers of Australia, Canada, Guyana, India, Nigeria, Tanzania, Zambia and Zimbabwe, with Joe Clark in the chair.[62]

In a persuasive analysis of the political manoeuvres behind the Vancouver meeting, Michael Valpy of *The Globe and Mail* wrote that a meeting in Tanzania of the six Front Line leaders before coming to Canada had pretty accurately predicted the outcome of the Vancouver meeting. As governments that were the targets of South African destabilization efforts and military incursions, they were entirely in sympathy with the popular movements in Southern Africa and the positions of the ANC. Like the liberation movements, they were also strong supporters of international comprehensive economic sanctions and the severance of diplomatic relations. Yet four of the Front Line leaders—two did not belong to the Commonwealth—had then gone to Vancouver and had accepted the Commonwealth communiqué which affirmed that sanctions were effective, but had adopted or recommended none. A senior official of one of the Front Line States explained to Valpy that it had been clear that Thatcher would absolutely rule out additional sanctions. In the changed atmosphere of 1987, the Front Line States had sensed that had they pressed for new economic sanctions or the end to diplomatic relations they would have forfeited not only Thatcher's but also Canada's and Australia's support. Valpy cited his interlocutor: "On this issue we are always dealing with very heavy odds. We don't have the power to move big countries.... And if you only have your mouth, then you've got to keep using it [as in the proposed CCFMSA]. The idea here was to make sure we didn't lose anything, to concretize what we already had." Acceptance of the Canadian proposal for the creation of a foreign ministers' committee had assured the Front Line States that instead of losing Canada to the British—who had refused to join—the new committee kept Canada's foreign minister on side with three veteran anti-apartheid governments, Tanzania, Zambia and Zimbabwe. Given the shift in the Canadian position, this had been for them the only victory possible.[63]

As chair of the CCFMSA, Clark acceded to an elevated status within the Commonwealth with increased powers to influence, monitor and control. On 2 November Clark communicated to the House of Commons the decisions taken in Vancouver and ended his speech once again with the incantation that "South Africa should be in no doubt that, if other measures fail, all of Canada's economic and diplomatic contacts will be terminated."[64]

Notes

1 The details here are from *Racism in Southern Africa*, p. 51.
2 Letter from W.R. Davis, chair, Taskforce on the Churches and Corporate Responsibility, to the Rt. Hon. Joe Clark, secretary of state for External Affairs, 30 October 1986; and a letter from Joe Clark to W.R. Davis, 10 April 1987.
3 Sheppard, "Ontario Probes South African Holdings."
4 The deputy director of the export controls division of External Affairs said that "Canadian businesses dodging trade restrictions with South Africa risk criminal prosecution under the Exports and Imports Controls Act." Indeed, Larry Camphaug of Aerovue Canada Ltd. and of Lajal Scientifique Ltd. was convicted and placed on two years' probation with a suspended sentence for shipping night-vision equipment to South Africa without a permit. The companies were each fined $10,000 (Brian Baxter, "South African Sanctions Dodged, Canadian Businessman Claims," *The Financial Post*, 4 May 1988.
5 *The Financial Times* (UK), 29 November 1985.
6 Exports Controls Policy, Department of External Affairs, "Export Controls Policy Background Paper," Communiqué no. 155, 10 September 1986, p. 3.
7 Ibid., "Question and Answers," p. 2.
8 Robert Matas, "Embargo Too Weak, Churches Say," *The Globe and Mail*, 2 April 1987.
9 Robert Matas, "Clark Rejects Accusations on Embargo," *The Globe and Mail*, 25 April 1987.
10 Taskforce on the Churches and Corporate Responsibility, "Notes on Information Given over the Telephone (March 5th and 8th) in Response to Enquiries on Canadian Government Response to United Nations Security Council Mandatory Arms Embargo against South Africa (UNSCR 418, Nov. 1977)," 26 March 1979 (mimeograph).
11 Gavin Cawthra, in his 1986 study *Brutal Force: The Apartheid War Machine*, wrote: "Three main [private] South African electronics companies, Altech, Reutech (Barlow Rand) and Grinaker Electronics, have established themselves by taking over the assets of overseas subsidiaries and have drawn heavily on military contracts. At least ten per cent of the South African electronics market is accounted for by military contracts" (p. 102).
12 The day Clark denied that Canada's embargo on sensitive military-related equipment to South Africa was too weak, South African helicopters carried commando raids to Zambia's border town of Livingstone where several Zambian citizens were killed before the raiders returned to South Africa, 660 km away. The raid was part of an election ploy that warned whites of an alleged imminent ANC attack on South Africa aimed at disrupting the 6 May white-only elections. Clark strongly condemned the raid (Peter Goodspeed [Johannesburg)], "Clark Blasts Pretoria for Raid on Zambia," *The Toronto Star*, 26 April 1987).

13 Moira Hutchinson, "Taking Sides in Southern Africa: Disinvestment, Divestment and Sanctions," a paper prepared for "Taking Sides in South Africa," a conference organized by the Canadian Council for International Cooperation, Montreal, 27 February to 1 March 1987, p. 5 (photocopy).

14 "Acted on" could but need not imply implementation of these sanctions. Clark therefore avoided the issue of continued exports of high-technology items to South Africa, contrary to the Nassau Accord.

15 "Canada's Role in Southern Africa," 28 February 1987 (no. 87/11), p. 2.

16 Ibid., p. 2.

17 Ibid., p. 3. By 1987 with sanctions adopted by the USA, the Nordic countries, the members of the Commonwealth—admittedly without Britain—and the EEC, the world had garnered considerable economic clout particularly if "market-led" (capital flight) and "people-led" (consumer boycotts) sanctions were added to the equation.

18 Ibid., p. 6.

19 Ibid., p. 6. Note that the sentiments expressed in this passage echo the statement made to the Taskforce by the Liberal secretary of state for External Affairs five years previous: "We remain convinced that societies which are isolated and deprived of external contact find it most difficult to change and to adopt new conceptions and new approaches." He too had insisted that "contact and dialogue ... strengthen Canada's capacity to encourage the process of change in South Africa" (see above, p. 76).

20 Nelson Mandela, *The Struggle Is My Life* (London: IDAF Publications, 1990), p. 118.

21 Chief Luthuli was stripped of his chieftainship in 1952 and banned shortly after; he died in 1967 (Meer, *Higher than Hope*, pp. 71, 280.

22 "Canada's Role in Southern Africa," 28 February 1987 (no. 87/11), pp. 1–2.

23 For details see Linda Freeman, "Canada, Aid and Peacemaking in Southern Africa," in Robert Miller, ed., *Aid as Peacemaker: Canadian Development Assistance and Third World Conflict* (Ottawa: Carlton University Press, 1992), pp. 37–38. Readers are also referred to Linda Freeman, *The Ambiguous Champion   Canada and South Africa in the Trudeau and Mulroney Years* (Toronto: University of Toronto Press, 1997).

24 "Canada's Role in Southern Africa," 28 February 1987 (no. 87/11), p. 5.

25 Ibid., p. 5.

26 Michael Valpy, "Understands ANC Use of Force, PM Says," *The Globe and Mail*, 31 January 1987.

27 Canadian Press, "Clark Says Time Not Yet Ripe for More Curbs on Pretoria," *The Globe and Mail*, 5 March 1987.

28 "Canada's Role in Southern Africa," 28 February 1987 (no. 87/11), p. 4.

29 *Weekly Mail* (SA), 8 May 1987, and *The Independent* (UK), 3 June 1987, quoted in *Focus on Political Repression in Southern Africa: A Newsletter of the International Defence and Aid Fund for Southern Africa*, no. 71 (July-August 1987), p. 4.

30 Peter Goodspeed, "Restore Right to Protest Canada Tells Pretoria," *The Toronto Star*, 16 April 1987.

31 Geoffrey Spaulding, South African special correspondent of *Southern Africa Report*, in an interview with members of the editorial board, made this comment: "This is a rather different situation from that of 1984–85 when it looked like some kind of tacit alliance of convenience might be beginning to take shape between the resistance movement and a significant grouping within the white community notably certain sections of big business. ... With the relative success of the Emergency ... the latter group has backed away from any strong criticism of the National Party. ... [I]t obviously feels that the political crisis has become much less urgent and, in any case, they are not about to move into the camp of liberation" (*Southern Africa Report*, 3, no. 3 [December 1987], 11–12).

32 Sampson, *Black and Gold*, p. 355.

33 Ibid., p. 361.
34 *Southscan: A Bulletin of South African Affairs* (London), 10 June 1987.
35 *Focus on Political Repression in Southern Africa*, no. 71 (July-August 1987).
36 Alan Cowell, "South Africa Without Apartheid," *New York Times*, 22 June 1986.
37 *Johannesburg Star*, 6 May 1987, quoted in "Elections Stay-at-Home," *Focus on Political Repression in Southern Africa*, no. 71 (July-August 1987), p. 3.
38 For a discussion of COSATU activities relating to these events see ibid., pp. 1–3, and *Southscan: A Bulletin of South African Affairs*, 10 June 1987 and 17 June 1987.
39 Ibid.
40 Michael Valpy, "Mulroney Trip Leaves Trail of Commitments," *The Globe and Mail*, 3 February 1987.
41 Richard Gwyn, "Canada's Contribution to Summits: Championing Cause of Less Fortunate," *The Toronto Star*, 11 June 1987.
42 For the prime minister's quotation as well as the comments attributed to "a senior government official," see John Fraser, "Statement by Summit Host on Apartheid Pleases PM," *The Globe and Mail*, 11 June 1987.
43 Paul Koring, "ANC Will Urge Clark to Cut Links with Pretoria," *The Globe and Mail*, 12 August 1987.
44 Paul Koring, "Clark, Botha Stay at Odds over the Release of Mandela," *The Globe and Mail*, 15 August 1987.
45 The group of South Africans included Frederik Van Zyl Slabbert, former leader of the Progressive Federal Party; Beyers Naudé, outgoing general secretary of the South African Council of Churches; author André Brink; historian Hermann Giliomee; Jakes Gerwel, dean of arts, University of Western Cape; the poet Breyten Breytenbach; and Tony Bloom, head of Premier Milling and the only businessman still interested enough to attend such a gathering (*Southscan: A Bulletin of South African Affairs*, 15 July 1987). Robert Price tabulates eleven occasions between September 1985 and July 1989 when groups of leading white South Africans—church, business students, academics, journalists, politicians—made the "Trek to Lusaka" (see Price, *The Apartheid State in Crisis*, Table 7.4, p. 240.
46 Hugh Winsor, "Canada Shows Signs of Softening Policy against Apartheid," *The Globe and Mail*, 7 September 1987.
47 Ibid.
48 Hugh Winsor, "Sanctions Could Cut Violence in S. Africa, ANC Head Says," *The Globe and Mail*, 29 August 1987.
49 Winsor, "Canada Shows Signs of Softening Policy against Apartheid,"
50 Notes taken by the author at the meeting with Oliver Tambo. For a full discussion of the meeting with Oliver Tambo, see "Toronto Committee for the Liberation of Southern Africa," *Southern Africa Report*, 3, no. 2 (October 1987), 19–22.
51 Mandela told the court that after fifty years of faithful non-violent and constitutional attempts to win political rights, this option had been closed by the outlawing of the ANC. The decision to turn to the armed struggle was taken: "precisely because the soil of South Africa is drenched with the blood of innocent Africans. ... [W]e felt it our duty to make preparations as a long-term undertaking, to use force in order to defend ourselves against force ... and the least risk of life to both parties was guerilla warfare."
   On "Communist domination in the ANC" Mandela made clear that in 1964 (as in 1987) the accusation was a propaganda ploy: "The suggestion made by the State, that the struggle in South Africa is under the influence of foreigners and Communists is wholly incorrect." The ANC's most important political document, Mandela said, was the "Freedom Charter," which did not advocate a socialist state. The ANC had never advocated revolutionary change nor condemned a capitalist society. The Communist Party

had joined the ANC to work for the "Freedom Charter" and thus shared a common goal in the short term. But Mandela specified: "The Communist Party sought to emphasize class distinction, the ANC seeks to harmonize them. . . . Cooperation . . . is merely proof of a common goal—in this case the removal of white supremacy—it is not proof of a complete community of interests." Mandela warned, however, that blacks increasingly equate freedom with Communism because of apartheid legislation which brands all exponents of democratic rule as Communists (Meer, *Higher than Hope*, pp. 234, 244, 250.

52 See Hilary MacKenzie, *Maclean's*, 21 September 1987, on the meeting in the Château Montebello between Sir Geoffrey Howe and Joe Clark circa 14 September 1987.

53 Carol Goar, "Why Clark Keeps the Pressure on South Africa," *The Toronto Star*, 15 September 1987. See also Jim Sheppard, "Canadians Anxious to Avoid Bitter Split over South Africa," *The Globe and Mail*, 17 August 1987.

54 The New Double Taxation Law effective 1 January 1988 was a provision of the *Omnibus Budget Reconciliation Act* of 1987. See Lawyer's Committee for Civil Rights under the Law, "The Efforts of the American People toward Namibian Independence, Presented to the United Nations Seminar on the International Responsibility for Namibia's Independence, Istanbul, 21–25 March 1988," 21 March 1988 (mimeograph), pp. 5–6.

55 Carol Goar, "Why Clark Keeps the Pressure on South Africa."

56 Ibid.

57 Editorial, *The Globe and Mail*, 11 September 1987.

58 See *Racism in Southern Africa*, pp. 70–75.

59 Ibid., p. 73.

60 Ibid., pp. 73–74.

61 The Nordic states, and particularly Sweden, contributed for decades to similar South African projects. Sweden had been the major contributor to the International Defence and Aid Fund for Southern Africa which assisted, in Clark's words, the "victims of apartheid" and supported opponents of the regime. The Swedish government had also contributed funds to NGO public education projects on apartheid Unlike Canada, though, Sweden had given a platform to the ANC and had given financial support to its non-military projects. None of these activities had required the consent of its Nordic colleagues, the United Nations or any other political grouping.

62 Ibid., pp. 74–75.

63 See Michael Valpy, "Statement Reflects Pragmatism on Sanctions," *The Globe and Mail*, 19 October 1987.

64 "Statement in the House of Commons by the Right Honourable Joe Clark, Secretary of State for External Affairs," Ottawa (Statement 87/64).

9 The Taskforce and the Abandonment of Canada's Sanctions Policy, 1988–90

De Klerk and the Defiance Campaign

In 1988 a new awareness had begun to take root among South Africa's white business elite. It was becoming evident that apartheid would not be able to withstand the impact of international economic sanctions, at least not without incurring intolerable economic costs. Three years earlier the business community had unsuccessfully attempted to stay international economic sanctions by advocating cosmetic reforms. We noted that after the major lurch to the radical right and Botha's 1987 electoral victory, the majority of business had closed ranks behind the Botha government. When international sanctions began to hurt, a fair number of business people at first predicted that their effect would soon be neutralized by "inward industrialization," which would make South Africa economically self-sufficient.[1] These predictions soon proved to be false. Moreover, the black business community, the very group Botha's "Total Strategy" had anticipated to serve as a buffer against black radicalism, was now itself calling for radical change. At the 1988 annual conference, the National African Federated Chambers of Commerce encouraged its members to support community-based anti-apartheid struggles and called for the release of black political prisoners as a precondition for negotiations for a new constitutional order.[2]

A timely reminder that even the military powers of the apartheid regime were not invincible had come in May 1988. At Cuito Cuanavale in South

---

Notes for chapter 9 are found on pp. 328–36.

East Angola, South Africa's army had exceeded its capacity and suffered a decisive defeat after four attempts to capture the town.[3] Pretoria was at long last forced into meaningful negotiations to relinquish its seventy-year occupation of Namibia, leading to that country's independence in March 1990.

In January 1989 President P.W. Botha suffered a stroke. His cabinet colleague F.W. de Klerk became acting president and head of the National Party and formally succeeded Botha as state president in August 1989. A shrewd pragmatist, de Klerk did not hesitate to renew the harsh state of emergency in June 1989 while also announcing his readiness for fundamental change. He saw that South Africa's isolation and economic decline urgently required such changes. De Klerk was determined to accomplish these as yet undefined changes without undermining white South Africa's socio-economic interests. In this limited but real interest in change he could count on the support of South Africa's business community and of increasing numbers from within the ruling party. Powerful voices now acknowledged the regime's great vulnerability to international economic sanctions—paradoxically echoing the chorus of international anti-apartheid movements of preceding decades. Henri de Villiers, chair of the Standard Bank Investment Corporation, warned in July 1988: "South Africa needs the world. It needs markets, it needs skills, it needs technology, and above all it needs capital."[4]

Such public hand-wringing over the impact of economic sanctions was greatly welcomed by the ANC and the internal opposition for whom effective international sanctions were important complements to their own persistent mobilization and defiance campaigns. We have seen that South Africa's popular forces had since 1987 seized the political initiative to which the regime's only response was spiralling repression. Yet as the crisis mounted the regime became increasingly frustrated in the exercise of repression by the very powers that it had arrogated to itself. In January 1989, twenty political prisoners who had been detained for lengthy periods without trial began a hunger strike, demanding their immediate release. In deliberately phased and cumulative actions, large numbers of detainees joined them and turned "detentions without trial," until then a major instrument of repression, into a political weapon against the state. By the end of February the number of hunger strikers had risen to 600.

The regime first sought to ignore them. As the physical condition of the hunger strikers deteriorated, fears for their lives generated widespread popular protests in South Africa and internationally. Eventually the government had to recognize that the combination of domestic and international mobilization was defining the limits of its powers. International exposure of the plight of the hunger strikers had stepped up demands for new international economic sanctions that the South African government could ill afford. In April 1989 the detained hunger strikers prevailed and 900 out of 1,100 political prisoners held without trial were released.[5] South Africa's anti-apartheid movements had won a major political victory. More than that, they had demonstrated to their supporters in the townships, to South Africa's business community and to the international community, the emerging vulnerability of the regime.

A new twist in the defiance campaign illustrated even more poignantly the growing self-confidence of the internal resistance. On 20 August, the sixth anniversary of the founding of the UDF, hundreds of UDF member organizations, which had been banned from all political activity since February 1988, held meetings all over South Africa proclaiming themselves "unbanned," their leaders defying their personal restriction orders. Soon the UDF, COSATU and other anti-apartheid organizations formed a loosely constituted Mass Democratic Movement (MDM) committed to intensifying the defiance campaign. As they sensed that a major shift in the regime's policy was in the offing, the MDM as well began to prepare "a unifying perspective" on constitutional negotiations. At its annual conference in June, the South African Council of Churches (SACC) renewed its pledge to challenge the restriction orders that had replaced detentions without trial, and urged intensified non-violent means to bring about the end of apartheid.[6] The SACC, along with the MDM and the ANC, urged that this was the time to place maximum pressure on the regime in order to demonstrate the strength and unity of the anti-apartheid movement and to disabuse it of any illusion that anything short of fundamental constitutional change would be acceptable.

In July 1989 under the auspices of the Organization of African Unity (OAU) meeting in Harare, the leadership of the ANC and the MDM formulated guidelines for a process of constitutional negotiations. They issued the *Harare Declaration*, a statement of great importance, which was then endorsed by the OAU. It insisted that constitutional negotiations could only begin after the apartheid regime had created a political climate that allowed the free exchange of political views:

> Accordingly, the present regime should, at the very least, release all political prisoners and detainees unconditionally and refrain from imposing restrictions on them; lift bans and restrictions on all proscribed and restricted organizations and persons; remove all troops from the townships; end the state of emergency and repeal all legislation, such as, and including, the Internal Security Act, designed to circumscribe political activity; and cease all political trials and political executions.[7]

On 14 December the essential elements of the *Harare Declaration* were adopted by the UN General Assembly which also enjoined state members "to ensure that the international community does not relax existing measures aimed at encouraging the South African regime to eradicate apartheid, until there is clear evidence of profound and irreversible changes."[8]

Such developments encouraged expectations of an early change in the political climate in South Africa. It should be remembered, however, that under de Klerk repression continued throughout this year. He not only renewed the state of emergency but as well during his presidency acts of extra-judicial executions and other forms of violent coercion by the security forces increased and were tolerated, to say the least.[9]

Since that time we have learned a great deal about the operations of the regime's death squads. Political murders continued throughout 1989. Among others, they felled David Webster, a human rights activist in South Africa, and Anton Lubowski, a SWAPO candidate in the first democratic elections in Namibia. We have also learned of a strategy to foment "black on black" violence in the townships. Its purpose was to generate international and domestic perception that black majority rule was premature.

Even as this study goes to press in early 1997, hard and compelling evidence and detailed confessions are being presented to the Truth and Reconciliation Commission in South Africa. They recount both the wide scope of these official acts of murder and of their sanction by the regime's highest political authorities.

In addition, major funding, military training and weapons were covertly made available to the KwaZulu "homeland" under Chief Buthelezi, the ANC's powerful black opponent.[10] In early 1990 de Klerk signed into law a new act that gave Buthelezi, who was also KwaZulu's minister of police, the right to have his police force operate not only in KwaZulu but in any part of South Africa, with grave and entirely foreseeable consequences of bloodshed. Zulus were also given the right to carry "traditional Zulu weapons."[11]

These developments did not augur well for early constitutional change. All progressive organizations in South Africa, including the South African Council of Churches, urged the international community to continue its economic pressure on Pretoria.

Canada's Policy Paralysis 1988–89

The Taskforce shared with their South African partners the conviction that the most important international contribution to a rapid transition to democratic rule with minimal further violence would be a major escalation of economic sanctions. Nevertheless the member churches had also to recognize the force of the sobering analysis, presented in chapter 8, that despite the intensifying struggle in South Africa, the Canadian government was unlikely to lend direct support to the liberation movements nor to impose the oft-promised comprehensive sanctions. There was no evidence that External Affairs was moderating its aversion to such moves. Moreover, in

1988 it was unlikely that Mulroney himself would press for stricter measures. Not only had he basically abandoned the issue, but with an election pending there was the added need to unite the party and to avoid alienating the business community.[12]

The Canadian churches' forebodings about Canadian policy were confirmed in February 1988 when Canada reacted minimally to the total ban on the activities of seventeen leading anti-apartheid bodies.[13] These included the United Democratic Front (UDF) with its over 800 affiliated organizations and all political actions—outside of state-defined union activities—of the Congress of South African Trade Unions (COSATU). This left the South African churches as virtually the only opposition voices not yet silenced. In a statement to the House of Commons, Clark announced that he was "disappointed" in the "response of the Government of South Africa" and asked rhetorically whether this was the time for Canada to end relations with South Africa altogether. Answering his own question, Clark concluded that this was "the wrong time for Canada to walk away." He committed the Canadian government to generous funding for some of the afflicted organizations and no one can quarrel with such largesse. But Canada's leadership role in the international community, and particularly in the Commonwealth, was faltering. Clark failed to respond to the regime's mass repression with appropriately tough sanctions.[14] He was silent on obvious alternatives to "walking away." Such procrastinations did not in fact go unnoticed in Pretoria: "In fact ... the slowing down of the international sanctions campaign made it possible for the Government [of South Africa] to get away with the crackdown with minimal internal opposition and ineffectual international reactions."[15]

In February 1988 Joe Clark chaired the first meeting of the new Commonwealth Committee of Foreign Ministers on Southern Africa (CFM) in Lusaka, Zambia. It did not recommend any new sanctions, but instead commissioned two studies on how to "widen, tighten and intensify economic and other sanctions against South Africa." One of these was to examine South Africa's international financial relationships and explore "effective action against South Africa in this area." The second would evaluate the impact of existing economic sanctions and propose areas where trade with South Africa could be further reduced and where investment in and trade with the Front Line States (FLS) could be enhanced. In addition, the Lusaka CFM agreed "as a matter of urgency" to seek more effective enforcement measures of the existing mandatory arms embargo. The Canadian government, still promoting the new focus for Commonwealth action which it had initiated at the Vancouver Commonwealth Heads of Government Meeting (CHOGM), volunteered to prepare a strategy paper on South Africa's censorship and propaganda.[16]

Efforts by the Taskforce to Widen, Tighten and Intensify Canadian Sanctions

Reacting to the intensifying repressions in South Africa and the inadequacy of Canadian government responses to them, the Taskforce set out once again to confront External Affairs with documented shortcomings in the implementation of existing sanctions, with policy recommendations for their improvements and with proposals for new sanctions. In April 1988 it wrote a detailed letter to Joe Clark requesting a meeting to discuss these issues. It had to settle instead for a meeting on 27 June 1988 with officials of the Southern Africa Task Force of External Affairs, without the minister.[17] The insights gained at this meeting were then incorporated into a major brief, which the Taskforce sent to Joe Clark on 20 July 1988. The title of the brief, *Widening, Tightening and Intensifying Economic and Other Sanctions against South Africa*, echoed the wording of the Okanagan Statement of October 1987. We review here several of the main issues of this substantial brief.[18]

Enforcement of the Arms Embargo against South Africa

The churches pointed out that no changes had been made to Canada's Export Controls Policy of 10 September 1986 in response to the Commonwealth call for more effective enforcement of the arms embargo. It still stated that "military and strategic goods are not exported to *military end users and government departments and agencies.*"[19] The brief noted that the churches had a verbal assurance from External Affairs officials that Canada did not permit the sale of military goods to *any* end user in South Africa. If this was the case, the churches wrote, then Canada's Export Controls Policy should be revised to reflect the changed policy.

The Taskforce brief also disagreed emphatically with the government's reliance on end-user certificates for the control of the uses in South Africa of these strategic exports. They questioned the assurances of the Export Controls Division that it was able to determine through "intelligence" that the exported items would not be diverted or converted for the use of South Africa's military and police. The churches contrasted Canada's policy on strategic exports to South Africa to its policy toward the Warsaw Pact states under the Coordinating Committee for Multilateral Export Controls (COCOM).[20]

> We fail to understand why the policy regarding the export of strategic goods to South Africa is not as stringent as the policy regarding exports to Warsaw Pact countries.... [They] are "denied all equipment and technology which would enhance their military potential." This policy ... bans not only military goods, but also all strategic goods in terms of their performance characteristics.... End-user certificates play no role—strategic goods are denied to *all* end users.[21]

Two seemingly innocuous examples illustrated the point. Recently a permit had been issued to export germanium crystals to a South African university. The crystals were essential in the manufacture of fibre optics technology for the South African military, but External Affairs held that this university was doing research on fibre optics for "civilian" purposes. The churches questioned External Affairs' conclusion that this research would not be made available to the military.[22]

Another permit for the export to South Africa of a ground terminal for a satellite-based global rescue system was pending. The churches conceded its humanitarian purpose, but noted that it could have been installed in a different country. In South Africa, the churches wrote, the system "would open the door for South Africa to obtain vital technology and information useful to its military and strategic applications." The churches recommended that the government "Revise the Export Control Policy to prohibit the export to *any* end user in South Africa of all strategic (dual purpose) goods which might assist South Africa to fill its strategic and military needs."[23] The Taskforce was also critical of Canada's consistently narrow interpretation of the Commonwealth "embargo on all military cooperation with Africa" to which the London Review Committee had agreed in August 1986. The churches urged the government to initiate a multilateral approach to the embargo and to press for the establishment of an effective "mechanism similar to COCOM" to screen international strategic exports to South Africa. Above all, the churches urged the Canadian government to tighten its own sanctions by preventing Canadian companies and organizations from aiding South Africa's military and strategic needs through consulting services, technology transfers, licenses and certain forms of investments.[24]

Financial Sanctions

When the Commonwealth had agreed in 1986 to halt all new loans to any borrower in South Africa, Canada and most member states had excluded trade credits from this ban. South Africa had been quick to take full advantage of this loophole and with the evident encouragement of South Africa's Reserve Bank negotiated ever longer terms of trade financing.[25] When the Taskforce met with External Affairs on 27 June, officials said that the government was aware of the situation, but did not want to ban trade credits altogether because it would then be imposing a "complete trade embargo by the back door."[26] As a "fall-back" position, the churches proposed that the study of financial sanctions commissioned by the Commonwealth foreign ministers' committee include an assessment of how best to insure that trade credits are not used as a substitute for loans now denied by international financial sanctions.

Enforcement of the Oil Embargo

The Taskforce also commented on the increase that had occurred in the export of petroleum products to South Africa since the voluntary ban on the sale of such products in September 1985. The churches noted that:

> External Affairs' information is that there is no internationally defined list of petrochemical products which were covered by the ban and that these petro-chemical products are more "chemical" than "petroleum." External Affairs has therefore asked Statistics Canada to consider . . . reclassifying them as man-ufactured chemical end products. They would then be exempt from the ban on petroleum exports.[27]

The Taskforce rejected such narrowing of the embargo and recommended a broad definition of what was covered by the oil embargo against South Africa.

This point was further pursued in March 1994. An official of Statistics Canada told the author that no record existed of any request by External Affairs in 1988 that the classification of petroleum products be redefined and that no such change had taken place. He also stated that Statistics Can-ada followed the Standard International Trade Classification of products where reclassification occurred from time to time, but not in response to requests by individual government departments.[28]

It is less clear what transpired. The Commonwealth recommendations of the oil embargo did not include an agreed definition of what should be treated as petroleum products in the implementation of the oil embargo. There was, however, an international agreement as part of the Standard International Trade Classification that treated lubricating oils and greases as petroleum products. External Affairs seems to have decided to ignore that international classification when interpreting the coverage of the oil embargo against South Africa, and instead to have chosen to regard these products as manufactured chemical end products, thus permitting their continued exportation to South Africa. A 1986 letter from J. M. MacLeod, president and chief executive officer of Shell Canada to Joe Clark bears out this assumption. He first assured Clark that Shell Canada was not involved in "direct petroleum trade with South Africa" and then went on to explain:

> we do have some direct and indirect sales to private sector buyers in South Africa of other petroleum-related products, namely sulphur and petrochemi-cals. We have not taken steps to stop these activities, and have had consulta-tions with your Department in this regard. Officials there are satisfied that Shell Canada is abiding by the law, and the spirit of the Canadian policy toward South Africa.[29]

This judgement of the officials expressed to Shell and possibly to other exporters of petroleum products to South Africa likely explains the increase in value of the export of these products to the Customs Union of South

Africa from $36,000 in 1985 to $425,000 in 1987.[30] It provides an additional indication of how diligently External Affairs sought to minimize the significance of trade sanctions against South Africa.

It was, moreover, not the only case. The Taskforce argued, for example, that the government should not have allowed the export of advanced technology drill bits for oil exploration and that it should have prevented Electrolyzer Corporation from exporting to South Africa hydrogen plants and parts applicable in the production of diesel fuel, a fuel that was in short supply and used extensively by the South African armed forces. The Canadian government should also have questioned a Winnipeg consultant who assisted, unencumbered, the South African production of ethanol, a fuel substitute.[31] The Taskforce urged that Canada's oil embargo should cover all activities such as financing, technology and equipment transfers, and consulting services that assisted South Africa's development of its own petroleum or alternative energy resources.[32]

Eldorado Nuclear Contracts for the Processing of Namibian Uranium

During their June 1988 meeting with External Affairs, the churches learned that the import of Namibian uranium and its "toll processing" by Eldorado Nuclear was continuing and was likely to be extended beyond the end of the year. The Taskforce argued that any extension of the contracts enabled the corporations involved, namely Rio Algom, Rio Tinto Zinc and other corporate shareholders of the Rossing Uranium Mine in Namibia, to evade attempts by the international community to end the trade in Namibian uranium. Further, as long as Canada continued to process Namibian uranium, American companies could import Namibian uranium processed in Canada as Canadian-processed uranium, thus bypassing the 1986 US ban on imports of South African and Namibian uranium.[33] The churches' brief, therefore, called for the termination of all processing contracts of Namibian uranium by the end of 1988.

The determination of the government to continue to pursue a vastly less engaged policy than the churches felt essential was quickly made clear by the role played by Canada at the August meeting of the Commonwealth Foreign Ministers' Committee.

Stand-off in Toronto—The August 1988 Meeting of the Commonwealth Foreign Ministers Committee

The Toronto meeting, which welcomed the foreign ministers of seven Commonwealth countries in a Canadian election year, is remembered for its public relations success and its gala entertainment of unusual proportions.[34] Joe Clark and External Affairs let it be known well in advance that this meeting was not about international economic sanctions but that it would centre on Canada's new focus of South African censorship and propaganda. News releases had been sent out, and External Affairs officers were at hand to inform the media about this change.[35] Commenting on the possible release of the Commonwealth's experts' studies that were commissioned in Lusaka, on "widening, tightening and intensifying" economic sanctions against South Africa, External Affairs officials told *The Globe and Mail*: "This is not going to be an occasion to consider new sanctions ... The meeting will devote particular attention to a Canadian strategy paper on propaganda and censorship."[36]

Clark's opening speech even contained a deft reordering of the sequence of issues the meeting was to address in order to downplay deliberations on sanctions. The "Okanagan Statement and Programme of Action on Southern Africa" had confirmed that: "With the exception of Britain we believe that economic and other sanctions have had a significant effect on South Africa and that their wider, tighter and more intensified application must remain an essential part of the international response to apartheid."[37] The next few paragraphs considered the means, including expert studies, by which the global application of economic sanctions could be enhanced and their impact assessed on an ongoing basis. This was followed by a section on the predicament of the Front Line States, their involuntary economic dependency on South Africa and their geographical vulnerability to South African attacks. Only then, under "Reaching into South Africa," did the Okanagan Statement deal with issues offered by Canada as an alternative to additional sanctions. Paragraphs 17-22 endorsed "individual and collective efforts" to support the victims and opponents of apartheid and "to promote real internal dialogue," while only the final paragraphs (23–24) acknowledged the need to "counteract South African propaganda and censorship."[38]

A short year later Clark welcomed his Commonwealth colleagues with this slight clouding of the order of priorities:

> At Vancouver our Committee was charged with pursuing Commonwealth goals to reach into South Africa to the victims and opponents of apartheid, to promote dialogue, and counteract South African censorship and propaganda; we were to widen, tighten and intensify sanctions to make them more effective; we were to increase our support to South Africa's neighbours in the face of destabilization by Pretoria; and we were to press for Namibian independence.[39]

Clark not only shifted the order of issues of the Okanagan Statement, but in the balance of his speech he barely touched on any initiative other than the censorship and propaganda issue. He hardly mentioned the two studies on trade and financial sanctions and avoided all further mention of the security needs of the Front Line States. Instead, Clark exercised his prerogative as convener of the conference and announced that the focus in Toronto would be South Africa's censorship and propaganda. He gave notice that a Canadian strategy paper on countering South African propaganda and censorship had been prepared to guide the discussions and he announced the various parallel events on censorship and propaganda that his government had organized during and following the meeting of the Commonwealth foreign ministers (CFM).

Although the CFM meetings were held behind closed doors, tensions and scepticism with regard to Canada's agenda seeped out. Sir Shridath Ramphal, general secretary of the Commonwealth, for example, warned that inaction by Canada and other Commonwealth countries was encouraging more censorship, more jailings and more killing of blacks by the apartheid regime.[40] Ramphal was emphatic on the need for tougher economic sanctions, as was Dr. Nhato Motlana, then head of the Soweto Civic Association and one of the government's invited guests. Motlana was quoted as saying: "The redirection by Sir Shridath was correct, I do not know if it is fair to accuse Canada. But if you do not get rid of apartheid, all your efforts against propaganda are wasted."[41]

Several African diplomats by now recognized that Canada was retreating from its previous advocacy of sanctions. They calculated—as they had done in Vancouver—that the best they could do under the circumstances was to keep Canada diplomatically in their corner. Nothing would be gained from their "publicly attacking Canada, or driving it into the arms of Mrs. Thatcher."[42] Canada's secretary of state for External Affairs seems to have relied on just that calculation.

In the Toronto meetings in August 1988 Clark defied with steely determination the Commonwealth Secretariat and several of his Commonwealth colleagues who were seeking tough new sanctions. Although the commissioned Commonwealth studies were at hand to assist in the choice of additional measures, Clark had found a way to minimize their impact. The most the "Concluding Statement" could record in the way of new sanctions was a recommendation that each country should ask the financial institutions operating within it to voluntarily agree not to expand their trade financing for South Africa and to press South Africa for rescheduling of its international debt at a rate of only one year at a time.[43]

No new trade sanctions were announced. Although the Interim Report on expanding trade sanctions was available at the Toronto meeting, it was kept under wraps.[44] It had responded to the Vancouver CHOGM request for the wider, tighter and more intensified application of economic sanctions, yet the "Concluding Statement" of the CFM meeting did not authorize the distribution of the Interim Report, not even of its relatively brief and challenging final chapter, "What Can Be Done Now?"[45]

The Toronto CFM meeting, following Clark's leadership, agreed to interpret the widening of sanctions that had been called for by the CHOGM in Vancouver to mean not the widening and intensifying of sanctions by Commonwealth states, but the attempt to multiply the number of states that were joining existing Commonwealth sanctions. The ministers limited themselves to inviting Commonwealth and other governments "to consider adopting" measures to which the Commonwealth had already agreed. For instance, governments could press other states that had not yet done so to adopt Commonwealth trade bans. They could seek stricter customs scrutiny and heavier penalties for violators of existing sanctions and they could consider prohibiting technology transfers that permitted South Africa to circumvent sanctions in the area of arms, oil and computers; they could consider redefining the meaning of "agricultural products" with a view to widen the scope of the ban on these South African imports; and they could increase publicity about companies that violated existing sanctions.[46]

The fifty-one pages of the Interim Report eventually surfaced in the press.[47] It then became clear that the suggestions to "governments" of what they could do, made at the close of the Toronto CFM meeting, bore some semblance to the Interim Report, but had lost their essential rationale. The experts' study had carefully connected one proposed measure to another and demonstrated the potential effect of this interlinking new set of sanctions on the ultimate goal of forcing the apartheid regime to abandon its policies and to enter into negotiations for constitutional changes. Its thoroughness and imagination had evidently convinced opponents of new sanctions that it was best not to give publicity to it during the Toronto CFM meeting.

For the "wider" application of sanctions, the experts had sought both a greater involvement of non-Commonwealth states in the sanctions campaign *and* a widening of the sanctions already applied. They called for strong diplomatic approaches to South Africa's remaining major trading partners, such as the UK, West Germany and Japan, to ask for an import ban of South African agricultural products as well as of coal, iron, steel and uranium, giving priority to coal as the most important South African export after gold. These commodities, the independent experts had reasoned, were readily available on the world market, making it hard for South Africa to find alternative markets and easy for importers to switch suppliers. The experts urged coordinated approaches also to a host of smaller states that had defied sanctions and had in fact increased their trade with South Africa.[48]

The Interim Report also proposed banning the import from South Africa of additional non-strategic base metals such as copper, lead, tin, zinc, aluminium and nickel, as well as iron ore and non-metallic minerals (except andalusite). These metals, the authors calculated, represented 5 percent of South African exports, they were not strategic substances and were readily available from alternate (non-Communist) suppliers, including Commonwealth members. The Interim Report urged swift action; it noted that the price of these South African exports had increased twofold over the preceding year and was threatening to undermine the overall effects of the other sanctions.

The independent experts proposed "Taking Advantage" legislation in all states where sanctions were in effect. Such legislation had been adopted in the US together with the Comprehensive Anti-Apartheid Act (1986). It permitted the imposition of trade restrictions on states that "took advantage" of products that South Africa was offering at a reduced price in an effort to break the sanctions against them.

For the tighter application of sanctions, the Commonwealth Interim Report had recommended penalties for sanctions violations such as falsification of labelling offenses or false country of origin declarations, far stronger than the minor penalties applied at the time. The experts specified that the penalties should equal those imposed for illegal trading with enemy countries [such as imposed by COCOM] or for drug smuggling. To enforce this, states should establish and adequately fund special units within their customs authorities.

The Interim Report had formulated several additional sanctions related to the arms and oil embargo. It advocated in no uncertain terms the prohibition of all technology transfers that were linked to South African attempts to gain self-sufficiency in oil, arms and computer technology. The prohibition was to include consultancy, sales and licenses of technology as well as sales of actual hardware.[49] "In the oil sector the prohibition would include anything that was linked to oil and gas exploration, production and processing, as well as gas and coal conversion."[50] As many of these proposals corresponded to those made by the churches in their July brief, their self-confidence and their resolve to continue their pressure were re-enforced.

To intensify economic sanctions the Interim Report had made several intriguing proposals. It called for complete transparency in commercial relations with respect to all South African transactions. This measure, already adopted by legislation in Sweden, was designed to intensify the economic isolation of South Africa and to serve as a deterrent for sanctions violations since, as the experts noted, many companies doing business with South Africa did so only as long as this remained confidential.[51]

We saw above that the CFM in their "Concluding Statement" agreed to ask the banks *not to expand* their South African trade credits. In contrast, the authors of the Interim Report categorically stated that there should be a broadly defined and *complete ban on export credits* to South Africa (emphasis added).[52] They confirmed the statement made by the Taskforce in its July brief to Joe Clark that export credits for South African trade were increasingly replacing non-available long-term credits.

The Interim Report had thus thoroughly reviewed every aspect of how the sanctions against South Africa could be "widened, tightened and intensified." Its authors nevertheless predicted that even with optimal compliance the measures they had proposed would not impose the "real discomfort" needed to force white South Africans to begin negotiations.

Yet they suggested that if these sanctions were adopted they would sharply intensify the pressure on the regime and would show that the Commonwealth was not prepared to stop where it was.[53] In August 1988, however, "where it was" was exactly where the Canadian government was determined to leave its sanctions policy. The decision not to release the Interim Report and the vast gap between the recommendations of the CFM and those proposed by the experts' study painfully illustrated that Canada had largely succeeded in bringing to a halt the Commonwealth movement toward increasing economic sanctions.

The Management of Politics in the Shadows of Apartheid in the Fall of 1988

In November 1988 the Mulroney government faced elections and needed to reassure its traditional supporters that it remained faithful to its own conservative ideology and loyal to its major international allies. We have seen that this argued against new economic sanctions. Yet two different sets of political considerations tempered this straightforward calculation. They called for a more nuanced response to the Southern Africa situation than Canada's poker-faced stance at the Toronto CFM meeting.

First, South Africa's repression had further increased throughout 1988 and could not be ignored. It had after all been Brian Mulroney who, three years earlier, had told the United Nations that if there were no fundamental changes in South Africa, Canada was prepared to invoke total sanctions against it. That decision had been postponed under one pretext or another while the situation in South Africa deteriorated from year to year.

South Africa's black townships had now been under armed siege for eighteen months, with 1988 seeing the creation of a new and deadly black police force called "kitskonstables" (instant police). Similar to the Koevoet units employed in Namibia, its members were recruited from impoverished rural areas and were deliberately left undertrained and undisciplined. They were rapidly brutalized as the regime ordered them into the townships. The often invisible networks of community organizations and street committees nevertheless remained strong. Their effectiveness was demonstrated in October 1988 when, despite the silencing of almost all opposition organizations, the detention of many activists and a government incentive program to boost voter participation, a near total boycott of the municipal elections in the black townships was achieved.[54] The regime's latest scheme to create a "multiethnic" National Council of "homeland" leaders and elected municipal councillors was thus stillborn.

We noted the ban in February 1988 of the activities of thirty-two opposition organizations and the detention of most of their leaders. South Africa's Human Rights Commission, a newly established independent organization, estimated that based on official figures, at the end of 1988,

1,500 people were in detention without trial; 1,000 of these had been held for over one year and 100, mainly UDF leaders, had been held for over two years.[55] More and more people were sentenced to death and executed for "unrest-related" offenses; in early 1988 alone, seven were hanged, and by the end of the year sixty persons were on "Death Row," sentenced for their participation in political protests. Although international outrage over South Africa's use of judicial executions as a means of repression had saved the lives of defendants of two well-publicized trials, sentencing remained extremely severe.[56] Convictions were increasingly obtained under a "Common Purpose" section of the law, which allowed for the conviction of persons for murder simply on the basis of their presence at the scene of the crime. Under this law the state was not required to prove that the accused had either committed the murder or intended to harm the victim.

The regime also resorted to arson and bombing attacks on the offices of opposition organizations. In May 1987 COSATU's headquarters had been totally demolished. On 31 August 1988, twenty-one people were injured when a powerful bomb severely damaged Khotso House in Johannesburg, which housed the South African Council of Churches, the Black Sash and other anti-apartheid organizations.[57] Then early on 12 October men broke into Khanya House, the Pretoria headquarters of the Southern African Catholic Bishops' Conference. They doused the first three floors with petrol and set the building alight, seriously endangering the lives of several sleeping churchworkers.[58]

Acts such as these were the subject of critical comment in official communiqués of the Canadian government. They were also monitored and publicized by an increasingly well-organized Canadian network of anti-apartheid organizations, which in turn had created a well-informed and critical public. Approaching an election, the Mulroney government could therefore not altogether ignore public opinion polls that consistently had shown substantial support for its economic sanctions and other measures against the apartheid regime.[59] This perhaps explains Joe Clark's announcement in the fall of 1988 during a speech at Laval University of long-overdue adjustments to several sanctions that Canadians had been led to believe had long been in place. The details are intriguing as they reveal a determination to appear to be doing more while doing little.

The Nassau Commonwealth Accord of October 1985 had contained "a programme of common action" consisting of two lists of economic sanctions. The first had been "agreed upon" and adopted right away. Adoption of the second list had been contingent on "adequate progress" within six months in South Africa's willingness to engage in constitutional negotiations. In August 1988 the London Review Committee, which followed South Africa's abrupt termination of the EPG mission, agreed to recommend the implementation of the second Nassau list.[60] In

Montreal in February 1987, Clark had claimed that: "Canada has acted on all the Commonwealth sanctions drawn up at Nassau and London. That means we ban airline links, new investment, agricultural imports, tourist promotion, imports of uranium, coal, iron, steel, and place restrictions on visas"[61]

This was in fact only partially true. Canada had not implemented paragraph 6 (d), the "ban on the sale and export of computer equipment capable of use by South African military forces, police or security forces." The Canadian government had left unchanged the wording of its very first set of sanctions in July 1985, which had preceded the Nassau meeting. Canadian exports of sensitive electronic equipment had thus remained restricted only to the South African military, police and government agencies, despite the possibility, indeed the probability, that once in South Africa such equipment would be used to enhance the capability of just these agencies.

It is clear from Clark's announcements at Laval University just how useful had been the Okanagan Statement for the Canadian government. He announced that Canada would "widen, tighten and intensify the application of sanctions" in accordance with agreements reached at the Vancouver Commonwealth meeting a year earlier. By simply announcing amendments to existing sanctions, he sought to soothe public demand for new sanctions and created the impression of a planned forward movement in Canada's South Africa policy.[62] For example, Clark told the students at Laval University that "[t]he ban on sales of high technology items on the Export Control List will be extended to private sector end-users in South Africa."[63] He did not remind his audience that with this step Canada would merely be catching up with the 1985 Nassau Accord and with equivalent sanctions already legislated in the USA and the Nordic states.

This is not the only illustration of the use of this strategy. At the 1986 London Review Committee, Canada had also agreed to, but had inadequately implemented, two further economic sanctions from the second list of the Nassau Accord. The first of these was paragraph 7(g), a ban on government contracts with majority-owned South African companies. At Laval University Clark promised to "tighten" this ban. The narrowest of definitions had, up to that moment, allowed Canadian officials to virtually ignore this clause of the Nassau Accord. Critical press reports had appeared two weeks before Clark's speech at Laval. They indicated that two majority-owned South African companies, Boart Canada Inc. of Mississauga and Longyear Canada Inc. of North Bay, had each received federal grants for export promotion while Longyear had as well received a Canadian government contract for replacement parts ordered by the Department of National Defence. As well, in September 1988, the federal Energy Department had included Hudson Bay Mining and Smelting in a lucrative research project on waste disposal, despite the fact that HBMS was ultimately controlled by Anglo American Corporation of South Africa through the Luxembourg registered MINORCO.[64]

External Affairs and the Department of Energy took these revelations in their stride. They denied that the federal ban on contracts with majority-owned South African companies applied in these cases. A confusion, they said, had arisen in 1986 over whether the federal ban on "contracts with such companies applied to all deals or only to procurement contracts." Clark made a virtue out of necessity. He announced that "the tightening of the rules is part of an effort that had long been planned." Orders were therefore issued that the bureaucracy find out henceforth whether companies were owned or controlled by South African interests before the federal government established business relations.[65] This in turn prompted the question of just how majority-owned South African companies had been identified before the recent new rules.

At Laval, Clark announced that in future the ban on government contracts with majority-owned South African companies would apply to "grants, contributions and sales including ... assistance under regional development programs," and to sales by agencies of the Canadian government "to all clients in South Africa ... [thus] terminating Petro Canada sulphur sales."[66] He also declared that "there will be no increase in trade credits to South Africa,"[67] Canadian banks having agreed to this voluntary curb.

The announcement at Laval of the tightening in these various Canadian economic sanctions served the interest of the Canadian government well beyond the votes it might thereby garner in the Canadian elections. A different election was pending in which Canada's anti-apartheid record would be critical. Canada was a contender once again for one of the rotating seats of non-permanent members on the United Nations Security Council. When Canada held this seat in 1977, major efforts had been made by Don Jamieson, then secretary of state for External Affairs, to polish Canada's tarnished record on Southern Africa in order to add credibility to the Contact Group of States (see above, pp. 51–56). In 1988 a similar stratagem was in place. It appears that the Canadian government had held back on the implementation of these Commonwealth measures in order to have a maximum impact in the United Nations General Assembly when appealing for votes in the election for a seat on the Security Council.

As part of this campaign, Prime Minister Mulroney attended the opening of the fall session of the United Nations General Assembly. It was the first time that he had returned to this forum since his pledge in 1985 that if there were no fundamental changes in South Africa, "we are prepared to invoke total sanctions against that country ...," a pledge that had earned him a standing ovation.

This time Mulroney was more constrained in his options. He was involved in two election campaigns that required conflicting political credibilities. For a Conservative victory in the Canadian elections it was considered best to be discreet about the government's involvements in Southern Africa. However, to win enough votes in the United Nations General Assembly for a seat on the Security Council, convincing evidence was needed that Canada would champion Third World causes, none more topical in the fall of 1988, than the urgency to strengthen international pressure on the apartheid regime.

Aided by Yves Fortier, who had replaced Stephen Lewis as Canada's permanent representative at the United Nations, Mulroney first laid the groundwork to disabuse in advance all expectations that he would call for total sanctions in 1988. He had several private meetings with President Robert Mugabe of Zimbabwe, who was then reported by Canadian officials to be content with the level of Canadian sanctions, suggesting that Canada needed "to go no further at this time with sanctions against South Africa." Mugabe's advice to Canada was quoted by Yves Fortier in terms that echoed almost word for word the position of External Affairs: "Canada is moving step by step toward a crescendo, but this is not the time to turn off the light." A spectacular reception attended by nearly all UN delegations earned Mulroney good will and indulgence when he addressed the General Assembly the following day. With Mugabe's explicit support for Canada's election to the Security Council, with all that this implied for other Third World support votes, Mulroney was able with ease to pull back from his 1985 promise of total sanctions.[68]

Mulroney's nine-page address to the General Assembly on 29 September devoted but six short paragraphs to Southern Africa.[69] He repeated Clark's assertion that "from the outset, we have applied all the sanctions agreed within the Commonwealth" and disclosed the new measures that Clark had announced earlier in the week at Laval University. He then, albeit framed in the vaguest of terms, announced Canadian security assistance to the Front Line States, a policy development of major importance to Mugabe: "Because of threats to major development projects in the Front Line States we intend to provide assistance, in concert with others, to preserve these development initiatives."[70]

The media paid scant attention to this part of Mulroney's speech, so preoccupied was it with Mulroney's ability to extricate himself without loss of face from his 1985 pledge to invoke total sanctions. A communiqué on the subject released simultaneously by External Affairs did not fare any better. It reported that: "[T]oday Canada has agreed to respond to requests for assistance for the protection of infrastructure projects in Southern Africa. Projects funded by [CIDA] ... have increasingly become susceptible to sabotage. Destabilization and insurgency activities continue to be a threat to major development projects."[71] The communiqué spelled out that this was Canada's response to requests for security assistance and that Canada planned to provide logistical support such as clothes, fuel, spare parts and communications equipment and to increase, for countries "experiencing these difficulties," balance-of-payment support. Canada also offered military training of FLS personnel through assistance already funded by Canada's External Affairs and National Defence.[72]

The Canadian media was still slow in picking up the significance of the release, possibly because it stressed, not unintentionally, that the new assistance was development aid offered by CIDA. To the Front Line States, however, it was clear that this was the kind of commitment they had been requesting since 1986. Action along such lines had been denied first at the 1987 Commonwealth Heads of Government Meeting in Vancouver and more recently when General Olusegun Obasanjo's report was ignored at the Toronto Commonwealth Foreign Ministers' meeting in early August 1988. It is reasonable to assume that in their private meetings in New York Mulroney and Mugabe had struck a deal: The FLS would not press for new Canadian sanctions, would not hold Mulroney to his 1985 pledge on total sanctions and would support Canada's candidature for a Security Council seat in return for a public announcement of official Canadian assistance for their security needs. Mugabe may well have considered that Canada's commitment to provide security assistance to these states was more important by far, both materially and politically, than would be Canadian promises for new or total sanctions that might remain as elusive as Mulroney's 1985 promise.

On his return to Zimbabwe, Mugabe met the press. To Mulroney's consternation, the headlines in Harare's *The Herald* announced "Canada pledges frontline military aid."[73] What Canada had wished to keep understated was now overstated. Canada's aid to the military was not "military aid" in the conventional sense, but under the circumstances it was a notable departure from previous Canadian policy on the issue and should have been announced with a sense of purpose and self-confidence. Instead, Mulroney's announcement at the United Nations as well as External Affairs' communiqué had been so convoluted that Canadian journalists had missed its significance. The Zimbabwean press in contrast, close as it was to the scene of South African attacks and with forthright information in hand, had seen at once the importance of the Canadian decision. Mugabe, for his part, was anxious to justify to his allies that his personal negotiations with Mulroney and his support for Canada's bid for a Security Council seat had achieved a valuable objective for the FLS. Thus while Mugabe praised Mulroney for his "bold stand," Mulroney sought to deny that there had been any change of policy.[74] On 26 October 1988 Joe Clark announced Canada's election to the United Nations Security Council for a two-year period beginning in January 1989.[75] Clark made this announcement from Edmonton where he had been opening an international conference entitled, "Tourism, a vital force for peace." There was bitter irony in this.

When Clark spoke at Laval University a month earlier he had promised the tightening of several Commonwealth sanctions and Mulroney had repeated Canada's commitment to these improvements at the United Nations three days later. Both men, however, overlooked the tightening of another Commonwealth measure that they had sorely neglected. Among the measures agreed to by the Review Committee meeting in London in August 1986 was a ban on the promotion of tourism to South Africa (paragraph 7[h] of the Nassau Accord). Subsequently, Canada had asked the tourist industry for voluntary compliance with the ban and had closed the offices of the South African Airlines. The Taskforce had protested almost at once that the voluntary ban was clearly ineffectual when a month later a half-page advertisement in *The Globe and Mail* promoted travel tours to South Africa.[76] In 1988 the churches had pressed again for a tightening of the tourism ban, especially given the Canadian government's new policy initiative of fighting South Africa's propaganda. They pointed to the fact that: "advertisements for tours to South Africa continue to appear in violation of the voluntary ban, and service groups and others are enticed to take tours to South Africa."[77] This, they suggested was clearly a propaganda victory for apartheid and should be halted by legislation to enforce the ban.

It was incredible then and remains so now that just as Canada was elected to the Security Council, Canada's ban on tourism was publicly voided. The Canadian government was cosponsoring a five-day international conference on tourism, which included South African participation and which devoted one session on tourism development in South Africa. Joe Clark himself welcomed the delegates with a speech and a reception. E. T. Heath, chief researcher for South Africa's Institute of Planning and Research in Port Elizabeth who led the opening session, insisted that he was not involved in politics. He nevertheless suggested that tourists to South Africa were more sensitive to the complexities of the country and that "obviously sanctions cut off markets and cut off opportunities." Yet again, External Affairs, when confronted with these obvious contradictions in Canadian policy showed itself adept in narrowing the definition of Commonwealth sanctions. Georges Rioux, a senior official in Ottawa, was quoted as saying that Canada had a ban on visits to this country by South African government officials, but did not prohibit visits by South African academics and that Canadian officials did not feel Heath was promoting South African tourism.[78]

At year's end the Taskforce was gratified to see at long last a willingness on the part of the government to implement adequately a ban on contracts with South African majority-owned companies and to terminate Petro Canada's sulphur exports to South Africa. The churches were also pleased that the government planned to extend the ban on high-technology sales to private sector end-users in South Africa, thus imposing a virtual total ban of such exports. These decisions addressed at least in part the concerns the churches had raised in their July 1988 brief to Clark. The experience, however, of watching sanction measures reduced to the minimum that domestic politics permitted and that political alliances dictated, was a troubling one.

The Harare Debacle, 1989, and Its Consequences

Increase in Canada-South Africa Trade

It was inevitable that Ottawa's lack of commitment to economic sanctions translated in time into embarrassing statistics on Canadian/South African trade. On 25 January 1989 Statistics Canada reported that Canadian imports from South Africa had totalled $149 million in the first eleven months of 1988, an increase of $59 million over the same period in 1987. In descending order of value the main categories of these imports were iron and steel products; precious stones and metals; turbines, motor parts, and nuclear reactor equipment; wool, fabrics and other animal hair products; inorganic chemicals, radioactive elements and other compounds.[79] A July 1989 update of trade statistics showed that imports from South Africa continued to grow. In the first three months of 1989 Canadians had imported $76.9 million worth of South African goods compared with $33.3 million during the same months in 1988.[80]

With the benefit of statistics not available at the time we can now consider the final Canada/South Africa trade figures for the years 1985 to 1990 (tables 2 and 3 below). They show that Canadian sanctions appear to have had a significant impact on Canada/South Africa trade in the first year after the main sanctions had been adopted but that this trade then began to regain importance in 1988 and 1989. Although Canadian imports from South Africa had seriously declined between 1989 and 1990, Canadian exports to South Africa as a percentage of total Canadian exports, had almost regained its 1985 level.

Table 2: Canadian Exports to South Africa, 1985–90

Year	Canadian Exports to South Africa (in Mill. of Dollars)	Total Canadian Exports (in Mill. of Dollars)	Exports to South Africa as Percentage of Total Canadian Exports
1985	155	119,474	0.13
1986	154	120,669	0.13
1987	105˙	125,086	0.08˙
1988	135˙	138,498	0.10˙
1989	106	138,701	0.07
1990	180	148,979	0.12

* Between 1987 and 1988 there was an increase of 25 percent in the percentage share of total Canadian exports that were constituted by exports to South Africa.

Table 3: Canadian Imports from South Africa, 1985–90

Year	Canadian Imports from South Africa (in Mill. of Dollars)	Total Canadian Imports (in Mill. of Dollars)	Imports from South Africa as Percentage of Total Canadian Imports
1985	228	104,355	0.2
1986	328	112,511	0.3
1987	100*	116,238	0.08*
1988	158*	131,171	0.14*
1989	206*	135,191	0.15*
1990	141	136,245	0.1

* Between 1987 and 1988 there was an increase of 75 percent in the percentage share of total Canadian imports which were constituted by imports from South Africa. There was a further increase of more than 7 percent in 1989 over the total 1988 imports.

No wonder that Canadian commentators of diverse ideologies could agree that Canada's commitment to economic sanctions was unconvincing. Peter Cook of *The Globe and Mail* suggested that the bans imposed in 1986 on finished steel, uranium and coal had been welcomed by Canadian suppliers and steel makers. However, ferrochrome, used in the manufacture of stainless steel, had not been banned, thanks to the successful lobbying of the steel companies. Thus, since 1986 ferrochrome imports from South Africa had tripled in value. Sharp increases in South African imports should have been expected, Cook wrote, "when the most valued commodities were exempted from sanctions." "If one wants to be patriotic, it can be said that Canada is doing its best to show its dislike of South Africa and is doing a better job than Margaret Thatcher's Britain or Helmut Kohl's Germany. If one were to tell it like it is, then Canada's stance is more than a mite hypocritical."[81] Stephen Lewis, now no longer Canada's permanent representative to the United Nations, angrily condemned the increase in trade with South Africa which, he said, severely undermined "Canada's credibility." He predicted that "until you move to comprehensive and mandatory sanctions our trade, although small with South Africa, will belie our rhetoric." Lewis warned that other countries which were pressing for stronger action against South Africa would be bitterly disappointed.[82]

Lewis's predictions proved to be only too true. In early February 1989, when Clark arrived in Harare to chair the third meeting of the Commonwealth Committee of Foreign Ministers on Southern Africa, the mood of irritation was unmistakable. In Toronto in August 1988, Clark had been able to contain the impatience of the Commonwealth Secretariat and his

Third World colleagues who had pressed for new and stronger sanctions against Pretoria. They had acquiesced without much conviction in Canada's project to combat South African propaganda and censorship, and in October had supported Canada's successful bid for a seat on the United Nations Security Council. However, the news of the sharp increase in Canadian trade with the apartheid regime, and particularly the rise of Canadian imports from South Africa, had snapped the patience of Clark's Zimbabwean host.

Nathan Shamuyarira, Zimbabwe's foreign minister, was still disturbed during an interview in 1994, when he remembered the 1989 CFM meeting in Harare. He recalled his consternation that "at a time when many third world nations and particularly black Africa were looking to Canada as a Commonwealth ally in the fight against apartheid; when we were expecting Canada to be reducing its trade with South Africa, Canada instead was increasing it."[83] But Shamuyarira was not the only African foreign minister deeply perturbed by the Canadian trade statistics. Benjamin Mkapa of Tanzania and Ike Nwachukwu of Nigeria were similarly displeased. The willingness of these three to voice publicly their frustrations in interviews with Oakland Ross of *The Globe and Mail* was an indication of their deep resentment. Shamuyarira detailed the high cost to Zimbabwe of having to protect itself from South African military raids. He told Ross that the $1 million that Canada had committed to counter South African censorship and propaganda "is peanuts compared to what we are spending every day [to protect Zimbabweans from South African attacks]."[84] Canada's shift on sanctions worried Tanzania as well: "If they are going to put emphasis on countering propaganda, at the expense of sanctions, then we may part ways," Mkapa warned.[85] On behalf of Nigeria, Nwachukwu called on Canada to honour Mulroney's commitment of 1985 to impose mandatory trade sanctions against the apartheid regime.[86] In May 1988, when Archbishop Desmond Tutu accepted an honorary degree from New Brunswick's Mount Allison University, he had pleaded with Canada to make good on its 1985 promises. In unusual bitterness he had asked: "What does the world still want to see about our pain and suffering that it has not yet seen? What must we say that has not yet been said? Canada should cut down the rhetoric and move to effective action. . . What would the world have done if the complexions were reversed—if white children were detained by—say—Mugabe?"[87] After Canada's increased trade with South Africa was exposed in Harare, Tutu spoke to Canadian journalists in Cape Town. In December 1984 it had been Tutu who had assured the churches that Mulroney was determined to adopt a more forthright policy on South Africa. He now shared the Canadian churches' chagrin, and expressed his deep disappointment with Canada's "credibility gap between utterance and performance." However he was generous in the confidence that he expressed for the work of the Canadian anti-apartheid movement: "I know that the church in Canada and other groups are not going to let your government rest."[88]

Clark was stung by all this adverse publicity on Canada's trade increase with South Africa. Soon after his return from Harare, he met with representatives of the Canadian steel industry about their apparent high degree of dependence on South African minerals and alloys and with representatives of the Canadian sulphur industry about the recent expansion of sulphur exports to South Africa. Two industry/government working groups were established in April 1989. The first was to examine the feasibility of importing "essential" minerals from suppliers elsewhere, and the second was to report on the effect of diversifying markets for Canadian sulphur away from South Africa. Both reports were to be completed before the end of 1989 when they would be tabled in the House of Commons.[89]

Yet again, performance did not measure up to promise. From the autumn of 1989 on, the Taskforce periodically enquired about the outcome of these deliberations. Eventually, in *September 1992*, the Department of External Affairs informed the churches that "while it is true that the reports were completed in 1989, they were not tabled in 1990 as initially contemplated, nor were they acted upon."[90] Attached to the letter were a forty-seven page report on the import of essential minerals from South Africa dated 18 December 1989 and a three-page summary of the findings of the working group on sulphur exports.[91] Given the authors, it was predictable that both reports essentially stressed the negative impact on the industries as well as attendant high costs to the government should the latter attempt to change the prevailing trading patterns with South Africa. Although the reports were not published and never acted upon, the public relations value in 1989 of announcing that they were in progress was no doubt worth their cost, for they held at bay impatient Canadian and international critics.

Last Minute Repair to Canada's Arms Embargo

In Harare, Clark was also greeted by Zimbabwe's allegations that military equipment and high technology items were still being sold to South Africa by Canada and other industrialized members of the Commonwealth, largely because these states interpreted too narrowly the existing agreements to ban such exports.

In 1989 there were in force three important international agreements on this issue: The United Nations' mandatory arms embargo of 1977 (UNSCR 418); the 1985 Nassau Commonwealth Accord banning the sale of computer equipment capable of use by South Africa's military, police or security forces; and the 1986 UN Security Council Resolution 591 seeking to prevent military equipment from reaching South Africa via third countries. UNSCR 591 had also included in this ban the export of spare parts for embargoed aircraft, electronics, telecommunications equipment, computers and other high-technology items.

Abdul Minty, director of the Oslo-based World Campaign against Military and Nuclear Collaboration with South Africa, was consulted during the Harare meetings. He addressed in particular third-country exports as major loopholes in the application of these several arms embargoes, particularly where members of the North Atlantic Treaty Organization (NATO) permitted trade in military equipment among its members without restrictions on subsequent resale.[92]

The Export Controls Policy that Canada had adopted in September 1986 explicitly illustrated Minty's point (see above, chap. 8, pp. 266–67). In the communiqué that launched the 1986 policy, Joe Clark referred to Canada's obligations to its NATO allies and described Canada as an important producer,

> particularly of components and sub-assemblies of larger military systems. Canadian firms will now be authorized to export these components and assemblies to all countries with which Canada has a suitable government-to-government agreement and where there exists a *bona fide* joint venture arrangement between the Canadian and the foreign manufacturer. In such cases, *the authorization to export the completely assembled product will now rest with the country of final manufacture.* (Emphasis added)[93]

Clark had contrasted this policy to the export restrictions "of civilian strategic equipment to COCOM proscribed destinations—the Soviet Union, its Warsaw allies—and to countries where there is a risk of diversion to those destinations."[94] Despite the risk of diversion to South Africa, Canada had not restricted the resale by its NATO allies of Canadian military equipment, high technology or assembled products.

The final communiqué of the Harare Commonwealth Foreign Ministers' meeting called for a tightening of the arms embargo against South Africa. The ministers recommended to their governments that UNSCR 591 be made mandatory and that the definition of "arms related material" that was banned for export to South Africa be tightened. It was to include strategic or tactical items that assisted the maintenance of repression in South Africa and "exports of high technology such as aircraft, their engines and parts, data processing equipment and four wheel drive vehicles."[95]

For the members of the Taskforce, the 1989 definitions of exports to be banned made strange reading. In 1981 the Taskforce had presented the Canadian government with a nearly identical list of items that should not be exported to South Africa. That list had been prepared at the time by the UN 421 Committee, which had attempted—but clearly failed—to make UN member states more responsive to the 1977 mandatory arms embargo. As well, in 1984–85 the government had rejected a request from the Taskforce that an export permit for the sale of Control Data computers to the Iron and Steel Company of South Africa be denied for precisely the reasons now listed by the foreign ministers in Harare.

With a similar sense of lost opportunities to reduce at a much earlier date South Africa's military capabilities, the Taskforce also noted that another section of the Harare "Statement on the Arms Embargo against South Africa" recommended "that measures be considered … for subsidiaries in South Africa of overseas companies being prohibited from manufacturing or supplying any items having a strategic or tactical value which would enhance the capability of the military and security forces; and … that UNSCR 418 relating to licences be strictly applied with a view to all licences being terminated."[96] This too paralleled the long-standing effort by the churches to convince successive Canadian governments that they disallow those activities in the South African operations of Ford Canada, Alcan and Varity, which had enhanced, in the words of 1989 statement, "the capability of the military and security forces." Repeatedly External Affairs officials and secretaries of state had sternly corrected the churches that such measures could not be considered because they would breach Canada's policy on "extra-territorial jurisdiction."

On 6 March 1989, only a short month after the Harare meetings, Canada announced a dramatic change in its export controls policy on South Africa. Clark reported that he was recommending to Cabinet that South Africa be placed on the Area Control List. All exports to countries on this list were subject to export control requirements. In the case of South Africa, Clark said this meant that all items on the Export Control List will be controlled, plus "all high-technology products including computers, software, telecommunications equipment, all aircraft, helicopters and parts and four-wheel drive vehicles."[97]

Canada's anti-apartheid organizations were satisfied that at long last a resolute step had been taken on this crucial issue. Yet three months later, to their astonishment, Joe Clark defended "the right" of South African arms dealers to attend ARMX, an international weapons exhibition in Ottawa. Clark called the fair a "private sector matter" that did not warrant his intervention. He told reporters "if they want to be there, they have a right to be there." ARMX featured products from 400 arms manufacturers and attracted about 13,000 buyers from sixty countries.[98] Three months after the Harare "Statement on the Arms Embargo against South Africa," which had, without exempting the private sector, newly defined the "strategic or tactical nature" of goods that assisted in the maintenance of repression in South Africa, Clark invited Canadians to accept once more the fictitious difference between South Africa's official and private sector arms merchants.

In parenthesis it should be noted that the 6 March 1989 decision to place South Africa on the Area Control List to restrict all high-technology exports was the very last and easily the most important of Canada's sanctions against South Africa. It was also the first of the serious government sanctions to be lifted in 1992.

Following Nelson Mandela's release from prison in February 1990, the South African Council of Churches (SACC), after consultations with the ANC, agreed to a set of South African circumstances that would permit international economic sanctions to be lifted. In June 1990 SACC agreed that sanctions should remain until "clear and irreversible change" had occurred in South Africa. This moment would arrive, the South African churches declared, "when the sovereign power is removed from the existing apartheid legislative structures and invested either in the constituent assembly or another agreed interim structure which the white minority cannot legally reverse or veto through a process of the present unrepresentative legislative structures."[99] On 28 February 1991 Joe Clark reported to the House of Commons that the Commonwealth foreign ministers had decided that "our strongest sanctions should remain until the system [of apartheid] is effectively abolished but that lesser sanctions should be lifted in response to tangible proof of a determination to end apartheid irreversibly."[100]

When the Commonwealth Heads of Government met in Harare the following October, they approved the removal of "people-to-people" sanctions. They lifted consular and visa restrictions, boycotts on cultural and scientific contacts and restrictions on tourism and direct air links. There was no mention of lifting the export ban on high-technology equipment.

Nevertheless, three months later on 9 January 1992, Canada removed South Africa from the Area Control List. The Notice to Exporters went further, much further than lifting "people-to-people sanctions:

> In line with Canada's sanctions policies and those of its Commonwealth partners, the Canadian Government has modified the application to its controls on the export of strategic goods to South Africa ... goods of United States origin will be assessed on the basis of standard export controls policy ... [as] will be accorded applications for the export of civilian aircraft (including helicopters), aircraft parts and engines, electronic and telecommunications equipment and software, and four wheel drive vehicles.[101]

Applicants were asked for "end-user" statements to assure the Department that the exports were for civilian purposes and would not end up in the hands of the military or police. This change, the "Notice" unjustifiably claimed, was "in keeping with commitments made to the Commonwealth Heads of Government and Commonwealth Committee of Foreign Ministers."[102]

That same year, 1992, was also marked by the world's revulsion at the violence unleashed in South Africa against the ANC and its allies, which was supported and tolerated by the apartheid regime and forces on its payroll. In the summer of 1992 the escalation of violence was discussed in a seminar for anti-apartheid organizations at the United Nations' Special Committee against Apartheid. The death toll attributed to such political violence had reached 8,000 in just two years, 1,700 alone between January and July 1992. There was unanimity that this unchecked breakdown of law and order could only occur when members of the security and the civilian population believed that they could engage in illicit activity without fear of being called to account.[103]

It was just at this time that the Canadian government chose to return to its 1986 exports policy and relied once again on non-verifiable pieces of paper to justify the return to near normal trading practices with South Africa.

The Limits of Canada's Financial Sanctions

In February 1989, during the Commonwealth Foreign Ministers' meeting in Harare, Clark had been faced with a second embarrassment. He had to account for a major Canadian bank loan to a private South African company in an apparent breach of financial sanctions.

In September 1988 Minorco, a South African company controlled by Anglo American Corporation and associated firms and registered in Luxembourg, had launched a $4.4 billion bid to take over Consolidated Gold-fields PLC of the UK, a rival giant in gold production.[104] The Bank of Nova Scotia had joined Swiss, German and American banks to finance the take-over with a $600 million loan.[105] Minorco's bid eventually failed, but not before the minimalist nature of Canada's commitment to sanctions was once more confirmed.

Because Minorco was South African-controlled, financial commentators quickly identified the loan as constituting a contravention of the voluntary ban to which Canadian commercial banks had agreed in 1986. This was no trivial issue; South African subsidiaries abroad could and did function as channels for the evasion of sanctions. In Harare, Clark was obliged to reveal to the international press and to his Commonwealth colleagues that he had known about the Scotiabank's loan, but had decided that it was "in bounds." He demonstrated the usefulness of writing your own definition of general Commonwealth commitments. Clark said: "We were aware of the transaction and we were also aware of the *Canadian definition* of the ban. And the *Canadian definition of the ban* allows a loan to a Luxembourg company (emphasis added)."[106] Press reports had confirmed that the BNS had discussed the Minorco loan with External Affairs: "Bank [of Nova Scotia] spokesman Nick Douloff, senior manager of public and corporate affairs, said that the bank was told by External Affairs that the government would view the transaction as a "European to European" deal."[107]

On 3 March the Taskforce wrote Joe Clark. They were critical of the Minorco loan and the obvious possibility of similar indirect bank loans to South African-controlled companies abroad.[108] Clark's reply was crisp though it hardly allayed the churches' unease. He wrote that there had been no government monitoring of bank compliance. External Affairs had only reacted after the Minorco loans had been publicized:

> I want to set the record straight about the question of Government giving "permission" to the Bank to proceed with the loan. Permission was neither sought nor given. . . . Rather, when the loan became public last fall, officials of my Department contacted the Bank to determine whether it violated the terms of the Canadian and Commonwealth ban . . . It was our interpretation that the ban specifically related to companies located inside South Africa. This was the basis of our original agreement with Canadian banks on their voluntary compliance. As Minorco is registered in Luxembourg, we did not consider that the loan contravened the ban.[109]

The Canadian loan to Minorco had been a wake-up call within the Commonwealth and it was given priority at the fourth meeting of the CCFMSA from 7-9 August 1989 in Canberra. The ministers redefined the Commonwealth ban on loans to South Africa's private sector by including loans to "South African-controlled" entities to clarify the international scope of the ban. As was the case with all financial sanctions affecting private banks, the newly defined ban was voluntary. It left it to the banks to establish, through a series of complicated enquiries that, "all circumstances considered, the loan would not significantly benefit economic interests in South Africa or its economy as a whole."[110] The new definition was unlikely to restrain a determined lender, but only those who were already hesitant. Clark explained the Canadian implementation procedure to the Taskforce in these terms: "we agreed upon guidelines to banks to be used in lending to an entity outside South Africa which may have South African connections. These were adopted in order that banks can be fully satisfied that the funds are not being obtained to circumvent sanctions . . . [The guidelines] have been brought to the attention of the banks operating in Canada."[111]

The Canberra meeting also dealt with South Africa's continued misuse of international trade credits to cushion its balance of payment. Since the August 1988 CFM meeting in Toronto, banks had been asked to cap voluntarily short-term South African trade credits at current levels. The Canberra CFM meeting recommended that henceforth the terms of these trade credits be limited to ninety days. This recommendation was accepted by the Commonwealth Heads of Government (Britain excepted) who met in Kuala Lumpur from 18–24 October. As before, the Canadian government assured the Taskforce that it had "asked the Canadian banks for their cooperation."[112] As the government either did not know or would not reveal the current terms of South African trade credits offered by Canadian banks, the churches asked the banks directly.

The Taskforce published the result of this enquiry. The Royal Bank, the Bank of Nova Scotia and the Toronto Dominion Bank reported that they were in fact not extending any South African trade credits; the Bank of Montreal stated that it would not increase the level of its trade credits, and the Canadian Imperial Bank of Commerce said that it had drastically reduced such credits and would not increase them. These two banks did not reveal their terms. Although these statements could not be confirmed independently, data of international researchers tracing South African loans at the time did not contradict the low level of activity of Canadian banks with regard to South Africa.[113]

Rescheduling of South Africa's Debt[114]

Following South Africa's default in September 1985 on $13.6 billion (US) debt to international lenders, the creditor banks took steps at once to bring the situation under control. A "Technical Committee" was established, comprising fourteen of the largest creditor banks to negotiate a repayment schedule and to act on behalf of the 330 international banks whose loans were also involved. Fritz Leutweiler, a retired Swiss banker, agreed to be its chair, and convened the first meeting on 23 October 1985. (There was no Canadian bank on the Technical Committee.)[115]

For this brief moment, South Africa's creditor banks had potentially the greatest international leverage for the dismantling of apartheid. They could have fully exploited South Africa's acute need for external finance by offering a phased program of relief in exchange for bold political changes. Indeed major figures in the anti-apartheid struggle, such as Archbishop Trevor Huddleston, Archbishop Desmond Tutu and Dr. Beyers Naudé, at once wrote to the bankers to remind them of their opportunity to make rescheduling of the debt conditional on the abandonment of apartheid.[116]

The banks themselves were cognizant of these internationally held positions, and Leutweiler let it be known that he was looking for a "positive statement at the highest level" in South Africa before proceeding with negotiations. But just how profoundly Leutweiler's views diverged from those of the eminent churchmen and the international anti-apartheid movement was captured in a warning he issued in a Swiss newspaper: "If South Africa delays much longer certain clients, particularly those of American, British and other banks, will say they will be satisfied only by the principle of one man, one vote."[117]

The moment of maximum opportunity for the international bankers passed. Botha's vague promises "to walk the road of reform and justice," which he made at the opening of parliament on 31 January 1986, were all too readily accepted. They cleared the way for the first rescheduling agreement in February 1986. The loans were renewed for fifteen months on terms entirely manageable for South Africa.[118]

At the second rescheduling in June 1987, the bankers again settled for accommodating terms and planned the next rescheduling for 30 June

1990. In June 1987, Botha's repression under continuing emergency rule had intensified, but the bankers no longer mentioned change.

The third debt rescheduling cast a long shadow ahead. Between 1989 and 1991 the apartheid regime was due to repay a major confluence of loans. These comprised the short-term loans rescheduled by Leutweiler's Technical Committee; and a large segment of long-term loans and bonds due to be repaid between 1989 and 1990, which had been only tangentially involved in South Africa's 1985 financial crisis. From early 1989 on, internal and international anti-apartheid organizations saw this "bunching up" of short-term and long-term debt obligations as an opportune time to push hard for constitutional changes and the dismantling of apartheid. In February, the Harare CCFMSA meeting had called on the international financial community to deny rescheduling arrangements of South Africa's loans beyond one year at a time. The Canberra CCFMSA meeting in August then dispatched delegates to call on banks of the Technical Committee to insist on tough terms in a renewed debt rescheduling agreement.

In South Africa, the African National Congress and the Mass Democratic Movement joined the South African Council of Churches in their opposition to any rescheduling of the debt. South African church leaders again wrote to the banks on the "Technical Committee," warning that a rescheduling of the loans at this crucial time would amount to "collaboration in the funding of apartheid." The World Council of Churches mobilized their members while anti-apartheid organizations sought directly to influence the banks on the Technical Committee in their own countries and indirectly to pressure the 330 international lenders not on the Committee. Members of the Taskforce wrote to the Canadian banks, urging them to support a rescheduling agreement that obliged South Africa to repay at least 15 percent of its debt annually.[119] These various international campaigns embarrassed the creditor banks. They were anxious to complete an early and long-term deal with South Africa that would minimize their risks and would remove them from the intense international spotlight for as long as possible.[120] In a surprise move, the banks' Technical Committee concluded a loan rescheduling agreement with South Africa the day *before* the Kuala Lumpur Commonwealth meetings opened on 18 October 1989. Chris Stals, the governor of the South African reserve bank, announced the new agreement, widely judged to be more favourable to South Africa than the previous ones. It provided for the repayment of only 20.5 percent over three-and-a-half years of US$8 billion of the short-term loans. This arrangement also aided South Africa to deal more comfortably with the large additional obligations of its long-term debt.[121]

Only briefly, in 1985, had the interests of South Africa's international creditor banks and those of the anti-apartheid movements coincided. In that year the banks had ceased lending because the unremitting popular uprisings had weakened business confidence in the economic future of apartheid. At home the international banks could no longer defend their South African loans to their critical shareholders and customers who had become part of the growing activism of the international anti-apartheid movements. As South Africa's *Weekly Mail* argued:

> the 1985 debt crisis was due to a combination of economic and political pre-cipitants and their interaction made it doubly dangerous to apartheid. It was not governments which were responsible for withholding debt roll overs and new loans from South Africa in August 1985, but a combination of banks' own decisions based on economic criteria and the work of grassroots pressure groups in the US, UK and elsewhere.[122]

The refusal to renew international short-term loans and the resulting collapse of the South African rand had temporarily exposed the banks' formidable power and potential leverage. At the time optimism seemed to be justified that this virtual end to new loans, and to renewal of existing loans, would materially contribute to the dismantling of apartheid. When several years later Commonwealth foreign ministers asserted that financial sanctions had been the most effective form of sanctions, they had these events in mind. However, they were ignoring the unusual convergence of interests of the international creditor banks and the anti-apartheid movements that had existed in 1985. The attempt by Commonwealth governments in 1989 to harness the power of the creditor banks for the purpose of strengthening international financial sanctions was in fact bound to fail. At this time the business interests of the banks were no longer compatible with the immediate goals of the Commonwealth. Clearly reflected in the accelerated rescheduling decisions of the Technical Committee was its overriding concern to minimize the risks for the banks. They had no interest in new lending and therefore had no problem with capping South African trade credits. They had no quarrel with the 1989 extension of Commonwealth guidelines to cover lending to South African-controlled entities abroad because their implementation was left to them. The banks' interest, however, would not have been served had they used the regime's debt to them as a lever to force it into constitutional negotiations. This might have increased their risks, the very circumstance they wished to avoid.

The efforts of Commonwealth governments to involve South Africa's creditor banks in the tightening of international financial sanctions had thus been thwarted. However there were additional and potentially effective options to tighten and intensify financial sanctions against South Africa. Nothing, for example, should have prevented individual governments from applying direct pressure on those international banks which, in 1989, were still extending loans to the apartheid government. The Task-force therefore sought to convince Ottawa to follow this course of action.

Since the early eighties the members of the Taskforce had supported anti-apartheid organizations in Britain, Germany and Switzerland in their campaigns against loans to South Africa by banks in their own countries. The Canadian churches had thus contacted the Canadian subsidiaries of Barclay's Bank, the Dresdner Bank, the Deutsche Bank, the Union Bank of Switzerland, Credit Suisse and others. The German and Swiss banks were among the largest lenders to South Africa and had persisted in doing business with the apartheid regime long after Canadian and other international banks had ceased lending. The Taskforce had protested that these continuing loans helped maintain the regime's ability to countenance international censure and sanctions. However, until the Government of Ontario decided to act, no Canadian authority had exerted tangible pressure on the European banks.

In 1985 the new Liberal government of Ontario had adopted several trade sanctions against South Africa. It banned the import from South Africa of wines and agricultural products under provincial jurisdiction. It also decided that it would utilize the services only of those Canadian or international firms that could satisfy the provincial government that they and their associate companies had not engaged in business deals with the government of South Africa since 1985. The province required assurances from each candidate firm that it met Ontario's South Africa requirements before economic considerations were reviewed and a choice made regarding the inclusion of a firm in a business syndicate.[123]

In February 1989 the Ontario government thus excluded two Swiss banks from among eighteen international financial institutions involved in a major Eurobond issue of $500 million by Ontario Hydro. The decision made news not only in *The Globe and Mail* but also in the *Wall Street Journal*, the *Journal de Genève*, *The Johannesburg Star* and likely others.[124] The Taskforce was pleased to see Ontario remain consistent in its approach. It wrote to Robert Nixon, treasurer of the Ontario government:

> While effective financial sanction could not be put in place without the participation of the international banks, it has been difficult for the churches and anti-apartheid groups in Canada to find ways of bringing pressure on the banks in Europe. The action of the Government of Ontario in relation to the Swiss banks has shown what can be done by those in a position to make their actions count.[125]

The Taskforce also wrote to Joe Clark and later to each of the other provincial premiers. It explained that the churches were supporting their European colleagues in a campaign to tighten international financial sanctions—a priority of the Commonwealth—and recommended that the federal and provincial governments follow the example of the Ontario government when awarding contracts to international financial institution.[126] They requested that the Government of Canada "refrain from using Swiss or German banks in bond issues until such time as those banks adopt public policies of offering no further financial assistance to South Africa."[127]

Federal officials had already declared that Ottawa had no intention of boycotting Swiss banks over South Africa "because it would be interfering in another country's affairs."[128] Most premiers followed this line of reasoning. Newfoundland, New Brunswick, Saskatchewan and British Columbia wrote that secondary boycotts were inappropriate, complicated and against federal policy. A telephone follow-up with the Quebec administration yielded a similar verbal reply. The premier of Prince Edward Island expressed support for the Ontario position, but noted that the island did little international banking. From Manitoba, where anti-apartheid organizations had lobbied in favour of the Taskforce proposal, several replies were received. Premier Filmon wrote that he had spoken to the Swiss banks; the Liberal opposition had requested disclosure of banks with which Manitoba did business and the Manitoba NDP had promised public support for the Ontario position.

These responses demonstrated an overwhelming reliance on the advice of the federal government on this issue. Considering the large amount of capital raised by Canadian jurisdictions on international capital markets, an important dimension to Canadian financial sanctions had thus been rejected by the federal government and—as provincial responses showed— by most of the provinces as well.[129]

Correspondence with Joe Clark on this issue continued into July 1990. Clark echoed the views of his officials. He wrote that he was opposed to such "secondary boycotts" which could have "extraterritorial implications." He also suggested that such actions would "detract from South Africa which was, after all, the main target." Without elaborating, he suggested that his "demarche" to the Swiss government had been "an effective approach to dealing with foreign banks." He advised the Taskforce that the Kuala Lumpur CHOGM in October 1989 had widened financial sanctions by establishing a monitoring agency to "increase awareness of South Africa's financial links."[130] This did not in the least impress the members of the Taskforce, who saw in the establishment of a monitoring agency the means to further delay action.

Reviewing initiatives in the United States that were comparable to Ontario's position, the Taskforce noted that by the end of 1989, twenty-five states, nineteen counties and eighty-two cities had taken economic measures against companies and banks that continued to do business with South Africa. The majority gave preference to banks and financial services without business ties to South Africa. These measures were not "deflecting from the target which is South Africa," as Clark had suggested. To the contrary, they helped create awareness of the financial links between apartheid and US enterprises and encouraged others to act far more effectively than any Commonwealth monitoring agency could.[131]

In 1989 Joe Clark and External Affairs officials claimed that the Government of Canada could not avoid dealing with international banks that were still lending to the apartheid regime. To do so would "undercut" Canada's policy of opposing the enforcement in Canada of another government's laws or policies: "Is it reasonable to impose on the government of Switzerland, through sanctions against Swiss banks, a foreign policy we wish them to follow? ... No matter how reprehensible apartheid is, we do not want to undercut our position that governments should not seek to enforce their policies extraterritorially."[132] The churches rejected this interpretation of their proposal. To have followed the Ontario example would have amounted to no more than an exercise in consumer choice for Canada's purchase of financial services from a variety of international options. It had nothing to do with imposing "on the government of Switzerland ... a foreign policy we wish them to follow." The matter would have been debatable had there been Canadian banks in Switzerland which, despite legislated sanctions in Canada, were making loans to South Africa and Canada was attempting to enforce its laws on Canadian banks under Swiss jurisdiction. This was clearly not the case. What was proposed was something quite different and entirely feasible. To the member churches of the Taskforce it was incomprehensible that the Canadian government "should be so reluctant to take itself the logical step of choosing its financial agents from among the many financial institutions which have, in compliance with Canadian and Commonwealth policy, voluntarily opted out of further loans to South Africa."[133]

Canada Proposes Pause in Sanctions

On 18 October 1989, the opening day of the Kuala Lumpur CHOGM, Canada called for a lessening of pressure on South Africa. Joe Clark proposed a six-to-seven-month breathing space from additional sanctions, "to give F.W. de Klerk a chance to deliver on his promises." Clark told the press that this had been the consensus of the CCFMSA and that this position had reversed a decision to significantly increase sanctions made in Canberra.[134]

What were these promises to which Clark had referred? On 13 October 1989 de Klerk had at long last released from prison eight political prisoners who had served life terms since 1964.[135] His "promises" for change at that time were in fact limited to visions of constitutional changes that would preserve "group rights" and would promote a constellation of political groupings that ensured "a white veto to limit the extent of change by policies supported by the majority."[136] This vision was totally unacceptable to the major anti-apartheid movements that were coalescing in South Africa and was seriously in conflict with the terms of the "Harare Declaration" signed by the Mass Democratic Movement and the ANC two months earlier.

Joe Clark, however, was impatient; he maintained that there was no need for new sanctions, no need to increase the pressure on the apartheid regime. He dismissed as ANC posturing the insistence of Thabo Mbeki, then the ANC's head of information services, that sanctions be intensified and that de Klerk did not need "to be given time to avoid doing what he must do."[137] Clark, relying on reports that Reverend Allan Boesak had supported a six-month sanctions freeze, was quoted as saying that privately, Mbeki and other black leaders "are of one mind on what is appropriate."[138]

Clark must have ventured considerably further than what he could substantiate. A day later, when presenting his report to the full Commonwealth meeting, he was obliged to preface his remarks with an awkward account of an informal meeting with Boesak and Mbeki. Clark explained that "at no time did Mr. Boesak suggest that it would be appropriate to relax Commonwealth pressure on South Africa now. He believes it is essential that pressure be maintained, and that the mere promise of reform should not be rewarded by any relaxation of pressure."[139]

The Kuala Lumpur CHOGM did not produce any new sanctions nor any meaningful tightening of existing ones. Canadian leadership in the Commonwealth had come full circle. In Nassau in 1985 and in London in 1986 Canada had provided leadership when sanctions were being proposed. In 1989, as chair of the Commonwealth committee of foreign ministers for Southern Africa, Canada led in the opposite direction away from further sanctions and toward renewed belief in the benevolent leadership of the white minority government.

After Mandela's Release

The Kuala Lumpur meeting was to be the last of the Commonwealth meetings before the historic release from prison of Nelson Mandela on 11 February 1990. During five hours of jubilant celebrations on 16 April in London's Wembley Stadium, Mandela told his 70,000 supporters that they must reject any suggestions of winding down international sanctions against South Africa. No rewards should be offered to the South African government, he said, neither for his own release nor for the unbanning of the ANC until the country was transformed into a non-racial democracy.[140] As preparations for the Wembley stadium celebrations were under way in London, Joe Clark contacted Archbishop Trevor Huddleston, president of the British Anti-Apartheid Movement and chair of the Council of Trustees of the International Defence and Aid Fund for Southern Africa. Clark sought to convince Huddleston that it would be more appropriate to move the celebrations to Canada because the Canadian government had been far more supportive of international sanctions and other anti-apartheid measures than the British government.[141]

This celebration, however, belonged to no foreign government. It belonged to Mandela, the ANC and to the international anti-apartheid movements whom he recognized as partners in the struggle. "We are here today" he told them,

> because for almost three decades you sustained the campaign for the unconditional release of all South African political prisoners. . . . You are allies in the common struggle to bring freedom, democracy and peace to all the people of South Africa. You chose many years ago to be on the side of those in our country who fight for this perspective. You elected to support the ANC, the Mass Democratic Movement and others who have been willing to give up their lives for justice and liberty.[142]

Four years of struggle, of sacrifices and betrayals, of further enormous bloodshed and suffering and long and patient negotiations were yet to come before Mandela became the first South African president elected in non-racial elections. But on that day in Wembley stadium, an early dawn of the new South Africa could be glimpsed.

In May 1990 the Commonwealth Committee of Foreign Ministers on Southern Africa (CFMSA) met in Abuja, Nigeria. Mandela and leaders of South Africa's popular opposition were on hand for consultations. *The Abuja Commitment* issued at the end of their meetings reflected a clear and focused goal for South Africa, "[where] democratization must be based on the principle of universal adult franchise leading to the establishment of a non-racial, democratic, non-fragmented South Africa."[143]

The CCFMSA also endorsed Mandela's position that "the trend to relax sanctions should be stopped"; that they were still necessary to safeguard continuous progress toward constitutional negotiations. The Commonwealth foreign ministers sent a letter bearing their individual signatures, to warn particularly members of the EC and the G7 countries against prematurely lifting sanctions:

> We understand, but do not accept, the suggestion that white South Africans will be encouraged to accept necessary fundamental change by relieving them now from some of the economic and psychological pressures so manifestly still pressing upon them. . . . We call upon you . . . to halt and reverse the effort to untimely and wrongly lift sanctions against the South African government. If this trend is not reversed all our gains will be reversed.[144]

A new chapter had begun in South Africa. Nelson Mandela, his senior colleagues and increasingly the rank and file of political prisoners and detainees were released. The ban imposed in the early 1960s on the ANC, the PAC and myriads of anti-apartheid organizations was lifted, and media restrictions were increasingly ignored and rescinded. Leadership and direction of the democratic forces was once again in the hands of South Africans silenced for decades by the apartheid regime. Different resources from those at the disposal of the Taskforce were now needed to support the changed requirements of the struggle.

The Taskforce saw that it must let go of its Southern African agenda. It did so with a sense of accomplishment. The member churches and religious orders had kept faith with their South African partners and with their own deep conviction that apartheid was an outrage and a heresy and that only its complete dismantling could restore human dignity to all the people of South Africa.

Notes

1 These views were rejected by less ideologically driven business executives such as Henri de Villiers, then chair of the Standard Bank of South Africa. He noted the growing lobby of South African "men of eminence and influence" who propagated the view that "somehow sanctions are good for us," and commented: "I consider that view dangerously misguided" (*Johannesburg Star*, 20 July 1988).

2 For details of these developments in South Africa see Price, *The Apartheid State in Crisis*, pp. 272–73.

3 The US-backed UNITA forces and the South African Defence Forces were defeated in their bid to capture sufficient territory in South Eastern Angola to install a provincial UNITA government to be recognized as the "legitimate" Angolan government. The bid was thwarted by a combination of Angolan, Cuban and PLAN (Peoples Liberation Army of Namibia) forces.

4 Price, *The Apartheid State in Crisis*, p.274.

5 South African Institute of Race Relations, "Race Relations Survey 1988–89," quoted in Price, *The Apartheid State in Crisis*, p. 268. Admittedly the released political detainees were placed under severe restrictions after their release and such restrictions were used henceforth increasingly in place of detentions without trial. Nevertheless, opportunities to remain involved in community actions were much greater under these restrictions than they had been in prison.

6 International Defence and Aid Fund, *Review of 1989: Repression and Resistance in South Africa and Namibia*, pp. 7–9.

7 Harare Declaration of the OAU Ad Hoc Committee on Southern Africa, 21 August 1989, cited in International Defence and Aid Fund, *Apartheid: The Facts*, p. 113.

8 Ibid.

9 For example, between April and June 1989 there were several attempts on the life of the Rev. Frank Chikane, general secretary of the South African Council of Churches. Highly toxic insecticide had been applied to his suitcase and travelling clothes, causing collapse and respiratory arrests during his visits to Namibia and the USA. At the University of Wisconsin Hospital tests uncovered the presence of the toxins in his suitcase and clothes and his symptoms were judged to be consistent with exposure to the toxins. See "Statement by the Reverend Chikane, General Secretary of the South African Council of Churches, Madison, University of Wisconsin, Wisconsin, USA," 8 June 1989 (mimeograph), 13 pages.

10 John Carling, "Former Officer Alleges Campaign of Dirty Tricks," *The Independent* (London), 11 June 1991, and "Notes and Comment," *The New Yorker*, 27 May 1991.

11 *The kwa-Zulu-Police Amendment Act* was signed by de Klerk in April 1990 (Carmel Rickard, "New Law May Give Buthelezi Power to Launch SA Raids," *The Weekly Mail*, 7–13 September 1990.

12 Hendrik de Klerk, South Africa's Ambassador to Canada, had not been idle, shoring up resentment among Conservative MPs against the official anti-apartheid policies of the government. His (anti-sanction) view, he told *The Toronto Star*, "has many supporters among Canadian members of Parliament, particularly within the Progressive Conservative Party" (John Deverell, "Clark Accused of Betrayal over South Africa," *The Toronto Star*, 7 August 1988).

13 Organizations affected included regional and national organizations such as five civic organizations; the National Education Crisis Committee of parent, teacher and student groups; two national Detainees Support Committees either aiding the families of detainees or providing post-detention assistance; political organizations such as the Azanian People's Organization and several youth congresses. Also banned were all activities of the Release Mandela Committee. See John D. Battersby, "South Africa Bans Most Anti-Apartheid Activities," *New York Times*, 25 February 1988.

14 "Statement in the House of Commons by the Right Honourable Joe Clark, Secretary of State for External Affairs, on South Africa," Ottawa, 2 March 1988 (Statement 88/17), In a public statement on 16 June 1988 timed for Soweto Day, Clark deplored the renewal on 9 June 1988 of the South Africa's state of emergency which further restricted the news media and proscribed international financing of South African opposition organizations. Clark expressed "deep concern" about the ongoing repression in South Africa and asked for clemency for the "Sharpeville Six." See Department of External Affairs, News Release no. 116, 16 June 1988. Absent from Clark's statements on South Africa were condemnations of the regime at the increasing number of murders or attempted murders of ANC representatives abroad—six in the first four months of 1988 alone—including the fatal shooting in Paris of Dulcie September, 19 March 1988, and the attempted murder of Albie Sachs in Maputo almost a month later.

15 Philip van Niekerk, "South Africa Cracks Down on Moderates," *The Globe and Mail*, 27 February 1988.

16 "Statement in the House of Commons by the Right Honourable Joe Clark, Secretary of State for External Affairs, Following the First Meeting of the Commonwealth Committee of Foreign Ministers on Southern Africa," Ottawa, 5 February 1988 (Statement 88/08).

17 "Notes of the Taskforce Meeting with the Southern Africa Taskforce of External Affairs," 27 June 1988 (mimeograph), 12 pages. Participating for the Taskforce were Ann Abraham (ACC), chair; Philip LeBlanc (UCC); Michael McBane (CCCB); David Pfrimmer (ELCIC); Moira Hutchinson and Marjorie Ross (staff). Present for External Affairs were John Schoiler (chair); Bethany Armstrong (deputy chair); Victor Rakmil (assistant to Armstrong); Marcel Saucier (permit officer, Export Control Division); Anthony Berger (International Financial and Investment Affairs Division); Reid Henry (Energy and Environment Division—Oil); B.E. Berton (Nuclear Division); M.S. Doyon (Francophone deputy director, Africa Trade Division); Ken McCartney (Namibian Desk—bilateral).

18 Taskforce on the Churches and Corporate Responsibility, "Widening, Tightening and Intensifying Economic and Other Sanctions against South Africa: A Brief to the Right Honourable Joe Clark, Secretary of State for External Affairs," 20 July 1988 (mimeograph), 17 pages.

19 Ibid., p. 1. The emphasis had been added by the Taskforce.

20 As early as 1983 the Taskforce had researched the comparative restrictions of strategic exports to human rights violator countries in the socialist block states and to human rights violator countries associated with Western democracies such as South Africa, Chile and the Philippines. It found that COCOM was established in 1950, with membership of NATO

member states minus Iceland but including Japan, to prevent the shipment of military and strategic goods and technologies from reaching socialist block states. A COCOM International Control List for Industrial, Munitions and Atomic Energy items defined goods and technologies considered to be strategic. Canada's "Area Control List" (ACL) contained the names of states, including the Warsaw Pact members, that were covered by COCOM rules. See "General Notice—Canadian Export Law and Policy and Information Requirements in Support of Export Permit Applications," Serial no. 12, 6 July 1982.

21 Ibid., p. 1.
22 Ibid., p. 1.
23 Ibid., p. 2.
24 Ibid., p. 3.
25 See John E. Lind and David J. Koistinen, CANICOR Research, "Financing South Africa's Foreign Trade," San Francisco, March 1988 (mimeograph), and Anthony Robinson, "Credits Ease Constraints on Balance of Payments," *The Financial Times*, 6 July 1988.
26 "Notes of the Taskforce Meeting with the Southern Africa Taskforce of External Affairs," 27 June 1988, p. 7.
27 Taskforce, "Widening, Tightening and Intensifying Economic and Other Sanctions against South Africa," 20 July 1988, p. 5.
28 Telephone interview with Gordon L. Blaney, Client Services Section, International Trade Division, Statistics Canada, 15 March 1994. After a high in 1987 the value of Canadian exports to South Africa of lubrication oils and greases dropped in 1988 to $252,000 and in 1989 to $228,000 (Statistics Canada, Merchandise Trade Data, 1988 and 1989).
29 Letter from J.M. MacLeod, president and chief executive officer of Shell Canada Ltd., to the Rt. Hon. Joe Clark, secretary of state for External Affairs, 4 March 1986.
30 See Statistics Canada (Cat. 65.202, 1987 edition), Exports by Commodity and Country, Table 4, p. 274.
31 Taskforce, "Widening, Tightening and Intensifying Economic and Other Sanctions against South Africa," 20 July 1988, p. 6.
32 Ibid., p. 6.
33 Ibid., p. 11.
34 The cost to Canadian taxpayers of the candle-lighting program and the anti-apartheid "festival" amounted to (Can.)$250,000. Another (Can.)$1 million was set aside for the implementation by Canada of its "Strategy to Counter South African Propaganda and Censorship" (John F. Burns, "Canada's Candles to Defeat Apartheid," *New York Times*, 3 August 1988).
35 "Public Forum on South African Censorship and Propaganda" was to take place parallel to the foreign ministers' meeting, all day on 2 August in Toronto's City Hall with prominent guests as moderators and panelists. In addition "Arts Against Apartheid," announced jointly by Joe Clark and Flora MacDonald, the latter then minister of Communications, was sponsored by the Department of External Affairs and was hosted, the News Release said, "by the Toronto arts and entertainment community." Its theme "Rekindle the Light" featured "over thirty events" including film, jazz and a mixed-media exhibit on South African censorship. According to the News Release, the day was to end with "15,000 Torontonians being involved in simultaneous candlelighting ceremonies across the city at 10:04 P.M." See Department of External Affairs, News Release no. 156, 20 July 1988, and Government of Canada, News Release no. 157, 26 July 1988.
36 "Propaganda from S. Africa Is Chief Target for Committee," *The Globe and Mail* (dateline Ottawa), 1 August 1988. This article also noted that the "anti-apartheid festival" was sponsored by the "Ministry of External Affairs and several private businesses, including the *Globe and Mail*."
37 Quoted in *Racism in Southern Africa*, p. 71.

38 Ibid., pp. 73–74.

39 "Statement by the Right Honourable Joe Clark, Secretary of State for External Affairs, at the Opening Session of the Commonwealth Foreign Ministers Meeting on Southern Africa," in Canada, Department of External Affairs and International Trade, *Statement and Speeches*, Toronto, 2 August 1988, p. 1.

40 John Deverell, "Canada, African States Divided over Measures to Fight Apartheid," *The Toronto Star*, 3 August 1988.

41 Ross Howard, "Ottawa Stand on S. Africa Queried after Toronto Meeting," *The Globe and Mail*, 5 August 1988.

42 Ibid.

43 Commonwealth Committee of Foreign Ministers on Southern Africa, "Concluding Statement," reprinted in *The Round Table*, no. 308 (October 1988), p. 414.

44 "Interim Report of the Expert Study on the Evaluation of the Application and Impact of Sanctions to the Commonwealth Committee of Foreign Ministers on Southern Africa," 11 July 1988 (confidential).

45 Although the "Concluding Statement" quoted the view of the "Interim Report" that sanctions were effective and had a "discernible impact on South Africa," no additional sanctions were announced and the "Interim Report" was not released (Commonwealth Committee of Foreign Ministers on Southern Africa, "Concluding Statement," p. 410.

46 Ibid., pp. 409–10.

47 The December issue of *Southern Africa Report* reproduced the "Interim Report's concluding section, "What Can Be Done Now." Details attributed to the "Interim Report" are taken from "South Africa Confidential: Document Underscores Canadian Backsliding," *Southern Africa Report*, 4, no. 3 (December 1988), 9–12.

48 Turkey, Switzerland, Austria, Belgium, Netherlands, Spain, Portugal, Hong Kong and Taiwan and possibly South Korea. See ibid., p. 10.

49 The technology licensee agreement between Perkins Engines, Varity's British subsidiary, and South Africa's state-owned Atlantis Diesel Engines Company was, of course, a case in point. See above, chap. 4, p. 119.

50 "South Africa Confidential," p. 11.

51 The measure would rescind all regulations that normally protected commercial confidentiality, such as licences, export permits and trade credits. It would apply to penalties for sanctions violations. A register should be opened for all transactions with South Africa including sales and purchases of goods and lists of ships that sailed to South Africa (ibid., p. 12).

52 Ibid.

53 Ibid.

54 International Defence and Aid Fund, *Review of 1988: Repression and Resistance in South Africa and Namibia* (London: IDAF Publications, 1988), p. 27.

55 Ibid., p. 29.

56 The lives of the "Sharpeville Six" in November and likely also the lives of those convicted in the "Delmas Treason Trial" in December were thus saved. See ibid., p. 31.

57 As this book was in production, evidence given by South Africa's past chief of police at the hearings of the Truth and Reconciliation Commission revealed that the order to bomb Khotso House had come from P.W. Botha, president of South Africa at the time.

58 Joe Clark publicly deplored these attacks and offered assistance to restore the church buildings. He expressed the hope that those responsible "would soon be brought to justice" (Department of External Affairs, Communiqué no. 221, 12 October 1988).

In January 1989 Law and Order Minister Adriaan Vlok made public these explanations offered by the police: COSATU House was likely to have been destroyed by residents or frequent visitors to the building; Khotso House was probably bombed by recent visitors, such as Shirley Renee Gunn, a social worker and alleged ANC terrorist. Also, in the past guerrillas had stored explosives there; and Khanya House may have been attacked by a white extremist who also planted the explosives left behind. The churches and COSATU rejected these bizarre speculations. No arrests were ever made. See *After the Fire: The Attack on Khanya House* (Pretoria: Southern African Catholic Bishop's Conference, 1989), p. 17.

59 An Angus Reid Poll in July 1988 showed that 29 percent of Canadians thought that Canada's sanctions were "about right"; 41 percent thought they "should be tougher," while 11 percent thought they were "already too tough" (with 19 percent DK) (*The Toronto Star*, 31 July 1988). A Gallup Poll released on 24 October 1988 showed national support of 46 percent for Mulroney's announced increase "in aid to black-ruled countries bordering South Africa who oppose South Africa's apartheid policy of racial segregation and white rule" (31 percent disapproved; 10 percent disapproved for other reasons; 13 percent DK). The poll also showed that 55 percent of those between eighteen and twenty-nine years of age and 50 percent of those between thirty and forty nine years old approved and so did 54 percent of those earning incomes of over $40,000, representing younger and affluent voters. Oddly enough, Gallup announced dismissively that "*only* 46% back Prime Minister's Mulroney's recent proposal" (Lorne Bozinoff and Peter MacIntosh, "Canadians Divided on Best Approach to South Africa," Gallup Canada Inc. (Toronto), 24 October 1988.

60 *Racism in Southern Africa*, pp. 63–64.

61 "Canada's Role in Southern Africa," 28 February 1987 (no. 87/11), pp. 1–2.

62 This ability to manipulate the phrase "wider, tighter and intensified application" of sanctions is at once apparent in the different interpretation given to it by the committee of experts appointed by the Commonwealth Secretariat who had prepared the "Interim Report of the Expert Study on the Evaluation of the Application and Impact of Sanctions" for the 1988 CFM meeting. The experts had recommended additional participants in the international application of sanctions (wider); additional aspects to existing sanctions and new means of their enforcement (tighter and intensified). Canada, with one important exception, used the phrase to correct improper enforcement of those sanctions which the government had announced since 1985.

63 Department of External Affairs, "Notes for a Speech" by the Rt. Hon. Joe Clark, secretary of state for External Affairs, at the Centre de Ressources Universitaires en Développement International, Laval University, Quebec, 26 September 1988 (Statement 88/44), p. 6.

64 Charlotte Montgomery and Susan Delacourt, "South Africa Sanctions Will Tighten, Clark Says," *The Globe and Mail*, 14 September 1988, and Charlotte Montgomery, "Ottawa to Join Project that Includes S. Africa-Controlled Firm," *The Globe and Mail*, 27 September 1988.

65 Ibid.

66 Department of External Affairs, "Notes for a Speech," 26 September 1988 (Statement 88/44), p. 6.

67 Ibid.

68 The details and quotations in the above paragraph are drawn from Val Sears, "Don't Press Sanctions against South Africa Mugabe Tells Mulroney," *The Toronto Star*, 29 September 1988.

69 Canada, Office of the Prime Minister, *Notes for an Address by the Right Honourable Brian Mulroney, Prime Minister of Canada before the United Nations General Assembly, United Nations, New York*, 29 September 1988, pp. 2–3.

70 Ibid., p. 3.

71 Department of External Affairs, "Canada Will Help Protect Development Projects in Southern Africa," News Release no. 213, 29 September 1988.

72 Ibid.

73 "Mulroney even went so far as to insist that 'there has been no change' in policy when asked by reporters on the campaign trail in Calgary" (John Bierman with Dan Baum in Harare and Chris Erasmus in Cape Town, "South Africa: On the Front Lines, Canada's New Aid to Black Africa," *Maclean's*, 17 October 1988, p. 27).

74 Ibid.

75 Department of External Affairs, News Release no. 230, 26 October 1988.

76 Taskforce, *Annual Report, 1986–1987*, p. 13.

77 Taskforce, "Widening, Tightening and Intensifying Economic and Other Sanctions against South Africa," 20 July 1988, p. 14.

78 Robert Matas, "South African Attends Ottawa-Backed Talks," *The Globe and Mail*, 27 October 1988.

79 Paul Watson, "Our South African Imports Up 68% in '88," *The Toronto Star*, 26 January 1989.

80 Charlotte Montgomery, "South African Exports to Canada Double," *The Globe and Mail*, 13 July 1989.

81 Peter Cook, Report on Business, "Too Sanguine and Soft-headed on Sanctions," *The Globe and Mail*, 10 February 1989.

82 Watson, "Our South African Imports Up 68% in '88."

83 Interview with the author, 1 January 1994.

84 Oakland Ross, "Ottawa-Pretoria Trade Jump Alarms African Nations," *The Globe and Mail*, 6 February 1989.

85 Ibid.

86 Oakland Ross, "Calling Canada to Account," *The Globe and Mail*, 7 February 1989.

87 Malcolm Dunlop, "Tutu Warns of Blood Bath," *Halifax Chronicle*, 10 May 1988.

88 John Bierman, *Maclean's* senior writer in Cape Town, cited in Mary Nemeth with Dan Baum and Margaret Knox "Canada in a Hot Seat: Joe Clark Has Showdown in Harare," *Maclean's*, 20 February 1989, p. 21.

89 Letter from Lucie Edwards, Department of External Affairs, chairperson, Southern Africa Task Force, to Marjorie Ross, associate coordinator of the Taskforce on the Churches and Corporate Responsibility, 17 November 1989.

90 Letter to W.R. Davis, coordinator of the Taskforce on the Churches and Corporate Responsibility, from John Schram, Department of External Affairs, Eastern and Southern Africa Division, on behalf of Barbara McDougall, who had meanwhile succeeded Joe Clark as secretary of state for External Affairs, 18 September 1992.

91 "Essential Mineral Imports from South Africa: A Report by the Industry-Government Task Force on Essential Minerals," 18 December 1989 (mimeograph), 47 pages, and Annex II, "Summary of Findings: Industry/Government Working Group on Sulphur Exports to Southern Africa," April 1990 (mimeograph), 3 pages.

92 Oakland Ross, "South Africa Stockpiling Armaments, Commonwealth Ministers Told," *The Globe and Mail*, 8 February 1989.

93 Department of External Affairs, Communiqué no. 155, 10 September 1986, p. 2.

94 Ibid.

95 External Affairs Ottawa, Press Office, Commonwealth Committee of Foreign Ministers on Southern Africa, "Statement on the Arms Embargo Against South Africa," Annex, 14 February 1989.

96 Ibid.

97 Simultaneously Clark announced "that the nine Warsaw Pact countries along with Vietnam and North Korea will be removed from the ACL. See Department of External Affairs, News Release no. 050, 6 March 1989.

98 Linda Diebel, "Clark Won't Bar South Africans from Ottawa Arms Convention," *The Toronto Star*, 11–12 May 1989.

99 South African Council of Churches, National Conference, 25–26 June 1990, cited in Taskforce on the Churches and Corporate Responsibility, *Annual Report, 1989–1990*, p. 36.

100 Department of External Affairs, "Notes for a Speech by the Secretary of State for External Affairs, the Right Honourable Joe Clark, in the House of Commons on the Results of the Commonwealth Foreign Ministers' Meeting in London," 28 February 1991 (Statement 91/13, p. 1.

101 External Affairs and International Trade Canada, "Notice to Exporters," Serial no. 59, 9 January 1992, p. 2.

102 Ibid., p. 4.

103 United Nations Special Committee against Apartheid, Seminar on the Role of the NGO's in Addressing Politically-Motivated Violence in South Africa, New York, 29–30 June 1992.

104 In 1980 members of the Taskforce had, without success, protested when Cedric Ritchie, head of the Bank of Nova Scotia, had accepted a seat on the board of Minorco, fearing that this would draw the Bank ever closer to this large and powerful South African corporation.

105 Charlotte Montgomery, "Sanctions Not Violated by Loan, Ottawa Says," *The Globe and Mail*, 8 February 1989, and Ross, "South Africa Stockpiling Armaments, Commonwealth Ministers Told."

106 Oakland Ross, "Clark to Caution Canadian Banks on Loans to S. African Companies," *The Globe and Mail*, 9 February 1989. See also Montgomery, "Sanctions Not Violated by Loan, Ottawa Says"; she cited Nick Douloff, senior manager of Public and Corporate Affairs of the Bank of Nova Scotia. He said that the bank was told that the government would view the transaction as a "European to European" deal.

107 Montgomery, "Sanctions Not Violated by Loan, Ottawa Says."

108 Letter from David Pfrimmer, chair, International Issues Committee, to Joe Clark, secretary of state for External Affairs, 3 March 1989.

109 Letter from Joe Clark, secretary of state for External Affairs, to David Pfrimmer, chair, Taskforce on the Churches and Corporate Responsibility, International Issues Committee, 14 June 1989.

110 A "Dear Friends" letter from Joseph Hanlon, co-ordinator of the Commonwealth Expert Study Group, to Commonwealth NGOs, including the Taskforce, which were engaged in anti-apartheid work, 24 August 1989. Hanlon encouraged pressure on governments to push for tighter trade and financial sanctions in anticipation of decisions at the CHOGM at Kuala Lumpur in October.

111 Letter from Joe Clark, secretary of state for External Affairs, to Ann Abraham, chair, Taskforce on the Churches and Corporate Responsibility, 11 December 1989.

112 Ibid.

113 Taskforce on the Churches and Corporate Responsibility, "Canadian Banks and South Africa," pamphlet (Toronto: Taskforce on the Churches and Corporate Responsibility, December 1989) (photocopy).

114 For further details see "Debt Repayment Schedules," "Analysis of South Africa's Balance of Payments (1985 through 1988)" and "What Payment Rate Could South Africa Pay?" in John E. Lind, "How Much Could South Africa Repay on Its Debt 1990–1993" (San Francisco: CANICOR Research, 1989) (photocopy), 14 pages; and Taskforce on the Churches and Corporate Responsibility, "International Financial Sanctions against South Africa: Canada's Position and Recommendations for Action, Prepared for the Inter Agency Anti-Apartheid Conference, Ottawa, May 1990" (Toronto, 1990), pp. 4–6.

115 Ibid. Members of the Technical Committee were: Banque Indo Suez and Credit Lyonnais of France; Commerzbank, Dresdner Bank and Deutsche Bank of West Germany;

Union Bank of Switzerland, Swiss Bank Corporation and Credit Suisse of Switzerland; Barclay's Bank, National Westminster Bank and Standard Chartered Bank of the United Kingdom; Citibank; Manufacturers Hanover and Morgan Guaranty of the United States. Five banks were singled out for international pressure by the ANC for their close relationship to the apartheid regime: Union Bank of Switzerland, National Westminster Bank, Manufacturers Hanover, Dresdner Bank and Credit Lyonnais.

116 Sampson, *Black and Gold*, p. 50.
117 *Tages Anzeiger* (Zürich), 14 November 1985, cited in ibid., p. 52.
118 Sampson, *Black and Gold*, p. 298.
119 This position was adopted by a consensus of anti-apartheid campaigners in North America and Europe (letter from Ann Abraham, chair of the Taskforce on the Churches and Corporate Responsibility, to Joe Clark, secretary of state for External Affairs, 27 July 1989).
120 "Lending Banks under Pressure: Anti-Apartheid Pressures on Banks Increase as Rescheduling Deadline Nears," *Southscan: A Bulletin of South African Affairs* (London), 6 October 1989.
121 Lind, "How Much Could South Africa Repay on Its Debt 1990–1993," pp. 12–14.
122 Alan Hirsch, "The Paperback which Reveals a More Likely Commonwealth Line," *Weekly Mail* (SA), 18–24 August 1989, p. 14.
123 Telephone interview between the author and Sandra Tychsen, director, Finance Policy, Government of Ontario, 12 April 1990. See also a letter from the Hon. Robert Nixon to Sheila Kappler, chair, Taskforce on the Churches and Corporate Responsibility, 27 April 1990.
124 *The Globe and Mail*, 25 February 1989; *Wall Street Journal*, 27 February 1989; *Journal de Genève*, 28 February 1989; and *Johannesburg Star*, 12 March 1989. The policy was continued by the incoming NDP government which in 1991 barred McLean McCarthy Ltd. from underwriting Ontario government bonds because its parent, the Deutsche Bank, was the lead underwriter of a $275 million bond issue floated by the South African government in September 1991. Banque Paribas, also a participant in the South African bond issue, was excluded as well from doing business with the Ontario government (Konrad Yakabuski, "Ontario Bars Firm over South Africa," *The Toronto Star*, 26 September 1991).
125 Letter from Ann Abraham, chair of the Taskforce on the Churches and Corporate Responsibility, to the Hon. Robert Nixon, treasurer, The Government of Ontario, 3 March 1989.
126 At the time Swiss banks had been exceptionally successful in their search for Canadian business. They had been involved in a $650 million Euro-Canadian bond issue of the Alberta government; a $500 million issue by Hydro Quebec (January 1989); and a $75 million issue for the federal Business Development Bank, a Crown corporation whose guidelines stressed the importance of using Canadian firms as much as possible for Canadian dollar issues. See Brian Milner, "Ottawa Rules Out Bank Boycott for Swiss Loans to South Africa," *The Globe and Mail*, 25 February 1989.
127 Letter from Sheila Kappler, chair of the Taskforce, to the Rt. Hon Joe Clark, secretary of state for External Affairs, 27 July 1989.
128 Milner, "Ottawa Rules Out Bank Boycott for Swiss Loans to South Africa."
129 Taskforce, *Annual Report, 1989–1990*, p. 44.
130 Letter from Joe Clark, secretary of state for External Affairs, to Ann Abraham, chair, Taskforce on the Churches and Corporate Responsibility, 11 December 1989.
131 "Dear Friends" letter from Jenifer Davis, Executive Director, The American Committee on Africa (ACOA), "States, Counties and Cities that Have Taken Economic Action against Apartheid," November 1989.

132 Milner, "Ottawa Rules Out Bank Boycott for Swiss Loans to South Africa."
133 Letter from the Rev. Dan Gennarelli, chair, International Issues, Taskforce on the Churches and Corporate Responsibility, to the Rt. Hon. Joe Clark, Secretary of State for External Affairs, 24 May 1990.
134 Ross Howard, "Clark Urges Commonwealth Heads to Freeze Sanctions on South Africa," *The Globe and Mail*, 18 October 1989.
135 Those released were five who had been sentenced to life imprisonment in 1964 with Nelson Mandela: 77-year-old Walter Sisulu; Ahmed Kathrada, 60; Andrew Mlangeni, 63; Elias Motsoaledi, 65; and Raymond Mhlaba, 69. Others were ANC members Oscar Mpheta, 80, and Wilton Mkwayi, 66; and PAC member, Jafta Masemola. See *Southscan: A Bulletin of Southern African Affairs*, 13 October 1989, p. 289.
136 See International Defence and Aid Fund, *Review of 1989: Repression and Resistance in South Africa and Namibia*, pp. 26–31.
137 Howard, "Clark Urges Commonwealth Heads to Freeze Sanctions on South Africa."
138 Ibid.
139 Department of External Affairs, "Notes for Remarks by the Secretary of State for External Affairs, The Right Honourable Joe Clark, Upon Presentation of the Report of the Committee of Foreign Ministers to the Commonwealth Heads of Government Meeting, Kuala Lumpur, Malaysia," 19 October 1989 (Statement 89/55), p. 1.
140 International Defence and Aid Fund, "Nelson Mandela's Address to the International Tribute for a Free South Africa," 16 April 1990, IDAF Information Notes and Briefings 90/2 (London: IDAF Research and Information Department, 1990).
141 As a member of the Council of Trustees of the International Defence and Aid Fund for Southern Africa, I was aware of these approaches in early 1990.
142 "Nelson Mandela's Address."
143 The Abuja Commitment, Commonwealth Committee of Foreign Ministers on Southern Africa, Abuja, Nigeria, 17 May 1990.
144 Ibid.

10   Final Reflections

The efforts of the Taskforce on the Churches and Corporate Responsibility to influence Canadian banks, corporations and the federal government to change their policies toward apartheid in Southern Africa constituted one of the most sustained social actions undertaken by the Canadian ecumenical community in recent history. These efforts had outlasted numerous cabinet rotations and indeed several changes of federal governments. From its creation in 1975 to the dramatic release from prison of Nelson Mandela in 1990, the Taskforce had acquired, I think it is fair to say, a knowledge of the issues that was widely respected and had explored, alone and in cooperation with others, many different strategies to persuade and at times to convince Canada's business community and governments to sever the ties that mortgaged them to the apartheid state.

The members of the Taskforce were realist enough always to recognize that its anti-apartheid work needed as well an important public education component, for, as has been made clear throughout this study, resistance to its advocacy in both business circles and government was powerful and substantial. The member churches of the Taskforce were therefore pleased to be able to work within a growing body of informed public opinion in Canada and internationally to which they were able to contribute their expertise and insights.

Five operational lessons that emerged from these fifteen years of experience of the Taskforce can be articulated most easily:

   (1) to remain effective, the churches' commitment had to be sustained even through periods of public disinterest, government indifference and corporate hostility;

Note for chapter 10 is found on p. 346.

(2) the detailed knowledge acquired by the Taskforce made it hard for their advocacy to be ignored or casually dismissed and gradually won for the Taskforce a recognition within the media, which greatly assisted its work;

(3) the Taskforce quickly developed the practice of always preparing its submissions and proposals in ways that made them immediately comprehensible to other organizations and individuals. These documents could thus also be used for public education and advocacy by others;

(4) the Taskforce took care that its work could not be dismissed as the work of activists distant from the positions of the churches on whose behalf they claimed to speak; its initiatives were therefore kept strictly within the framework of the official policies of its member churches; and

(5) finally, the board of the Taskforce was (and is) a "working board." Its members decide on the use of their proxies in shareholder meetings and represent their own denominations and orders in discussions with companies and government; they also respond to media enquiries. They "own" the work of the Taskforce.

Why the Concentration on Apartheid?

To be sure, apartheid was not at all the only international issue that offended Christian teachings and received church attention during the period covered here. Yet it clearly was an issue of special concern for the churches. One may therefore legitimately ask what were the additional compelling reasons for this prolonged commitment to the liberation of South Africa. The answer is without doubt related to the fact that the Christian faith and its sacred texts were claimed by the Nederduitse Gereformeerde Kerk (NGK), the Dutch Reformed Church of South Africa, to provide the foundation for racial separation and eventually for the total suppression of all rights and freedoms of the black majority. The NGK of South Africa, with a membership of 70 percent of the white Afrikaner population, had played a crucial role in forming, enhancing and sustaining the apartheid system since 1948, the year the National Party came to power. Throughout the "cold war," this theology had bestowed on the white minority regime of South Africa the image of the West's Christian bulwark against Communism on the African continent.

This was deeply offensive to Christians the world over. In chapter 5 we examined in detail how international church alliances such as the World Council of Churches, the Lutheran World Federation and the World Alliance of Reformed Churches, with the full participation of South Africa's anti-apartheid churches, had dealt with this unacceptable theological justification of apartheid. The resolute commitment on the part of South African and international church leaders and a myriad of Christian organizations around the world to end apartheid cannot be separated from their determination to reject this false theology and to restore the integrity of their faith.[1]

The Unifying Features of the Anti-Apartheid Work of the Churches

From the beginning, in Canada as elsewhere, two major components of the anti-apartheid activities of the churches were manifest. First, they allied themselves emotionally and morally with the black South African community and its allies in their struggle against apartheid. They thus skirted a barrier to effective action so prevalent in both government and corporate approaches to change in South Africa. This was a tendency to consult the white South African government or sources close to it and the South African business elite, and to react to their assessment of what ought to be done. In contrast, the actions by the churches were based on their solidarity with South African church partners who were themselves deeply involved in the struggle.

Second, the churches were concerned to promote a rapid but non-violent dismantling of South Africa's apartheid system. From the start, and throughout the activities of the Taskforce, this was recognized to involve above all the mobilization of economic pressures on the South African regime. A halt to bank loans to, and investment in South Africa, an end to exports useful to South Africa's military and police and the suspension of scientific exchanges with the regime and similar objectives were the primary focus of the member churches of the Taskforce. This emphasis was supported by their South African partner churches and was stressed by the ANC as an important contribution that the international anti-apartheid movement could make to the struggle.

The Taskforce and Canadian Investors in South Africa

The degree to which the work of the Taskforce actually contributed to ending the apartheid system is difficult to assess and should be neither exaggerated nor belittled. Relatively few Canadian-based companies held South African investments and none held majority ownership. Thus, even the celebrated 1986 sale of Alcan's South African investment in Hulett Aluminium was a minor success compared with the accelerated disinvestments of majority-owned American companies during this period. Nevertheless, Alcan's withdrawal and that of other Canadian investments added to the ripple effect on similar business decisions. Both internationally and in South Africa, such withdrawals contributed to an undermining of business confidence in the future of the apartheid regime. This was the objective of the international disinvestment campaign. The efforts of the Taskforce on this issue should be recognized as a contribution to that international campaign.

The Taskforce's persistent monitoring of corporate activity in South Africa and Namibia, its probing into Canadian links with South Africa's military industries and its research into black working conditions were each important. The material assembled aided discussion with senior management, making it difficult for management to dismiss the churches as ill-informed meddlers. It informed the formulation of credible shareholder proposals which in turn generated important publicity, even when the church proposals were voted down. Taskforce research also generated valuable data for the preparation of government briefs and was an important reason for the good relations the Taskforce developed with the public media.

From the early 1980s on, Canadian anti-apartheid organizations were growing steadily in number and strength. Enquiries into Canadian business links with South Africa multiplied as calls for consumer boycotts and disinvestment gained currency. There was in consequence increasing demand for specific information the Taskforce had to offer and a widening interest in the actions taken by its member churches. The Taskforce thus contributed to greater Canadian understanding and to a more pervasive pressure on corporations and banks to discontinue business with the apartheid regime.

The Taskforce and Canadian Bank Loans to South Africa

If Canadian corporate investment was small compared to the American or British presence in South Africa, the involvement of Canadian chartered banks in South Africa was on a major scale. Syndicated long-term loans had benefited South African government departments, state-owned enterprises and private companies. Leaked information from within the European American Banking Corporation in 1974 had presented the Taskforce with evidence of the dimensions of such financial support and of its importance for the staying power of the regime. The churches' campaigns to halt all lending until apartheid was abolished lasted eleven years and were successful. In 1985, when the government called for voluntary sanctions on new loans to the South African government, the five large Canadian chartered banks had long ceased making new loans.

The bank campaigns well illustrated that the Taskforce's actions are perhaps best understood within the context of the international anti-apartheid movement. The South African resistance movements, the South African church partners and the international anti-apartheid activists agreed that bank loans to the regime must cease. The call was taken up by activists in almost every Western industrialized state, with the Canadian churches assuming this role in Canada as early as 1974, even before the Taskforce was formally established. They were soon joined by other national organizations and by numerous local church, civic, municipal and university organizations that played a major role in keeping the pressure on the banks.

As popular uprisings intensified in South Africa, the regime's repression became ever more obvious and the economic climate more uncertain. The repercussions were felt in the boardrooms of international businesses. Senior executives facing activist shareholders and other anti-apartheid organizations could no longer justify continued loans to, or investment in, the apartheid state. If we search for the original impetus responsible for the ultimate decision of the banks to halt lending to South Africa, we find it in the popular uprisings against apartheid in South Africa's black townships. We would claim on behalf of the Taskforce only that it helped to accelerate this process.

The Taskforce and the Government of Canada
1975–84: The Trudeau Years

The churches were less able to convince successive Canadian governments to add their weight to the pursuit of sanctions in the struggle against apartheid. From the first Taskforce brief to the government prepared for the meeting on 12 November 1975 with Allan MacEachen as secretary of state for External Affairs to the last communication recorded here from Joe Clark in 1990, the Taskforce, to its profound regret, was more often engaged in a battle of wits than in a joint enterprise to find the fastest and most peaceful way of dismantling apartheid.

For the Taskforce, relations with the Department of External Affairs and the Department of Industry, Trade and Commerce during the balance of the Trudeau governments (ignoring the brief Clark government in 1979–80) were a continuous learning process. Early in this period the Taskforce accumulated a wealth of information relating to the operations of Canadian companies in South Africa and Namibia. Details concerning the origins, the scale and the recipients of commercial bank loans to these countries were brought to light, as were the details of Canadian investments there. In discussions with business executives about these activities, the churches were assured that all was entirely legal and would continue unless there was a change in Canadian government policy. The churches therefore sought through briefs to the Department of External Affairs and Industry, Trade and Commerce and in meetings with government ministers to ensure, at the very least, that the government did not encourage or support business relations with South Africa and Namibia. This continuing dialogue with successive secretaries of state for External Affairs convinced the members of the Taskforce that the government was not interested in mounting any significant economic pressure on the South African regime and exposed them to the range of arguments used by the government to defend its deep-rooted aversion to the application of economic pressures. They learned that far from questioning corporate links to the apartheid regime, the government encouraged them, even when these involved transactions that might benefit South Africa's military and police. Where corporate or indeed government ties demonstrated an unbecoming closeness, the government swiftly minimized or explained away their significance.

By 1983 the churches had become confident in their judgement and analyses of Canadian policy positions, disheartening as were their implications.

1985–90: The Mulroney Years

When in 1985 Mulroney decided to embark on an explicit anti-apartheid policy, he was assured of the support of a strong and well-grounded anti-apartheid movement in Canada. His most important policy change was the decision to adopt selective economic sanctions to which he added an unambiguous promise that Canada would impose total sanctions if no fundamental changes took place in South Africa. In April-May 1985 the Taskforce, likely because of its long experience in monitoring South African developments and Canadian business activities in South Africa and Namibia, briefly played a prominent role. It provided Joe Clark, Mulroney's secretary of state for External Affairs with proposals for specific economic sanctions, proposals which apparently were not available from External Affairs.

The first set of sanctions of July 1985 thus bore the imprint of the Taskforce's recommendations, but as discussed, they had been softened in ways that minimized their scope and effect. With few exceptions, this tendency of the Department of External Affairs to select economic sanctions and then to lessen their effectiveness was evident throughout the years in which sanctions were applied. This was done by relying on compliance that was voluntary rather than mandatory, by weakening their impact through the use of ambiguous language, by excluding crucial components or by recurrent announcements of "furthering" or "tightening" of sanctions evidently not adequately implemented in the first place.

By 1987 the Taskforce and most Canadian anti-apartheid organizations were losing patience with the government. It had become clear to them that no serious additional economic sanctions, let alone "total" sanctions, were contemplated, despite the well publicized intensifying repression in South Africa. Joe Clark's efforts from 1987 on to lower public expectations of additional economic sanctions and to concentrate instead on softer options such as the promotion of better race relations within South Africa and the fight against South African propaganda and censorship, suggested a managed retreat from economic sanctions. Although there were two more economic interventions after 1987, when Canada gave aid to Zimbabwe in 1988 and when it placed South Africa on the Area Control List in 1989, the era of Canadian leadership regarding economic sanctions had essentially ended in 1987.

As one considers Canada's policy towards South Africa in the Mulroney years, one must seek to explain both what had triggered Mulroney's initial interest in a new and more aggressive policy on South Africa and then what had caused its early abandonment.

With the 1984 appointment of Stephen Lewis as Canada's permanent representative at the United Nations, Mulroney had given a clear signal that he was touched by the racism of apartheid and was likely to act on it. When, much against the wishes of the Department of External Affairs, Mulroney met Archbishop Tutu in December 1984, the eloquence of Tutu, an early advocate and supporter of international economic sanctions, was bound to have influenced the prime minister. External Affairs' rigid antipathy to such initiatives forced Clark and Mulroney first to obtain a list of possible sanctions from the Taskforce and later to seek assistance outside the Department to prepare for the Nassau Commonwealth and the United Nations meetings later in the year. All these are indicators that Mulroney, the prime minister, and Mulroney, the person, from late 1984 on, was engaged in this issue and sought a role for himself and for Canada in the international arena.

However, in addition, influences from a very different source, which were likely to have reinforced Mulroney's early resolve to act, can be identified. This was the position at the time of South Africa's white business elite. In early January 1985 it had presented Senator Edward Kennedy with its first political manifesto which, although calling for vaguely defined and limited political reforms, seemed to signal discontent with the apartheid system. After international financing had been suspended, the white South African business community intensified its pressure on Botha and even hoped for his removal from office. The business community's most pronounced fear was that Botha's enduring brutal repression was radicalizing the educated young leaders of the black resistance to the point of threatening destruction of the free-enterprise economy in a future South Africa. One can but hypothesize that Mulroney found these arguments persuasive.

Thus the twin impulses, Tutu's plea for justice for the black majority on the one hand, and the business call for reforms to safeguard the free-market economy on the other, may well have convinced Mulroney in 1984–85 that the sooner international economic sanctions forced Botha to abandon his politics, the more likely both objectives could be achieved. That considerations of this order were centrally important is made apparent also in the speeches given by both Mulroney and Clark in the fall of 1985. Each spoke in identical terms. They reduced the significance of black popular resistance in South Africa to three individualized black personalities, Tutu, Boesak and Mandela, paying tribute only to them. Their emphasis, however, was placed elsewhere. Clark stressed that the consequences of the efforts of South Africa's business community "can not be overstated," and that Canada's contribution to this new reality was well recognized. Mulroney, speaking at the United Nations, repeated the tribute to Tutu,

Boesak and Mandela. He also forbore any mention of either the exiled liberation movements or of the struggle of popular forces within South Africa. Like Clark, he praised South Africa's business community, which he credited with "unprecedented opposition to apartheid." Here then is tangible evidence for the trust placed in 1985 by both Mulroney and Clark in the efforts of the business elite to save South Africa's free-market economy through pressure on the Botha regime to adopt reforms.

By the same token, the circumstances in 1987 that led Mulroney and Clark to abandon their emphasis on international economic sanctions were associated, at least in part, with the retreat of the South African business elite from its reformist position during Botha's May 1987 (white-only) elections. Business had backed the imposition of new and even tougher states of emergency. The sentiments that had given rise to the 1985 conciliatory meeting with the ANC were replaced by an acceptance of the regime's propaganda of the ANC as a Communist terror organization. In short, the South African business elite had returned to the fold.

At this point one of the major flaws in the analysis of Mulroney's anti-apartheid policies came to the fore: the almost total absence of any official Canadian acknowledgment of the central importance of the black liberation struggle. In a peculiar contradiction, even though Nelson Mandela, the imprisoned leader of the ANC, was given prominence and praise, the ANC itself was either ignored or denounced for its ideological makeup and for its 1964 decision to embark on guerilla warfare. Consistent with this, Oliver Tambo, in Ottawa in August 1987 on Mulroney's invitation, was treated by his host and the secretary of state for External Affairs with outlandish discourtesy and disrespect. Yet Tambo was president of the ANC, the largest, the oldest and the most unifying force in the black struggle. The Mulroney government, given its ideological configuration, was simply unwilling and unable to transform its shallow commitment to the reform goals of the liberal wing of white South Africa's business elite into a lasting and profound support of the black struggle.

The Canadian government had failed to recognize or had chosen to ignore, the powerful role of the many composite parts of the popular resistance in South Africa who were to merge into the Mass Democratic Movement in support of the ANC. A major commitment to these forces would have led Canada to follow the example of the Nordic states, particularly Sweden, with major non-military support for the ANC, a downgrading of its embassy to consular status and an adherence to total sanctions until apartheid was dismantled. Canada could certainly have done this, but it would thereby have risked alienating its partners in the Group of Seven and this the government preferred not to do.

From 1987 on, therefore, many in the Canadian anti-apartheid community felt manipulated. They had observed the various lapses in the implementation of Canada's sanctions and were no longer confident that Canada was acting in good faith in its anti-apartheid activities. The member churches of the Taskforce continued to challenge corporate activities in South Africa that clearly supported the apartheid regime, and to emphasize to the government the importance of sustained economic sanctions. The churches were confident that apartheid would be ended and that international economic pressures on the regime were the most effective non-violent support that could be offered from outside. They took heart from the fact that this was exactly what their South African partners and the ANC had asked them to do.

From Repression to Negotiations

Because the anti-apartheid struggle was so long and arduous, it is hard to be certain about what convinced President F.W. de Klerk, who had succeeded P.W. Botha in 1989, finally to release South Africa's political prisoners and sit down with them to negotiate a new constitution. It does seem clear to this anti-apartheid activist that the continuous and intensifying popular uprisings, which defied armed repression, finally persuaded de Klerk that he could not contain them any longer without simultaneously jeopardizing the present and future interests of the white South African community.

International economic sanctions had in fact contributed quite substantially to this judgement. There had been a brief period after Botha's 1987 electoral victory when some members of the white business elite had attempted "inward industrialization," to make South Africa immune against sanctions and economically self-sufficient. But they had failed. As early as July 1988 powerful voices contradicted such notions. Henri de Villiers, chair of the Standard Bank Investment Corporation, dismissed these efforts and warned that South Africa needed markets, skills, technology and capital, plainly enumerating all areas severely affected by international economic sanctions. With each additional repressive measure, more companies withdrew, more white professionals and capital left the country.

The international anti-apartheid movements in all their various forms, from research and information agencies to hands-on support activities in South Africa, provided a sort of fifth column whose members, each in their own area of competence, brought the South African struggle to prominence in their own countries and prompted protest actions. In this way they contributed to the internationalization of the struggle. The organized disinvestment and bank campaigns undertaken in Canada, as elsewhere, did not force the apartheid regime to seek negotiations, nor were they the primary cause of the disinvestment and the outflow of capital from South Africa. However, they constituted an important international auxiliary factor in the disintegration of business confidence in apartheid South Africa, which eventually left the regime no option but to negotiate.

The history of the last years of apartheid and its final dismantling very much suggests that the emphasis on sustained international economic sanctions that marked the advocacy of a very wide range of church and secular international anti-apartheid movements, far from being an indulgence in self-righteousness, was in fact strategically sound and appropriate. It gave evidence to the South African popular forces that there was mounting international acceptance of the legitimacy of their struggle, and became a further reinforcing reason for disinvestment and capital flight. Next to the defiant resistance in South Africa, economic sanctions were the most important reason why that resistance led to the negotiations that ended apartheid and to a democratically elected majority government, and not to a protracted and unresolved civil war.

The churches and religious orders that constituted the Taskforce can be proud that they were associated with this great historic victory over injustice.

Note

1   An indication that at long last the theological bases for apartheid were to be renounced by the NGK came at a conference in Rustenburg, South Africa, in November 1990. It brought together delegates from the white NGK and representatives of those South African churches that had been active in the anti-apartheid struggle. Professor Willie Jonkers, a leading Afrikaner theologian at the University of Stellenbosch, made this statement: "I confess before you and before the Lord, not only my own sin and guilt, and my personal responsibility for the political, social, economic and structural wrongs that have been done to many of you and the results from which you and your whole country are still suffering, but vicariously I dare to do that in the name of the NGK [the white Dutch Reformed Church of South Africa] of which I am a member, and for the Afrikaans people as a whole" (Desmond Tutu, in John Allen, ed., *The Rainbow People of God: The Making of a Peaceful Revolution* [New York: Doubleday, 1994], p. 222).

Selected Bibliography

Adam, Heribert, and Kogila Moodley. *Democratizing Southern Africa: Challenges for Canadian Policy.* Ottawa and Toronto: Canadian Institute for International Peace and Security, 1992.

Administration and Observance of the Code of Conduct Concerning the Employment Practices of Canadian Companies Operation in South Africa, The: Annual Reports 1985–91. Ottawa. Photocopy (distributed by the Department of Foreign Affairs and International Trade).

After the Fire: The Attack on Khanya House. Pretoria: Southern African Catholic Bishops' Conference, 1989.

Allen, John, ed. *The Rainbow People of God: The Making of a Peaceful Revolution.* New York: Doubleday, 1994.

Amnesty International. *South Africa: State of Fear, Security Force Complicity in Torture and Political Killings, 1990–1992*: New York: Amnesty International, 1992.

Anglin, Douglas, ed. *Canada and South Africa: Challenge and Response.* Ottawa: The Norman Patterson School of International Affairs, Carleton University, 1986.

Anglin, Douglas, et al. *Canada, Scandinavia and Southern Africa.* Upsala: Scandinavian Institute of African Studies, 1978.

"Bank Bows to Church over Sale of Krugerrand." *Financial Times* (London), 29 November 1984.

Bierman, John, with Dan Baum and Chris Erasmus. "South Africa: On the Front Lines, Canada's New Aid to Black Africa." *MacLean's,* 17 October 1988, p. 27.

Bratcher, Diane. "The Neptune Strategy: SHELL in South Africa." *ICCR Brief,* 16, no. 7 (1987).

Bunting, Brian. *The Rise of the South African Reich.* Harmondsworth: Penguin Books, 1964 and 1969. Reprint London: International Defence and Aid Fund for Southern Africa, 1986.

Business Day (Johannesburg), 20 September 1985.

Canada. *Independence and Internationalism: Report of the Special Joint Committee on Canada's International Relations.* Ottawa: Queen's Printer, 1986.

———. Department of External Affairs and International Trade. *Communiqué,* 1975 to 1993.

———. Department of External Affairs and International Trade. *News Release,* 1975 to 1993.

———. Department of External Affairs and International Trade. *Statements and Speeches,* 1975 to 1992.

———. House of Commons. *Debates,* 19 December 1977 and 14 October 1981.

———. House of Commons. Standing Committee on Finance, Trade and Economic Affairs. *Minutes of Proceedings and Evidence,* 23 January 1979.

———. House of Commons. Standing Committee on Human Rights. *Minutes of Proceedings and Evidence,* 17 July 1986.

———. Office of the Prime Minister. *Notes for an Address by the Right Honourable Brian Mulroney, Prime Minister of Canada, United Nations General Assembly, New York, October 23rd 1985,* undated.

———. Secretary of State for External Affairs. *Foreign Policy for Canadians: United Nations.* Ottawa: Queen's Printer, 1970.

Canadian Council of Churches (in conjunction with TCCR and the Inter-Church Coalition on Africa). "Recommendations for Canadian Policy in Southern Africa." Toronto: Canadian Council of Churches, 1987. Photocopy.

Carling, John, "Former Officer Alleges Campaign of Dirty Tricks." *The Independent* (London), 11 June 1991.

Cawthra, Gavin. *Brutal Force: The Apartheid War Machine.* London: International Defence and Aid Fund for Southern Africa, 1986.

Commonwealth Committee of Foreign Ministers on Southern Africa. "Concluding Statement." Reprinted in *The Round Table,* no. 308, pp. 408–15.

Desmond, Cosmas. *The Discarded People.* Harmondsworth: Penguin Books, 1971.

———. "Stonewalling the Future: Thatcher's 'No'." *Southern Africa Report,* 2, no. 2 (1986), 9–12.

Drainville, Gérard, et al. *No Neutral Ground: Report of the Visit to South Africa and Zambia of the Delegation of the Canadian Catholic Church*. Toronto: Canadian Catholic Organization for Development and Peace, 1986. Photocopy.

Focus on Political Repression in Southern Africa: A Newsletter of the International Defence and Aid Fund for Southern Africa, nos. 1 to 93, 1976 to 1991.

Fraser, Malcolm, "Statement on the Report and Recommendations of the Panel of Eminent Persons on the Activities of Transnational Corporations in South Africa and Namibia to the Second Committee of the General Assembly of the United Nations." New York: United Nations Centre on Transnational Corporations, 1985. Photocopy.

Freeman, Linda. *The Ambiguous Champion – Canada and South Africa in the Trudeau and Mulroney Years*. Toronto: University of Toronto Press, 1997.

———. "Canada, Aid and Peacemaking in Southern Africa." In Robert Miller, ed., *Aid as Peacemaker: Canadian Development Assistance and Third World Conflict*, pp. 33–49. Ottawa: Carleton University Press, 1992.

———. "Keeping Up with the Joneses: Canada and South Africa 1985." *Southern Africa Report*, 1, no. 2 (October 1985), 4–8.

———. "What's Right with Mulroney? Canada & Sanctions, 1986." *Southern Africa Report*, 2, no. 2 (October 1986), 3–8.

———. "Where's the Beef? Canada and South Africa, 1987." *Southern Africa Report*, 3, no. 3 (December 1987), 3–8.

———. "Rescuing Credibility? Canadian Policy towards South Africa, 1988." *Southern Africa Report*, 4, no. 3 (December 1988), 3–8.

———. "Leading from the Rear: Canada and South Africa 1989." *Southern Africa Report*, 5, no. 3 (December 1989), 4–8.

———. "Getting Rich Together: Canada and South Africa 1990." *Southern Africa Report*, 6, no. 3 (December 1990), 4–9.

Globe and Mail, The (Toronto), 1975 to 1993.

Hanlon, Joseph, ed. *South Africa: The Sanctions Report – Documents and Statistics*. London: Commonwealth Secretariat, 1990.

Harber, Anton, and Barbara Ludman, eds. *A-Z of South African Politics, Weekly Mail & Guardian*. Harmondsworth: Penguin Books, 1994.

Horrell, Muriel, ed. *A Survey of Race Relations* (Annual Survey). Johannesburg: The South African Institute of Race Relations, 1969 to 1979.

———. *South Africa's Workers*. Johannesburg: The South African Institute of Race Relations, 1969.

———. *Action, Reaction and Counteraction*. Johannesburg: The South African Institute of Race Relations, 1971.

Howard, Rhoda. "Black Africa and South Africa." In Robert Mathews and Cranford Pratt, eds., *Human Rights and Candian Foreign Policy*, pp. 265–84. Montreal and Kingston: McGill-Queen's University Press. 1988.

Hutchinson, Moira. "Taking Sides in Southern Africa: Disinvestment, Divestment and Sanctions." A paper prepared for "Taking Sides in Southern Africa," a conference organized by the Canadian Council for International Cooperation, Montreal, 27 February to 1 March 1987. Photocopy.

Hutchinson, Roger, "Missiology." In Christopher Lind and Joe Mihevc, eds., *Coalitions for Justice*, pp. 320–32. Ottawa: Novalis, 1994.

———. "The Just War Tradition: Human Rights and Public Moral Discourse." *McMaster Journal of Theology*, 2 (Spring 1991), 30–42.

———. "Social Action and Mission in the Eighties." In Terry Brown and Christopher Lind, *Justice as Mission*. Burlington: Trinity Press, 1985.

Independent Expert Study on the Evaluation of the Application and Impact of Sanctions, Final Report to the Commonwealth Committee on Southern Africa. London: Commonwealth Secretariat, 1989. Photocopy.

International Defence and Aid Fund. *Apartheid's Violence against Children*. London: IDAF Publications, 1988.

―――. *Review of 1988: Repression and Resistance in South Africa and Namibia*. London: IDAF Publications, 1988.

―――. *Review of 1989: Repression and Resistance in South Africa and Namibia*. London: IDAF Publications, 1989.

―――. *Namibia: The Facts*. London: IDAF Publications, 1989.

―――. *Apartheid: The Facts*. London: IDAF Publications, 1991.

ISCOR Survey. Supplement to *The Financial Mail* (Johannesburg), 7 November 1980.

Johannesburg Star, 4 December 1984.

Johnston, Douglas, and Sampson, Cynthia, eds. *Religion, The Missing Dimension in State-craft*. New York: Oxford University Press, 1994.

Kairos Document, The: A Theological Comment on the Political Crisis in South Africa. Third World Theology Series. 2nd rev. ed. London: Catholic Institute for International Relations in association with the official international development agencies of the Roman Catholic Church in Australia, Canada, England and Wales, Ireland, New Zealand and Scotland, 1986. Originally published September 1985; reprinted 1989.

Keenleyside, T.A. "Canada-South Africa Commercial Relations: 1977–1982: Business as Usual?" *Canadian Journal of African Studies*, 17 no. 3 (1983), 449–67.

―――, and Patricia Taylor. "The Impact of Human Rights Violations: A Contemporary Dilemma." *Behind the Headlines* (November 1984).

Klein, Beate. *United States and Canadian Involvement in Loans to South Africa from 1979 to May 1984*. In United Nations, *Notes and Documents*. New York: United Nations Centre against Apartheid, 1984.

Kovak, Catherine M. "Fuelling the Machines of Apartheid." *ICCR Brief*, 15, no. 5 (1986).

Lind, John E. "How Much Could South Africa Repay on Its Debt 1990–1993." San Francisco: CANICOR Research, 1989. Photocopy.

Mandela, Nelson. *The Struggle Is My Life*. London: IDAF Publications, 1990.

McGovern, Edmond. *International Trade Regulation: GATT, The United States and the European Community*. Exeter: Globefield Press, 1986.

Meer, Fatima. *Higher than Hope: The Authorized Biography of Nelson Mandela*. London: Penguin Books, 1990.

Mission to South Africa: The Commonwealth Report – The Findings of the Commonwealth Eminent Persons Group on Southern Africa. Harmondsworth: Penguin Books, 1986.

Mulvihill, Conlin. "The Role of QIT-Fer et Titane in the Development of South Africa's Titanium Industry." Toronto: Taskforce on the Churches and Corporate Responsibility, 1985. Photocopy.

Newsletter on the Oil Embargo against South Africa. Amsterdam: Shipping Research Bureau. Occasional publication circa 1980 to 1990.

New York Times, 1980 to 1990.

Nossal, Kim Richard. *Rain Dancing: Sanctions in Canadian and Australian Foreign Policy*. Toronto: University of Toronto Press, 1994.

Pfrimmer, David. *The Evangelical Lutheran Church in Canada: Position on South Africa and Namibia*. Edited by Pat Simonson. Winnipeg: The Division for Church and Society of the Evangelical Lutheran Church in Canada, 1987.

Pratt, Cranford, ed. "An Exchange between the Secretary of State for External Affairs and the Taskforce on the Churches and Corporate Responsibility." *Canadian Journal of African Studies*, 17, no. 3 (1983), 497–525.

Pratt, Cranford, and Roger Hutchinson, eds. *Christian Faith & Economic Justice: Toward a Canadian Perspective*. Burlington, Ontario: Trinity Press, 1988.

Pratt, Renate. "Codes of Conduct: South Africa and the Corporate World." *The Canadian Forum*, 63, no. 731 (August/September 1983), 33–36.

———. "The Costs of Procrastination: Canada's Policy towards Namibia." *Southern Africa Report*, 3, no. 2 (1987, 9–12.

———. "International Financial Institutions." In Robert Matthews and Cranford Pratt, eds., *Human Rights and Candian Foreign Policy*, pp. 159–84. Montreal and Kingston: McGill-Queen's University Press: 1988.

———. "Betrayal of a Sacred Trust: A Review of Namibia's History." A paper presented to the Conference on "Apartheid, the Beginning of the End," University of Western Ontario, February 1990. Photocopy.

———. "From the Goldmines to Bay Street." In Bonnie Greene, ed., *Canadian Churches and Foreign Policy*, pp. 103–25. Toronto: James Lorimer & Company, 1990.

Price, Robert M. *The Apartheid State in Crisis: Political Transformation in South Africa 1975–1990*. New York and Oxford: Oxford University Press, 1991.

Racism in Southern Africa: The Commonwealth Stand. London: Commonwealth Secretariat, 1989.

Redekop, Clarence. "Commerce over Conscience: The Trudeau Government and South Africa, 1968–84." *Journal of Canadian Studies*, 19 (Winter, 1984–85), 82–105.

———. "The Mulroney Government and South Africa." *Behind the Headlines*, 44, no. 2 (1986), 1–16.

Report of the Panel for Hearings on Namibian Uranium, Part Two. In United Nations, *Notes and Documents*. New York: United Nations Centre against Apartheid, 1980. Photocopy.

Republic of South Africa. "National Key Points Act." *Government Gazette* (Cape Town), 181, no. 7134 (1980).

Rikard, Carmel. "New Law May Give Buthelezi Power to Launch SA Raids." *The Weekly Mail*, 7–13 September 1990.

Ryan, Colleen. *Beyers Naudé: Pilgrimage of Faith*. Claremont: David Philip Publishers, 1990.

Sampson, Anthony. *Black and Gold: Tycoons, Revolutionaries and Apartheid*. Sevenoaks: Hodder and Stoughton, 1987.

Saul, John S. *Socialist Ideology and the Struggle for Southern Africa*. Trenton, NJ: Africa World Press, 1990.

———. "The Southern African Revolution." A paper presented to the Annual Meeting of the Canadian African Studies Association, Carlton University, Ottawa, May 1989. Photocopy.

———. "South Africa: Between Barbarism and 'Structural Reform'." *New Left Review*, 188 (July/August), 3–44.

Save Robert McBride: No Apartheid Executions. London: Southern Africa, The Imprisoned Society, 1988.

Shipping Research Bureau. *Oil to South Africa: Apartheid's Friends and Partners*. Amsterdam: Shipping Research Bureau, 1988.

Sindab, Jean. *Shell Shock: The Churches and the Oil Embargo*. Geneva: World Council of Churches Programme to Combat Racism, 1989.

Smith, Timothy. "Chrysler, Ford, and General Motors in South Africa." *Newsletter, Council on Economic Priorities* (New York), no. 5 (October-November 1970), 20–23.

South Africa: The Case for Mandatory Economic Sanctions. In United Nations, *Notes and Documents*. New York: United Nations Centre against Apartheid, 1986.

South Africa: The Sanctions Report. Prepared for the Commonwealth Committee of Foreign Ministers on Southern Africa. London: Penguin Books, 1989.

South African Council of Churches and Southern African Catholic Bishops' Conference. *Relocations: The Churches' Report on Forced Removals in South Africa*. Johannesburg: South African Council of Churches and Southern African Catholic Bishops' Conference, 1984.

Southern Africa Report (Toronto), 1985 to 1992.

Southscan: A Bulletin of South African Affairs (London), 1985 to 1991.

"Statement by the Synod of Bishops of the Church of the Province of Southern Africa." News Release from the Church of the Province of Southern Africa, Cape Town, 4 December 1988. Archives, Anglican Church of Canada.

Study and Action Committee of the World Relationship Committee of Young Women's Christian Association of Canada. *Investment in Oppression.* Toronto: YWCA of Canada, 1973.

Sweden. *Prohibition of Investments in South Africa and Namibia and Other Measures against Apartheid – An Unofficial Translation of the Swedish Government's New Bill on Prohibition of Investment in South Africa and Namibia.* Stockholm: Ministry of Foreign Affairs, February 1985.

Taskforce on the Churches and Corporate Responsibility. *Annual Reports.* Toronto, 1975 to 1992.

———. Records of communications with Canadian financial institutions regarding loans to South African borrowers and the sale of Krugerrand in Canada and related documents. Archives and current files of the Taskforce on the Churches and Corporate Responsibility, 1974 to 1992.

———. Records of communications with Canadian corporations with investments in, and other links to, South Africa and Namibia and related documents. Archives and current files of the Taskforce on the Churches and Corporate Responsibility, 1974 to 1992.

———. Records of communications with the Department of External Affairs and International Trade and other departments of the Canadian government on issues related to Canadian policy toward South Africa and Namibia. Archives and current files of the Taskforce on the Churches and Corporate Responsibility, 1975 to 1992.

———. Records of communications with the Royal Bank of Canada, the Canadian Imperial Bank of Commerce, the Toronto Dominion Bank, the Bank of Nova Scotia, the Bank of Montreal and other financial institutions and related documents. Archives and current files of the Taskforce on the Churches and Corporate Responsibility, 1974 to 1992.

———. "Banking on Apartheid" (Pamphlet). Toronto: Taskforce on the Churches and Corporate Responsibility, 1977. Photocopy.

———. *Investment in Oppression: Canadian Responses to Apartheid.* Toronto: Taskforce on the Churches and Corporate Responsibility, 1979. Rev. ed. of Study and Action Committee of the YWCA of Canada, *Investment in Oppression* (1973).

———. "A Few Words from the Canadian Banks about Loans to South Africa" (Pamphlet). Toronto: Taskforce on the Churches and Corporate Responsibility, 1981. Photocopy.

———. "Canadian Policy toward Southern Africa: A Brief to the Secretary of State for External Affairs and the Minister of Industry Trade and Commerce." Toronto: Taskforce on the Churches and Corporate Responsibility, 5 May 1981. Photocopy.

———. "Proposals Relating to Human Rights Violations in South Africa: A Brief to the Select Committee on the Ombudsman of the Ontario Legislature." Toronto: Taskforce on the Churches and Corporate Responsibility, 1982. Photocopy.

———. "Comments on the Evolution of Codes of Conduct for Companies Investing in South Africa Prepared for the United Nations Seminar in Montreal on the Role of Canadian TNC's in South Africa and Namibia." Toronto: Taskforce on the Churches and Corporate Responsibility, 1982. Photocopy.

———. "Canada and Namibian Uranium." Toronto: Taskforce on the Churches and Corporate Responsibility, 1982. Photocopy.

———. "Canadian Policy towards Southern Africa: An Analysis of the Canadian Government's Response of 15 June 1982 to the Brief of the Taskforce of 5 May 1981." Toronto: Taskforce on the Churches and Corporate Responsibility, March 1983. Photocopy.

———. "Analysis of the May 1982 and May 1983 Statements Concerning Employment Practices in Huletts Aluminium Limited, Alcan's Affiliate in South Africa." Toronto: Taskforce on the Churches and Corporate Responsibility, November 1983. Photocopy.

———. "Canadian Policy toward Southern Africa: A Brief Presented to the Rt. Hon. Joe Clark, Secretary of State for External Affairs." Toronto: Taskforce on the Churches and Corporate Responsibility, May 1985. Photocopy.

———. "A Few Words from the Canadian Banks about Loans to South Africa" (Pamphlet). Toronto: Taskforce on the Churches and Corporate Responsibility, February 1985, updated September 1985. Photocopy.

———. "The Role of the TNC's in the Military and Nuclear Sectors of South Africa and Namibia: Aspects Related to Canadian Involvement." Submitted to the United Nations Centre on Transnational Corporations. Toronto: Taskforce on the Churches and Corporate Responsibility, September 1985. Photocopy. Updated for submission to the Special Joint Committee on Canada's International Relations, Toronto, November 1985.

———. "A Few Words from the Canadian Banks about Loans to South Africa" (Pamphlet). Toronto: Taskforce on the Churches and Corporate Responsibility, May 1987. Photocopy.

———. "Widening, Tightening and Intensifying Economic and Other Sanctions against South Africa: A Brief," 20 July 1988.

———. "Canadian Banks and South Africa" (Pamphlet). Toronto: Taskforce on the Churches and Corporate Responsibility, December 1989. Photocopy.

———. "Correspondence between the Secretary of State for External Affairs and TCCR on Financial Sanctions, July-December 1989." Toronto: Taskforce on the Churches and Corporate Responsibility, 1990. Photocopy.

———. "International Financial Sanctions against South Africa: Canada's Position and Recommendations for Action, Prepared for the Inter Agency Anti-Apartheid Conference, Ottawa, May 1990." Toronto, 1990.

Toronto Star, The, 1975 to 1992.

Truth Shall Make You Free, The: The Lambeth Conference, 1988. The Reports, Resolutions and Pastoral Letters from the Bishops. London: Anglican Church, 1989.

United Nations. Notes and Documents. New York: United Nations Centre against Apartheid, 1976 to 1989.

Valpy, Michael. "Singing External's Song: Journalism Conference Controversy." *Southern Africa Report,* 4, no. 5 (1989), 26–27.

Webb, Pauline, ed. *A Long Struggle: The Involvement of the World Council of Churches in South Africa.* Geneva, World Council of Churches, 1994.

Wood, Bernard. "Canada and Southern Africa: A Return to Middle Power Activism." *The Round Table,* 315 (1990), 280–90.

Index

Johannesburg Consolidated Investment (JCI), 145
The Johannesburg Star, 323
Jos. E. Seagram & Sons, 253
Jotcham, Denis, 222
Journal de Genève, 323
JKS Boyles International, 253
Juneau, Pierre, 105–106

The Kairos Document, 154–55
Kappler, Sheila, 235
Keenleyside, T.A., 53
Kekane, Rev., 153
Kennedy, Edward, 139, 147, 174, 343
Kennecott Corporation, 40, 41
Khanya House, 305, 332n
Khotso House 305, 331n
Kibira, Joseph, 17
Kierans, Tom, 104
Koeberg nuclear reactors, 93
Kohl, Helmut, 278, 312
Kruger, Paulus, 31
Krugerrand, 31–33, 81, 99, 103, 105–106, 191–92
KwaNdebele, 9, 149
KaNgwane, 9
KwaZulu, 9, 39, 40, 115–16, 294
KwaZulu Shoe Company, 114

Lalonde, Marc, 90
Lambeth Conference, 251
Landis, Betsy, 47
Laurence, Margaret, 30
Lavoie, Jean, 102
Lebowa, 9, 34, 102
Leadership (S.A.), 141
Lee, Edward G., 115
Lelyveld, Joseph, 119
Leman, Paul, 222
Lesotho, 70, 77
Leutweiler, Fritz, 320
Levy Auto Parts, 84
Lewis, Stephen, 163, 164, 308, 343
Liberation of Southern Africa's Colonies (Toronto Committee), 30
liberation theology, 153, 154–55
London Review Committee, 297, 305–306, 310
Longyear Canada, 306
Lubowski, Anton, 294

Lumley, Ed, 76, 86, 106
Lutheran Church in America, Canada Section (LCA-CS), 2, 16–17
Lutheran World Federation (LWF), 157, 338
Luthuli, Chief Albert, 271

Macaulay, Colin, 242
MacDonald, Flora, 271
MacEachen, Allan, 50, 51, 52, 90–91, 222, 227, 341
MacGuigan, Mark, 55, 76, 82, 86, 88, 89
MacKay, Colin, 164
Mackay, Kenneth, 222
MacKenzie, Ian, 39
MacLean, Ronald, 273
MacLeod, Jim, 245, 247, 248, 249, 298
Maharaj, Mac, 141
Malan, D.F., 70
Mandela, Nelson: and ANC, 140, 142, 270–71; birthday, 30; championed by Clark, 193, 278, 343; and COSATU, 150; and EPG, 205; imprisoned, 139, 250, 317 326–27; Statement from the Dock, 281; and Taskforce, 156, 158
Mangope, Lucas, 225
Manufacturers Life-Insurance Company, 11
Marc Rich & Co. A.G., 244
Marobe, Murphy, 275
Marubeni, 244
Mass Democratic Movement (MDM), 282, 293, 321, 327, 344
Massey-Ferguson, 11, 44–46, 79–80, 118–21, 227–29, 237, 238, 265. *See also* Varity
McAvity, James M., 221, 222
Mbeki, Thabo, 141, 153, 326
McBride, Sean, 46
McCall, Christina, 30
McLeod Young Weir, 104, 264
McMurtry, Roy, 282, 283
McNeil, Fred, 16, 29
Metropolitan Toronto Board of Education, 107
Milliken, Frank, 41
"Minimum Living Level" (University of S.A.), 226
Minorco (Mineral and Resources Corporation), 32–33, 103, 307, 318–19
Minty, Abdul, 315
Mitterand, Danielle, 279
Mkhatschwa, Smangaliso, 149, 152

www.ingramcontent.com/pod-product-compliance
Lightning Source LLC
Chambersburg PA
CBHW072045020426
42334CB00017B/1396